Also in the Variorum Collected Studies Series:

GERALD BONNER
God's Decree and Man's Destiny: Studies on the Thought of Augustine of Hippo

R.A. MARKUS
Sacred and Secular: Studies on Augustine and Latin Christianity

R.A. MARKUS
From Augustine to Gregory the Great: History and Christianity in Late Antiquity

T.D. BARNES
From Eusebius to Augustine

T.D. BARNES
Early Christianity and the Roman Empire

W.H.C. FREND
Archaeology and History in the Study of Early Christianity

LUISE ABRAMOWSKI
Formula and Context: Studies in Early Christian Thought

HENRY CHADWICK
Heresy and Orthodoxy in the Early Church

HENRY CHADWICK
History and Thought of the Early Church

CAROLINE BAMMEL
Tradition and Exegesis in Early Christian Writers

VICTOR SAXER
Pères saints et culte chrétien dans l'Eglise des premiers siècles

CHARLES MUNIER
Autorité épiscopale et sollicitude pastorale (IIe–VIe siècles)

CHRISTOPHER STEAD
Substance and Illusion in the Christian Fathers

CHARLES KANNENGIESSER
Arius and Athanasius: Two Alexandrian Theologians

A.H. ARMSTRONG
Hellenic and Christian Studies

COLLECTED STUDIES SERIES

Church and Faith in the Patristic Tradition

Gerald Bonner

Gerald Bonner

Church and Faith in the Patristic Tradition

Augustine, Pelagianism, and Early Christian Northumbria

VARIORUM
1996

Published by VARIORUM
Ashgate Publishing Limited
Gower House, Croft Road,
Aldershot, Hampshire GU11 3HR
Great Britain

Ashgate Publishing Company
Old Post Road,
Brookfield, Vermont 05036–9704
USA

ISBN 0–86078–557–2

British Library CIP Data
Bonner, Gerald
Church and Faith in the Patristic Tradition: Augustine,
Pelagianism, and Early Christian Northumbria.
(Variorum Collected Studies Series: 521)
1. Pelagianism. 2. Heresies, Christian—History—Early Church.
3. Northumbria (England)—Church History. I. Title II. Series
273.5

US Library of Congress CIP Data
Bonner, Gerald
Church and Faith in the Patristic Tradition: Augustine,
Pelagianism, and Early Christian Northumbria / Gerald Bonner.
p. cm. — (Variorum Collected Studies Series: CS521)
Includes bibliographical references and index. (cloth)
1. Augustine, Saint, Bishop of Hippo. 2. Pelagianism.
3. Northumbria (England: region)—Church History. 4. Bede, the
Venerable, Saint, 673–735. 5. Cuthbert, Saint, Bishop of
Lindisfarne, ca. 635–687. 6. Church History—Primitive and Early
Church, ca. 30–600. I. Title. II. Series: Collected Studies: CS518.
BR1720.A9B62 1996 95–45631
270.2–dc20 CIP

The paper used in this publication meets the minimum requirements of the American National Standard for Information Sciences - Permanence of Paper for Printed Library Materials, ANSI Z39.48-1984. ™

Printed by Galliard (Printers) Ltd
Great Yarmouth, Norfolk, Great Britain

COLLECTED STUDIES SERIES CS521

CONTENTS

This volume contains xiv+ 316 pages.

PUBLISHER'S NOTE

The articles in this volume, as in all others in the Collected Studies Series, have not been given a new, continuous pagination. In order to avoid confusion, and to facilitate their use where these same studies have been referred to elsewhere, the original pagination has been maintained wherever possible.

Each article has been given a Roman number in order of appearance, as listed in the Contents. This number is repeated on each page and quoted in the index entries.

Corrections, for which it was not possible to make amendment in the text, are noted at the end of the relevant article with a Corrigenda; additions by the author are refered to in the Additional Notes. Both corrections and additions are marked by an asterisk in the margin.

PREFACE

This volume comprises three parts. The first continues the studies of Augustine of Hippo published by Variorum Reprints in *God's Decree and Man's Destiny* in 1987. Although it is overwhelmingly devoted to the Pelagian Controversey, an episode which has been a preoccupation of mine for thirty years, I have nevertheless sought to draw attention to two other aspects of the saint's theology, namely the concept of deification, which is so often alleged to be peculiar to the Greek East, and his doctrine of sacrifice. In his teaching on deification, as in other fields, it is the resemblance between Augustine's thought and that of the Greek Fathers, and not the difference, which impresses me.

The second part includes writings on early Christianity in the North-East of England, where I have lived since 1964, and particularly on two outstanding figures: St Cuthbert, the great saint of the North, an English ascetic in the Irish devotional tradition, and Bede, the scholar and priest, who has attracted so many admirers down the centuries. These studies stem from feelings of personal devotion, though I have always endeavoured to control my affection by the disciplines of historical study. If I am more confident than some other scholars, whose learning I respect, of painting a pen-portrait of Cuthbert as a man, and not simply as a hagiographer's icon, it is because the evidence seems to justify my confidence. There is much to be said for a sceptical approach to historical investigation, but this does not require us to abandon all hope of knowing anything about the personalities of men and women who lived a millenium or more ago.

The third part of the collection touches on certain issues which have attracted my attention and interest, either spontaneously or at the invitation of others. My consideration of the process of the extinction of Greco-Roman paganism helped me to appreciate Robert Markus's characteristically learned work on *The End of Ancient Christianity*. The essay 'Christianity and the Modern World-View' is a defence – I hope a modest one – of Latin Christendom, of reason in theologizing, and of Western technological achievement against dogmatic *a priori* disparagement. In doing this I have no desire uncritically to commend Western industrialised capitalism as an ideal, or even as a particularly desirable form of human society. I am well aware of its faults: but it seems to me foolish to indulge in nostalgia for past ages which were by no means themselves free from greed, selfishness, savage cruelty and oppression, at the expense of advances in the material quality of life on earth brought about by human experience and skill.

I have dedicated this volume to The Catholic University of America and The Atonement Seminary, both of Washington, DC, as an expression of gratitude for hospitality enjoyed in the years 1991–94, a hospitality which I shall never forget and will certainly never be able to repay, but I am also very well aware of many other friends to whom I am indebted for help and encouragement. I cannot list them all, but would especially mention Robert Markus, George Lawless, OSA, Robert Dodaro, OSA, Allan Fitzgerald, OSA, John Rotelle, OSA, Sidney Griffith, ST, John Smedley, Ruth Peters and their colleagues at Variorum, my wife Jane, and our children, Jeremy and Damaris. To them, and to all my other benefactors, my grateful thanks.

GERALD BONNER

Durham, England
August 1995

ACKNOWLEDGEMENTS

The permission of the following journals and institutions to reproduce the various articles and reviews which originally appeared in them is gratefully acknowledged: *The Journal of Theological Studies* and the Clarendon Press, Oxford (I, XIII & XVIII); the Cambridge University Press (II); *Studia Patristica* and the Berlin Academy and Peeters Press, Leuven (III & V); the Institut Historique Augustinien, Louvain and *Augustiniana* (IV); *Augustinian Studies*, Villanova, PA (VI & VII); *The Journal of Ecclesiastical History* and the Cambridge University Press (VIII & XVII); *Anglo-Saxon England* and the Cambridge University Press (XI); the Rector and Churchwardens of St Paul's, Jarrow-upon-Tyne (XII); the Dean and Chapter of Durham (IX); the Council of the University of Durham and *The Durham University Journal* (X & XIV); the Council of the Fellowship of St Alban & St Sergius and *Sobornost* and the *Eastern Churches Review* (XV & XIX); and the Society for the Promotion of Christian Knowledge (XVI). Grateful thanks are extended to Penguin Books, Harmondsworth, Middlesex, for permission to make use of the translation of St Augustine, *The City of God*, by Henry Bettenson (II).

THIS VOLUME IS DEDICATED TO
THE CATHOLIC UNIVERSITY OF AMERICA, WASHINGTON, DC
AND TO THE
ATONEMENT SEMINARY IN THE SAME CITY
AS SOME EXPRESSION OF GRATITUDE
FOR THEIR UNFAILING KINDNESS
DURING THE THREE YEARS OF MY SERVICE
IN THE
EARLY CHRISTIAN STUDIES PROGRAM
OF THE UNIVERSITY
1991–1994

I

AUGUSTINE'S CONCEPTION OF DEIFICATION

AUGUSTINE's use of the concept of deification tends to be neglected by students of his theology. Not only do general works on patristics ignore it, but even specialized studies pass it by. Indeed it was possible, as recently as 1975, for a British scholar,[1] buttressing himself on the assertions of Dr Philip Sherrard[2] and Mme Myrrha Lot-Borodine,[3] to write as if deification played no part in Augustinian theology, in ignorance of the magisterial article by Victorino Capánaga in 1954[4] and G. B. Ladner's admirable study, *The Idea of Reform*, which appeared in 1959.[5]

Ignorance of Augustine's teaching by writers on deification may be deemed culpable; neglect by Augustinian scholars as a whole is more readily forgivable, given the relative sparsity of references in the saint's writings. The computer serving the contributors to the forthcoming *Augustinus Lexikon*, when asked to furnish references to the use of the words DEIFICARI and DEIFICATUS and their various forms in Augustine's work, was able to supply only fifteen examples, seven of which are irrelevant to the theology of deification.[6] It should in fairness be recognized that the computer was not programmed to identify phrases such as occur in Augustine's exegesis of Ps. 81 [82]: 6: *Dixi, dii estis*; or his declaration, echoing Irenaeus and Athanasius, that Christ became man that we might become gods, which teaches deification without actually employing the word; but the fact remains that references to deification are rare in Augustine, so that the case for their importance must be made from their content, and from their relation to Augustine's theology as a whole, rather than from their frequency. The fact that Augustine is prepared to speak of deification at all is in itself significant, and one can understand the scepticism of those scholars who, having read widely in the anti-Pelagian writings, interpreting them from the

[1] B. Drewery, 'Deification' in *Christian Spirituality. Essays in Honour of Gordon Rupp*, ed. Peter Brooks (London, 1975), pp. 35–62.

[2] *The Greek East and the Latin West* (London, 1959), pp. 43 f.

[3] *La déification de l'homme* (Paris, 1970), pp. 39 ff., quoted by Drewery, art. cit., p. 37.

[4] 'La deificación en la soteriología agustiniana' in *Augustinus Magister* ii (Paris, 1954), 745–54.

[5] 'St Augustine's Conception of the Reformation of Man to the Image of God' in *Aug. Mag.* ii. 867–88; *The Idea of Reform* (Cambridge, Mass., 1959).

[6] Namely *Contra Faustum* xxxii. 7; xxxii. 19; *Contra Felicem* i. 13; *De Baptismo* VI. xv. 24; *Contra Cresconium* III. lxix. 80 (twice); *De Patientia* xvii. 14. Relevant are *Ep.* 10. 2; *De Civitate Dei* xix. 23; *Enarratio in Ps.* 49. 2 (three times); 117. 11; *Serm.* 126. x. 14; 166. iv. 4.

[Journal of Theological Studies, NS, Vol. 37, Pt. 2, October 1986]

classical Protestant position, find it hard to believe that Augustine would ever have embraced a doctrine which seems to stem from Graeco-Roman paganism rather than from the Bible.

Such scepticism can only be reinforced by the arguments of the distinguished Eastern Orthodox theologian, Vladimir Lossky, who has argued that, while the Eastern Fathers teach deification, Augustine and the Latins have seen man's final perfection in redemption through justification by faith,[7] or in a rationalistic understanding of the Beatific Vision,[8] disregarding the consideration that some later Western Catholic theologians, such as Bernard of Clairvaux and St John of the Cross,[9] have taught a doctrine of deification as part of their theology—a fact which should serve as a warning against any temptation to make generalized contrasts between the Greek East and the Latin West. If distinctions are to be made, it should be on the basis of all the available historical evidence; and this suggests that the resemblances between the two traditions, on this issue at least, are greater than their differences.

Before, however, we turn to Augustine's teaching on deification, it must be admitted that the doctrine taken by itself and without any further definition, is a curious one, and justifies the suspicions of Protestant critics, who feel that it is unchristian. The notion of the worship of a human being, although acceptable in the Greek East during the Hellenistic age, was distasteful to the Roman mind and repulsive to Jews and Christians. When King Herod Agrippa I accepted the applause of the people of Caesarea, who cried out that he was a god and not a man, the angel of the Lord smote him, and he died miserably. This incident, recorded in the book of Acts (12: 19–23), must obviously inhibit any talk of deification in Christian circles which is not based on a theology which would exclude the otherwise inevitable accusation of blasphemy. Furthermore, the

[7] Vladimir Lossky, 'Redemption and Deification' in *In the Image and Likeness of God*, Eng. tr. (London and Oxford, 1975), pp. 71–110; cf. Jouko Martikainen, 'Man's Salvation: Deification or Justification?' in *Sobornost*, series 7, no. 3 (1976), p. 189: 'The Eastern tradition uses concepts which are mainly connected with ontology and regards salvation as deification. The Lutheran tradition, on the contrary, employs personalistic concepts and considers that justification by grace alone is most central to salvation.'

[8] Lossky, *The Vision of God*, ET (London, 1963), pp. 9–20. For a development of this view see Christos Yannaras, 'Orthodoxy and the West' in *Eastern Churches Review* iii, n. 3 (1971), 286–300, who sees the development of Western rationalistic secularism as a consequence of the methodology of Western theologians, including Augustine, Anselm, and Aquinas, and associates this rationalism with the absence of any doctrine of deification on Palamite lines in the Latin West.

[9] Bernard, *De Diligendo Deo* 10. 28; see E. Gilson, *The Mystical Theology of St Bernard*, ET (London, 1940); for John of the Cross, see E. Allison Peers, *Spirit of Flame* (London, 1943), pp. 141–4.

biblical authority can fairly be described as scanty. The words of the serpent in Gen. 3: 3: *Ye shall be as gods*, coming from such a source, are hardly to be counted authoritative. The phrase in 2 Peter 1: 4: *partakers of the divine nature*, although an obvious text, stands in a magnificent isolation, and in any case Augustine, so far as I am aware, does not seek to base his theology upon it. The text which Augustine, in common with the Greek Fathers, takes as specifically teaching deification is Ps. 81 [82]: 6: *I said, ye are gods*—words which are quoted by Jesus in John 10: 34. It is, however, clear that in the original context of this passage there was no thought of teaching deification of humanity, and it would seem that in quoting it Christ was making a debating point against those who were preparing to stone Him for the blasphemy of declaring Himself to be the Son of God, rather than proclaiming a doctrine. Here opponents of the idea of deification like Dr Drewery[10] may be said to have made their case—no modern scholar could build a theology of deification on such a scriptural foundation and expect to be taken seriously. With the Fathers, however, the case was different. They did not read the Bible with the eyes of a modern critic, but were prepared to find in it meanings which were not intended by the author of the text. As Augustine put it: 'When two or more meanings are to be found in the words of Scripture, even if the meaning of the author remains hidden, there will be no risk in teaching any of those which agree with the truth derived from other scriptural passages.'[11] Augustine certainly believed that his teaching on deification was based on Scripture; but he was not constrained by the literal and historical considerations which condition the modern exegete.

Nevertheless, there is reason to think that Augustine's first encounter with the concept of deification came in the context of Neoplatonist philosophy, rather than from the Christian Scriptures. In an important article published in 1962 Père Georges Folliet discussed the phrase *deificari in otio*,[12] which occurs in Augustine's tenth letter, written to his friend, Nebridius, in 389 or 390, after his return to Africa from Italy.[13] Nebridius, a sick man, had been begging Augustine to come to live with him at Carthage.

[10] Art. cit. n. 1 above, pp. 49–50.

[11] *De Doctrina Christiana* III. xxvii. 38. *CCSL* xxxii. 99–100.

[12] Folliet, '*Deificari in otio*. Augustin, *Epistula* 10. 2' in *Recherches Augustiniennes* ii (1962), 225–36.

[13] *Ep.* 10. 2: '. . . sed neque his, qui ad huius modi administrationes temporalis honoris amore raptantur, neque rursum his, qui cum sint privati, negotiosam vitam appetunt, hoc tantum bonum concedi arbitror, ut inter strepitus inquietosque conventus atque discursus cum morte familiaritatem, quam quaerimus, faciant; deificari enim utrisque in otio licebat.' *CSEL* xxxiv (1), 23–4.

Augustine replied that he could not abandon his community at Thagaste, which needed his presence, and further pleaded his own poor health; but the essential factor in his refusal was the desire to be made like God in *otium*—leisure; not the leisure of a wealthy landowner, but rather the freedom from worldly affairs of the philosopher, for which the Christian equivalent would be the *anapausis* of the desert monk in his cell in Nitria or Scete, of whom Augustine had learned from Ponticianus at Milan on the eve of his conversion.[14] However, Folliet argued, with a wealth of evidence, that Augustine was here citing from the *Sententiae ad intelligibilia ducentes* of the anti-Christian Porphyry, who teaches detachment from the material world for the sake of contemplation, and purgation of the soul and self-knowledge, to lead to that freedom which makes the soul like God. Folliet also drew attention to the passage in Porphyry's *Philosophy of Oracles*, quoted by Augustine in Book XIX of *The City of God*, in which the Neoplatonist philosopher declares that enquiry about God purges the soul, while imitation deifies it by bringing our disposition into harmony with God's.[15]

By the time, however, that Augustine came to write the nineteenth book of *The City of God* (about 427), his outlook had undergone a radical change from that which he had displayed in writing to Nebridius in 389/390. Porphyry was now an enemy, the Platonist who was too proud to accept the grace of the Incarnation,[16] and who for that reason saw deification as a state which is to be achieved by the philosopher's own efforts. Such a view was now wholly unacceptable to Augustine, the defender of the grace of God against the Pelagians, the *inimici gratiae*. Deification can come only from a participation in God made possible by divine initiative.

It might be said that Augustine's mature understanding of deification is based upon a theological datum and a philosophical conception. The theological datum is, of course, the God-man Jesus Christ, by whom, and by whom alone, we come to the Father.[17] The Christocentricity of Augustine's thought need not be laboured here, but it is integral to his doctrine of deification, because Christ, being God and man, is therefore the mediator between God and man.

[14] *Conf.* VIII. vi. 15. *Bibliothèque Augustinienne* xiv. 36–8.

[15] *De Civ. Dei* xix. 23: 'Nam Deus quidem, utpote omnium Pater, nullius indiget; sed nobis est bene, cum eum per iustitiam et castitatem aliasque virtutes adoramus, ipsam vitam precem ad ipsum facientes per imitationem et inquisitionem de ipso. Inquisitio enim purgat, inquit; imitatio deificat adfectionem ad ipsum operando.' *CSEL* xl (2), 416. See the remarks of John T. O'Meara, *Porphyry's Philosophy from Oracles in Augustine* (Paris, 1959), p. 57.

[16] *De Civ. Dei* x. 28. *CSEL* xl (1), 495, 496.

[17] *De Doct. Christ.* I. xxxiv. 38. *CCSL* xxxii. 28.

There cannot be a mediator between God and God because God is one, but *a mediator is not of one* (Gal. 3: 20), because he is in the midst between others. . . . And so the only Son of God was made the mediator of God and man, when being the Word of God with God, He both brought down His majesty to human affairs and raised human lowliness to the realms of the divine, that He might be a mediator between God and men, being made a man by God above men.[18]

Christ, then, is the theological datum; the philosophical conception is that of participation by man in God. Here Augustine, in common with the Greek Fathers, draws upon Platonic thought, 'spoiling the Egyptians', as he would have put it. The notion of participation—μετοχή, μέθεξις, μετουσία—is common enough in Greek patristic writing, and Augustine similarly uses the word *participatio* to explain that man exists by participating in God, who is both Being and the source of Being. Thus, in an often-quoted passage in *De LXXXIII Quaestionibus*, he identifies the Platonic ideas with thoughts in the mind of God and declares that it is by participating in them that every created thing exists.[19] Augustine takes this essentially philosophical understanding of participation and radically Christianizes it: man derives his spiritual life from participation in God, but this participation is made possible only by the Incarnation and flesh-taking of Christ the Mediator. Thus in the twenty-third tractate on the Gospel of John he declares:

The Lord Jesus . . . has declared to us that the human soul and reasonable mind, which is in man and not in animals, is not animated, not made happy and blessed, not illuminated, except by the very substance of God. . . . But the soul's beatitude, by which it is made happy, cannot be, except by participation of that ever-living life and unchanging and eternal substance which is God. . . . This is the Christian religion, that one God is to be worshipped, and not many gods, because the soul is not made blessed except by one God. It is made blessed by participation in God. The weak soul is not made blessed by participation in a holy soul, nor is a holy soul made blessed by participation in an angel; but if the weak soul seeks to be made blessed, let it seek that by which the holy soul is made blessed. You yourself are not made blessed by an angel, but from whence an angel is made blessed, thence are you also. With these truths most firmly established in advance: that the reasonable soul is not made blessed except by God, and the body not animated except by the soul, and that the soul is a kind of middle term between God and the body, direct your thoughts and

[18] *Ep. ad Galatas Exp.* 24. 5: 'Mediator inter deum et deum esse non posset, quia unus est deus, *mediator autem unius non est*, quia inter aliquos medius est. . . . (8) Sic itaque unicus filius dei, mediator dei et hominum factus est, cum verbum dei deus apud deum et maiestatem suam usque ad humana deposuit et humilitatem humanam usque ad divina subvexit, ut mediator esset inter deum et homines, homo per deum ultra homines.' *CSEL* lxxxiv. 86, 87.

[19] *De LXXXIII Quaest.*, q. 46. 2. *CCSL* xliv A, 72–3.

remember with me . . . and let us delve with all our powers until we come to the rock: Christ the Word, Christ the Word of God with God, the Word Christ and God the Word, Christ and God and the Word one God. . . . But not only was the Word Christ, but *the Word was made flesh and dwelt among us*. Therefore Christ is both Word and flesh.[20]

Again, and more succinctly, in his first sermon on Ps. 58, he says:

The teacher of humility and sharer of our infirmity, giving us participation of His divinity, coming down that He might both teach and be the Way, has deigned most highly to commend His humility to us.[21]

In this phase: 'the sharer (*particeps*) of our infirmity, giving us participation of His divinity', we can see the manner in which Augustine conceives of deification: it comes about, not because the human soul is naturally divine (which is impossible because of its creaturely status), nor even because it is made in the image and likeness of God (though this gives man a special place in creation, above the level of the beasts), but because God has taken our humanity into Himself: '. . . the Word was made flesh through the assuming of flesh by divinity, not by the conversion of divinity into flesh.'[22] This had, as G. B. Ladner has pointed out, profound consequences for the Christian doctrine of man: 'If God really was crucified as man, man could never again be quite the same',[23] for by taking upon Himself man's sin, and by participating in man's penal suffering, which did not pertain to sinless manhood, God joined humanity to His nature in a degree—if we may employ a theological hyperbole—which went beyond the hypostatic union. Thus it comes about that the crucified God becomes peculiarly the object

[20] *In Iohannis Evang. Tr.* 23. 5: 'Dominus Iesus . . . insinuavit nobis animam humanam et mentem rationalem, quae inest homini, non inest pecori, non vegetari, non beatificari, non illuminari, nisi ab ipsa substantia Dei; . . . beatitudinem tamen eius qua fit beata ipsa anima, non fieri nisi participatione illius vitae semper vivae, incommutabilis aeternamque substantiae, quae Deus est. . . . Haec est religio christiana, ut colatur unus Deus, non multi dii; quia non facit animam beatam nisi unus Deus. Participatione Dei fit beata. Non participatione sanctae animae fit beata infirma anima, nec participatione angeli fit beata sancta anima; sed si quaerit beata esse infirma anima, quaerat unde beata sit sancta anima. Non enim beatus efficeris ex angelo tu; sed unde angelus, inde et tu. (6) His praemissis atque firmissime constitutis, animam rationalem non beatificari nisi a Deo, corpus non vegetari nisi per animam, atque esse quamdam medietatem inter Deum et corpus, animam; intendite et recolite mecum . . . et pro viribus fodimus, donec ad petram perveniamus. Verbum Christus, Verbum Dei Christus apud Deum, Verbum Christus et Deus Verbum, Christus et Deus et Verbum unus Deus . . .; sed non tantum Verbum Christus, sed *Verbum caro factum est, et habitavit in nobis*; ergo et Verbum et caro Christus.' *CCSL* xxxvi. 235–6.

[21] *Enar. in Ps.* 58, s. 1. 7: 'Doctor autem humilitatis, particeps nostrae infirmitatis, donans participationem suae divinitatis, ad hoc descendens ut viam doceret et via fieret, maxime suam humilitatem nobis commendare dignatus est.' *CCSL* xxxix. 734.

[22] *Ench.* x. 34. *BA* 9. 166.

[23] Ladner, *The Idea of Reform*, p. 154.

of Christian devotion, and the Risen Christ the pledge of man's deification, of the 'In-Godding' of man, to borrow a phrase of Dr Pusey.[24] So Augustine declares:

Christ's deformity forms you, for if He had not willed to be deformed, you would not have recovered the form which you lost. He, therefore, hung upon the cross deformed; but His deformity was our beauty. In this life, therefore, let us hold the deformed Christ.[25]

And again, in a work addressed to the less educated of his flock:

And so the Son of God assumed manhood and in Himself steadfastly endured human miseries. This medicine for men's sins is so great that it passes imagination. For what pride is able to be cured, if it is not cured by the humility of the Son of God? What avarice can be cured, if it is not cured by the poverty of the Son of God? What anger can be cured, if it is not cured by the patience of the Son of God? What impiety can be cured, if it is not cured by the charity of the Son of God? Finally, what fear can be cured, if it is not cured by the resurrection of Christ's body? Let the human race lift up its hope and recognise its nature and see what a place it has in the works of God![26]

There is, however, a further dimension to Christ's assumption of humanity in the thought of Augustine: the Body of Christ, which is the Catholic Church. The unity of Christ with His Church is one of the dominating themes in Augustinian theology and receives majestic exposition in Book X of *The City of God*, where Christ is shown as the great Priest who offers as a universal sacrifice to God the whole redeemed community, the body of which He is the head.[27] Again, in one of his sermons, Augustine declares:

Therefore, because that flesh has received resurrection and eternal life, which arose and being made alive ascended into heaven, this has been promised to us also. For we expect the inheritance itself, eternal life. But hitherto the whole body has not received it, for the head is in heaven, but the members still upon earth. Nor shall the head alone receive the inheritance and the body be left. The whole Christ will receive the inheritance—the whole according to the manhood, that is, head and body.[28]

This picture drawn by Augustine of Christ's assumption of our flesh both elevating humanity and embracing, not only the individual believer, but the whole Church, 'the whole redeemed community, that is to say, the congregation and fellowship of the

[24] E. B. Pusey, *Sermons during the Season from Advent to Whitsuntide* (Oxford, 1848), p. 63: 'If He have so taken our poor nature into Himself, that in Him it is In-Godded, Deitate', quoted by Y. Brilioth, *The Anglican Revival* (London, 1933), p. 223 n. 1.

[25] *Serm.* 27. vi. 6. *CCSL* xli. 365.

[26] *De Agone Christ.* xi. 12. *CSEL* xli. 115.

[27] *De Civ. Dei* x. 6. *CSEL* xl (1), 456.

[28] *Serm.* 22. x. 10. *CCSL* xli. 300–1.

saints',[29] prepares the way for an examination of a number of texts in which Augustine specifically teaches his doctrine of deification.

1. To make gods those who were men, He was made man who is God.[30]

This is, obviously, a decisive text, echoing Irenaeus: '. . . who for His immense love was made what we are, that He might bring us to perfection, to be what He himself is'[31] and, almost literally, Athanasius: 'He was made man that we might be deified.'[32] Whether Augustine had actually read either Irenaeus or Athanasius cannot be established, and does not greatly matter. What is important is that he is plainly in full agreement with the two Greek-writing Fathers.

In this declaration, Augustine illustrates G. B. Ladner's observation, that if God became man and died on the cross, manhood could never be quite the same again. Capánaga speaks of 'the great antithesis of Christianity', declaring that 'the deification of men is the master-work of Christ and Christianity, revealed above all in the Psalms and the books of the New Testament'.[33] Augustine himself amplifies the brief assertion of Sermon 192, quoted above, in Book IV of *De Trinitate*:

We are not divine by nature; by nature we are men, and through sin we are not righteous men. And so God, being made a righteous man, interceded with God for man who is a sinner. The sinner has nothing in common with the Righteous One, but man has humanity in common with man. Therefore joining to us the likeness of His humanity, He took away the unlikeness of our iniquity, and being made a sharer (*particeps*) of our mortality, He made us sharers of His divinity.[34]

This passage provides an admirable exposition of how Augustine conceives of deification. It owes nothing to man, considered in his

[29] *De Civ. Dei* x. 6.

[30] *Serm.* 192. i. 1: 'Deos facturus qui homines erant, homo factus est qui Deus erat.' *PL* xxxviii. 1012.

[31] Irenaeus, *Adv. Haereses* v, *Praef.*: . . . *τῷ Λόγῳ Θεοῦ Ἰησοῦ Χριστῷ τῷ Κυρίῳ ἡμῶν, τῷ διὰ τὴν ὑπερβάλλουσαν αὐτοῦ ἀγάπην γεγονότι τοῦτο ὅπερ ἐσμέν, ἵνα ἡμᾶς εἶναι καταρτώῃ ἐκεῖνο ὅπερ ἐστὶν αὐτός*. *Lat.* '. . . Verbum Dei Iesum Christum Dominum nostrum, qui propter immensam suam dilectionem factus est quod sumus nos, uti nos perficeret esse quod est ipse.' *SC* 153. 14.

[32] Athanasius, *De Incarnatione* 54. 3: *Αὐτὸς γὰρ ἐνηνθρώπησεν, ἵνα ἡμεῖς θεοποιηθῶμεν*. *PG* xxvii. 192 B.

[33] Capánaga, art. cit., p. 746 n. 4.

[34] *De Trin.* IV. ii. 4: 'Deus enim natura non sumus; homines natura sumus; iusti peccato non sumus. Deus itaque factus homo iustus intercessit deo pro homine peccatore. Non enim congruit peccator iusto, sed congruit homini homo. Adiungens ergo nobis similitudinem humanitatis suae abstulit dissimilitudinem iniquitatis nostrae, et factus particeps mortalitatis nostrae fecit nos participes divinitatis suae.' *CCSL* l. 164.

own being—that is obvious, given Augustine's insistence on the absolute primacy of grace; yet it does owe something to man, in that it comes about through the divine humanity of Christ. Christ is the Mediator between God and man. By being incorporate in His Body through baptism, our humanity is joined to His divinity through His humanity. In Augustine's own words:

And so the only Son of God was thus made the mediator of God and man, when being the Word of God with God, He both brought down His majesty to human affairs and raised human lowliness to the realm of the divine, that He might be a mediator between God and man, being made a man by God above men.[35]

2. *That we might receive the adoption*, says the Apostle, *of sons*. He says *adoption* for this reason, that we may clearly understand the Son of God to be the only Son. For we are sons of God by the favour and esteem of His mercy; but He is by nature the Son, who is what the Father is. Nor does he say *that we might accept* but *that we might receive*, to signify that we have lost this sonship in Adam, from whom we are mortals. . . . Hence we receive adoption because He, the Only-Begotten, has not disdained to participate in our nature, having been made out of woman, that He should not only be the Only-Begotten where He has no brethren, but also be made the First-Begotten of many brethren.[36]

This is a major, perhaps the palmary, text for understanding Augustine's doctrine of deification. It is true that the term deification does not occur in it; what we have is an assertion of the brotherhood of the elect with Christ, because of His assumption of humanity. This does not mean that human nature is changed in its essence; it remains something created, but the created being is raised to a peculiar relationship with its creator by adoption. So Augustine, in the *Tractates on St John's Gospel*, can speak of God's generosity in adopting men as His heirs:

If anyone has an only son he rejoices in him the more, because he alone will possess all his goods, and will not have anyone else to divide the inheritance with him, which will leave him the poorer. Not so God. He sent the selfsame Only Son whom He had begotten and by whom He created all things, into this world, that He might not be one alone, but have adopted brothers. For we are not born of God, as is the Only-Begotten, but adopted by his grace.[37]

[35] *Epist. ad Galatas Exp*. 24. 8, cited above, n. 18.

[36] Ibid. 30. 6: '*Ut adoptionem*, inquit, *filiorum recipiamus*. Adoptionem propterea dicit ut distincte intelligamus unicum dei filium. Nos enim beneficio et dignatione misericordiae eius filii dei sumus, ille natura est filius, quid hoc est quod pater. (7) Nec dixit: accipiamus sed *recipiamus*, ut significaret hoc nos amisisse in Adam, ex quo mortales sumus. . . . (10) Hinc enim adoptionem recipimus, quod ille unicus non dedignatus est participationem naturae nostrae factus ex muliere, ut non solum unigenitus esset, ubi fratres non habet, sed etiam primogenitus in multis fratribus fieret.' *CSEL* lxxxiv. 96.

[37] *In Io. Ev. Tr*. 2. 13. *CCSL* xxxvi. 17.

What is implied here is that for Augustine, as for the Greek Fathers, deification is nothing more, but also nothing less, than what is implied by the New Testament doctrine of *uiothesia*, sonship by adoption and not by nature, through the Incarnation. This does not mean that we may discount the remission of sins brought about by the same Incarnation; on the contrary, the remission of sins was the condition of our adoption, as Augustine says, quite specifically:

The Only-Begotten came to abolish sins, by which we were held in bondage, nor would He adopt us because of their impediment. Those whom He wished to make His brothers, He Himself released and made co-heirs.[38]

3. *I have said, Ye are gods; and ye are all the children of the most Highest. But ye shall die like men: and fall like one of the princes.* It is clear that He calls men *gods* through their being deified by His grace and not born of His substance. For He justifies, who is just of Himself and not of another; and He deifies, who is God of Himself and not by participation in another. Now He who justifies, Himself deifies, because by justifying He makes sons of God. For *to them gave He power to become the sons of God.* If we are made *sons of God*, we are also made *gods*; but this is done by grace of adoption, and not by generation.[39]

This passage might be said to be the corollary to, and the amplification of, the passage from the *Epistulae ad Galatas expositio* cited above. Here Augustine makes a clear identification of adoption and deification, which is echoed in other passages:

God wishes to make you a god, not by nature, like Him whom He begot, but by His gift and adoption. For just as He through His humanity was made a partaker of your mortality, so He makes you a partaker of His immortality by exaltation;[40]

and again:

Therefore if He Himself is the Selfsame and cannot in any way be changed, by participating in His divinity we too shall be made immortal in eternal life; and this pledge has been given to us by the Son of God . . . that before

[38] *CCSL* xxxvi. 17.

[39] *Enar. in Ps.* 49. i. 2: '*Ego dixi: Dii estis, et filii Excelsi omnes; vos autem ut homines moriemini, et sicut unus ex principibus cadetis.* Manifestum est ergo, quia homines dixit deos, ex gratia sua deificatos, non de substantia sua natos. Ille enim iustificat, qui per semetipsum non ex alio iustus est; et ille deificat, qui per seipsum non alterius participatione Deus est. Qui autem iustificat, ipse deificat, quia iustificando, filios Dei facit. *Dedit* enim *eis potestatem filios Dei fieri.* Si filii Dei facti sumus, et dii facti sumus; sed hoc gratiae est adoptantis non naturae generantis.' *CCSL* xxxviii. 575–6.

[40] *Serm.* 166. iv. 4: 'Deus enim deum te vult facere: non natura, sicut est ille quem genuit; sed dono suo et adoptione. Sicut enim ille per humanitatem factus est particeps mortalitatis tuae; sic te per exaltationem facit participem immortalitatis suae.' *PL* xxxviii. 909.

we should be made partakers of His immortality, He should Himself first be made a partaker of our mortality. For just as He was mortal, not of His substance but of ours, so we shall be immortal, not of our substance but of His.[41]

The text on which Augustine founded his proof of deification: *I have said, Ye are gods*, seemed to him to be so self-evident in its meaning that, commenting on the text of John 10: 35 and 36: *If he called them gods, unto whom the word of God came (and scripture cannot be broken), do you say of him whom the Father sanctified and sent into the world, Thou blasphemest, because I said, I am the Son of God*, he was prepared to argue from the deification of man by grace as proof of the deification by nature of the Son:

If the word (*sermo*) of God was so made to men that they should be called gods, how can the Word (*verbum*) of God Himself, who is with God, not be God? If men are made gods by the word of God (*per sermonem Dei*), if by participating (*participando*) they are made gods, is not He in whom they participate not God? If lights which are kindled are gods, is the light which enlightens not God? If they are made gods being warmed in a certain fashion by the saving fire, is He by whom they are warmed not God? You come to the light and are illuminated and numbered among the sons of God. If you draw back from the light you are darkened and reckoned to be in darkness. But that light does not come to Itself, because it does not draw back from itself. If therefore the word (*sermo*) of God makes you gods, how is the Word (*verbum*) of God not God?[42]

Clearly, there is in this argument a philosophical strand derived from Platonism: man's being depends upon his participation in God; but Augustine develops this theologically by appealing to Scripture to argue that man's sanctity depends upon his participation in God and that that participation is of such an order as to justify the language of deification.

[41] *Enar. in Ps.* 146. v. 11: 'Igitur si ipse idem ipse est, et mutari ex nulla parte potest; participando eius divinitatem erimus et nos immortales in vitam aeternam. Et hoc nobis pignus datum est de Filio Dei, quod iam dixi Sanctitati vestrae, ut antequam efficeremur participes immortalitatis ipsius, fieret ipse prius particeps mortalitatis nostrae. Sicut autem ille mortalis, non de sua substantia, sed de nostra, sic nos immortales, non de nostra substantia, sed de ipsius.' *CCSL* xl. 2130.

[42] *In Io. Ev. Tr.* 48. 9: 'Si sermo Dei factus est ad homines ut dicerentur dii, ipsum Verbum Dei quod est apud Deum, quomodo non est Deus? Si per sermonem Dei fiunt homines dii, si participando fiunt dii, unde participant non est Deus? Si lumina illuminata dii sunt, lumen quod illuminat non est Deus? Si calefacti quodammodo igne salutari dii efficiuntur, unde calefiunt non est Deus? Accedis ad lumen et illuminaris, et inter filios Dei numeraris; si recedis a lumine, obscuraris, et in tenebris computaris; illud tamen lumen nec accedit ad se, quia non recedit a se. Si ergo vos deos facit sermo Dei, quomodo non est Deus Verbum Dei?' *CCSL* xxxvi. 417–18.

4. We too are made by His grace what we were not, that is, sons of God. Yet we were something else, and this much inferior, that is, sons of men. Therefore He descended that we might ascend, and remaining in His nature was made a partaker of our nature, that we remaining in our nature might be made partakers of His nature. But not simply thus; for His participation in our nature did not make Him worse, while participating in His nature makes us better.[43]

Here, in the letter to Honoratus *On the Grace of the New Testament*, written in 412 at the very beginning of the Pelagian Controversy, we have an admirable expression of the Augustinian doctrine of man's deification by adoption, by participation in God through the mediation of Jesus Christ. There is an obvious parallel of thought between this passage and the passage from the *Tractates of John*, quoted immediately above. Christ descends to heal fallen man; but the healing is not merely a return to Adam's primal state, an *apokatastasis eis to archeion*, but an elevation, so that the Church may truly say: *O felix culpa, quae talem ac tantum meruit habere Redemptorem!* The image of God in fallen man is renewed *in melius*, to a better condition than that in which Adam was created. So Augustine declares to his congregation:

You hear in the Psalms: *I have said, Ye are gods, and ye are all the children of the Most Highest*. God is therefore calling us, not to be men. But in the future, in a better state, we shall not be men, if we first recognise ourselves to be men, and so rise to that high state by humility. Otherwise, by thinking ourselves to be something when we are nothing, we shall not simply fail to become what we are not, but will in addition lose what we already are.[44]

5. *Putting away lying*, therefore, *speak truth*, so that this mortal flesh which you have up to now from Adam may, after *the reformation of the spirit*, itself deserve renewal and transformation in the time of its resurrection; and thus the whole man, being deified, may cleave to the perpetual and unchanging truth.[45]

[43] *Ep.* 140. iv. 10: 'nos quoque per eius gratiam facti sumus, quod non eramus, id est filii dei; sed tamen aliquid eramus, et hoc ipsum aliquid multo inferius, hoc est filii hominum. descendit ergo ille, ut nos ascenderemus, et manens in sua natura factus est particeps naturae nostrae, ut nos manentes in natura nostra efficeremur participes naturae ipsius, non tamen sic; nam illum naturae nostrae participatio non fecit deteriorem, nos autem facit naturae illius participatio meliores.' *CSEL* xliv. 162.

[44] *In Io. Ev. Tr.* 1. 4: 'Audite in psalmis: *Ego dixi, dii estis, et filii Excelsi omnes*. Ad hoc ergo vocat nos Deus, ne simus homines. Sed tunc in melius non erimus homines, si prius nos homines esse agnoscamus, id est, ut ad illam celsitudinem ab humilitate surgamus: ne cum putamus nos aliquid esse, cum nihil simus, non solum non accipiamus quod non sumus, sed et amittamus quod sumus.' *CCSL* xxxvi. 2.

[45] *Serm.* 166. iv. 4: '*Deponentes* ergo *mendacium, loquimini veritatem* (Eph. 4: 25), ut et caro ista mortalis quam adhuc habetis de Adam, praecedente novitate spiritus, mereatur et ipsa innovationem et commutationem tempore resurrectionis suae: ac sic totus homo deificatus inhaereat perpetuae atque incommutabili veritati.' *PL* xxxviii. 909.

In this passage Augustine makes it clear that deification is a state which will be attained only in the life to come. No one with any experience of Augustine's thinking would expect otherwise, for Augustine insists that our renewal and reform to the image of God is a process which, begun in baptism, is the work of a lifetime. As he puts it in the *De Trinitate*:

Of course, the renewal of which we speak is not effected in the single moment of return, like the renewal which takes place in baptism in a single moment through the remission of all sins—none whatsoever remaining unremitted. But it is one thing to be relieved of fevers, and another to regain health after the weakness which fevers have caused. It is one thing to withdraw a dart from a body, and another to heal by further treatment the wound it has inflicted. So here, cure's beginning is to remove the cause of sickness; and that is done through the forgiveness of sins. Its furtherance is the healing of the sickness itself, which takes effect by gradual progress in the renewal of the image.[46]

Augustine's experience during the ten years which elapsed between his conversion at Milan and the writing of the *Confessions* had left him wary of any claims either to sudden perfection or to final perfection in this life. An example of his caution is to be found in his discussion in *De Genesi ad Litteram* of what we receive in the renovation of what Adam lost.

How then, men say, are we said to be renewed, if we do not receive [in baptism] what the first man lost, *in whom all die*? This we both clearly receive in one way and do not receive in another. Thus, we do not receive the immortality of a spiritual body, which that man did not yet have; but we receive righteousness, from which that man fell by sin. We shall therefore be renewed from the old nature of sin, not into that first animal body in which Adam was, but into a better state, that is a spiritual body, when we shall be made equal to the angels of God, fitted for our heavenly habitation, where we shall have no need of the food which corrupts. We are therefore renewed in *the spirit of our mind* according to the image of Him who created us, which Adam lost by sin. We shall also be renewed in the flesh, when this *corruptible* body *shall put on incorruption*, that it may be a spiritual body, into which Adam was not yet changed but destined to be changed, if he had not deserved the death of his animal body by sinning.[47]

The essence of Augustine's doctrine of deification, as depicted in the texts which we have just examined, may be described as man's participation in God through the humanity of Christ, after this earthly life is ended and without any alteration of man's creaturely status. It is implied by the New Testament doctrine of *uiothesia*,

[46] *De Trin.* XIV. xvii. 25. *CCSL* 1 (A), 454. Tr. John Burnaby.
[47] *De Gen. ad Litt.* VI. xxiv. 35. *CSEL* xxviii (1), 196–7.

sonship by adoption, and is the measure of God's grace to fallen humanity. What features are to be noticed about this doctrine in relation to other Christian thinkers who teach it?

Perhaps the most obvious feature of Augustine's teaching is, that so far as he is concerned, deification pertains to the realm of dogmatic, rather than contemplative, theology; it describes the consequence of the saving work of Christ rather than a mystical state enjoyed by a contemplative. It is of course true that the question of Augustine's personal mysticism is a controversial one, with a great gulf fixed between those scholars who maintain that he * was a mystic and those who deny it. The present writer inclines to denial rather than to affirmation; but in this particular case, opinions on this point are irrelevant, in view of Augustine's direct assertion that deification will take place only in the life to come. As he puts it in *De Peccatorum Meritis et Remissione*:

> Our full adoption as sons will take place *in the redemption of our body*. We now have the *firstfruits of the spirit*, by which we are indeed made sons of God; but in other respects we are sons of God as saved and made new by hope. In the event, however, since we are not yet finally saved, we are therefore not yet fully made new nor yet sons of God, but children of this world.[48]

In this context it is perhaps relevant that in the Vision of Ostia, the most obvious example of an apparently mystical experience enjoyed by Augustine, the saint speaks of himself and Monica as touching, in an instant, the Divine wisdom,

> . . . and leaving the firstfruits of our spirit bound to It, we returned to the sound of our own tongue, in which a word has both beginning and ending.[49]

The experience is transitory (*attigimus eam modice toto ictu cordis*) and the contemplatives leave behind, bound, the firstfruits of the spirit (*et relinquimus ibi religatas primitias spiritus*). Thus, they may be deemed to have had a foretaste of the joys of heaven, but no more; they return to the present world. The firstfruits of the spirit of the Vision of Ostia resemble those of the passage quoted from *De Peccatorum Meritis et Remissione*: they are a pledge, but not a guarantee.

Andrew Louth has noted Augustine's distinction between ecstasy, of which the Vision of Ostia is an example, and the beatific vision, which I would regard as the state which deification implies, and observes that for Augustine, ecstasy '*if it went on for ever*, would be indistinguishable from the joys of heaven. But it does not'.[50] Louth

[48] *De Pecc. Mer. et Rem.* II. viii. 10. *CSEL* lx. 81.
[49] *Conf.* IX. x. 24. *BA* 14. 118.
[50] *The Origins of the Christian Mystical Tradition* (Oxford, 1981), p. 137.

also makes the very interesting suggestion that Augustine is far more aware of the fact of human mortality than the Greek Fathers. 'For Augustine, ecstasy is a breach of that qualification [i.e. that man must die], and its very fleetingness emphasizes the fact.'[51] Louth is certainly correct about Augustine's sense of human mortality. We may remember Possidius' account of how, in the last weeks of his life, with the Vandal army around the walls of Hippo, Augustine was heard to quote the words of Plotinus: 'No great man will think it a great matter when sticks and stones fall and mortals die.'[52] It may be that Augustine's experience of the deaths of those nearest and dearest to him in the early years of his life as a Catholic Christian—Monica, so soon after the Vision of Ostia; Nebridius;[53] and Adeodatus, whose loss must have brought back vivid and bitter memories of past years—had a decisive effect on his theology, which could only have been strengthened in his maturity by the challenge presented by the sack of Rome. Significantly, commenting on Ps. 67: 21 [68: 20]: *Domini exitus mortis*, he declares:

Now *by hope are we saved; but if we hope for what we see not, let us wait for it with patience* (Rom. 8: 24, 25). Let us therefore bear death itself with patience, taking for our example Christ who, although He was not liable to death by any sin, and was the Lord, whose life no one could take away, Himself laid down His life, so that even for Him there was *an issue of death*.[54]

Furthermore, for Augustine deification is an ecclesial process, in that it takes place within the communion of the Church, to which the Christian is admitted by baptism. For this reason, it can be called a sacramental process, in that the Christian grows in grace by being nourished by the eucharist, which he receives as part of the worship of the Church. Augustine in his writings speaks movingly of the sacrifice of Christians, in which the faithful are offered to God by Christ, the great High Priest; but I have not discovered in him

[51] Ibid., p. 138.

[52] Possidius, *Vita Augustini* 28. 12 (ed. Pellegrino, Milan, 1955, p. 154). Tr. F. R. Hoare. The quotation is from Plotinus, *Enneads* I. 4. 7.

[53] Folliet, art. cit., n. 12 above, pp. 227 ff., draws attention to Augustine's concern for preparation for death at the time of his correspondence with Nebridius in 389/390. The fact that Nebridius should have died so soon afterwards, earning a moving tribute in *Conf.* IX. iii. 6, must have had its effect upon Augustine's memories.

[54] *Enar. in Ps.* 67. xx. 29: '. . . *et Domini exitus mortis. Spe enim salvi facti sumus; si autem quod non videmus speramus, per patientiam exspectamus.* Patienter ergo etiam ipsam mortem feramus, illius exemplo qui, licet nullo peccato esset debitor mortis, et Dominus esset a quo nemo animam tolleret, sed ipse eam a semetipso poneret, etiam ipsius fuit *exitus mortis*.' *CCSL* xxxix. 890.

the notion of the Eucharist as the medicine of immortality[55] that we find in the famous passage in Gregory of Nyssa's *Catechetical Oration*,[56] in which the reception of Christ's body and blood divinizes the recipient. It is conceivable that the passage in the *Confessions*: 'I am the food of the full-grown: grow, and you shall feed upon Me, and you shall not change Me into yourself as bodily food, but into Me you shall be changed'[57] may indicate a Eucharistic theology of deification similar to that of Gregory of Nyssa, but this is by no means certain. Augustine certainly teaches a Eucharistic doctrine of the Real Presence, side by side with his doctrine of signs;[58] but his thought seems to be more of the faithful who, as the Body of Christ, are themselves offered on the altar and receive their own mystery[59] than of the divinization of the individual by the life-giving mysteries.

Again, it has been argued that for Augustine deification is equivalent to the New Testament idea of sonship by adoption. It is surely significant that Augustine should have continued to speak of deification when he had an unambiguously scriptural expression available, to use exclusively, if he had so chosen. Are we to see here evidence of the continuing influence of Neoplatonism in his thought, even after he had come to see that there was no way to wisdom save by Christ?[60] Or should we rather see the influence of the Greek Fathers, whose words seem to be echoed by Augustine? What is particularly interesting, in view of the alleged division between East and West on this matter, is that Augustine was apparently prepared to equate justification and deification, regarding both as the consequence of man's adoption.

For He justifies, who is just of Himself and not of another; and He deifies, who is God of Himself and not by participation in another. Now He who justifies, Himself deifies, because by justifying He makes sons of God.[61]

It would be misleading to claim that this passage reconciles the theological differences between East and West on the issue of

[55] Ignatius, *Ad Ephesios*, 20. 2: *Φάρμακον ἀθανασίας* (ed. Kirsopp Lake, *The Apostolic Fathers* i (Loeb edn.), 194).

[56] Gregory of Nyssa, *Oratio Catechetica*, 37. *PG* xlv. 93A–97B.

[57] *Conf*. VII. x. 16: 'Cibus sum grandium: cresce et manducabis me. nec tu me in te mutabis sicut cibum carnis tuae, sed tu mutaberis in me.' *BA* xiii. 616.

[58] See A. Sage, 'L'Eucharistie dans la pensée de saint Augustin' in *Revue des Études Augustiniennes* xv (1969), 208–40.

[59] *Serm*. 272. *PL* xxxviii. 1247.

[60] *Retract*. i. 4. 3: '. . . item quod dixi: *ad sapientiae coniunctionem non una via perveniri* [*Solil*. I. xiii. 23] non bene sonat; quasi alia via sit praeter Christum, qui dixit: *ego sum via*.' *CSEL* xxxvi. 23–4.

[61] *Enar. in Ps*. 49. i. 2 quoted above, n. 39.

deification.[62] One swallow does not make a summer, and it is unlikely that a convinced Protestant will be won to an acceptance of Eastern Orthodox theology by the authority of Augustine, or that disciples of Vladimir Lossky will, with any enthusiasm, accept Augustine as the theological mediator between Orthodoxy and Western Christendom. Nevertheless, the Augustinian passage is interesting, in that it appears to embrace both theological approaches while being at the same time in harmony with the general tone of Augustine's teaching on deification.

This being said, it is necessary to exercise caution. It must be borne in mind that, for Augustine, deification is the privilege of the elect, a small minority, while the great majority of the human race pertains to the *massa damnata*. This may seem to be a mere statement of the obvious, so far as Augustine is concerned; but it must be remembered, to avoid reading into the Augustinian doctrine of deification any of the optimism about human destiny which is sometimes, rightly or wrongly, ascribed to the Greek Fathers. It is, after all, Augustine's rigorous predestinarian theology which made him, for many centuries, the great doctor of Protestantism after St Paul and John Calvin, and inspired the Jansenist movement, which exercised so powerful an influence over French Catholicism. Predestination theology is today out of fashion; indeed, more than a century ago William Bright, introducing a collection of Augustine's anti-Pelagian writings for the use of students of theology at Oxford, felt constrained to speak of the 'vehement and destructive' recoil from Calvinism,[63] which characterized so much of the religious and intellectual history of the nineteenth century. Predestination is, however, too fundamental to Augustine's mature theology, and too much a part of the heritage of Western Christian theology, to be ignored in serious ecumenical debate. If East and West are to come to a common theological mind, as opposed to publishing agreed statements of doctrine, the issues raised by the doctrines of deification and predestination have alike to be faced, and not lightly dismissed as being, in the one case, unchristian, and in the other as being the rationalization of the mystery of human freedom and divine grace.[64]

[62] See the remarks of Jouko Martikainen, n. 7 above.

[63] *Select Anti-Pelagian Treatises of St Augustine and the Acts of the Second Council of Orange* with an introduction by William Bright (Oxford, 1880), p. xiii. Bright specifically mentioned the case of James Mill.

[64] As does Lossky, *The Mystical Theology of the Eastern Church*, ET (London, 1957), p. 198: 'The fundamental error of Pelagius was that of transposing the mystery of grace on to a rational plane, by which process grace and liberty, realities of the spiritual order, are transformed into two mutually exclusive concepts which then have to be reconciled, as if they were two objects exterior to one another. St

[*note 64 continued overleaf*

Augustine, in his attack on Pelagianism, followed the example of his adversary in taking his stand on the same rational ground, where there was no possibility of the question ever being resolved.' This assertion fails to do justice to Pelagius, still less to Augustine; and the problems raised by the question of divine decree and human freedom are not to be resolved by a simple enunciation of the concept of synergism, as Lossky seems to imply.

II

THE DOCTRINE OF SACRIFICE: AUGUSTINE AND THE LATIN PATRISTIC TRADITION

Thus the true sacrifice is offered in every act which is designed to unite us to God in a holy fellowship, every act, that is, which is directed to that Final Good which makes possible our true felicity.[1]

This familiar, and comprehensive, definition of sacrifice is typical of Augustine's thought: he sees it as an action directed to union with God, which alone makes us truly happy. The eudaemonistic element in this definition is characteristically Augustinian: although Augustine has generally little concern for the transitory happiness of the present age ('in huius vitae infelicitate'), in his desire for eternal beatitude he is a thorough hedonist. 'Nulla est homini causa philosophandi nisi ut beatus sit' – the only purpose man has in philosophizing is the attainment of happiness. Yet Augustine is clear that happiness without God is impossible: 'that which makes man happy is the Supreme Good itself'.[2] Furthermore, the only way to attain to the Supreme Good is through the mediation of the God-man, Jesus Christ.[3] From this it follows inevitably that Augustine's approach to sacrifice will be determined by his christocentricity and that he will, without hesitation, accept the earlier tradition which understood the eucharist, the great action of Christian unity, in sacrificial terms. Not every sacrifice, in Augustine's theology, is the eucharist; but every eucharist is a sacrifice.

It is very easy, when dealing with Augustine or with any great thinker, to overestimate his originality and to neglect his debt to the past; but Augustine would have been the first to reject any suggestion that he sought to introduce new doctrine, like some theological Paracelsus burning the books of his predecessors and making a fresh start. Augustine's originality is not iconoclastic. Rather, he amplifies and enriches the thought and feeling of earlier generations. No Christian thinker is more aware of, and more concerned to follow, the tradition of the Catholic Church.

This consideration governs Augustine's attitude to his sources and their possible influence upon him. Of the place of the Bible in his thought there can be no doubt but there remains the question of non-Christian influences, and especially that of pagan philosophy, whether read in translations of the Neoplatonists or mediated by Cicero.[4] To these should be added the actuality of pagan sacrificial worship in Augustine's own day. Although banned by the laws of Christian emperors, paganism remained a force in Roman Africa, and it was possible to find Christians who held that pagan sacrifices, no less than Jewish, had been legitimate in their time and had only become otiose – and illegal – with the rise of Christianity.[5] Such a view forced Augustine to distinguish between Jewish and pagan sacrifice and to maintain the validity of the former before the coming of Christ, while asserting that the latter had always been illegitimate, being directed not to the one true God but to the demons, who had fraudulently appropriated what was due to God alone. A large part of *De Civitate Dei* is devoted to precisely this sort of refutation. Nevertheless, Augustine could not fail to take account of pagan philosophical argument, particularly when he found it in a thinker like Porphyry, whose good qualities he was very ready to recognize. It is, however, unwise to ascribe an Augustinian idea to a pagan source when the Bible provides a likely inspiration. To give an example, in *De Civitate Dei* Augustine writes:

> There are some who suppose that these visible [pagan] sacrifices are suitable for other gods, but that for the One God, as He is invisible, greatest and best, only the invisible, the greatest and the best sacrifices are proper; and such sacrifices are the services of a pure mind and a good will. But such people evidently do not realize that the visible sacrifices are the symbols of the invisible offerings, just as spoken words are the symbols of things. Therefore in our prayers and praises we address significant sounds to Him, as we render to Him in our hearts the realities thus signified. In the same way, in offering our [Christian] sacrifices we shall be more aware that visible sacrifice must be offered only to Him, to whom we ourselves ought to be an invisible sacrifice in our hearts.[6]

The most obvious subject of these remarks is Porphyry who, in his treatise *De Abstinentia*, rejected any sort of sacrifice to the supreme gods and declared that the intelligible gods should only be worshipped by hymns and that to the gods of the world and to the astral gods – the planets and the fixed stars – there should be no bloody sacrifices, but only offerings of corn, honey, fruits and flowers.[7] In similar fashion a saying ascribed to Apollonius of Tyana, preserved by Eusebius of Caesarea, asserts that the highest god has no need of sacrifices at all, and that the only fitting offering is man's reason (*logos*), not the word that comes out of his mouth: 'We men should ask the best of beings through the best thing in us for what is good – I mean by means of the mind, for mind needs no material things to make its prayer.'[8] It is very likely that Augustine was familiar with sentiments like those of Porphyry and Apollonius from his reading; but it is improbable that they exercised much influence on his thinking, if only because the whole point of the polemic against the Neoplatonists in Book x of *De Civitate Dei* is that sacrifice may only be offered to the One God and that *any* offering to an inferior being is idolatry. The horror of pagan sacrifices lies precisely in the fact that they have been usurped by the demons from the One True God.

Accordingly, in his maintaining that God has no need of sacrifice, even though He desires it of men, it is more likely that Augustine's inspiration came from biblical texts like Ps. 15[16]: 2: 'Thou art my God, my goods are nothing unto thee', which he quotes repeatedly,[9] than from any Neoplatonic author. 'The sacrifice of God is a troubled spirit: a broken and contrite heart, O God, shalt thou not despise' (Ps. 50: 19[51: 17]).[10]

Again, it is possible that Augustine's doctrine of the mediation of Christ by his sufferings and death, shown forth in the sacrifice of the altar,[11] could have been influenced by Neoplatonic ideas. There is a passage in the curious handbook of pagan doctrine, *De Diis et Mundo*, by the fourth-century Neoplatonist theologian Salutius (Sallustius), relating to sacrifice. In the best Neoplatonic tradition Salutius declares that the divine has no need of anything and that human worship is offered for man's advantage, and not for the benefit of the gods. Divine Providence is everywhere, and it requires only worthiness, by imitation (*mimesis*) and likeness (*homoiotēs*), to receive its benefits. Hence the apparatus of religious worship imitates its archetypes: temples copy heaven, altars the earth, and statues represent life, which is why they are made in the image of living beings.[12] This leads Salutius to a discussion of how sacrifices unite men with the gods. The primordial and highest life, he declares, is that of the gods. Human life is life of some sort, and in order for communion to exist between these two lives, there must be a mediator (*mesotēs*) to join them. But the mediator must be like the two natures which are to communicate. It therefore follows that life is needed to mediate between divine and human life and hence the need for a mediating victim.[13]

There is here a certain resemblance to Augustine's teaching with regard to the mediation of Christ, and there is no reason to reject the supposition that this particular aspect of Neoplatonic thinking (though not necessarily this particular text) might have been familiar to him. However, similar doctrine was available to Augustine in the Epistle to the Hebrews (especially 2: 14) which, in default of positive evidence to the contrary, would seem a more obviously immediate source of inspiration.

More generally, it may safely be assumed that the Platonic conception of the relation between existing things and the archetypes which they resemble – the more nearly an image approaches its archetype, the more closely it resembles it – played its part in Augustine's theology: 'Everything', says Salutius, 'rejoices in what it resembles and turns away from unlikeness'.[14] The efficacity of any image depends upon its relation to its original. Such a philosophy would harmonize with Augustine's understanding of the relation between Old Testament sacrifices, Christ's final and definitive sacrificial offering and the efficacious signs of bread and wine by which that offering is now shown forth in the Christian eucharist. Yet Augustine could equally well, and actually did, point to the words of St Paul: 'figurae nostrae fuerunt' – 'these things were our types *or* images' (1 Cor. 10: 6) – to explain their significance:

> With all this, you dare to denounce the sacrifices of the Old Testament [he tells Faustus the Manichee] and to call them idolatry, and to attribute to us the same impious notion. To answer for ourselves: in the first place, while we no longer consider it a duty to offer sacrifice, we recognise sacrifices as part of the mysteries of Revelation, by which the things prophesied were foreshadowed. For *they were our images* [*figurae*], and in many and various ways they all pointed to the One Sacrifice which we now commemorate.[15]

And again:

> As regards animal sacrifices, every Christian knows that they were enjoined as suitable to a perverse people, and not because God had any pleasure in them. Still, even in these sacrifices *there were types* [*figurae*] of what we enjoy, for we cannot obtain purification or the propitiation of God without blood. The fulfilment of these types [*figurarum*] is Christ, who is the Truth, by whose blood we are purified and redeemed.[16]

The conclusion which may reasonably be drawn from the foregoing is, then, that while Augustine was unquestionably influenced by Neoplatonic thought – an influence which he never denied – it is not necessary, and may indeed be positively misleading, to emphasize that influence at the expense of the more obviously immediate influence of the Bible, on which his mature theology is fundamentally based.

In his understanding of the idea of sacrifice, Augustine had to take account of three particular connotations of the word in his own day: the physical sacrifices of the pagans, now illegal, and of the Jews, now discontinued; the self-offering of Christ on Calvary, the great sacrifice, which had fulfilled and rendered redundant the Jewish sacrifices;[17] and the Christian eucharist, which had long been regarded as re-presenting or re-actualising the sacrifice of the cross.[18] In his consideration of this third aspect Augustine followed a tradition to which Tertullian, Cyprian and Ambrose had borne witness, and one moreover which was sustained by popular practice. The principle that the law of prayer is the law of belief was never more strikingly illustrated than by the attitude of the early Church to the commemoration of the departed at the offering of the eucharist: 'sacrificium pretii nostri' ('the sacrifice of our redemption'), as Augustine was to call it, when describing the burial of his mother.[19] Furthermore, popular devotion to the dead, as exemplified in the feasts at the tombs of the martyrs, had a superstitious element inherited from paganism, which caused bishops like Ambrose and Augustine to seek to transfer it to orthodox public worship, in which the sacrifice of the altar would replace unregulated devotion, and the enthusiasm of the worshipper be more surely directed from the martyr to the One True God.[20]

It was the actuality of animal sacrifice in a dying but still tenacious paganism – Augustine had, in his youth, refused the offer of a sorcerer to offer victims to ensure his success in a rhetorical competition[21] – and the fact that it had been practised by the saints of the Old Testament, to whom the Christian Church looked for example, that brought an element into the patristic treatment of sacrifice which is not easily intelligible to later ages, for whom animal sacrifice is a matter for the anthropologist and the student of primitive religion. This was not the case in the fourth and fifth centuries. A hostile critic of Catholic Christianity, like the Manichaean bishop Faustus, could accuse the Catholics of being the heirs of both paganism and Judaism;[22] yet there was a very real pastoral problem confronting the Catholic episcopate: to what extent was it permissible to identify Christian practice with the ideas derived from pagan society and from the Judaism described in the Bible, of which the Church claimed to be the only legitimate heir? Here, the crucial decision, made in the second Christian century, to regard the Old Testament as authoritative, played a vital role. If the Catholic Church had decided, like the Gnostics, to reject the Old Testament, many of the problems which arose from the Christian polemic against paganism would never have existed.

The theological key for understanding Augustine's doctrine of sacrifice is his conception of Christ the Mediator, the God-man, who is the great high priest after the order of Melchizedek.[23] In this approach Augustine was not original. Such an attitude was common to his predecessors, such as Cyprian[24] and Ambrose of Milan.[25] What was original in Augustine was his ability to bring together different elements in traditional theology and to weave them into a coherent whole. This is especially apparent in the tenth book of *De Civitate Dei*, a wonderful *tour de force* in which dogmatic and speculative theology is applied to anti-pagan polemic to produce one of the most profound discussions of the nature of sacrifice in Christian literature.

It may be said at the outset that for Augustine the one, true, perfect and sufficient sacrifice, oblation and satisfaction, upon which all others depend, is that offered on Calvary:

> By his death, which is indeed the one and most true sacrifice offered for us, he purged, abolished and extinguished whatever guilt there was by which the *principalities and powers* lawfully detained us to pay the penalty; and by his resurrection he called us, *whom he had predestined*, to new life, *justified those whom he had called, and glorified those whom he had justified* [Rom. 8:30].[26]

It is upon this act of self-oblation that Augustine bases Christ's priesthood. He offered himself, the one sinless victim, for humanity, of whom he had become one:

Who then is so righteous and holy a priest as the only Son of God, who had no need of sacrifice to purge his own sins, either Original or the sins which are added in the course of human life? And what could he take more fittingly from men to offer on their behalf than human flesh? And what was more suitable for such sacrificial offering than mortal flesh? And what was so pure for purifying the vices of mortals than the flesh born without any infection of fleshly lust within and from the womb of the Virgin? And what could more acceptably be offered and received than the flesh of * our Sacrifice, made the Body of our Priest? Since there are four things to be considered in any sacrifice: to whom it is offered, by whom it is offered, what it is that is offered, and for whom it is offered, so the One True Mediator, who reconciles us to God by the sacrifice of peace, remained one with him to whom he offered; made one in himself those for whom he offered; and was himself both the offerer and the thing which was offered.[27]

It is in the tenth book of *De Civitate Dei* that Augustine gives his definition of sacrifice as 'every act which is designed to unite us to God in holy fellowship', which, combined with his earlier statement that 'The visible sacrifice is the sacrament, the sacred sign, of the invisible sacrifice',[28] may be said to epitomize Augustine's understanding. One may note here the comprehensive character of the definition: a sacrifice is 'omne opus' – every act – and not simply the visible sacrifice of the eucharist.[29] Here Augustine is in accord with African tradition, for the word 'sacrifice' had early been applied in Africa to the oblations of the faithful, and St Cyprian can rebuke a rich woman who comes to church 'sine sacrificio' – 'without an offering' – and who therefore communicates from the offerings of the poor.[30] Nevertheless, the notion of sacrifice had simultaneously a more technical sense, being applied to the eucharist, in which Christ's self-offering on Calvary is shown forth. Thus Tertullian can urge those who are observing a fast not to fear that it will be broken by attendance at the Sacrifice and the reception of the body of the Lord.[31] By the time of Cyprian, *sacrificium* is the regular word for the eucharist, instituted by Christ,[32] celebrated by the bishops, 'who daily as priests solemnize the sacrifices of God',[33] and offered for the departed.[34] The same language is found in Optatus of Mileve, Augustine's predecessor as a Catholic apologist against the Donatists,[35] and in Ambrose of Milan.[36]

Nevertheless, the eucharist is a sacrifice only because of its relation to Christ's self-offering as a propitiation for human sin.[37] Foreshadowing this great and supreme sacrifice[38] were the sin-offerings of the Jews, offered by the high priest, both for himself as a sinner and for his sinful people. Christ's sacrifice differs from, and completes, the earlier sacrifices, because here the priest and the offering are one and the same, and the priest, no less than the victim, is pure:

... by the grace of God he was in a marvellous and ineffable manner conjoined and interknit in unity of person with the Father's only-begotten Word, who is not by grace but by nature the Son, and therefore himself committed no sin. Yet because of the *likeness of sinful flesh* [Rom. 8: 3] in which he came, he was himself described as sin [2 Cor. 5: 21], seeing he was to be sacrificed for the washing away of sins. In fact in the old Law, sacrifices for sins were called by the name of sins [Lev. 6: 25; Num. 8: 8; Hos. 4: 8]; and he became that in truth of which those sacrifices were shadows.[39]

Christ was not, however, only the victim, but the priest as well. Augustine was helped here by the fact that in the Old Latin Bible which he used the word 'propitiation' (*hilasmos*) of 1 John 4: 10: 'and sent his Son as the propitiation for our sins', was translated by *litator*, 'an offerer of sacrifices'.

And he sent his Son to be the propitiator for our sins – propitiator, that is, offerer of sacrifice. He offered sacrifice for our sins. Where did he find the offering, the pure victim that he would offer? Because he could find no other, he offered himself.[40]

It is this sort of understanding of the character of Christ's sacrifice which underlies the famous passage in Book x of *De Civitate Dei* which is, perhaps, the finest short statement of Augustine's thought in the whole of his writings:[41]

Hence it is that the true Mediator, insofar as he *took the form of a servant* and was thus made the *mediator between God and mankind, the man Christ Jesus* [1 Tim. 2: 5], receives the sacrifice *in the form of God* [Phil. 2: 6, 7], in union with the Father, with whom he is one God. And yet *in the form of a servant* he preferred to be himself the sacrifice than to receive it, to prevent anyone from supposing that sacrifice, even in this circumstance, should be offered to any created being. Thus he is both the priest, himself making the offering, and the oblation. This is the reality, and he intended the daily sacrifice of the Church to be the sacramental symbol of this; for the Church, being the Body of which he is the Head, learns to offer herself through him. This is the true sacrifice, and the sacrifices of the saints in earlier times were many different symbols of it. This one sacrifice was prefigured by many rites, just as many words are used to refer to one thing, to emphasize a point without inducing boredom. This was the supreme sacrifice and all the false sacrifices yielded place to it.[42]

Given the patristic view that the Old Testament writings are prophetic, not only in the specifically prophetic books but as a whole, it was desirable to find in them a figure who would foreshadow the coming of Christ and anticipate the ending of animal sacrifices and their replacement by the offering of bread and wine, instituted by Christ at the Last Supper. Such a figure was found in the person of Melchizedek, king and priest, from the letter to the Hebrews. Here again, Augustine was by no means the first Latin Christian author to dwell on his significance. The relation between him and Christ, 'the pontifex of the uncircumcised priesthood', had already been urged by Tertullian:[43] but it was to be richly developed by St Cyprian in his sixty-third letter, the earliest extended study of the eucharist, cited by Augustine.[44] Cyprian was concerned to denounce the practice of some bishops who used water in the eucharist instead of the traditional mixed chalice. His argument turns upon his conception of Christ as the true priest of which Melchizedek was a type.[45]

The influence of the figure of Melchizedek as a type of Christ in relation to the understanding of the eucharist in African theology was immense.[46] In the first place, by seeing Melchizedek as a prophetic image of Christ, it was possible to explain why the Aaronic sacrifices of the Old Testament had ceased, superseded by the unbloody rites of the Christians – a useful argument in controversy with the Jews. So Augustine could write:

[Abraham] received at that time a public blessing from Melchizedek, who was the priest of the Most High God. Many important things are written about Melchizedek in the epistle entitled *To the Hebrews* . . . Here we certainly see the first manifestation of the sacrifice which is now offered to God by Christians in the whole world, in which is fulfilled what is said in prophecy, long after the event, to Christ who was yet to come in the flesh: *Thou art a priest for ever after the order of Melchizedek.* Not, it is to be observed, in the line of Aaron, for that line was to be abolished when the events prefigured by these shadows came to the light of day.[47]

Again, in a sermon, he could declare:

There was formerly, as you know, animal sacrifice among the Jews after the order of Aaron, and this was allegorical, for there was not, as yet, the sacrifice of the Body and Blood of the Lord, which the Faithful and those who read the Gospel know – a sacrifice now spread over the whole world. Therefore set before your eyes two sacrifices, the one after the order of Aaron, the other *after the order of Melchizedek,* for it is written: *The Lord sware and will not repent: thou art a priest for ever after the order of Melchizedek.* About whom is it said: *Thou art a priest for ever after the order of Melchizedek?* About our Lord Jesus Christ. Who was Melchizedek? The king of Salem. Salem was a city of former times which afterwards, as learned men have shown, was called Jerusalem. Therefore before the Jews ruled there, there was that priest Melchizedek, who is described in Genesis as *the priest of the Most High God.* He met Abraham when he had freed Lot from the hand of those who pursued him, and had laid low those by whom Lot was held; after the liberation of his kinsman, Melchizedek met him. And Melchizedek, by whom Abraham was blessed, was very great. *He brought forth bread and wine* and blessed Abraham, and Abraham gave him tithes. You see what he brought forth and whom he blessed; and afterwards it was said: *Thou art a priest for ever after the order of Melchizedek.* David said this in the spirit long after Abraham, for Melchizedek was contemporary with Abraham. About whom else does he say: *Thou art a priest for ever after the order of Melchizedek* except about Him whose sacrifice you know? So the sacrifice of Aaron has been taken away and the sacrifice *after the order of Melchizedek* has begun.[48]

Augustine, however, owed more to Cyprian than the conception of the prophetic character of Melchizedek fulfilled in the person of Christ, whose passion and resurrection are shown forth in the eucharist, which is now the universal and only valid sacrifice. In Cyprian Augustine also found the conception, which he was to develop in his arguments with the Donatists with regard to the validity of baptism administered by sinners, of Christ being the true priest at the eucharist, with the ordained minister being only his representative:

For if Christ Jesus, our Lord and God, is himself the great High Priest of God the Father, and if he offered himself as a sacrifice to the Father and directed that this should be done in remembrance of him, then without doubt that priest truly serves in Christ's place [*vice Christi*] who imitates what Christ did; and he offers up a true and complete sacrifice to God the Father in the Church when he proceeds to offer it just as he sees Christ himself to have offered it.[49]

In a similar spirit Augustine can write to the Donatists in 409:

Why then do we not speak the truth and rightly understand that, while the grace is of God and the sacrament of God, the ministry is always of a man who, if he is good, cleaves to God and works with God; but if he is bad, God works the visible form of the sacrament through him, but himself gives the invisible grace? Let us all understand this and let there be no schism among us.[50]

Yet Christ is not only the true priest, himself offering the sacrifice of the Faithful; he has also associated the Faithful with himself, offered in the bread and wine. So Augustine, preaching to the newly baptised on Easter Day, explaining to them the character of the sacrament, describes the action of the eucharist up to the consecration, and continues:

Then, after the sanctification of the sacrifice of God, because He has willed that we ourselves should offer sacrifice, as was clearly indicated at the first institution of that sacrifice of God which we are – or, rather, of which we are the sign – well then, when the sanctification has taken place, we say the Lord's Prayer.[51]

This passage, expressed by Augustine in rather disjointed phraseology, is clarified by *De Civitate Dei* 10, 6:

So then, the true sacrifices are acts of compassion, whether towards ourselves or towards our neighbours, when they are directed towards God; and acts of compassion are intended to free us from misery and thus to bring us to happiness – which is only attained by the Good of which it has been said: *As for me, my true good is to cling to God* [Ps. 72 [73]: 28]. This being so, it immediately follows that the whole redeemed community, that is to say the congregation and fellowship of the saints, is offered to God as a universal sacrifice, through the great Priest who offered himself in his suffering for us – so that we might be the Body of so great a head – under *the form of a servant* [Phil. 2: 7]. For it was this form he offered, and in this form he was offered, because it is under this form that he is the Mediator, in this form he is the Priest, in this form he is the Sacrifice.[52]

The complexity of construction of the argument of this passage is remarkable, even by Augustine's standards. Starting from his premiss that a sacrament is every act which is designed to unite us to God in holy fellowship, he argues that acts of compassion are sacrifices, and immediately applies this conception to the eucharist, in which Christ, the priest, offers his Body, which is at one and the same time the human body which suffered on Calvary; the bread and wine on the altar, which are offered by the Faithful; and the Faithful themselves. The result is an astonishing piece of theological exposition. Yet the thought underlying it had been formulated by Cyprian in his Letter 63 long before Augustine:

And this bonding and union between water and wine in the Lord's cup is achieved in such a way that nothing can therefore separate the union between Christ and the Church, that is, the people who are established within the Church and who steadfastly and faithfully persevere in their beliefs. Christ and his Church must remain ever attached and joined to each other by indissoluble love ... And just as the Lord's cup consists neither of water alone nor of wine alone but requires both to be intermingled together, so, too, the Lord's body can neither be flour alone nor water alone but requires that both be united and fused together so as to form the structure of one loaf of bread. And under this same sacred image our people are represented as having been made one, for just as numerous grains are gathered, ground, and mixed all together to make into one loaf of bread, so in Christ, who is the bread of heaven, we know there is but one Body, and that every one of us has been fused together and made one with It.[53]

The Cyprianic image of bread and wine as representing the unity of a multiplicity of individuals may well have been in Augustine's mind when he delivered his Sermon 227 to the newly baptised:

This bread which you see on the altar, sanctified by the word of God, is the Body of Christ. This cup – or, rather, what this cup contains – being sanctified by the word of God, is the Blood of Christ. Through these our Lord Jesus Christ willed to entrust to us his Body and Blood, which he poured out for us for the remission of sins. If you have received them in good faith, you are what you have received. Now the Apostle has said: *We, being many, are one bread, one body* [1 Cor. 10: 17]. Thus he has explained the sacrament of the Lord's table: *We, being many, are one bread, one body*. He has shown you in this bread how you ought to love unity. Was this bread made from one grain? Were there not rather many grains of wheat? But before they came to be one loaf they were separate; they have been conjoined after a sort of crushing, for unless the wheat is ground and sprinkled with water, it will by no means come to that form which is called bread. Such was your condition before being, as it were, ground by the humiliation of fasting and the sacrament of exorcism. Then came baptism and you were, so to say, moistened by the water so that you might come to the form of bread... The Holy Spirit came, fire after water [of baptism] and you became the bread which is the Body of Christ.[54]

This notion of unity with and in Christ in the eucharist, illustrated by the images of bread and wine made into his own Body and Blood by the high priest, who offers his people who make up his Body, had its effect upon Augustine's ecclesiology and, in particular, on the relation between the Church Militant and the City of God with regard to the faithful departed. Of the significance of the eucharist offered for the dead in the early Church, and in Roman Africa in particular, there is no question. Monica, on her deathbed, desired her sons, wherever they might be, to remember her at God's altar,[55] and when Augustine's own time came, 'the holy Sacrifice was offered up, commending his body to the earth, and he was buried'.[56] Augustine repeatedly declares that the departed receive much benefit from it, provided that they have been baptized and that their earthly lives have been such as to justify our intercession.[57] Deprivation of the help of the Sacrifice after death was a terrible penalty, to be imposed only for grave offences, such as making one of the clergy an executor or guardian (an appointment which could not legally be refused), 'for he does not deserve to be named at the altar of God in the prayers of the priests who would call the priests and ministers away from the altar'.[58] Indeed, so great was African confidence in the efficacy of funerary celebration that it became necessary to forbid the practice of placing the eucharist in the mouth of the corpse at burial, 'for it was said by the Lord: *Take and eat*; but corpses are not able either to take or to eat'.[59]

There was, clearly, a very considerable element of superstition in the popular attitude to the cult of the dead, of which Augustine disapproved. Of the propriety of the practice of eucharistic commemoration of the dead, however, he had no doubt:

> Accordingly, funerary ostentation, huge congregations, lavish expenditure on the burial, expensive construction of tombs – these are some sort of consolation to the living, but no help to the dead. But there is no doubt that the dead *are* helped by the prayers of Holy Church, by the saving Sacrifice, and by alms which are expended for their spirits, so that they may be more mercifully treated by God than their sins have deserved. The universal Church observes this custom, handed down by the Fathers, that prayer should be made for those who have died in the communion of the Body and Blood of Christ, when they are commemorated at the appropriate place in the Sacrifice, and also that it should be proclaimed that It is offered for them.[60]

It was this sense of the unity of all faithful Christians, the living and the departed alike, in the offering of the eucharist, which enabled Augustine to find a theological understanding to replace the old literal belief in a Thousand Year Reign of Christ with his saints before the Last Judgement, as described in Revelation 20:4. The passage of the centuries had made a literal interpretation of the Apocalypse less and less attractive; but this apart, it was not congenial to Augustine's mind to seek to define times and seasons:

> We are now in the Sixth Epoch [of the world], but that cannot be measured by the number of generations, because it is said: *It is not for you to know the dates: the Father has decided those by his own authority* [Acts 1:7].[61]

For this reason Augustine, although constrained by controversy with the Donatists to maintain that the Church Militant must, at the present time, be a mixed body, containing both good and bad Christians, is nevertheless prepared to identify her with the Kingdom of Christ:

For the souls of the pious dead are not separated from the Church, which is even now the Kingdom of Christ. Otherwise they would not be commemorated at the altar of God at the time of the partaking of the Body of Christ, nor would it be of any avail to have recourse to the Church's baptism in time of peril, for fear that this life should end without baptism, nor to have recourse to reconciliation at such time, if it happens that one is separated from this Body under penance or through one's own bad conscience. Why are such steps taken, unless it is because the Faithful are still members of this Body, even when they have departed this life? And therefore their souls, even though not yet with their bodies, already reign with Him while those thousand years are running their course. That is why we read, in another place in the same book: *Blessed are the dead who die in the Lord. Yes indeed, says the Spirit, from henceforth they may rest from their toils, for their deeds go with them* [Rev. 14: 13]. And so the Church now begins to reign with Christ among the living and the dead.[62]

It would be going too far to assert that this rejection of millenarianism and Augustine's unhesitating declaration that both the living and those who die in the peace of the Church are equally members of the Church Militant are directly derived from Augustine's doctrine of eucharistic sacrifice. What cannot reasonably be disputed is that they are in harmony with the whole tenor of his thought on the eucharistic sacrifice as revealed in his writings. The eucharist proclaims the self-offering of Christ on Calvary. It is not. however, a mere commemoration, but an active re-presentation by Christ himself, the true Minister who is in his own person both Priest and Victim. Hence, in the action of the eucharist, time impinges on eternity,

for sacrifice is a divine matter [*res divina*] in the phrase of the old Latin authors, even if it is performed or offered by a man . . .

and, significantly, Augustine adds:

Hence a man consecrated in the name of God, and vowed to God, is in himself a sacrifice, inasmuch as he *dies to the world* so that he may *live for God* [Rom. 6: 11].[63]

– a reminder that death enters into the notion of sacrifice,[64] and most appropriately into the priesthood of Christ, who has died and is alive again.

Such a train of thought leads Augustine, by a kind of theological inevitability, to the triumphant declaration:

This is the sacrifice of Christians, who are *many, making up one body in Christ* [Rom. 12: 5]. This is the sacrifice which the Church continually celebrates in the sacrament of the altar, a sacrament well-known to the faithful, where it is shown to the Church that she herself is offered in the offering which she presents to God.[65]

It has, in this essay, been argued that in his treatment of the notion of Christian sacrifice, Augustine is less original and more in harmony with earlier tradition than might have been expected, in view of his reputation as an innovator in Latin theology. In fact, comparison with his predecessors suggests that the character of Augustine's thought had already been determined by theologians of an earlier generation, with whom he was happy to agree. Nevertheless, it would be unreasonable and unfair not to recognize in Augustine's thinking a richness and an amplitude which justifies his peculiar reputation among the great theologians of the early Church. He draws out and amplifies what in his predecessors was only implicit or more briefly stated.

NOTES

Abbreviations

CCL	*Corpus Christianorum*. Series Latina, Turnhout
CSEL	*Corpus Scriptorum Ecclesiasticorum Latinorum*, Vienna
ep.	*epistola* (letter)
PL	*Patrologiae cursus completus*. Series Latina. Accurante J.-P. Migne, Paris
s.	*sermo* (sermon)
SC	*Sources chrétiennes*, Paris

1 *De Civitate Dei* (hereafter *Civ.*) 10, 6: 'Proinde verum sacrificium est omne opus, quo agitur, ut sancta societate inhaereamus Deo, relatum scilicet ad illum finem boni, quo veraciter beati esse possimus' (*CCL* XLVII, 278; trans., here and elsewhere, by Henry Bettenson (Penguin Classics, 1972); we gratefully acknowledge permission from Penguin Books to reprint these translations. Other translations below are mine, unless otherwise stated.) On sacrifice in the thought of Augustine see W. J. Sparrow-Simpson, *The Letters of St Augustine* (London, 1919), 276–300, Bonner (1978), Lécuyer (1954) and Cunningham (1886). This last contains *An Epistolary Dissertation Addressed to the Clergy of Middlesex wherein the Doctrine of St Austin concerning the Christian Sacrifice is set in a true Light. By Way of Reply to Dr Waterland's late Charge to them. By a Divine of the University of Cambridge*. This pamphlet, perhaps by the nonjuror George Smith (1693–1756), is a monument of erudition.

2 *Civ.* 19, 1, 3 (*CCL* XLVIII, 659).

3 *Expositio Epistulae ad Galatas* 24: 'Sic itaque unicus Filius Dei, mediator Dei et hominum factus est, cum Verbum Dei Deus apud Deum, et maiestatem suam usque ad humana deposuit, et humilitatem humanam usque ad divina subvexit, ut mediator esset inter Deum et homines, homo per Deum ultra homines' (*CSEL* LXXXIV, 87).

4 Note his reference (*Civ.* 19, 1, 1) to Cicero's treatise '*De finibus* enim *bonorum et malorum* multa et multipliciter inter se philosophi disputarunt' (*CCL* XLVIII, 657). It is all too easy to see Augustine as the pupil of Plotinus, and to neglect his continued and openly acknowledged debt to Cicero.

5 It was only in 399 that the temples at Carthage were finally closed; but paganism remained strong for years afterwards. See Charles-Picard 1965, 98–130; Hamman 1979, 170–93; and Bonner 1984, 347–50. On the attitude

of Christians who believed that pagan sacrifice had been valid before the coming of Christ, see *De Divinatione Daemonum* 2, 4: 'Contra hoc dictum est, iniusta quidem esse nunc ista, non tamen mala; et ideo iniusta, quia contra leges, quibus prohibentur, fiunt; ideo autem non mala, quia, si mala essent, numquam deo utique placuissent; porro si numquam placuissent, numquam et facta essent, illo non sinente, qui omnia potest, et qui talia non contemneret' (*CSEL* XLI, 601).

6 *Civ.* 10, 19 (*CCL* XLVII, 293).

7 Porphyry, *De Abstinentia* II, 34–7 (ed. J. Boffartigue and M. Patillon (Paris: Collection des Universités de France, Association Guillaume Budé, 1979), vol. II, pp. 100–4).

8 Eusebius, *Preparatio Evangelica* 4, 13 (*SC* CCLXII, 144; trans. G.R.S. Mead, *Apollonius of Tyana. The Philosopher-Reformer of the First Century A.D.* (New York, 1966), p. 154 (slightly modified).

9 *Civ.* 10, 5 (*CCL* XLVII, 276); 19, 23, 5 (*CCL* XLVIII, 694); *ep.* 102, 17 (*CSEL* XXXIV (2), 558–9); *ep.* 138, 1, 7 (*CSEL* XLIV, 132).

10 *Civ.* 10, 5 (*CCL* XLVII, 277). Note that Augustine quotes from the Old Latin version of the Psalms, made from the Greek version (the Septuagint), in which the numeration commonly differs from the Hebrew original, from which our English versions are made. I give both numbers here for ease of reference.

11 *Civ.* 10, 6: 'Hoc est sacrificium Christianorum: *multi unum corpus in Christo*. Quod etiam sacramento altaris fidelibus noto frequentat ecclesia, ubi ei demonstratur, quod in ea re, quam offert, ipsa offeratur' (*CCL* XLVII, 279).

12 *De Diis et Mundo*, 15, 1–3 (ed. G. Rochefort (Paris: Budé 1960), p. 20).

13 *Ibid.*, 16, 2; cf. 13, 5 (Rochefort edn, pp. 21; 19). Cf. Augustine, *De Trinitate* 8, 10, 14, providing an image of the Trinity: 'Quid est autem dilectio vel caritas quam tantopere scriptura divina laudat et praedicat nisi amor boni? Amor autem alicuius amantis est, et amore aliquid amatur. Ecce tria sunt, amans et quod amatur et amor. Quid est ergo amor nisi quaedam vita duo aliqua copulans vel copulari appetens, amantem scilicet et quod amatur?' ('What is the Love of Charity which Holy Scripture so greatly praises and preaches, except love of the good? But love supposes a lover and a beloved. So there are three things: the lover, the beloved, and love. And what is love *except a certain life, joining or seeking to join two beings*, the lover and the beloved?') (*CCL* L, 290–1). This would seem to be a clear instance of Neoplatonic thought affecting Augustine's imagery.

14 *De Diis et Mundo*, 3, 2 (Rochefort edn, p. 5). On the need for the image to be turned to the archetype, see Plotinus, *Enneads* V, 3, 7 (ed. A. H. Armstrong (Loeb Library; Cambridge, Mass.: Harvard University Press/London: William Heinemann, 1984), pp. 92–101).

15 *Contra Faustum Manicheum* 6, 5 (*CSEL* XXV (1), 290–1); trans. R. Stothert, *Augustine: Writings in Connection with the Manichacan Controversy* (Select Library of Nicene and Post-Nicene Fathers, 4; Buffalo (Christian Literature Company, 1887), p. 169), slightly modified). Here and below, italics in these quotations signify biblical quotations.

16 *Ibid.*, 18, 6 (*CSEL* XXV (1), 494–5).

17 *Enarrationes in Psalmos* 33, s. 1, 5 (*CCL* XXXVIII, 277), and *ibid.*, 39, 13: 'Det mihi modo gens iudaica sacerdotem. Ubi sunt sacrificia illorum? Certe perierunt,

certe ablata sunt nunc' (*CCL* XXXVIII, 435; *ep.* 138, 1, 7: '... scriptura dicit: *Mutabis ea et mutabuntur, tu autem idem idem ipse es* (Ps. 101:27, 28 [102:26, 27])) insinuandum est eis mutationem istam sacramentorum testamenti veteris et novi etiam praedictam fuisse propheticibus vocibus' (*CSEL* XLIV, 132); *Civ.* 17, 5, 2 (*CCL* XLVIII, 562–3).

18 Cyprian, *ep.* 63, 9: 'quomodo autem, de creatura vitis novum vinum cum Christo in regno patris bibemus, si in sacrifico Dei patris et Christi vinum non offerimus nec calicem Domini dominica traditione miscemus?'; 17: 'Et quia passionis eius mentionem in sacrificiis omnibus facimus, passio est enim Domini sacrificium quod offerimus' (*CSEL* III (2), 708; 714).

19 *Confessiones* 9, 12, 32 (*CCL* XXVII, 151).

20 On Ambrose, see Dassmann 1975, pp. 49–68, esp. pp. 54, 55. On Augustine, see his account of the ending of the *Laetitia* festival in *ep.* 29. For the attitude of a hostile critic, see the charge of Faustus: '... sacrificia vero eorum [paganorum] vertistis in agapes, idola in martyres, quos votis similibus colitis; defunctorum umbras vino placatis et dapibus, sollemnes gentium dies cum ipsis celebratis, ut Kalendas et solstitia. de vita certe mutastis nihil: estis sane schisma a matrice sua diversum nihil habens nisi conventum' (*Contra Faustum* 20, 4 (*CSEL* XXV (1), 538)).

21 *Confessiones* 4, 2, 3 (*CCL* XXVII, 41).

22 *Contra Faustum* 20, 4 (cited above, note 20); 6, 5 (*CSEL* XXV (1), 290–1).

23 *Enarrationes in Psalmos* 33, s. 1, 5, 6 (*CCL* XXXVIII, 276–7); *Civ.* 16, 22; 17, 5, 5; 18, 35, 3 (*CCL* XLVIII, 524–5; 565–6; 629–30).

24 Cyprian, *ep.* 63, 4 (*CSEL* III (2), 703–4).

25 On the figure of Melchizedek in Ambrose, see Johanny 1968, 240–3.

26 *De Trinitate* 4, 13, 17: 'Morte sua quippe uno verissimo sacrificio pro nobis oblato quidquid culparum erat unde nos principatus et potestates ad luenda supplicia iure detinebant purgavit, abolevit, exstinxit, et sua resurrectione in novam vitam nos *praedestinatos vocavit, vocatos iustificavit, iustificatos glorificavit*' (*CCL* L, 183).

27 *De Trinitate* 4, 14, 19 (*CCL* L, 186–7).

28 *Civ.* 10, 5: 'Sacrificium ergo visibile invisibilis sacrificii sacramentum, id est sacrum signum est' (*CCL* XLVII, 277).

29 Cf. *Enarrationes in Psalmos* 49, 23: 'Videte autem quod sequitur, fratres mei. Iam enim nescio quis, quia dixerat illi Deus: *Immola Deo sacrifium laudis*, et hoc quodammodo vectigal indixerat, meditabatur sibi, et dicebat: Surgam quotidie, pergam ad ecclesiam, dicam unum hymnum matutinum, alium vespertinum, tertium aut quartum in domo mea; quotidie sacrificio sacrifium laudis, et immolo Deo meo. Bene facis quidem, si hoc facis; sed vide ne iam securus sis, quia iam hoc facis, et forte lingua tua Deum benedicat, et vita tua Deo maledicat' (*CCL* XXXVIII, 593).

30 Cyprian, *De opere et eleemosynis* 15 (*CSEL* III (1), 384).

31 Tertullian, *De Oratione* 19 (*CCL* I, 267–8).

32 Cyprian, *ep.* 63, 1: 'Iesus Christus Dominus et Deus noster sacrificii huius auctor et doctor fecit et docuit' (*CSEL* III (2), 701).

33 Cyprian, *ep.* 57, 3: '... ut sacerdotes qui sacrificia Dei cotidie celebramus hostias Deo et victimas praeparemus' (*CSEL* III (2), 652).

34 Cyprian *ep.* 1, 2 (*CSEL* III (2), 466).
35 Optatus, 2, 12; 3, 4; 4, 3; 7, 6 (*CSEL* XXVI, 47; 85; 104; 179).
36 Ambrose, *Expositio Evangelii secundum Lucam* 1, 28 (*CCL* XIV, 20).
37 *De Trinitate* 4, 13, 17, quoted above, note 26.
38 *Civ.* 10, 20 (*CCL* XLVII, 294).
39 *Enchiridion* 13, 41 (*CCL* XLVI, 72; trans. E. Evans, *Saint Augustine's Enchiridion* (London, 1953), p. 39).
40 *In epistulam Iohannis ad Parthos tractatus decem* 7, 9 (*PL* XXXV, 2033; trans. John Burnaby, *Augustine: Later Works* (Library of Christian Classics, 8; London, 1955), pp. 316–17).
41 But cf. *De Trinitate* 4, 14, 19, quoted above, p. 106.
42 *Civ.* 10, 20 (*CCL* XLVII, 294).
43 Tertullian, *Adversus Marcionem* 5, 9, 9 (*CCL* I, 690–1).
44 *De Doctrina Christiana* 4, 21, 45 (*CCL* XXXII, 151–2).
45 See Cyprian, *ep.* 63, 4 (*CSEL* III (2), 703; trans. G. W. Clarke. *The Letters of St Cyprian of Carthage*, vol. III (Ancient Christian Writers, 46; New York/Mahwah: Paulist Press, p. 99). All quotations from Cyprian's letters at any length are from this version; we gratefully acknowledge permission from the Paulist Press to reproduce these.
46 And in Italy, in the writings of Ambrose; see Johanny 1968.
47 *Civ.* 16, 22 (*CCL* XLVIII, 524–5).
48 *Enarrationes in Psalmos* 33, *s.* 1, 5, 6 (*CCL* XXXVIII, 276–7). Cf. *Civ.* 17, 5, 3; 18, 35, 3 (*CCL* XLVIII, 565–6; 629–30).
49 Cyprian, *ep.* 63, 14: 'nam si Christus Iesus Dominus et Deus noster ipse est summus sacerdos Dei patris et sacrificium patri se ipsum optulit et hoc fieri in sui commemorationem praecepit, utique ille sacerdos vice Christi vere fungitur qui id quod Christus fecit imitatur et sacrificium verum et plenum tunc offert in ecclesia Deo patri, si sic incipiat offerre secundum quod ipsum Christum videat optulisse' (*CSEL* III (2), 713).
50 *Ep.* 105, 3, 12: 'quare ergo non verum dicimus et recte sapimus, quia semper dei est illa gratia et dei sacramentum, hominis autem solum ministerium, qui si bonus est, adhaeret deo, et operatur cum deo; si autem malus est, operatur per illum deus visibilem sacramenti formam, ipse autem donat invisibilem gratiam? hoc sapiamus omnes et non sint in nobis schismata' (*CESL* XXXIV (2), 604).
51 *S.* 227: 'Deinde post sanctificationem sacrificii dei, quia nos ipsos voluit esse sacrificium suum, quod demonstratum est ubi impositum est primum illud sacrificium dei et nos – id est signum rei – quod sumus, ecce ubi est peracta sanctificatio dicimus orationem dominicam' (ed. S. Poque, *SC* 116, p. 240).
52 *Civ.* 10, 6 (*CCL* XLVII, 279).
53 Cyprian, *ep.* 63, 13 (*CSEL* III (2). 711–12).
54 *S.* 227 (ed. Poque, pp. 234–8).
55 *Confessiones* 9, 11, 27 (*CCL* XXVII, 148–9).
56 Possidius, *Vita Augustini* 31, 5 (ed. M. Pellegrino (Alba: Edizioni Paolini, 1955), p. 190; trans. F.R. Hoare, *The Western Fathers* (London: Sheed and Ward, 1954), p. 243).
57 *De anima et eius origine* 1, 11, 13; 2, 15, 21 (*CSEL* LX, 313; 356); *Enchiridion* 29, 110 (*CCL* XLVI, 108); *s.* 159, 1 (*PL* 38, 867–8); *s.* 172, 2 (*PL* 38, 936–7).

58 Cyprian *ep.* I, 2 (*CSEL* III (2), 466).

59 *Brevarium Hipponense*, 4: 'Ut corporibus defunctis eucharistia non detur; dictum est enim a Domino: *Accipite et edite*; cadavera autem nec accipere possunt nec edere' (*CCL* CXLIX, 33–4).

60 *S.* 172, 2 (*PL* 38, 936–7). Cf. *Civ.* I, 12: 'Proinde ista omnia [id est] curatio funeris, conditio sepulturae, pompa exequiarum, magis sunt vivorum solacia quam subsidia mortuorum' (*CCL* XLVII, 14).

61 *Civ.* 22, 30 (*CCL* XLVIII, 865–6).

62 *Civ.* 20, 9, 2 (*CCL* XLVIII, 717).

63 *Civ.* 10, 6: 'Etsi enim ab homine fit vel offertur, tamen sacrificium res divina est, ita ut hoc quoque vocabulo id Latini veteres appellaverint. Unde ipse homo Dei nomine consecratus et Deo votus, in quantum mundo moritur ut Deo vivat, sacrificium est' (*CCL* XLVII, 278).

64 A point noted by Rickaby (1925, p. 43 note 1).

65 *Civ.* 10, 6, quoted above, note 11.

REFERENCES

Bonner, G. (1978). The Church and the Eucharist in the Theology of St. Augustine. *Sobornost* ser. 7, no. 6, 448–61 [reprinted 1987 in *God's Decree and Man's Destiny* (London: Variorum Reprints, 6)]

(1984). The Extinction of Paganism and the Church Historian. *Journal of Ecclesiastical History* 35, 347–50

Charles-Picard, G. (1965). *La Carthage de Saint Augustine*. Paris: Fayard

Cunningham, W. (1886). *St. Austin and his Place in the History of Christian Thought*. London: Clay and Sons

Dassmann, E. (1975). Ambrosius und die Martyrer. *Jahrbuch fur Antike und Christentum* 18, 49–68

Hamman, A.-G. (1979). *La vie quotidienne en Afrique du Nord*. Paris: Hachette

Johanny, R. (1968). *L'eucharistie: centre de l'histoire de salut chez Saint Ambroise de Milan*. Paris: Beauchesne

Lécuyer, J. (1954). Le sacrifice selon Saint Augustin. In *Augustinus Magister (Congres International Augustinien, Paris, 21–24 September 1954)*, vol. 2, pp. 905–14. Paris: Etudes Augustiniennes

Rickaby, J. (1925). *St. Augustine's City of God: A View of the Contents*. London: Burns & Oates

Corrigenda

p. 106, l. 9–10, please read: ... the Body of our Priest made the flesh of our Sacrifice?

III

How Pelagian was Pelagius?

An examination of the contentions of Torgny Bohlin

This paper does not profess to resolve the problem implied in its title, but merely to draw attention to the fact that, despite great advances in the study of Pelagius' life and writings, the heresiarch himself remains an enigmatic, one might almost say a shadowy, figure. A distinguished scholar has recently observed, when speaking of Pelagius, that "it is plain that we are in the presence of an outsize personality, whose extravagant opinions were felt in some way to match an extravagant physical appearance"[1], the reference being, of course, to the very unflattering description given by Jerome and Orosius of Pelagius' physical characteristics in his later years. But we should beware of taking too seriously the pen-portrait given by Jerome of any man he detested, or that of Orosius, anxious to represent himself as a new David, defying the Goliath of heresy[2]. Nor is the reference to an outsize personality one which can be easily sustained from the facts of history; for while Pelagius has given his name to one of the greatest controversies of Church history, which preoccupied western theologians for centuries after the deaths of the principal antagonists and whose effects are still with us, his whole tendency during the dispute was to avoid debate and to keep himself in the background. He lacked both the political acumen of Caelestius and the indefatigable journalistic enthusiasm of Julian of Eclanum. Indeed, far from regarding Pelagius as an outsize personality, it is tempting to echo Collingwood's uncompromising judgement: "It was the ineffective, unpractical man [Pelagius] who insisted on the freedom of the will; the strong

---

[1] J. N. L. Myres, Pelagius and the end of Roman rule in Britain, in: Journal of Roman Studies 50, 1960, 24.

[2] Cf. Georges de Plinval, Pélage: ses écrits, sa vie et sa réforme, Lausanne, 1943, 56.

man [Augustine] knew that such insistance was the unconscious betrayal of inner weakness"[1].

It will be generally conceded that Pelagius was a singularly unfortunate man. But for the controversy with which his name is inalienably associated, and into which he was precipitated by the importunity of his disciples, he might have lived a life of honourable mediocrity, and earned a place among Christian writers of the second or third rank of the patristic age. No one ever accused him of serious sin. Augustine, indeed, always spoke of his personal character with respect[2] and recognised the sincerity of his desire to rebuke those who urged human frailty as an excuse for their failure to amend their ways[3]. Yet he has gone down to history as an heresiarch, the more deplorable because the more subtle. The excesses of Caelestius and Julian of Eclanum are clear enough, but those of Pelagius, if we judge from what has been preserved in the writings of Augustine, may well appear to a modern critic with no axe to grind to be capable of an orthodox interpretation. It is significant that the Oxford scholar, J. B. Mozley, in a study of the Augustinian doctrine of predestination first published in 1855, was able to say: "It does not appear that [the Pelagian] limits the idea of grace to nature in the sense of the powers with which man was originally endowed at his creation, or to the outward helps of the law. On the contrary, he includes in it those internal Divine impulses and spiritual assistances commonly denoted by the word"[4]. Thus, as early as

[1] R. G. Collingwood and J. N. L. Myres, Roman Britain and the English Settlements, Oxford, 2nd ed., 1937, 309.

[2] See, for example, his remarks at the beginning of the dispute, De Pecc. Mer. et Rem. III 1, 1: *verum post paucissimos dies legi Pelagii quaedam scripta, sancti viri, ut audio, et non parvo provectu Christiani, quae in Pauli apostoli epistolas expositiones brevissimas continerent* . . . CSEL LX 129.

[3] Aug., De Nat. et Grat., I 1: *et vidi hominem zelo ardentissimo accensum adversus eos, qui cum in suis peccatis humanam voluntatem debeant accusare, naturam potius accusantes hominum per illam se excusare conantur*. CSEL LX 233.

[4] J. B. Mozley, A Treatise on the Augustinian Doctrine of Predestination, London, 1855, 54 (2nd ed., 1878, 50). Mozley is not here speaking of Pelagius alone, but of the followers of his system, including Julian of Eclanum; but of the two references which he gives, Op. Imperf. c. Iul. III 106 (PL XLV 1291) and De Grat. Christi VII 8: '*Adiuvat enim nos deus, inquit [Pelagius], per doctrinam et revelationem suam, dum cordis nostri oculos aperit; dum nobis, ne praesentibus occupemur, futura demonstrat; dum diaboli pandit insidias; dum nos multiformi et ineffabili dono gratiae caelestis illuminat*' (CSEL XLII 131), only the second, which refers to Pelagius alone, is sufficiently concrete to buttress his case.

the nineteenth century, it was possible, on the basis of the hostile evidence provided by Augustine, to suggest that Pelagius had been misjudged.

In the twentieth century, the researches of a number of scholars have opened the way to an entirely new reconsideration of Pelagius' rôle in the controversy which goes by his name. Among these, three names stand out: Alexander Souter; Georges de Plinval; and Torgny Bohlin. Thanks to the labours of Souter, we possess the authentic text of what is possibly Pelagius' greatest work and certainly the most important of those which have come down to us: his commentary on the Pauline Epistles, written before the commencement of the Pelagian controversy, and therefore of vital importance as evidence of the tendencies of his mind when no charge of unorthodoxy hung over him [1]. To Plinval we owe an admirable biography of Pelagius, which places him in his correct perspective in his own age as a reformer and teacher [2], and a study of Pelagius' language and style [3]. Finally, Bohlin has used Pelagius' commentary on St. Paul, as identified and edited by Souter, as the basis for a study of Pelagius' theological principles and the sources from which he drew them [4]. In so doing, Bohlin has provided a new point of departure for Pelagian studies, which future Church historians will neglect at their peril, for he raises issues which, as I hope to argue, go beyond the mere question of the good faith of Pelagius himself in the Pelagian controversy.

First, let me indicate, very briefly, the field of Bohlin's enquiry. His book falls into two parts: a description of the theology of Pelagius and an examination of the sources upon which he drew in formulating his doctrine, in a highly selective fashion which excluded whatever did not suit his own ideas [5]. This second

---

[1] Alexander Souter, Pelagius's Expositions of Thirteen Epistles of St Paul (Texts and Studies IX), Cambridge, 1922–1926. With Souter should be commemorated Heinrich Zimmer, Pelagius in Irland, Berlin, 1901 – an epoch-making work to whose importance Souter pays due homage.

[2] Plinval, op. cit.

[3] Idem, Essai sur le style et la langue de Pélage (Collectanea Friburgensia, N. S., Fasc. 31), Fribourg en Suisse, 1947.

[4] Torgny Bohlin, Die Theologie des Pelagius und ihre Genesis (Uppsala Universitets Årsskrift 1957, 9), Uppsala/Wiesbaden, 1957.

[5] Ibid., 56: "Aus einem Gedankensystem kann Pelagius einen bestimmten Aspekt herausgreifen und ihn herauskristallisieren und ihn dann in sein eigenes System einfügen, wobei er andere Tendenzen, die die so herauskristallisierten

part which, though important, does not immediately concern us, we will notice first. In this, Bohlin shows that Pelagius made use of a number of authors including Augustine (the early works); Hilarius (Ambrosiaster); St. Ambrose; and Origen, whom he studied in the translation of Rufinus of Aquileia. Pelagius thus read within two traditions: the western, represented by Augustine, Hilarius and St. Ambrose; and the eastern, represented by Origen-Rufinus. It was his genius to combine these two traditions to construct a theology to oppose his principal theological opponent: Manichaeism[1].

This brings us to the first part ot Bohlin's study. In his exposition of Pelagius' system, based primarily upon a detailed study of his commentaries upon the Pauline Epistles, he shows that Pelagius has two adversaries constantly in mind: Arianism, which denies the true Godhead of Christ, and Manichaeism, which denies His true humanity[2]. It is these two heresies, and especially the latter, which condition his approach and cause him, when speaking of Grace, to have constantly in mind Manichaean dualism, which declares evil to be a substance and the created world evil, and Manichaean determinism, which declares sin to be inevitable, since it is merely the operation of the evil principle within us.

With great care and clarity, Bohlin analyses Pelagius' reply to Manichaeism, expressed in his doctrine of Grace. He observes that Pelagius' thinking is dialectical: strictly speaking God alone is by nature wise and good, but God bestows goodness and wisdom upon man in creating him and so man, in a certain fashion, is wise and good[3]. Man's free will is the gift of God but, since it is free will, it can be regarded dialectically both as something God-given and divine and also as something specifically human[4]. Only on the human side can free will be abused and turn to sin

---

aufwiegen, vollständig vernachlässigt. Das hat Pelagius' Art, mit Augustins Gedanken umzugehen, bestätigt." [1] Ibid., 109–110.

[2] Ibid., 13: "Nach Pelagius sind sowohl der Arianismus als auch der Manichäismus mit ihrer Anschauung vom Schöpfer häretisch. Aber der Arianismus leugnet Christi wahre Gottheit, während der Manichäismus seine wahre Menschheit leugnet." [3] Ibid., 15.

[4] Ibid., 16: "Das Denken des Pelagius ist dialektisch: derselbe Wille, der von einem Gesichtspunkte her gottgeschenkte Natur ist, kann von einem anderen Gesichtspunkt her der Natur gegenüber gestellt werden als etwas spezifisch Menschliches. Die beiden Seiten dieser Dialektik sind gegen den Manichäismus gewandt."

and therefore, from the divine point of view, the God-given capacity to avoid sin can be termed a necessity of human nature[1]. Thus Pelagius is prepared to describe the transmission of the divine capacity to man in the creative act as Grace[2], and ask how anything, which stands in absolute dependence upon God, can be said to be without God's Grace[3]. This is one side of Grace conceived in terms of Creation, which Bohlin terms IA. Closely allied to it is the Grace of Conservation, IB, an aid *(auxilium)*, a word which, for Pelagius, is closely allied to Grace[4].

Secondly, Pelagius speaks of the Grace of Revelation. For him, reason and the will are closely allied. To live righteously is to live reasonably, but to follow Adam's example is to live unreasonably, so that the sinner needs the Graces of Revelation and Forgiveness to restore him[5]. The Grace of Revelation comes through the Law (Grace II A) and the Revelation of Christ (II B), which stands in the same relation to the Revelation given by the Law as the light of the sun to that of the moon[6]. The man who does not rightly believe in Christ cannot rightly believe in the prophets[7].

Finally, there is a third conception of Grace: that of the Remission of Sins. Here again, Pelagius' dialectical thinking plays its part. From one point of view man's nature, being the gift of God, cannot be injured by sin, and man can assert his free will at any time and receive the Grace of Revelation when he desires. Sin, from this point of view, is something external to man[8]. But, from another point of view – that of man – by choosing evil and falling into the custom of sin, man forfeits his free will, so that the Grace of Revelation is not enough. He requires something else – the Death and Resurrection of Christ.

Once again, the dialectic dominates Pelagius' thought. In one sense, Christ's Death and Resurrection are something outside man, models for him, and as such pertain to the Grace of Revela-

---

[1] Ibid., 18. [2] Ibid.

[3] Pelagius, De Natura, cited in Aug., De Nat. et Grat. XLV 53: *Nam cum dicitur ipsum posse arbitrii humani omnino non esse, sed naturae, sed auctoris naturae, dei scilicet, ecqui fieri potest ut absque dei gratia intellegatur, quod ad deum proprie pertinere censetur.* CSEL LX, 271–272.

[4] Bohlin, op. cit., 19. [5] Ibid., 25.

[6] Ibid., 27.

[7] Ibid.

[8] Ibid. 29–30.

tion. But in another, deeper sense, in the sacrament of Baptism, they are internal. In the sacrament of Baptism we suffer, die and rise again with Christ. This Grace (III B) was foreshadowed in the Old Testament in the faith of Abraham (III A).

By Baptism men are freed from the tyranny of custom and regain their freedom of action. It is, however, a freedom which depends upon God's gift in Creation. By this type of argument, Pelagius was able to meet those of the Manichees. As Bohlin observes, Pelagius' system stands or falls by its anti-Manichaean dialectic[1]. It was not intended to sustain the sort of analysis to which it was subjected by Augustine. Pelagius never discussed how faith takes its origin or the relation between God's contribution and man's response[2]. His aim was to refute the Manichees and his system, with its concept of nature and will, was clearly an effective anti-Manichaean apparatus.

So far, so good. But does this mean that Pelagius was essentially the victim of a great misunderstanding, and that he was not a Pelagian, as the word is commonly understood, just as Nestorius is held by some not to have been a Nestorian?

Before we consider this question, let us notice certain points about Bohlin's researches. He seems to me to have succeeded in killing two unfair, but popular prejudices about Pelagius. First, that his system was, at heart, godless, and secondly, that it borrowed heavily from Stoicism. I do not think that either of these views can now be maintained in the face of Bohlin's analysis of Pelagius' teaching. Again, Bohlin has made clear the object of Pelagius' arguments: the refutation of Manichaeism – a piece of elucidation which finds support from the fact that Pelagius' supporters, during the Pelagian controversy, affected to regard the Augustinian doctrine as being a new version of Manichaeism. Finally, Bohlin confirms the view that the doctrine of Pelagius is not identical with that of later Pelagianism, as exemplified by Caelestius and Julian of Eclanum[3]. The charge of rationalism, often levelled against these two, is not true of Pelagius.

Are we therefore justified in regarding Pelagius as being, in intention at least, innocent of the charges brought against him,

---

[1] Ibid., 40: "Mit der aus seinem Antimanichäismus herrührenden Dialektik scheint Pelagius' System zu stehen und zu fallen."

[2] Ibid. 40.

[3] Ibid. 9.

and was his disgrace and condemnation a tragic case of misunderstanding? Certain considerations seem to favour this view. Augustine himself records that at one point, when reading Pelagius' work *De Natura,* he came very near to believing that Pelagius admitted Grace in the sense in which Augustine understood it[1]. Again, Pelagius' general behaviour during the Pelagian controversy suggests that he rather missed the point of the attack. He never took the initiative and acted only in his own defence. At the Synod of Diospolis, when faced by statements made by Caelestius, he declined to enter into any controversy and merely proclaimed his own adherence to Catholic doctrine[2]. Again, the confession of faith which he prepared for Pope Innocent in which, as Augustine observed, he spoke of matters like the unity of the Trinity and the resurrection of the body, which were not in dispute[3], may well seem to be the marks of a puzzled man, not clear as to why he was being marked out for denunciation and anxious to show that his whole system was a defence of the Catholic faith against two of its chief enemies, Arianism and Manichaeism[4]. Viewed in this light, his famous retort to Orosius at Jerusalem in 415: "What is Augustine to me?"[5] is less a mark of overweening arrogance than the retort of a scholar who, without any desire to engage in polemics, is fully confident of his own judgement, and not prepared to alter it at the behest of another divine, however eminent.

There is, however, another side to the matter, which may make us hesitate to exculpate Pelagius as entirely as these reflections seem to recommend. In the first place, there is precisely the ambiguity of Pelagius' language on Grace; if he were really so near to what Augustine regarded as the mark of Catholic doctrine, why did he never make an unambiguous declaration of a true internal assisting Grace? It was not, after all, only St. Augustine who condemned Pelagius, but also Pope Zosimus who

---

[1] De Nat. et Grat. X 11–XI 12: *Dicit ergo* [Pelagius]: *sive per gratiam sive per adiutorium sive per misericordiam et quicquid illud est per quod esse homo absque peccato potest, confitetur quisquis rem ipsum fatetur. Fateor dilectioni vestrae, cum ista legerem, laetitia repente perfusus sum, quod dei gratiam non negaret, per quam solam homo iustificari potest; hoc enim in disputationibus talium maxime detestor et horreo.* CSEL LX 240.

[2] De Gestis Pel. XIV 30; XVIII 42–43. CSEL XLII 83–84. 97–98.

[3] De Grat. Christi XXXII 35. CSEL XLII 152.

[4] See Bohlin, op. cit., 14–15.

[5] Orosius, Liber Apologeticus 4: *et quis est mihi Augustinus?* CSEL V 607.

was, at one time, disposed to be lenient. Zosimus' change of heart, unless it is to be dismissed merely as a concession to anti-Pelagian feeling, is a guarantee that close acquaintance with the works of Pelagius raised doubts in the minds of his orthodox contemporaries.

Furthermore, we cannot fail to observe that, for all his retiring ways, it was Pelagius who was regarded as the leader and inspirer of the Pelagian heresy. It was not Rufinus of Syria, the man who, according to Marius Mercator, first introduced the heresy to Rome[1], nor Caelestius, who so vigorously proclaimed it, nor Julian of Eclanum, its most formidable apologist, who gave Pelagianism its name; and the word *Pelagiani*, which first appears in 415[2], is an indication that his contemporaries and posterity have alike agreed to see in Pelagius the Briton the inspirer of the heresy which denies the need for prevenient Grace. Without feeling obliged to accept J. N. L. Myres' view of an 'outsize personality', we are bound to recognise that Pelagius had ability to inspire bolder men to proclaim views which his opponents believed were his own.

I said at the beginning that this paper did not profess to resolve the problem which it proposed. No final judgement upon the personal views of Pelagius seems possible at the present state of our knowledge. Like Priscillian, Nestorius and other unfortunates in Christian history, he may have been simply unlucky in the circumstances of his writing, and been held responsible for the excesses of others. One thing, however, may be said: that his ingenious system for refuting Manichaeism does suffer from a deadly flaw in that, while it may be adequate with regard to Grace, it certainly does not provide adequately for the disastrous consequences for humanity of the Fall. Pelagius recognised the natural goodness of human nature as part of the divine creation, but his anti-Manichaean outlook prevented him from developing the other term of his dialectic: the extent of the cor-

[1] Marius Mercator, Liber Subnotationum in Verba Iuliani Praef. 2: *Hanc ineptam et non minus inimicam rectae fidei quaestionem, sub sanctae recordationis Anastasio Romanae Ecclesiae summo pontifice, Rufinus quidam natione Syrus Romam primus invexit, et ut erat argutus, se quidem ab eius invidia muniens, et per se proferre non ausus, Pelagium gente Brittanum monachum tunc decepit, eumque ad praedictam apprime imbuit atque instituit impiam vanitatem.* PL XLVIII 111 A.

[2] See Plinval, Pélage, 216 n. 3.

ruption brought about in human nature by the Fall. It is perhaps this blindness which prevented him from understanding the emphasis laid by Augustine upon the need for prevenient Grace, the *adiutorium a quo* as well as for the *adiutorium sine quo non* for which Pelagius' system abundantly provides. Perhaps, indeed, the clue to Pelagius' orthodoxy or heresy lies not so much in his concept of Grace as in that other, vehemently debated topic, the baptism of infants *in remissionem peccatorum.*

IV

THE SIGNIFICANCE OF AUGUSTINE'S *DE GRATIA NOVI TESTAMENTI*

Augustine's Letter 140, included by him among his longer treatises in the *Retractationes* (II, 62 [63]), is one of the most interesting of his compositions, in that it provides an insight into some of the fundamental assumptions of his theology. Although the work undoubtedly had the nascent Pelagian movement in mind, as the long concluding exhortation makes clear (37, 83-85), it has a range and comprehensiveness which goes beyond the immediate context and makes it, in certain respects, a microcosm of Augustine's theological thinking. The purpose of this article is to examine the development of the argument of the treatise, as an example of Augustine's views before they were hardened by the polemics of controversy, by an analysis of the text.

Of Honoratus, the inspirer of the letter, we know only what we are told by Augustine. There is no compelling reason to identify him with the recipient of the *De Utilitate Credendi*, though equally there is no evidence which would decisively exclude such identification[1]). The statement in Cassiodorus' *Institutes* that he was a presbyter[2]) is contradicted by the letter itself, which speaks of him as being not yet baptised (19, 48). It is conceivable that Cassiodorus was misled by Augustine's opening phrase, *dilectissime mi frater Honorate*, into supposing that he was in holy orders; but it may be that Augustine's use of the word *frater*, commonly employed in writing to his fellow

[1]) G. BARDY, *Les Révisions* (Bibliothèque Augustinienne 12) (Paris, 1950), 585: '*Le traité «De gratia noui Testamenti»* ... est adressé à ce même Honorat à qui avait été naguère dédié le *De Libero arbitrio* (*sic*!)'; John H.S. BURLEIGH, *Augustine: Earlier Writings* (The Library of Christian Classics Volume VI) (London, 1953), 287: 'There is nothing in the Epistle to suggest that the two men are identical, though they well may be. It would be pleasant to think that St Augustine won his case'; Mary Inez BOGAN, *Saint Augustine. The Retractations* (The Fathers of the Church Volume 60) (Washington, D.C., 1968), 63: 'It would be interesting to know more about this addressee [of *De Utilitate Credendi*] but it is not possible to do so with certainty, for we do not have definite grounds on which to identify him as ... the Honoratus whose five queries ... are answered by Augustine in ... *Letter* 140'.

[2]) *Institutiones* I, 16. 4: 'scripsit etiam quinque quaestiones de nouo Testamento ad Honoratum presbyterum ...' (ed. Mynors 54. 21-23).

clergyman, is to be here understood as being inspired by pastoral concern. In Letter 139, addressed to Count Marcellinus, Augustine refers to the heavy burden of urgent correspondence laid upon him and speaks of a letter to *Honoratus noster* which he has in hand for immediate reply, since the *ordo amandi* requires that those most in need of assistance should be helped first: 'for love deals with her sons as a nurse does with children, devoting her attention to them, not in the order of the love felt for each, but according to the urgency of each case'[3]).

So far as the dating of the letter is concerned, Augustine's own language in the *Retractationes* supplies fairly precise information. It was written, he says, 'at the time when I was strenuously engaged in controverting the Donatists and had already begun to oppose the Pelagians'[4]). Furthermore, he places the composition of the *De Gratia Novi Testamenti* after the *De Peccatorum Meritis et Remissione* but before the *De Spiritu et Littera*, which would locate it in the period 411-412. Such a date is confirmed by a reference in the work itself (5, 13) to *Enarratio in Ps.* 72, which was preached *nocte, qua inlucescebat sollemnitas beatissimi Cypriani*, that is, 13-14 September 411[5]); and by the reference in Letter 139, dated by Goldbacher to the winter of 411-412: 'Nunc in manibus habeo librum ad Honoratum nostrum de quaestionibus quibusdam quinque, quas mihi proposuit et per litteras intimauit, cui non continuo respondere uides quam minime oporteat'[6]). Altogether, the most satisfactory date would seem to be the early months of 412.

Honoratus had asked Augustine to explain the meaning of five passages of Scripture: the cry of dereliction from the Cross: *My God, my God, why hast thou forsaken me?*; the passage in Ephesians: ... *that you, being rooted and grounded in love, may have power to comprehend with all the saints what is the breadth and length and depth* ... (3: 17, 18); the significance of the parable of the five wise and the five foolish virgins (Matt. 25: 2); the outer darkness (Matt. 8: 12; 22: 13); and the declaration: *The Word was made flesh.* To these Augustine added a

[3]) *Ep.* 139, 3: '... sicut nunc in manibus habeo librum ad Honoratum nostrum de quaestionibus quibusdam quinque, quas mihi proposuit et per litteras intimauit, cui non continuo respondere uides quam minime oporteat. caritas enim, quae tamquam nutrix fouet filios suos, non ordine amandi sed ordine subueniendi infirmiores fortioribus anteponit'; ed. Goldbacher, *CSEL* xliv, 153. 7-12.

[4]) *Retr.* 2, 62 [63]. *CCSEL* lvii, 119. 3-4.

[5]) O. PERLER, *Les voyages de Saint Augustin* (Paris, 1969), 456-7.

[6]) *CSEL* xliv, 153. 7-10.

sixth of his own, designed to combine the questions into a coherent theological whole: What is the grace of the New Testament? The resulting treatise, based upon so variegated a collection of texts, is something of a *tour de force*, in view of the fact that Augustine did not choose the topics of his exegesis, but had them imposed by another. The one concession which he allowed himself in answering Honoratus' questions was to alter the order and to treat first the meaning of the declaration that *the Word was made flesh*, thus setting the tone of his discussion, which would be determined by the meaning of the Incarnation.

At the outset, however, Augustine makes a distinction between two possible human lives: the temporal life, which pursues transitory and sensual pleasures; and the life of the intellect, chosen by the reason and aided by divine providence, in order that the reasonable soul may so make use of temporal happiness that it may hereafter enjoy the eternal God. Although things temporal are not in themselves evil, since they are God's creation and are therefore naturally good, the reasonable soul must nevertheless love them with an ordered love, so that it may rise from the lower goods to the higher, and thence come to the God who is the source of all goodness.

This short passage (2, 3-4) is an exposition of familiar themes in Augustinian theology. We find them discussed in greater or lesser detail in earlier writings: in the Cassiciacan dialogues; in the first and second books of the *De Doctrina Christiana*; and in the *De Natura Boni*. In Letter 140 they serve as an introduction to the section (2, 5) in which Augustine introduces what will be a recurring theme throughout the whole work: temporal benefits and earthly happiness are in themselves good things and the gift of God; but they are not an end in themselves and are only shadows of higher goods — a truth which is made clear in the Old Testament, in which the true and lasting blessings of the New were prophesied and understood, though only by a few — the prophets who were made worthy by divine grace. It is by the prophets that the coming of Christ was foretold, which would teach mankind the truly good things, for whose sake earthly felicity should rightly be rejected.

This notion was not new for Augustine in 412. It had been expressed in a famous passage in the *De Vera Religione* (27, 50), composed at Thagaste in 389/90, in which Augustine speaks of the 'two lives' of the old and earthly man and the new and heavenly man (I Cor. 15: 47), revealed in a succession of people devoted to the one God.

> But from Adam to John the Baptist [the people of the one God] live the life of the earthly man under a kind of servile righteousness. Their history is called the Old Testament, which promised a sort of earthly kingdom, all of which was nothing more than an image of the new people and of the New Testament, which promises the Kingdom of Heaven[7]).

Augustine returns to this idea in *Ep.* 140, with a special emphasis. In the *De Vera Religione* he had spoken of the possibility of the 'old man' obtaining 'what the common herd calls happiness in a well-ordered earthly city' (26, 48: *quam uulgus uocat felicitatem in bene constituta terrena ciuitate*). In *Ep.* 140, 5, 13 he emphasises the fact that God has bestowed worldly felicity even on the wicked, to discourage Christians from worshipping Him for the sake of a material reward, which they see that the wicked may also enjoy, and refers Honoratus to his sermon on Psalm 72 for more detailed treatment. In this psalm, Augustine sees the Jews in the Old Dispensation as serving God rightly, but for earthly ends; while the heathen also seek the same good things, but from the demons[8]). Yet the good things enjoyed by the Jews were only symbols of the happiness of the New Testament. The psalmist sees the wicked in prosperity and almost loses faith in God, until he *comes into the sanctuary* and sees their final end at the Last Judgement[9]). Christ has come in the fulness of time to teach men to scorn the temporal, not to set a high value on what the wicked desire, and to endure what they fear. Christ has been made the Way. He has called men back to deep reflexion and has warned us what should be sought from God[10]). Earthly goods are to be despised, and things eternal

[7]) *Vera rel.* 27, 50: '... sed ab Adam usque ad Iohannem Baptistam terreni hominis uitam gerens seruili quadam iustitia. Cuius historia Vetus Testamentum uocatur, quasi terrenum pollicens regnum. Quae tota nihil est aliud quam imago noui populi et Noui Testamenti pollicentis regnum caelorum'. *CSEL* lxxvii, 36. 7-10.

[8]) *En. Ps.* 72, 6: 'Synagoga ergo, id est, qui Deum ibi pie colebant, sed tamen propter terrenas res, propter ista praesentia; sunt enim impii qui praesentium rerum bona a daemonibus quaerunt; hic autem populus ideo melior erat gentibus, quod quamuis praesentia bona et temporalia, tamen ab uno Deo quaerebat, qui est creator omnium, et spiritalium, et corporalium'. *CCSEL* xxxix, 990. 1-7.

[9]) Ibid., 23: 'Ego, inquit, de sanctuario Dei intendo oculum in finem; praesentia transgredior. Totum hoc quod uocatur humanum genus, omnis ista massa mortalitatis uentura est ad examen, uentura est ad libram; appendentur ibi opera hominum'. *CCSEL* xxxix, 998. 14-18.

[10]) Ibid., 16: '*Cum autem uenit plenitudo temporis, misit Deus Filium suum*. Ipsa est plenitudo temporis, quando uenit ille temporalia docere contemni, non habere magnum quidquid mali homines cupiunt, pati quidquid mali homines metuunt. Factus est uia, reuocauit ad cogitationem intimam, admonuit quid a Deo quaerendum esset'. *CCSL* xxxix, 995. 5-10.

desired[11]). While not condemning the possession of riches in themselves, Augustine holds out no hope for the proud rich man, who glories in his wealth and despises his poor brother.

> All our rich brethren abounding in money, gold, silver, family connexions and honours may well tremble at what has just now been said: *Thou, O Lord, shalt bring their image to naught in the city*. Do they not deserve to suffer in this way, that God *should bring their image to naught in* his *city*, because they themselves have brought the image of God [i.e. the poor, made in the image of God] to nothing in their own earthly city?[12])

It is to this exposition of Psalm 72 that Augustine refers Honoratus in Letter 140, to amplify his contention that the man Christ, in order to reveal the grace of the New Testament, was not recommended by earthly good fortune but by suffering and death, so that His faithful followers might learn what reward they ought to ask and expect for their devotion (*Ep.* 140, 5, 13). The grace of the New Testament — and in this context it would seem better to understand *gratia* as 'favour', as in Luke 1: 30 and Acts 7: 46 in the Vulgate version, rather than in the usual Augustinian sense of aid (*adiutorium*) — as revealed in the person of Jesus Christ, has nothing to do with material well-being or worldly happiness. The servant of Christ must, in the words of St Paul, be as those *having nothing and yet possessing all things* (II Cor. 6: 10).

This consideration suggests another approach — though by no means an exclusive one — for understanding the *De Gratia Novi Testamenti*, apart from Augustine's own account in the *Retractationes*. Augustine located the work as having been composed in the period when the Donatist Controversy was at its height and the Pelagian beginning, and he took care, at the conclusion of the treatise (37, 83-85) to utter a solemn warning against those who, although virtuous in their actions and orthodox in their beliefs, nevertheless put their confidence

[11]) Ibid., 20: '*Et fui flagellatus tota die.* A me non recedunt flagella Dei. Bene seruio, et flagellor; non seruit, et ornatur. Magnam quaestionem sibi fecit. Agitatur anima, transit anima transitura ad contemnenda terrena et concupiscenda aeterna. Transitus est ipsius animae in hac cogitatione; ubi fluctuat in quadam tempestate, peruentura est ad portum'. *CCSEL* xxxix, 996. 1-6.

[12]) Ibid., 26: 'Exhorrescant omnes fratres nostri diuites, abundantes pecunia, auro, argento, familia, honoribus; exhorrescant quod modo dictum est: *Domine, in ciuitate tua imaginem illorum ad nihilum rediges.* Nonne digni sunt haec pati, ut Deus in civitate sua imaginem illorum ad nihilum redigat, quia et ipsi in ciuitate sua terrena imaginem Dei ad nihilum redegerunt'. *CCSL* xxxix, 1000. 38-44.

in themselves, and not in the grace of God. When, however, he came to compose Letter 140, Augustine could, and did, have another consideration in mind: the theological problems raised by the sack of Rome in 410, which were eventually to lead to the composition of *The City of God.* In the first book of that work Augustine addresses himself to the complaints of those who considered that the profession of Christianity ought to have preserved Rome from the barbarians; and his answer is precisely that which he has already given in *Ep.* 140, 5, 13.

> It has pleased divine providence to prepare good things in the future for the righteous, which the wicked will not enjoy, and evil things for the ungodly, by which the good will not be tormented. However, God has willed that temporal goods and evils should be common to good and bad alike, so that good things should not be too eagerly sought, which the bad are also seen to have, nor evil things shamefully avoided, by which the good are very frequently afflicted[13]).

Although he makes no allusion to it, Augustine could hardly have been unaware of the implications of the sack of Rome, when he preached on Psalm 72 in September 411, and spoke of the Incarnation as teaching that earthly goods were to be despised, and the sufferings which the wicked fear were to be embraced[14]).

> But you — what are you doing? *It is good for me to cleave to God.* This is the sum of what is good. Do you want more? I am sorry for those who do. Brethren, what more do you want? Nothing is better than to cleave to God, when we shall see Him *face to face* (I Cor. 13: 12). What is better now? — because I speak being still a pilgrim. *It is good,* he says, *to cleave to God* — but now on our pilgrimage, because the reality has not yet come, it is good *to put my hope in God.* As long, therefore, as you do not cleave, put your hope there[15]).

[13]) *Ciu.* 1, 8: 'Placuit quippe diuinae prouidentiae praeparare in posterum bona iustis, quibus non fruentur iniusti, et mala impiis, quibus non excruciabuntur boni; ista uero temporalia bona et mala utrisque uoluit esse communia, ut nec bona cupidius adpetantur, quae mali quoque habere cernuntur; nec mala turpiter euitentur, quibus et boni plerumque adficiuntur'. *CCSL* xlvii, 7. 13-19.

[14]) *En. Ps.* 72, 16, cited above , note 10.

[15]) Ibid., 34: 'Tu autem quid facis? *Mihi autem adhaerere Deo bonum est.* Hoc est totum bonum. Vultis amplius? Doleo uolentes. Fratres, quid uultis amplius? Deo adhaerere nihil est melius, quando eum uidebimus facie ad faciem. Modo ergo quid? Quia adhuc peregrinus loquor: *Adhaerere*, inquit, *Deo Bonum est*; sed modo in peregrinatione, quia nondum uenit res, *Ponere in Deo spem meam.* Quamdiu ergo nondum adhaesisti, ibi pone spem'. *CCSL* xxxix, 1003. 1-8.

The same thought underlies Augustine's introduction to Letter 140 before he addresses himself to Honoratus' questions.

> These saints [of the Old Testament] proclaimed the Old Testament in a form adapted to their age, but they belonged in reality to the New Testament; for when they dealt with temporal felicity, they understood that the true and eternal felicity was to be set forth, and they declared the former in a mystery, so that they might attain to the latter in the reward. And if at any time they suffered misfortune, they suffered it to this end: that being set free by the most manifest divine aid, they might glorify God, the giver of all good things, not only those eternal things, for which they devoutly hoped, but also temporal things, which they administered in prophetic manner[16]).

This is the background to Augustine's treatment of the meaning of the declaration: *And the Word was made flesh*, the last of Honoratus' questions, which Augustine elected to treat first. As might be expected, he makes the Incarnation the centre of his exposition. Christ is God, the Word of God, the creator of all things and the unchangeable Son of God, omnipresent, even in the minds of the ungodly, although they do not see Him (*Ep.* 140, 3, 6). He assumed manhood; but in order that He might not be deemed to be no more than a holy man, John the Baptist was sent before to proclaim Him as the true light (3, 8). Then Christ came and gave to those who received Him the power to become sons of God.

> This is the grace of the New Testament, which lay hidden in the Old yet did not cease to be prophesied and foretold under obscure images, so that the soul might know its God and be reborn to Him by His grace. This is, indeed, a spiritual birth, and therefore *not of blood, nor of the will of man, nor of the will of the flesh, but of God.* It is also called adoption, for we were something before we were sons of God and we received the favour (*beneficium*) that we might be what we were not ... And the Son Himself must be distinguished from this begetting by grace, the Son who, when He was the Son of God, came in order that He might be the son of

[16]) *Ep.* 140, 2, 5: 'dispensabant ergo illi sancti pro congruentia temporis testamentum uetus, pertinebant uero ad testamentum nouum. nam et quando temporalem felicitatem agebant, aeternam ueram et praeferendam intellegebant et istam ministrabant in mysterio, ut illam consequerentur in praemio, et si quando patiebantur aduersa, ad hoc patiebantur, ut euidentissimo diuino adiutorio liberati glorificarent deum bonorum omnium largitorem non solum sempiternorum, quae pie sperabant, uerum etiam temporalium, quae prophetice gubernabant'. *CSEL* xliv, 158. 16-25.

Man and give to us, who were sons of men, [the power] to be made sons of God[17]).

This adoption, which Augustine elsewhere equated with deification[18]), is effected by participation: Christ was incarnate *ut participata natura filiorum hominum ad participandam etiam suam naturam adoptaret filios hominum* (4, 11). Augustine does not, of course, ignore the atoning power of the Incarnation; but his emphasis here is upon its deifying aspect, affected by participation. It need cause no surprise to find this Platonic conception operating in Augustine's mind at the beginning of the Pelagian Controversy. As late as 426/7, when he was completing *The City of God*, Augustine could still, in Athanasian fashion, refer to '*the mediator between God and man, the man Christ Jesus*, who was made partaker of our mortality to make us partakers of His divinity'[19]), but it is significant that he should make it the basis of his exegesis of *the Word was made flesh* in Letter 140.

> And so we, mutable beings who are to be changed to a better state (*in melius*), are made partakers of the Word; but the unchangeable Word itself, being in no way changed for the worse, was made a partaker of flesh with a reasonable soul acting between. For Christ the man did not, as the Apollinarian heretics thought, either not have a soul, or did not have a reasonable one; but Scripture, in its own fashion, put *flesh* for 'man', that it might the more clearly show Christ's humility, and not appear to avoid the name of flesh as though it was something unworthy[20]).

[17]) Ibid., 3, 9 - 4, 10: 'haec est gratia noui testamenti, quod in uetere latuit nec tamen figuris obumbrantibus prophetari praenuntiarique cessauit, ut intellegat anima deum suum et gratia eius renascatur illi. haec quippe natiuitas spiritalis est, ideo non ex sanguinibus, non ex uoluntate uiri nec ex uoluntate carnis sed ex deo (4, 10). Haec etiam adoptio uocatur. eramus enim aliquid ante, quam essemus filii dei, et accepimus beneficium, ut fieremus, quod non eramus ... et ab hac generatione gratiae discernitur ille filius, qui, cum esset filius dei, uenit, ut fieret filius hominis donaretque nobis, qui eramus filii hominis, filios dei fieri'. *CSEL* xliv, 161. 18-26; 28-162. 1-3.

[18]) *En. Ps.* 49, 2: '*Ego dixi: Dii estis, et filii Excelsi omnes; uos autem ut homines moriemini, et sicut unus ex principibus cadetis.* Manifestum est ergo, quia homines dixit deos, ex gratia sua deificatos, non de substantia sua natos. Ille enim iustificat, qui per semetipsum non ex alio iustus est; et ille deificat, qui per seipsum non alterius participatione Deus est. Qui autem iustificat, ipse deificat, quia iustificando, filios Dei facit. *Dedit enim eis potestatem filios Dei fieri.* Si filii Dei facti sumus, et dii facti sumus; sed hoc gratiae est adoptantis, non naturae generantis'. *CCSL* xxxviii, 574. 6 - 575. 15.

[19]) *Ciu.* 21, 16: '... per mediatorem Dei et hominum, hominem Christum Iesum, qui factus est particeps mortalitatis nostrae, ut nos participes faceret diuinitatis suae'. *CCSL* xlviii, 782. 28-30.

[20]) *Ep.* 140, 4, 12: 'Nos itaque mutabiles in melius commutandi participes efficimur uerbi; uerbum autem incommutabile nihil in deterius commutatum particeps carnis effectum est rationali anima mediante. neque enim homo Christus, ut Apollinaristae

So Christ, being made man, endured suffering and death to reveal that the grace of the New Testament does not pertain to temporal, but to eternal life (5, 13).

In this first section of his letter, which determines its subsequent orientation, Augustine has declared that the grace of the New Testament, the peculiar grace of Christ, bestows eternal felicity through participation in God's divinity made possible by the mediation of the divine humanity of Christ; but he is also at pains to show that this felicity is, in the present age, experienced in hope, not in fulfilment; *in spe* and not *in re*. This provides him with a theological basis for resolving the first of Honoratus' questions, discussed by Augustine secondly: the meaning of the cry of dereliction: *My God, my God, why hast thou forsaken me?*

Augustine's treatment of this text is preceded by a warning: just as the author of Psalm 72 could not resolve the problems which agonized him until he *went into the sanctuary of God*, so here it is necessary that our understanding should be enlightened by the gift of the Holy Spirit (5, 13). Augustine had already discussed Psalm 21 in a sermon of 407[21]), where his exposition, understandably, had an anti-Donatist orientation; but the fundamental principle of exegesis remained unchanged in 412: in the cry from the cross, Christ spoke with and for the voice of human infirmity, in which *our old man was crucified* with Him, so that the bond of sin *might be done away* (Rom. 6:6) (5, 14). In Psalm 21 Christ is said to represent His Body, the Church: *Haec Christus ex persona sui corporis dicit, quod est ecclesia* (6, 18) — an identification which Augustine had already made in 407: *Et cum Verbum Deus factum esset caro, pendebat in cruce et dicebat*: Deus meus, Deus meus, respice me: quare me dereliquisti? *Quare dicitur, nisi quia nos ibi eramus, nisi quia corpus Christi ecclesia?* (*en. Ps*. 21, *s*. 2, 3; cf. 4). For Augustine this whole psalm, to the exegesis of which he devotes the major part of Letter 140, is a prophetic declaration of the grace of the New Testament (6, 15). It reveals the hopes and desires of the Old Man, who is still of a carnal mind.

haeretici putauerunt, aut non habuit animam aut non habuit rationalem; sed more suo scriptura, ut Christi humilitatem magis ostenderet, ne carnis nomen quasi indignum aliquid refugisse uideretur, carnem pro homine posuit'. *CSEL* xliv, 163. 18-25. Augustine's notion of Christ's mediation requires him to assert the human soul of Christ and the union of the two natures, thus rejecting Apollinarianism openly and Nestorianism by anticipation.

[21]) *En. Ps*. 21, *s*. 2. For the date, see Anne-Marie LA BONNARDIÈRE, *Recherches de chronologie augustinienne* (Paris, 1965), 52, 54-6, who assigns it to Wednesday, 10 April 407.

> Among the good things of the Old Testament pertaining to the Old Man, length of life is principally desired, that it may be retained a little longer, because it cannot always be. All men know that the day of death will come, and yet all — or almost all — seek to defer it, even those who believe that they will live more happily after death, such great power has the sweet association of flesh and soul ... But these words, by which length of human life are desired, *are the words of transgressions* (v. 2) and are far from that salvation which we now have in hope, but not yet in actuality, concerning which it is written: *by hope were we saved; but hope that is seen is not hope* (Rom. 8: 24). And therefore in this psalm when He has said: *My God, my God, look upon me, why hast thou forsaken me?* He immediately adds: *the words of my transgressions are far from my salvation*, that is, these words of my transgressions are far removed from the salvation which is promised to me by the grace of the New Testament and not the Old[22]).

The space which Augustine devotes to the exegesis of Psalm 21 (some fifty-six pages out of the total of eighty occupied by Letter 140 in Goldbacher's edition) indicates the importance which he attributes to it as a prophecy of the grace of the New Testament. It is for this reason that he declines to understand the cry of dereliction as being uttered by Christ in His own person: 'the Church suffered in Him when He suffered for the Church, just as He also suffered in the Church when the Church suffered for Him'[23]). When we cry to God for temporal goods and are not heard, we are taught by Him to know what we ought to hope and ask (7, 19).

> This is the grace of the New Testament; for when You taught in the Old Testament that temporal and earthly felicity ought not to be sought and hoped for from anyone but You, then *our fathers*

[22]) *Ep.* 140, 6, 16-17: 'In illis autem ueteris testamenti bonis ad ueterem hominem pertinentibus praecipue concupiscitur uitae huius productio temporalis, ut aliquanto diutius teneatur, quia semper non potest. ideo mortis diem omnes quidem adfuturum sciunt et eum tamen omnes aut paene omnes differre conantur, etiam qui post mortem se beatius credunt esse uicturos; tantam habet uim carnis et animae dulce consortium ... Sed haec uerba, quibus humanus dies et uitae huius prolixitas concupiscitur, uerba sunt delictorum et longe sunt ab ea salute, cuius nondum rem sed iam spem gerimus, de qua scriptum est, quia *spe salui facti sumus: spes autem quae uidetur, non est spes.* ideoque et in isto psalmo cum dixisset: *Deus, deus meus, respice me; quare me dereliquisti?* continuo subiungit: *Longe a salute mea uerba delictorum meorum*, id est haec uerba delictorum meorum sunt et longe sunt ab illa salute mea, quam mihi non ueteris sed noui testamenti gratia pollicetur'. *CSEL* xliv, 166. 24 - 167. 4; 15-24.

[23]) Ibid., 6, 18: 'ecclesia in illo patiebatur, quando pro ecclesia patiebatur, sicut etiam ipse in ecclesia patiebatur, quando pro illo ecclesia patiebatur'. *CSEL* xliv, 169. 2-4.

hoped in thee, they hoped and thou didst deliver them; they cried to thee and were saved; they hoped in thee and were not confounded[24]).

Augustine gives a list of Old Testament saints who trusted in God and were saved: Isaac, for whom a ram was substituted as a sacrifice; Job, recompensed doubly for his sufferings; Daniel, delivered from the lions' den; and the three holy children in the furnace.

> The Jews expected that something like this would be done for Christ, from which they might test whether He was truly the Son of God ... Having regard to the time of the Old Testament and the temporal felicity of the Fathers, in which God showed them that such gifts were also His gifts, they did not see that the time had already come in which it would be revealed in Christ that God would bestow eternal good things upon the righteous alone, who bestows temporal goods upon the ungodly as well[25]).

Augustine sees a double mystery in the words: *I am a worm and no man* (v. 7), since they both express humility and also hint at the mystery of the virginal conception, 'because a worm is born [spontaneously] from [corrupting] flesh without copulation, so Christ was born of a virgin ... and the Son of Man was born like something putrid, as a worm from putrescense, that is to say, a mortal from mortality'[26]). Accordingly, the words: *I am a worm and no man* are to be understood as meaning: 'I am Christ, in whom *all* are *made alive*, and not *Adam*, in whom *all die*' (8, 21).

> By this grace of thc New Testament learn, O men, to desire eternal life. Why do you so greatly wish to be set free by the Lord from death, as our fathers were set free, when God has revealed that there is no other giver, even of worldly felicity, than Himself? That felicity has to do with the Old Man, with the old age beginning from Adam; *but I am a worm and no man*, Christ, not Adam. You were old men from the Old Man; be new men from the New Man; men from Adam, Sons of Men from Christ[27]).

[24]) Ibid., 7, 20: 'Haec est gratia testamenti noui. nam in uetere testamento quando commendabas nonnisi a te peti sperarique debere etiam ipsam terrenam temporalemque felicitatem, *in te sperauerunt patres nostri, sperauerunt et eruisti eos; ad te clamauerunt et saluti facti sunt; in te sperauerunt et non sunt confusi*'. *CSEL* xliv, 170. 8-13.

[25]) Ibid.: 'tale aliquid in Christo expectabant fieri Iudaei, unde probarent, si uere filius dei esset ... adtendentes quippe tempus ueteris testamenti et illam patrum etiam temporalem felicitatem, in qua illis exhibenda demonstrauit deus etiam talia dona sua esse, non uiderunt iam esse tempus, quo reuelaretur in Christo bona aeterna proprie deum praestare iustis, qui bona temporalia praestat et impiis'. *CSEL* xliv, 170. 19-21; 171. 2-7.

[26]) Ibid., 8, 21: 'quia uermis de carne sine concubitu nascitur, sicut natus est ille de uirgine ... et filium hominis uermem natum de putredine quasi putrem, hoc est de mortalitate mortalem'. *CSEL* xliv, 171. 18-19; 172. 1-2.

[27]) Ibid., 8, 22: 'Ac per hoc discite, homines, per gratiam testamenti noui iam uitam

Christ's humiliation, and the mockery to which He was subjected on the cross, were according to His own will. He wished to suffer in the sight of his enemies so that they should think Him abandoned, and by this the grace of the New Testament would be commended, by which we might learn to seek another felicity, which is now by faith, but which will afterwards be by sight (9, 24). Again, Christ's resurrection, by which the faithful learn from His flesh what they ought to hope for in their own, was revealed only to His own followers, and not to aliens:

> ... to aliens, I say, not by nature but by vice, which is always contrary to nature. For He died in the sight of men but rose again in the sight of the Sons of Men, because death pertained to the man, but resurrection to the Son of Man, *for as in Adam all die, even so in Christ shall all be made alive* (I Cor. 15: 22)[28]).

Christ's Passion and Resurrection provide an example for His faithful followers to despise temporal good things for the sake of eternal happiness (9, 25).

Augustine recognises that there were, in the Old Testament, a very few saints who endured to the death without being accorded relief, just as under the New Covenant there were and are many enjoying worldly prosperity; but he reminds the rich of the Apostolic injunction, that *they should not be highminded, nor have their hope set on the uncertainty of riches, but on the living God, who gives us richly all things to enjoy* (I Tim. 6: 17) (10, 27). Here, as in his later writings against the Pelagians[29]), Augustine does not regard the possession of riches as being in itself wrong; it is the use made of the riches, and the attitude to them, by which the rich man is justified or condemned. Augustine knew only too well that in his own day there were many persons who became Christian only from the hope of temporal well-being and, when disappointed in this, fell away (11, 29).

The verses: *Thou art he that took me out of the womb, thou wast my*

concupiscere sempiternam. quid pro magno ita uos uultis a domino de morte liberari, sicut liberati sunt patres nostri, quando commendebat eius etiam terrenae felicitatis praeter se non esse alium largitorem? illa felicitas ad ueterem hominem pertinet, quae uetustas ab Adam coepit. *ego autem sum uermis et non homo,* Christus, non Adam. a ueteri ueteres fuistis, a nouo noui estote; ab Adam homines, a Christo filii hominum'. *CSEL* xliv, 172. 17 - 173. 1.

[28]) Ibid., 9, 25: 'alienis dico non natura sed uitio, quod semper contra naturam est. mortuus est ergo in conspectu hominum, resurrexit autem in conspectu filiorum hominum, quia mors ad hominem pertinebat, resurrectio ad filium hominis; *sicut enim in Adam omnes moriuntur, sic et in Christo omnes uiuificabuntur. CSEL* xliv, 175. 18-23.

[29]) See, for example, *ep.* 157, 4, 23 ff.

hope from my mother's breasts. I was cast out of the womb upon thee; from the belly of my mother thou art my God (vv. 10, 11), Augustine understands, in conformity with the general pattern of his exegesis, both as showing that God is the source of all good things, earthly as well heavenly, and also as revealing how we have been brought by grace from terrestrial felicity to that of heaven.

> Therefore *from the belly of my mother*, that is, from the good things of the flesh, which I drew upon in my mother's womb, *thou art my God*, so that apart from these You may be my good. It is spoken thus as if, for example, it should be said: I dwell in heaven from the earth, that is, I have removed here from thence; and this is our transfiguration in Him, those of us who, by the grace of the New Testament, change our life, passing from the Old to the New. For He, indicating this truth in the mystery of His Passion and Resurrection, changed His flesh from mortality to immortality, though He did not change His life from the old to the new, since He never lived in impiety, from whence He should pass to piety[30]).

The apparent contradiction between the petition: *Go not from me, for trouble is hard at hand* and the opening words of the psalm: *Why hast thou forsaken me?* is resolved, for Augustine, by his distinction between temporal and eternal felicity. The cry of dereliction refers to the loss of earthly good things; the petition: *Go not from me*, asks that the psalmist may not be deprived of the hope of eternal life[31]). Furthermore, the loss of temporal benefits exposes the faithful soul to temptation, which was the reason why the devil, in tempting Job, began by despoiling him of material possessions and then afflicted his body (13, 34). So the martyr, when he begins to suffer in his body, may say to God: *Go not from me, for trouble is hard at hand* (13, 35).

In his exposition of the following verses (12-22), Augustine continues to apply them to the Church, as the Body of Christ (14, 36;

[30]) *Ep.* 140, 12, 30: 'ideoque *de uentre matris meae*, id est de bonis carnis, quam sumpsi in uentre matris meae, *deus meus es tu*, ut de his tu sis bonum meum. ea locutione dictum est, ac si diceretur uerbi gratia: De terra caelum habito, hoc est hinc illo emigraui; et ista nostra in illum transfiguratio est, qui per gratiam testamenti noui mutamus uitam transeuntes de uetere ad nouam. nam ille hanc rem sacramento suae passionis resurrectionisque significans carnem mutauit de mortalitate ad inmortalitatem, uitam uero non mutauit de uetustate in nouitatem, qui numquam fuit in impietate, unde transiret ad pietatem'. *CSEL* xliv, 181. 2-12.

[31]) Ibid., 13, 33: 'Iam illud, quod sequitur: *Ne discedas a me, quoniam tribulatio proxima est*, uide, ut inluminet, quem ad modum dictum sit: *Quare me dereliquisti?* quo modo enim dereliquit, cui dicitur: *Ne discedas*, nisi quia dereliquit uitae ueteris temporalem felicitatem? Rogatur autem, ne discedat et deserat spem uitae aeternae'. *CSEL* xliv, 183. 7-12. Cf. 17, 43.

16, 41-42), while recognising that certain of them are better related to His Person (16, 39), and others to both (16, 40). His conclusion is that Psalm 21 is a declaration of the grace of the New Testament, which Christians now experience in the Catholic Church.

> *I will declare*, he says, *thy name unto my brethren; in the midst of the Church will I praise thee*. The *brethren* are those with regard to whom He says in the Gospel: *Go and say to my brethren...* (Ioh. 20: 17). The Church is she whom He has just now called His only One (Ps. 21: 21). This is the one Catholic Church, which is widely spread over the whole world and which by growth extends to the farthest nations. On this account He says in the Gospel: *And this gospel shall be preached in the whole world for a testimony to the nations: and then the end will come*[32]).

The notion of praise of God and proclamation of the Gospel by the one Catholic Church is applied by Augustine to the words: *Magnify him all ye seed of Jacob* (v. 24), and he is concerned to show that, in the words of the Apostle: *It is not the children of the flesh that are children of God, but the children of the promise are reckoned as a seed; for this is the word of promise: At this time I will come and Sarah shall have a son* (Rom. 9: 8, 9) (19, 47). The elect are the seed of Abraham and Isaac by grace, and not by works.

> Therefore the sons of the promise are the sons of God's favour (*beneficii*). This is grace, which is given gratis, not for the merits of the worker, but by the mercy of the giver. Hence we give thanks to our God, which act of thanksgiving, *Gratias agimus*, is a great mystery (*sacramentum*) in the sacrifice of the New Testament, with regard to where and when and in what manner it is offered, you will find out when you have been baptised[33]).

We have here a characteristic statement of Augustine's doctrine of grace, which he will be concerned to maintain in his later debates with the Pelagians. Augustine is not, however, here concerned to develop it, except by emphasising, for Honaratus' benefit, that the Gentiles are

[32]) Ibid., 17, 43: '*narrabo*, inquit, *nomen tuum fratribus meis; in medio ecclesiae cantabo te*. fratres illi sunt, de quibus in euangelio ait: *Vade et dic fratribus meis*. ecclesia illa est, quam modo dixit unicam suam; haec est unica catholica, quae toto orbe copiosa diffunditur, quae usque ad ultimas gentes crescendo porrigitur, unde in euangelio dicit: *Et praedicabitur hoc euangelium in uniuerso orbe in testimonium omnibus gentibus et tunc ueniet finis*'. *CSEL* xliv, 191. 20 - 192. 5.

[33]) Ibid., 19, 48: 'filii ergo promissionis filii sunt beneficii. haec est gratia, quae gratis datur non meritis operantis sed miseratione donantis. hinc gratias agimus domino deo nostro, quod est magnum sacramentum in sacrificio noui testamenti, quod et ubi et quando et quo modo offeratur, cum fueris baptizatus, inuenies'. *CSEL* xliv, 195. 26 - 196. 3.

reckoned as belonging to the seed of Israel by the mercy of God, who has grafted them in, like a wild olive into a cultivated tree (Rom. 11: 17-20), on account of the pride of the natural branches, and not for any merit of their own (20, 49-50). It was pride which has caused the children of Abraham after the flesh to go into the outward darkness,

> ... because, boasting themselves to be of the seed of Abraham, they did not wish to be made the [true] seed of Abraham, that they might be *sons of the promise*; because they did not receive the faith of the New Testament, where the righteousness of God is commended, *seeking to establish their own*, that is, as though trusting too much in their own merits and works, they scorned to be *sons of the promise*, that is, sons of grace, sons of mercy. *So let him who glories, glory in the Lord* (I Cor. 1: 31), believing in Him who *justifies the ungodly* (Rom. 4: 5), that is, who makes a godly man out of the ungodly, so that *his faith* may be *reckoned for righteousness* and that there may be fulfilled in him, not what his merit sought, but what has been promised by the Lord as a favour ... On this account, although the Apostle may say to the faithful, with regard to the New Testament, what I cited a little earlier [20, 49]: *You have not received the spirit of bondage again unto fear; but you received the spirit of adoption, whereby we cry: Abba, Father* (Rom. 8: 15); that is, that the *faith* may be in us, *which works by love* (Gal. 5: 6), not by fearing punishment, but by loving righteousness (cf. I Ioh. 4: 18). Yet because the soul is not made righteousness except by participation in a Better, who *justifies the ungodly* — for what does it have, which it has not received? (cf. I Cor. 4: 7) — it ought not, by attributing to itself what is of God, so to glory as if it had not received[34])

Augustine has here linked two themes which are characteristic of, and fundamental to, his theology: the doctrine of grace, and the need for humility. In this sense we have here a classical piece of Augustinian argument; but to it, in Letter 140, Augustine joins the notion of

[34]) Ibid., 20, 50 - 21, 52: '... quia iactantes se de semine Abrahae semen Abrahae fieri noluerunt, *ut essent filii promissionis*; quia fidem noui testamenti non receperunt, ubi dei iustitia commendatur, *suam constituere uolentes*, id est tamquam de suis meritis et operibus praefidentes spreuerunt esse *filii promissionis*, hoc est filii gratiae, filii misericordiae, *ut, qui gloriatur, in domino glorietur* credens in eum, *qui iustificat impium*, hoc est qui ex impio facit pium, ut deputetur *fides eius ad iustitiam* et impleatur in eo, non quod postulabat eius meritum, sed quod a domino promissum est beneficium ... (21, 52). Quapropter quamuis fidelibus ad nouum testamentum pertinentibus dicat apostolus, quod paulo ante commemoraui: *Non enim accepistis spiritum seruitutis iterum in timorem, sed accepistis spiritum adoptionis filiorum, in quo clamamus: «Abba, pater»*, id est ut *fides* in nobis sit, *quae per dilectionem operatur*, non tam timendo poenam quam amando iustitiam, tamen, quia non fit anima iusta nisi participatione melioris, qui iustificat impium — quid enim habet, quod non accepit? — non debet sibi tribuendo, quod dei est, ita gloriari, tamquam non acceperit'. *CSEL* xliv, 197. 20 - 198.2; 198. 18 - 199. 2.

participation, introduced in his discussion of the text: *the Word was made flesh* (4, 11). God was made man that men might be made gods; by His participation in our humanity, we may come to that condition described in the First Epistle of St John in which love, being made perfect, casts out fear - the servile fear of punishment, not the chaste fear of losing the grace by which it delights in refraining from sin (19, 53).

> This is the righteousness of God, that is, what God gives to man when He justifies the ungodly. The proud Jews, *being ignorant of God's righteousness and seeking to establish their own, did not subject themselves to the righteousness of God* (Rom. 10: 3). By this pride they were cast down, that the humble wild olive might be grafted in; and they will go *into the outer darkness* (Matt. 8: 12), about which, among other matters, you enquired, with *many coming from the east and the west*, who *will sit down with Abraham and Isaac and Jacob in the kingdom of heaven*[35]).

Augustine now introduces the penultimate of Honoratus' questions, which he elects to treat within the context of his exposition of Psalm 21. He makes a distinction between the outer darkness (*tenebrae exterae*) which is the present condition of souls which have not received light and grace and which is capable of being cured, and the more outward darkness (*tenebrae exteriores*), where healing is impossible, the darkness into which the devil and his angels have fallen by pride (22, 54). In language which is curiously reminiscent of Origen's account of the fall of souls in the *De Principiis* Augustine declares:

> The devil and his angels, having turned away from the light and warmth of love and gone too far in pride and envy, have become numb with a kind of glacial hardness[36]).

[35]) Ibid., 22, 54: 'Haec est iustitia dei; hoc est, quod deus donat homini, cum iustificat impium; hanc *dei iustitiam ignorantes* superbi Iudaei *et suam uolentes constituere iustitiae dei non sunt subiecti*; hac superbia deiciuntur, ut humilis inseratur oleaster. et illi *ibunt in tenebras exteriores*, de quibus inter alia requisisti, uenientibus ab oriente et occidente multis, qui recumbant *cum Abraham, Isaac et Iacob in regno caelorum*'. *CSEL* xliv, 200. 11-18.

[36]) Ibid., 22, 55: 'Diabolus igitur et angeli eius a luce atque feruore caritatis auersi et nimis in superbiam inuidiamque progressi uelut glaciali duritia torpuerunt'. *CSEL* xliv, 201. 15-17. Cf. *De Princ.* 3, 8, 3: 'Si ergo ea quidem, quae sancta sunt, ignis et lumen et feruentia nominantur, quae autem contraria sunt, frigida, et «caritas» peccatorum dicitur «refrigescere», requirendum est ne forte et nomen animae, quod graece dicitur *psyche*, a refrigescendo de statu diuiniore ac meliore dictum sit et translatum inde, quod ex calore illo naturali et diuino refrixisse uideatur, et ideo in hoc quo nunc est et statu et uocabulo sita sit'. *GCS*: Origenes, 5er Bd., 157. 12 - 158. 2.

Men, however, may still be warmed, and so it is said in the Song of Songs, speaking of the grace of the Saviour which is to come: *Awake, O north wind, and come thou south; blow upon my garden, that the spices thereof may flow out* (Cant. 4: 16), and in the Psalms: *Turn, O Lord, our captivity, as the rivers of the south* (Ps. 125: 4) (22, 55).

The thought behind these images of the *auersio-conuersio* conception arises from the idea of participation.

> Accordingly the reasonable creature, whether an angelic spirit or a human soul, has been so made that it cannot itself be its own good by which it may be made happy; but its mutable nature, if it is turned to the unchanging Good, may be made happy, from which, if it is turned away, it is wretched. Its aversion is its vice and its conversion its virtue ... But just as among corporal bodies, those that are inferior, like earth and water and the air itself, are made better by participation in something better — that is, when they are illuminated by light and enlivened by heat — so bodiless creatures, endowed with reason, are made better by participation in their creator, when they cleave to Him with the purest and most holy love, which, if they wholly lose, they become, in a certain manner, darkened and hardened.
> Accordingly, unbelievers are darkness; but those who are converted to God through faith are made light, by a certain illumination bestowed upon them. If they come from faith to sight by going forward in that light, so as to deserve the sight of what they believe — so far as so great a good is able to be seen — they will receive the perfected image of God[37]).

The wicked, on the other hand, will go to the more outward darkness of the devil and his angels (23, 57), where there will be no such delights as they are able to enjoy in the present world (23, 58). Therefore the Psalmist says: *Let all the seed of Israel fear the Lord, for he has not despised or scorned the prayer of the poor* (v. 25). Augustine identifies *the poor* with the humble, who resemble Christ who, *though he was rich became poor for* our *sake so that by his poverty* we *might*

[37]) Ibid., 23, 56-57: 'Proinde rationalis creatura siue in angelico spiritu siue in anima humana ita facta est, ut sibi ipsa bonum, quo beata fiat, esse non possit, sed mutabilitas eius, si conuertatur ad incommutabile bonum, fiat beata; unde si auertatur, misera est. auersio eius uitium eius et conuersio uirtus eius est ... sed quem ad modum in ipsis corporibus ea, quae inferiora sunt, sicut terra et aqua et ipse aer, meliora fiunt participatione melioris, id est cum luce inluminantur et feruore uegetantur, sic incorporeae creaturae rationales ipsius creatoris fiunt participatione meliores, cum ei cohaerent purissima et sanctissima caritate; quam omni modo si caruerint, tenebrescent et obdurescent quodam modo (57). Proinde infideles homines tenebrae sunt, qui per fidem conuersi ad deum quadam praemissa inluminatione lux fiunt, in qua proficiendo si ex fide ad speciem peruenerint, ut id, quod credunt, etiam conspicere, sicut tantum bonum potest conspici, mereantur, perfectam recipient imaginem dei'. *CSEL* xliv, 202. 12-16; 202. 24 - 203. 12.

become rich (II Cor. 8: 9). The prayer of the poor is: *Go not from me, for trouble is hard at hand* (24, 59).Once again Augustine urges that it is not the loss of earthly goods which constitutes abandonment by God. *My praise is of thee in the great Church; I will pay my vows before those who fear thee* (v. 26). Augustine contrasts the synagogue, which mocked Christ upon the cross, apparently abandoned by God, with the great Church, extended among all the nations, which believes in the resurrection of Him who was not abandoned (24, 60). The *vows* are the sacrifice of Christ's body, which is the sacrament of the faithful. *The poor*, who *shall eat and be filled* with *the bread which comes down from heaven* (Ioh. 6: 50), are those who imitate Christ's humility by cleaving to Him and maintaining His peace and love. Those *who seek the Lord and will praise him* (v. 27) are *the poor* who understand that it is by His grace and not by their own merits that they have been *filled. Their hearts shall live for ever*, even though their flesh may suffer temporal tribulation while they praise Him. These are the poor who follow the precept of charity and do not give way to pride (24, 61).

> *The beginning of all sin is pride* (Eccli. 10: 15), by which the devil has irrevocably proceeded into the more outward darkness and by envying man and persuading him to similar pride hast cast him down. To that man in a certain writing it is said: *Why is earth and ashes proud, since in his life he has cast away his inmost parts?* (Eccli. 10: 9, 10). *In his life* is said as though it meant 'in his own possessions' or 'in his private affairs,' in which all pride delights.
> It is on this account that love, having regard to the common, rather than to the private good, is said *not to seek her own* (I Cor. 13: 4). Their *hearts live for ever* by her, as though *filled* with heavenly bread, of which the filler Himself says: *Unless you eat* my *flesh and drink* my *blood, you will not have life within you* (Ioh. 6: 54). Justly then do *the hearts* of those *that are filled, live for ever*. For their life is Christ, who dwells in their hearts, for the time being by faith, and afterwards by sight also[38]).

[38]) Ibid., 24, 61 - 25, 62: '*initium* autem *omnis peccati superbia*, qua diabolus irreuocabiliter in exteriora progressus est hominemque inuidendo et ei simile aliquid suadendo deiecit. cui homini in quadam scriptura dicitur: *Quid superbit terra et cinis, quoniam in uita sua proiecit intima sua?* «in uita sua» dictum est tamquam in propria sua et quasi priuata, qua delectatur omnis superbia (25, 62). Unde caritas in commune magis quam in priuatum consulens dicitur non quaerere, quae sua sunt, hac uiuunt corda in saeculum saeculi tamquam saturata pane caelesti, de qua dicit ipse saturator: *Nisi manducaueritis carnem meam et sanguinem biberitis, non habebitis uitam in uobis.* merito ergo istorum, qui saturantur, *uiuent corda in saeculum saeculi.* uita enim Christus est, qui habitat in cordibus eorum interim per fidem post etiam per speciem'. *CSEL* xliv, 207. 11 - 208. 1.

It is from this notion of love, brought into the hearts of the faithful by the indwelling of Christ, that Augustine turns to consider the meaning of the passage of Ephesians on *the length and breadth and height and depth*, which he sees in the activity of love: extending itself in good works — the width; enduring adversity — the length; doing all this for the sake of eternal life, which is promised on high — the height; and the hidden grace of God, of which the Apostle cries: *O the depth of the riches both of the wisdom and the knowledge of God! How unsearchable are his judgements and his ways past finding out! For who hath known the mind of the Lord?* (Rom. 11. 33, 34) — the depth (25, 62; cf. 26, 63). Augustine's citation of the *O altitudo!* warns the reader that the saint regards the passage in Ephesians as signifying a mystery, which Augustine finds expressed in the figure of the cross[39]).

Augustine has not, however, come to the end of his exposition of Psalm 21.

> *All the ends of the earth shall remember and turn to the Lord and all the nations of the peoples shall worship in his sight, for the kingdom is the Lord's and he shall rule over the peoples* (vv. 28, 29). He who was mocked, He who was crucified, He who was abandoned, has acquired this kingdom and will, at the end, deliver it up to God the Father, not as though He should lose it, but rather that what He sowed in faith when He came lower than the Father, He should bring to sight, in which sight He, being equal, did not withdraw from the Father[40]).

In verse 30: *All the rich of the earth have eaten and adored*, Augustine sees a reference to the proud, who approach Christ's table and receive His Flesh and Blood, but only adore and are not filled, as are the poor — that is, the poor in spirit, the humble — because they do not *hunger and thirst after righteousness* (Matt. 5: 6). It is those who hunger and thirst who are filled.

[39]) Ibid., 26, 64: 'In hoc mysterio figura crucis ostenditur. qui enim, quia uoluit, mortuus est, quo modo uoluit, mortuus est. non frustra igitur tale genus mortis elegit, nisi in eo quoque latitudinis huius et longitudinis et altitudinis et profunditatis magister existeret'. *CSEL* xliv, 211. 11-15.

[40]) Ibid., 27, 66: '*Commemorabuntur*, inquit, *et conuertentur ad dominum uniuersi fines terrae et adorabunt in conspectu eius uniuersae patriae gentium, quoniam domini est regnum et ipse dominabitur gentium.* ille inrisus, ille crucifixus, ille derelictus hoc regnum adquirit et tradet in fine deo et patri, non ut ipse amittat, sed, quod in fide seminauit, cum uenit minor patre, hoc perducat ad speciem, in qua aequalis non recessit a patre'. *CSEL* xliv, 212. 11 - 18.

> Although perfect fulness will be in that life eternal, when we shall have come out of this pilgrimage *from faith to sight*, from the *mirror, face to face* (I Cor. 13: 12), from riddles to manifest truth, the man may not unfittingly be said to be filled by the poverty of Christ (cf. II Cor. 8: 9) who, for the righteousness of Christ, that is, for participation in the Eternal Word, which he has now begun by faith, not only temperately sets little value on temporal goods, but also patiently endures evils[41]).

Such were the fishermen and publicans who were Christ's disciples. They were the poor, who ate and were filled; but through their preaching, *all the ends of the earth* remembered and turned to the Lord and *all the nations of the earth* worshipped in His sight. Through the extension of the Church *the rich of the earth* — that is, the proud — *have eaten* and, although they have not been filled, *have adored*. These are they *who fall down prostrate in his sight, who go down into the earth* (v. 30), that is, all those who, by loving earthly goods, do not ascend into heaven. Indeed, it is to the extent by which, through earthly possessions, they seem the happier that they *go down into the earth* and so *fall prostrate in his sight* (27, 67).

Accordingly, the psalmist says: *My soul lives to him; my seed shall serve him* (v. 31). The Apostle exhorts us, not to live to ourselves but to Him who for our sakes died and rose again (II Cor. 5: 11).

> For by this He was made a Mediator, to reconcile us to God by humility to God, from whom we had fallen away by ungodly pride[42]).

We have here the familiar Augistinian conception of the 'region of unlikeness'[43]), from which fallen humanity needs to be recalled to the Father's house, a conception which admirably harmonises with the idea of participation in the Word, by which we are made children of God by adoption (4, 10-12). It is pride which has caused our falling away from God, and the cure is, not to live to ourselves but for Christ. By

[41]) Ibid.: 'quamquam perfecta saturitas in illa uita aeterna erit, cum ex ista peregrinatione uenerimus ex fide ad speciem, ab speculo ad faciem, ab aenigmate ad perspicuam ueritatem, non tamen inconuenienter saturatus dicitur paupertate Christi, qui pro iustitia eius, hoc est pro participatione uerbi aeterni, quam inchoauit interim fide, omnia temporalia non solum temperanter contemnit bona, uerum etiam patienter sustinet mala'. *CSEL* xliv, 213. 24 - 215. 5.

[42]) Ibid., 28, 68: 'per hoc enim mediator effectus est, ut nos reconciliet deo per humilitatem, a quo per impiam superbiam longe recesseramus'.*CSEL* xliv, 215. 13-15.

[43]) *Conf.* 7, 10, 16. On this see P. Courcelle, *Recherches sur les* Confessions *de Saint Augustin dans la tradition littéraire* (Paris, 1963), Appendix V, pp. 623-40.

following our own will we were made darkness; by coming to Him, *the light which enlightens every man coming into the world* (Ioh. 1: 9), we are enlightened (28, 68).

The prophetic character of Psalm 21 is proved for Augustine in the concluding verses, 30 and 31: *Adnuntiabitur domino generatio uentura et adnuntiabunt iustitiam eius populo, qui nascetur, quem fecit dominus.* He observes that the phrase *Adnuntiabitur domino generatio uentura* can be understood in two ways: it can mean: 'the coming generation will be pleasing to the Lord which ascribes its good works not to itself but to Him by whose grace they are done', or: 'the generation will be declared which will come to the Lord', that is, the generation of the devout and holy, for it is only by participation in God, the Self-same (Ps. 121: 3: *cuius participatio eius in idipsum*)[44]), that the reasonable creature, being mutable, can be made happy, being freed from pride by coming to the unchanging Good which is common to all. When the faithful soul has been converted by coming to God, whatever good it does is done to His praise, by whose grace it is done: 'whence comes that act of thanksgiving, which is celebrated in the most secret mystery of the faithful' (29, 70).

Such an understanding is confirmed by the words: *And they shall declare his righteousness to the people which shall be born, whom the Lord hath made.* Ours is not the righteousness by which God Himself is just; but we are made righteous by His grace, not by works (30, 71), just as we were made whole (*salui*), not by the wholeness (*salus*) which God is, but by that by which He saves us (30, 72).

> Thus, when we read of the righteousness of God in the verse: *Being ignorant of the righteousness of God and wishing to establish their own* (Rom. 10: 3), we should not understand the reference to be to the righteousness by which God is righteous, but that by which men are righteous ... Pride is the contrary of this righteousness of God, which puts its trust as though in its own works, and therefore there follows: *Let not the foot of pride come upon me* (Ps. 35: 12). This righteousness is the grace of the New Testament, by which God's faithful are made righteous, while still living by faith, until with their salvation made perfect, they also come to bodily immortality[45]).

[44]) Cf. *En. Ps.* 121, 5: '... Quid est *idipsum?* Quod semper eodem modo est; quod non modo aliud, et modo aliud est. Quid est ergo *idipsum*, nisi, quod est? Quid est quod est? Quod aeternum est. Nam quod semper aliter atque aliter est, non est, quia non manet; non omnino non est, sed non summe est. Et quid est quod est, nisi ille qui quando mittebat Moysen, dixit illi: *Ego sum qui sum?*'. *CCSL* xl, 1805. 11-17.

[45]) *Ep.* 140, 30, 72-73: '... sic, cum legitur dei iustitia in eo, quod scriptum est:

Augustine has here combined two theological conceptions. The notion of participation, which might outside a Christian context be effected by the powers of the individual himself, is modified by the Pauline conception of unmerited grace, without which participation is impossible. Again, Augustine has been careful to emphasise that human righteousness is not the same as the righteousness of God; we are justified by grace of adoption, and not by nature. The radical gulf between the Creator and the created is maintained, even though the Creator has bridged that gulf by the Incarnation.

> *Him who knew no sin he made to be sin in our behalf* (II Cor. 5: 21) — that is, a sacrifice for sin, for the things which were offered for sins were called sins in the Law — that we might be the righteousness of God in Him, that is, in His Body, which is the Church, of which He is the Head[46]).

It is within the Church that we participate in the righteousness of God. The characteristic of the created being, and the weakness which brought about the Fall, is its instability.

> The mutability of the reasonable soul teaches it that it cannot be righteous, whole, wise and happy, except by participation in the unchanging Good; nor by its own will can it be a good to itself, but an evil. By its own will the soul is turned away from the unchanging Good, and by that turning away it is corrupted. Nor can it be healed by itself, but only by the unmerited mercy of its Creator, which establishes it in this life, living by faith, in hope of eternal salvation. On this account, let it *not be highminded, but fear* (Rom. 11: 20), and by that chaste fear let it cleave to God, who has cleansed it from its impurity, by which it loved inferior good things in an unordered fashion, as though by a kind of spiritual fornication. Let it not be numbered among those foolish virgins rejoicing in the praise of others — and this remains the final one of your questions for consideration[47]).

Ignorantes dei iustitiam et suam uolentes constituere, non est illa intellegenda, qua deus iustus est, sed qua iusti sunt homines ... huic igitur iustitiae dei contraria superbia est, qua fiditur tamquam de operibus propriis, ideoque ibi sequitur: *Non ueniat mihi pes superbiae* (73). Haec iustitia, qua eius fideles iusti sunt interim uiuentes ex fide, donec perfecta iustitia perducantur ad speciem sicut salute perfecta etiam ad ipsius corporis immortalitatem, gratia testamenti noui'. *CSEL* xliv, 219. 25 - 220. 1; 220. 15-21.

[46]) Ibid., 30, 73: '*Eum, qui non nouerat peccatum, peccatum pro nobis fecit* — id est sacrificium pro peccatis; nam et ipsa in lege peccata appellabantur, quae pro peccatis offerebantur — *ut nos simus iustitia dei in ipso*,; id est in eius corpore, quod est ecclesia, cui caput est'. *CSEL* xliv, 221. 1-5. Augustine's reference is to Gen. 20: 9 and Ps. 39 [40]: 7 (Hebr. *ḥaṭā'āh*) (I owe this information to my colleague, Dr Robert Hayward).

[47]) Ibid., 31, 74: 'Animae igitur rationalis mutabilitas admonetur, quo nouerit nisi participatione incommutabilis boni iustam, saluam, sapientem, beatam se esse non posse

Augustine has contrived to bring his discussion to Honoratus' last question, which is (once again) to be discussed in terms of humility. He has argued that the good things of the New Testament are spiritual and not material; he has understood *the poor* as meaning the humble, and has urged the rich not to be puffed up with pride of possession. He now sees the foolish virgins as symbolising those Christians who put their trust in their own virtues, and the merchants of oil as the flatterers, who sell their praise to the proud and foolish as if it were oil (31, 74). The saying: *Perhaps there will not be enough for us and you* (Matt. 25: 9), he understands as an expression of humility; no one can safely trust in his own merits; the wise virgins wish that their good deeds may be seen by men, not to their own glory, but to the glory of God, of whom comes the grace by which they do good (31, 75). The foolish virgins, on the other hand, do good for the sake of human praise, and therefore their lamps go out when that oil is taken away. The sleep which overcomes the virgins while they wait for the bridegroom is the sleep of death (32, 76). Their lamps are their good works; the oil, participation in the highest Good.

> The man who, having participated to some degree in the highest Good, with the intention of participating yet more; who performs good works, and lives in the sight of men in praiseworthy fashion, has with him the oil through which the good works which he performs in the sight of men are not put out, because love does not grow *cold* in his heart *when iniquity is multiplied* (Matt. 24: 12) but *endures to the end* (Matt. 10; 22)[48]).

The coming of the bridegroom is the resurrection to judgement (34, 78), when all the consolations of human praise will be taken away and everyone must *bear his own burden* (Gal. 6: 5) and give account of his own work (34, 79). The wise virgins will enter *into the joy of the Lord* (Matt. 25: 21; 23).

nec sibi eam bonum esse posse propria uoluntate sed malum. propria quippe uoluntate auertitur a bono incommutabili eaque auersione uitiatur; nec sanari per se ipsam potest sed gratuita misericordia sui creatoris, quae in hac uita eam ex fide uiuentem in spe constituit salutis aeternae. unde *non altum* sapiat, *sed* timeat eoque timore casto inhaereat deo, qui eam a propria inmunditia, qua inordinate bona inferiora dilexit, uelut a quadam spiritali fornicatione mundauit; nec humanis laudibus extollatur, ne sit in uirginibus stultis aliena laude laetantibus — hoc enim de quaestionibus tuis restat extremum...'. *CSEL* xliv, 221. 20 - 222. 5.

[48]) Ibid., 33, 77: 'cuius boni aliquantum participati et plenius perfectiusque participandi intentione qui bene operatur et laudabiliter etiam in conspectu hominum conuersatur, habet oleum secum, quo bona opera eius etiam in conspectu hominum lucentia non extinguantur, quia non in eius *corde* caritas refrigescit abundante iniquitate, sed perseuerat usque in finem'. *CSEL* xliv, 226. 1-7.

> ... where participation in the unchangeable good will have been made perfect, of which a kind of pledge is now held, as it were, by faith, so that we may live according to this grace, in as much as we live to God and not to ourselves[49]).

The foolish virgins will be rejected, and the words: *I know you not* (Matt. 25: 12), mean nothing other than: 'You do not know Me, because you chose to trust in yourselves rather than in Me'.

> For when it is said that God knows us, He furnishes knowledge of Himself to us, that by this we may know that not even the fact that we know God is to be attributed to ourselves, but that we should also ascribe that knowledge to His mercy. On that account, when the Apostle said in a certain place: *Now that you have come to know God*, he corrected himself and said, *or, rather, to be known of God* (Gal. 4: 9). What else does he wish to be understood, except that God Himself has made them know Him? For no one knows God, except him who understands God to be that highest and unchanging Good, by whose participation he is made good, as is stated in the conclusion of this psalm: *And they shall declare his righteousness to the people which shall be born, whom the Lord hath made*, from whence comes the saying in another psalm: *It is he that hath made us and not we ourselves* (Ps. 99: 3). But this saying should not be applied to the nature by which we are human, although He is Himself the creator of that nature, as He is of heaven and earth and the stars and all living things, but rather to that of which the Apostle says: *For we are his workmanship, created in Christ Jesus for good works, which God prepared that we should walk in them* (Eph. 2: 10)[50]).

Augustine concludes his discussion of Honaratus' five questions by returning to his own, concerning the grace of the New Testament, for

[49]) Ibid., 34, 80: '... ubi erit perfecta participatio incommutabilis boni, cuius modo uelut arra quaedam per fidem tenetur, ut secundum hanc gratiam uiuamus, in quantum deo non nobis uiuimus'. *CSEL* xliv, 229. 5-8.

[50]) Ibid., 35, 81: 'cum enim dicitur, quod nos cognoscit deus, cognitionem sui nobis praestat, ut per hoc intellegamus ne hoc quidem nobis esse tribuendum, quod nos scimus deum, sed eam quoque scientiam illius misericordiae tribuamus. unde, cum quodam loco apostolus diceret: *Nunc autem cognoscentes deum*, correxit et ait: *Immo cogniti a deo* quid aliud uolens intellegi, nisi quod eos ipse fecerit cognitores suos? nemo autem cognoscit deum, nisi qui intellegit illud esse summum atque incommutabile bonum, cuius participatione fit bonus, quod in huius psalmi conclusione positum est: *Adnuntiabant iustitiam eius populo, qui nascetur, quem fecit dominus*; inde est et illud, quod in alio psalmo: *Ipse fecit nos et non ipsi nos*. hoc enim non ad eam naturam, qua homines sumus, cuius naturae idem ipse creator est, qui caeli et terrae et siderum omniumque animantium, sed ad illud potius referendum est, quod apostolus ait: *Ipsius enim sumus figmentum creati in Christo Iesu in operibus bonis, quae praeparauit deus, ut in illis ambulemus*'. *CSEL* xliv, 229. 17 - 230. 11.

which the starting point of his answer was the Johannine declaration that *the Word was made flesh.*

> ... that is, that He that was the Son of God was made man, by taking our nature and not losing His own, by which the power is given to us who receive Him that we who were men should be made *sons of God*, having been changed to a better state by participation in the unchanging Good, not to temporal felicity but by adoption to eternal life, which alone is happy. On this account I decided to go through the prophetic psalm, whose first verse Christ recalled in His Passion, showing how God has in one way forsaken us, and in another has not gone from us, drawing us on to eternal good things, and sometimes usefully furnishing us with temporal goods, and at other times usefully withdrawing them, that we should learn not to cleave to them lest, having despised the interior light which pertains to the new life ... we should gladly dwell in outer darkness [51]).

Augustine concludes Letter 140 with a warning against the opponents of the Grace of the New Testament, who wish to attribute the fact that they are good to themselves, and not to God. He recognises that they are continent and deserving of praise for their good works, and that they are orthodox in belief; but they are *ignorant of the righteousness of God and wish to establish their own*, so that, at the last, God will say to them, as to the foolish virgins: *I do not know you* (37, 83). Like the foolish virgins, they do not recognise God as the giver of all good (37, 84).

> For it is necessary that he loves God too little, who thinks himself made good, not by God but by himself [52]).

There can be no doubt about the identity of these opponents of the grace of the New testament.

Nevertheless, the *De Gratia Novi Testamenti* is more than merely an anti-Pelagian treatise. Although composed just after the *De*

[51]) Ibid., 36, 82: '*uerbum caro factum est*, id est, qui dei filius erat, homo factus est naturam suscipiendo nostram non amittendo suam, per quod et nobis recipientibus eum *potestas* daretur, ut, qui eramus homines, *filii dei* fieremus participatione incommutabilis boni in melius commutati non ad temporalem felicitatem sed ad uitae aeternae, quae sola beata est, adoptionem. unde placuit etiam propheticum psalmum percurrere, cuius primum uersum in passione commemorauit ostendens, quo modo nos derelinquat et quo alio modo non recedat a nobis, ad bona aeterna nos colligens temporalia uero aliquando utiliter tribuens et aliquando utiliter subtrahens, ut eis non haerere discamus, ne contempta luce interiore, quae ad nouam pertinet uitam ... ne in exteris tenebris libenter habitemus'. *CSEL* xliv, 230. 14 - 231. 1-2, 4-5.

[52]) Ibid., 37, 85: 'necesse est autem, ut parum diligat deum, qui non ab illo sed a se ipso bonum se arbitratur effectum'. *CSEL* xliv, 233. 20-21.

Peccatorum Meritis et Remissione, it is not concerned with Original Sin and the need for baptism. Its approach is closer to that of the *De Spiritu et Littera* which followed it, the two having in common the doctrine of participation in the unchangeable Good which is God, *ut ex illo ei bene sit, a quo habet ut sit*[53]). This notion of participation constantly recurs in Letter 140[54]), and is made possible by the Incarnation. Christ the Word became partaker in our flesh that we might be made partakers of Him and so be changed *in melius*, to a better condition.

If the inspiration of Letter 140 is the Incarnation, the text of Scripture from which the grace of the New Testament is understood is Psalm 21. Indeed, it would hardly be too much to say that the whole letter is an extended commentary on this one psalm, with two short excursuses on Ephesians 3: 18 and the *outer darkness*, and a longer concluding section on the Wise and Foolish Virgins. Christ's cry of dereliction provides the theme; and it is here that we may notice a change from the exegesis of Psalm 21 given in 407. In both of his expositions Augustine recognised that the words uttered by Christ were spoken on behalf of his Body, the Church; but in 407 he was concerned to preach against Donatism[55]). In Letter 140 his intention was rather to emphasise that Christians should not expect material favours from God while living in this world, and he refers Honoratus to his sermon on Psalm 76 for a more extended treatment of the theme (rather unnecessarily, it might be thought, in view of the space which he was to devote to the topic in his letter). This, however, indicates that Augustine's initial conception of his treatment of the grace of the New testament in the letter to Honoratus was to expound it in terms of divine favour: material favour in the Old Testament, which symbolised and prophesied the spiritual favour bestowed in the New through the Incarnation. While Augustine does not say that this treatment was

[53]) *Spir. et litt.* 3, 5: 'Nos autem dicimus humanam uoluntatem sic diuinitus adiuuari ad faciendam iustitiam, ut praeter quod creatus est homo cum libero arbitrio praeterque doctrinam qua ei praecipitur quemadmodum uiuere debeat accipiat spiritum sanctum, quo fiat in animo eius delectatio dilectioque summi illius atque incommutabilis boni, quod deus est, etiam nunc cum per fidem ambulatur, nondum per speciem, ut hac sibi uelut arra data gratuiti muneris inardescat inhaerere creatori atque inflammetur accedere ad participationem illius ueri luminis, ut ex illo ei bene sit, a quo habet ut sit'. *CSEL* lx, 157. 10-19. Cf. *ep.* 140, 23, 56-57 (quoted above, note 37); 34, 80 (quoted above, note 49); 35, 81 (quoted above, note 50) and 36, 82 (quoted above, note 51).

[54]) *Ep.* 140, 3, 7; 3, 9 - 4, 11; 23, 56; 27, 66; 29, 69; 29, 70; 31, 74; 33, 77; 34, 80; 36, 82.

[55]) *En. Ps.* 21, *s.* 2, 2; 31. *CCSL* xxxviii, 122-3; 132-4.

inspired by reflections on the theological implications of the sack of a Christian Rome, which were to find later expression in *The City of God*, all probabilities would seem to point in that direction.

Augustine's development of this process of theologial exegesis of Honoratus' five questions, by which the apologetic of *The City of God* is turned to a moderately-expressed anti-Pelagian polemic, is extremely skilful. The transition occurs during his discussion of the meaning of the outer darkness. Here he argues that created beings who turn aside from the light of the highest Good, their creator and the source of their well-being (23, 56-57), fall into spiritual darkness through the sin of pride, the head and fount of all sin (24, 61 - 25, 62). The cure for this sin is humility, shown forth supremely in the Incarnation and Christ's death upon the Cross; and in a brief paragraph Augustine sees the Cross as the great example of the mystery of divine grace (26, 64). Christ, by His sufferings, has obtained the kingdom (27, 66). The thought here, if not the language, anticipates the devotion to the Cross of later Latin hymnography.

> Hic acetum, fel, arundo, sputa, clavi, lancea;
> Mite corpus perforatur; sanguis, unda profluit,
> Terra, pontus, astra, mundus quo lavantur flumine.

> ... per hoc enim mediator effectus est, ut nos
> reconciliet deo per humilitatem, a quo per impiam
> superbiam longe recesseramus (28, 68).

The restoration of fallen humanity and its exaltation in Christ is begun on earth in the fellowship of the Church. It is not without interest that, although the fact that he was writing to a catechumen imposed a restriction on his language, Augustine more than once in the *De Gratia Novi Testamenti* refers to the eucharist, the act of thanksgiving in the Church which anticipates on earth the united worship eternally offered by the Church in heaven[56]). Unhappily, not all of those who accept the message of the Gospel understand the lesson of the Cross, but prefer to put their trust in their own works (30, 73). Such Christians resemble the

[56]) *Ep.* 140, 19, 48: 'hinc gratias agimus domino nostro, quod est magnum sacramentum in sacrificio noui testamenti, quod et ubi et quando et quo modo offeratur, cum fueris baptizatus, inuenies'; 24, 61: 'Vota ergo sua sacrificium uult intellegi corporis sui, quod est fidelium sacramentum'; 27, 66: 'et ipsi quippe adducti sunt ad mensam Christi et accipiunt de corpore et sanguine eius, sed adorant tantum, non enim saturantur'; 29, 70: '... unde est actio gratiarum, quae intimo fidelium mysterio celebratur'. *CSEL* xliv, 195. 28 - 196. 3; 206. 18-19; 213. 7-9; 218. 7-8.

foolish Virgins and rejoice in human praise (31, 74) and to them the Lord, at the Last Judgement, will say: *I know you not*, because you trust in yourselves rather than in Me (35, 81). These are the rich, the proud, who have *eaten and adored* but, unlike the poor in spirit, have not been filled, because they do not hunger and thirst for the righteousness which comes from God alone (27, 66).

Considered as a document illustrating the course of the development of Augustine's theology during the Pelagian Controversy, Letter 140 does not reveal any of that implacable hostility which will characterise him after the shock caused by the acquittal of Pelagius at the synods of Jerusalem and Diospolis. Although well aware of the Pelagian denial of Original Sin and the need for infant baptism on that account, Augustine makes no mention of these issues. His concern is far more with Christian living and with the danger of the sin of pride, which goes wholly counter to the humility of the Incarnation and blights the lives of those who, although virtuous in conduct and orthodox in belief, put their confidence in themselves, rather than in the grace of Christ, upon which they depend, not only to be, but also to be virtuous. If, as has been asserted in a well known study, 'Pelagianism as we know it, that consistent body of ideas of momentous consequences, had come into existence [by the winter of 411-412] ... in the mind of Augustine'[57]), it can only be said that this is not apparent in the letter to Honoratus. Augustine, at the time of writing, and for some time afterwards, regarded the Pelagians as 'brethren to be reasoned with and, if possible, retained in the fellowship of the Church rather than heretics to be denounced'[58]). Accordingly, he urged Honoratus not to be persuaded by the emptiness of their vessels, but rather to persuade them by the fulness of his own. *Necesse est autem, ut parum diligat deum, qui non ab illo sed a se ipso bonum se arbitratur effectum* (37, 85). This is what is to be understood by the grace of the New Testament.

It was suggested at the beginning of this analysis that the *De Gratia Novi Testamenti* represents a microcosm of Augustine's theological thinking, with its emphasis on God as the source of all good, and on the absolute dependence of man upon Him, which commends and enjoins the virtue of humility, supremely revealed in the Incarnation and in the death of the Cross. Yet with this there is also a sense of the

[57]) Peter BROWN, *Augustine of Hippo* (London, 1967), 345.

[58]) Gerald BONNER, *Augustine and Pelagianism in the Light of Modern Research* (Augustine Lecture 1970) (Villanova, Pa., 1972), 40.

glorification of humanity, brought about by participation in Christ, the God-Man and Mediator between man and God. Consideration of such themes seems particularly appropriate in a study offered to Tarsicius van Bavel, in whose theological thinking Christology has always occupied a central, and determining, place.

V

Pelagianism Reconsidered

An invitation to supply an article on Pelagianism for the *Theologische Realenzyklopädie* caused me to think again about the controversy as an historical phenomenon, and to try to consider its significance at the time, in contrast to its long-term effects. Of the importance of these there can be no question, and this is largely due to Augustine's voluminous writings and the challenge of his opponents, notably Julian of Eclanum. Because of this, and because of the vast residual literature inspired by Pelagianism, which is currently being explored in depth by patristic scholars, it would be unwise to adopt any unduly simplistic view of the theology of the movement. Pelagianism may start from a common repudiation of the doctrine of Original Sin; but its various exponents and defenders are individual thinkers who are not open to simple categorisation. No doubt the time will come when some scholar will give us a volume on Pelagian theology which will take account of the many contributors to this particular school of Christian thought[1].

At the moment, however, I am concerned with the actual events which set the controversy in motion and would like to suggest that there is a remarkable element of contingency about the whole Pelagian affair — that it might easily never have come about. Let me begin by raising the question of the actual strength of the movement. Augustine seems to speak as though there were hordes of Pelagians in Africa[2]; but if this was indeed the case, one can only say that they kept remarkably quiet after Caelestius' condemnation at Carthage in 411. There were enough of them at Rome in 418 to produce a riot; but given the taste for rioting in the ancient world, which resembled that of eighteenth century London, England, or Boston, Massachusetts, one may suspect that a good many of the rioters were as much motivated by the fun of the thing as by any particular devotion to Pelagian dogma. The same might well be true of those who sacked Jerome's monastery at Bethlehem in 416 (if they were indeed Pelagians, which is no more than an assumption) — not a few people might have been glad to attack Jerome for his own sake, without

[1] There are already a number of admirable investigations of individual Pelagian writers. What I have in mind is a general study which would comprehend them all, noting their similarities and disagreements.

[2] *De Gestis Pelagii* xxxv,62: 'Ista haeresis cum plurimos decepisset et fratres, quos non deceperat, conturbaret, Caelestius quidam talia sentiens ad iudicium Carthaginensis ecclesiae perductus episcoporum sententia condemnatus est' (CSEL 42,116).

regard to his theology. Sicily appears to have been a Pelagian centre, judging from the literature which it produced; and there seems to have been a Pelagian cell at Constantinople, which was harassed and expelled by the Patriarch Atticus[3]; but the overall picture does not encourage us to regard Pelagianism as a mass-movement. On the contrary, its character would rather seem to have been aristocratic and exclusive. Julian of Eclanum had no use for the hosts of simpletons whom he saw as constituting the mass of the Catholic party[4].

There would therefore seem to be no reason to see Pelagianism as enjoying anything like the mass support later enjoyed by Nestorianism or Monophysitism. Caelestius may have made converts to his way of thinking in North Africa, but no body of resistance emerged after he was denounced and condemned. Augustine, it is true, was moved to embark on the composition of *De Peccatorum Meritis et Remissione*, but that was at the request of his zealous patron, Count Marcellinus, when he was more than adequately engaged with the Donatists. What the condemnation of Caelestius did, however, was to arouse a suspicion of Pelagius in the minds of the African bishops. J.A. Davids long ago made the suggestion[5] that one of the purposes of Orosius' visit to Palestine in 415 was to warn Jerome (unnecessarily, as it happened) about the dangers of Pelagian theology, which were becoming clear from the reports of Hilary of Syracuse about propaganda in Sicily, and Pelagius' own *De Natura*, sent to Augustine by Timasius and James in 415. The Africans were quick to link Pelagius with his more aggressive disciple, an association of names which was to have profound consequences in the later stages of the controversy.

I find it difficult not to feel that Orosius, despite his relatively small part in the drama, is one of the key-figures in the Pelagian Controversy. By his aggressive behaviour and lack of tact in dealing with the Jerusalem synod Orosius contrived to alienate, not only himself, but the whole African tradition from John of Jerusalem. His famous exhortation: 'If you represent Augustine follow his faith!' suggested to John, already disenchanted with that other Latin luminary, Jerome, that he was been commanded to learn his theology from Africa. His resentment must have been profound if, as seems likely, he ignored Augustine's later request for the minutes of the Synod of Diospolis[6]. There can be no question that a concern for the prestige of individual sees played its part in determining the course of the Pelagian

[3] See G. Bonner, 'Some remarks on Letters 4* and 6*' in *Les lettres de Saint Augustin découvertes par Johannes Divjak. Communications présentées au colloque des 20 et 21 Septembre 1982* (Paris, 1983), 160-161.

[4] *Contra Iulianum* V,i,4 (PL 44,783).

[5] J.A. Davids, *De Orosio et sancto Augustino Priscillianistarum aduersariis commentatio historica et philologica* (The Hague, 1930), 23.

[6] See Bonner, *art. cit.*, note 3 above, 155-158.

Controversy. What is surprising is the degree to which a single individual, and an individual of no particular standing, could so effectively alienate the see of Jerusalem from the Church of Africa.

The Synod of Diospolis was marked by the absence of the principal accusers — the one ill, the other unwilling to come without him. This left Pelagius in possession of the field, and he made good use of his opportunities. As a result he was cleared of the charges brought against him and reached the pinnacle of his fortunes in the controversy.

The sequel to Pelagius' brief triumph was the African campaign which led to his excommunication and that of Caelestius by Pope Innocent I on 27 January 417. What was the reason for this African vehemence? It should be remembered that African prestige was involved: African conviction of the rightness of its beliefs — the bishops of Proconsular Africa could tolerate the prospect of Pelagius being acquitted by the pope, but only provided that the doctrines urged against him were condemned[7] — and African conviction of the universality of its understanding of the necessity of infant baptism for the remission of Original Sin. This last consideration must particularly have moved Augustine, since he had so constantly urged against the Donatists the uniformity of Catholic belief throughout the Christian world. The events of the year 415 must have come as an appalling shock to Augustine: Pelagius quoting his earlier writings in the *De Natura* to defend his own doctrine and the Synod of Diospolis apparently finding no fault in Pelagius' teaching. From 416 onwards Augustine was to be implacable in his campaign against Pelagius and in so doing he had the full support of his African colleagues.

The reaction of Pope Zosimus against Innocent's condemnation of the two Pelagian leaders is open to a number of interpretations: sympathy for two men who had been condemned without being accorded a chance to defend themselves; suspicion of African attempts to impose their particular theology on the Church as a whole — the clash between Stephen and Cyprian indicated that this was nothing new; and, it must be added, personal hostility to Heros and Lazarus, on account of his relations with Patroclus, Heros' supplanter in the see of Arles. To this may be added zeal for maintaining the prestige of the Roman Church. It was unfortunate for Zosimus that in the African bishops he encountered divines whose professed respect for the authority of the Apostolic See was tempered by a conviction of their own rightness. Whether a more cautious handling of the dispute by Zosimus could have brought about some sort of compromise solution which would have saved the dignity of both parties must remain an open question. As it was the

[7] Inter Aug., *Ep.* 175,4: 'Si ergo Pelagius episcopalibus gestis quae in oriente confecta dicuntur, etiam tuae Venerationi iuste uisus fuerit absolutus, error tamen ipse et impietas, quae iam multos assertores habet, per diuersa dispersos, etiam auctoritate apostolicae sedis anathemanda est' (CSEL 44, 658).

Africans, supported by the emperor, were able to maintain their own extreme traducian position, even if they were unable to constrain Zosimus to reproduce it exactly in his *Epistola tractoria*.

It is, however, the sequel to the events of the year 418 which is particularly important for any evaluation of the significance of the Pelagian Controversy in its own day. Unlike the later Christological disputes in the East, there was no surge of support for the Pelagian position — only a handful of clerics, of whom only one, Julian of Eclanum, had any outstanding theological ability. Augustine's long literary duel with Julian provided material for doctrinal discussion in future centuries; it hardly inflamed the Christian world in his own lifetime. The real debate was with the Massilian divines of southern Gaul and was provoked, not by any sympathy with Pelagianism on their part, but by dismay at what seemed to be the appalling consequences of Augustine's theological principles when carried, as Augustine was prepared to carry them, to their logical conclusion. To say that the debate was maintained by Augustine's sheer obstinacy may seem hard, but his incapacity to recognise any point of view other than his own was prodigious; as John Burnaby observed: 'Augustine never realised that his own conception of grace required nothing less than a revolution in his thought of the divine omnipotence'[8]. Perhaps John Cassian and his supporters, where this particular issue was concerned, understood the genius of Augustine better than Augustine himself.

The enduring concern with the issues raised by the Pelagian Controversy in Western Christendom in later centuries is obvious enough: from Gottschalk to Jonathan Edwards and George Whitefield there has been no lack of theologians prepared to understand extreme Augustinian theology in its starkest terms. In this field Augustine's influence has been enormous; but to recognise this need not mean that we are thereby committed to a species of historical determinism, which sees the Pelagian Controversy as the natural and inevitable goal of Augustine's career. On the contrary, the aspect of the Pelagian affair most calculated to strike the uncommitted observer is the element of chance and contingency which characterised its course. If Pelagius had actually encountered Augustine when he arrived at Hippo; if Caelestius had departed for Palestine with his master; if Paulinus of Milan had not decided to bring an ecclesiastical action against Caelestius; if Orosius had shown more restraint and more common sense at Jerusalem in 415; if Heros and Lazarus had been able to be present at the Synod of Diospolis; if someone other than Zosimus had succeeded Innocent; if Zosimus had shown greater diplomatic skill and the Africans less concern for their own prestige; if Julian of Eclanum had not emerged from a respectable obscurity to present Augustine with the most formidable antagonist that he ever encountered, the whole course of Christian Church history and Christian theology would have

[8] Burnaby, *Amor Dei. A Study of the Religion of Saint Augustine* (London, 1938), 230.

been very different. William Frend has even declared that 'except for the fall of Rome, Pelagius would never have been condemned'[9]. So Alaric the Goth adds to his laurels the distinction of having precipitated the Pelagian Controversy.

This is not to say that, but for Pelagianism, Augustine would never have written on Grace, Free Will and Original Sin. On the contrary, his doctrine of the *massa* had been expressed before 395 in Question 68 of *De diuersis quaestionibus LXXXIII* and the intellectual illumination which made clear to him the implications of 1 Cor. 4.7, to which he would several times refer during the Pelagian Controversy[10], had occurred when writing *De diuersis quaestionibus ad Simplicianum*. It is conceivable that, even without the spur of religious polemic, he would have written on the theme of God's decree and man's destiny; but we may guess that it would have been in the spirit of the *De Gratia Noui Testamenti* or the *De Spiritu et Littera* rather than that of the *De Correptione et Gratia* or the *Opus Imperfectum*. Controversy hardened Augustine, as it is apt to harden controversialists.

It would be too much to claim that the Pelagian Controversy was an accident, but I am inclined to see it as a succession of accidentals. It may be argued that the same holds true of a great many incidents of history, secular as well as ecclesiastical, and I would be disposed to agree. As Winston Churchill once said in another context, 'the terrible ifs accumulate'.

[9] Frend, *Saints and sinners in the Early Church* (London, 1985), 139.

[10] Aug., *Retract.* II,i[27] (CSEL 36,131-32). *De Praedestinatione Sanctorum* iv,8 (quoting *Retract.* II,i[27]) (PL 44,965-966); *De Dono Perseuerantiae* xx,52-53; xxi,55 (PL 45,1025-1027).

VI

Pelagianism and Augustine*

Among the many achievements of twentieth-century ecclesiastico-historical research has been the advance made in Pelagian studies. By this I do not mean simply, or even primarily, the identification and publication of Pelagian writings, fundamental as such researches are, but even more the attempt to understand the phenomenon of Pelagianism as the Pelagians understood it, to see them as they saw themselves. In company with other theological schools, like Arianism and Nestorianism, condemned in their own age as heresies and for centuries treated as such by scholars, we now seek to see Pelagianism as a religious tendency existing in its own right and not as mere opposition to prevailing doctrine; believing itself to be orthodox and not setting out deliberately to pervert Christian truth – it has, after all, been fairly remarked that the one sin to which one cannot logically admit is that of being, as opposed to having been, a heretic, because this would imply that one is deliberately believing doctrines which one recognizes to be false. This does not mean, of course, that it is now impossible for a scholar to hold that the ancient heresies were erroneous; but it does require that they must be allowed a fair hearing on their own terms, and not on what their opponents regarded as their own terms. I think that B. R. Rees, in the title of his book, *Pelagius: A Reluctant Heretic*, has very fairly caught the spirit of the contemporary approach to Pelagianism by scholars who would still wish to regard themselves as orthodox Christian believers.

It is for this reason that in these two lectures I want to begin from a consideration of Pelagianism as a movement in itself and not to see it, as it has so often in the past been seen, as a kind of appendage to the career of Augustine. This does not mean that Augustine now becomes irrelevant to the history of Pelagianism. On the contrary, as I hope to suggest later on, it was he, more than any other individual, who ensured that it was to have a permanent place as an event in ecclesiastical history; but it does mean that, in considering the Pelagian movement, we should avoid the temptation of seeing it negatively, as being aimed primarily at Augustine, and try to understand it in positive terms, as seeking to build, rather than to destroy. It may, of course, be our final conclusion that Pelagianism was, in essence, a negative influence, that its assumptions, carried to their logical conclusion, would have turned the Catholic Church into a tiny assembly of saints rather than a large school for sinners; but it would be unfair to the Pelagians to suppose that their goal was anything other than the advancement of Christian truth and morals, as they understood them. A generation ago the Swedish scholar, Torgny Bohlin, drew attention to the fact that Pelagius, in his Pauline commentaries, had two theological opponents principally in mind: Arianism and Manichaeism. In choosing these two, Pelagius displayed a concern for Christian doctrine as well as for Christian morals. The Arians denied the full divinity of the Word and so assailed the foundation of Christian faith. The Manichees, as dualists, denied the goodness of matter and therefore, since they saw man as a compound of matter and spirit, it logically followed that he must inevitably sin because of the material element in his nature. It was this assumption of the inevitability of sin because human beings have material bodies that Pelagius and his supporters attacked. Against Manichaean determinism they asserted the freedom of the human will, and it was because of their determination to assert the freedom of the human will that they denied the doctrine of Original Sin, which they saw as impugning the goodness of God as creator and as implying a Manichaean view of the human body as being something evil. Unless we keep this double concern in Pelagian theology in mind: to maintain right doctrine and to encourage men and women to live the Christian life in accordance with what they believed to be the teaching of the Gospel, we shall fail to understand the movement. In their appeal to Pope Zosimus in 418 both Pelagius and Caelestius submitted professions of faith in which, said Augustine, Pelagius held forth upon many matters which were irrelevant to the dispute.[1] We may reasonably hold that they did not seem so to Pelagius, who sought to vindicate himself in respect of both faith and works, in the belief that the one depends upon the other.

It was this emphasis upon man's essential goodness which, being God's creation, cannot be destroyed by sin, and upon the freedom of the human will, given by God and equally invulnerable, that constituted the foundation of Pelagian ethics, and explains why Pelagius, even before controversy began, reacted so violently to Augustine's prayer in the *Confessions*: "Give what Thou dost command and command what thou wilt."[2] It was not, I suggest, simply that it seemed to give excuse to the slothful and hypocritical; rather, that it struck at the whole basis of moral theology as Pelagius understood it. The Pelagians were not innocently unaware of human weakness.[3] They knew that, in practice, even good Christians sinned and needed to do penance; but they were utterly opposed to making human weakness the measure of human achievement: the only acceptable goal was perfection and, as the Pelagian author whom I call the Sicilian Anonymous says, in his treatise *On the Possibility of Not Sinning*,[4] if someone is told that he is capable of avoiding sin, he will be encouraged to make every effort to avoid it, with the result that, even if he does sin, his sins will be less frequent and less serious.[5] The traducian theory of the physical transmission of Adam's primal sin seemed to the Pelagians a recipe for disaster. If you start off persuaded that you are going to fail, then fail you undoubtedly will.

It is the denial of any doctrine of Original Sin which constituted the one essential article of belief for any would-be Pelagian. Once there is agreement on that point there is a reasonable margin for different tendencies and emphases. In general Pelagianism seems to have commended a strong asceticism, though Pelagius himself took care to defend the lawfulness of marriage, even though, like other, more orthodox theologians, he preferred virginity and chaste widowhood.[6] Again, although their denial of Original Sin removed the urgent necessity for infant baptism felt by Augustine, the Pelagians were quite prepared to accept the practice as part of the custom of the Catholic Church. They certainly did not regard their own foundation doctrine of the denial of Original Sin as a ground for separation from the Great Church. At his trial at Carthage in 411 Caelestius, perhaps the ablest Pelagian leader, charged with holding that the sin of Adam injured only himself and not the human race, was content to argue that doctrine concerning the transmission of sin as a matter of opinion, not of heresy. "I have always said that infants need baptism and ought to be baptized. What more does he want from me?" he demanded.[7]

The Pelagians, then were a body within the Church, holding opinions which they sought to commend to their fellow-Christians though without any desire to depart from Catholic unity. One might, in modern terminology, call them a pressure-group. But how strong was this pressure group? It is here that we encounter a question which is rarely discussed, presumably because of the sparsity of evidence, but which is of great importance in evaluating the movement. Augustine apparently considered that Pelagians were very numerous in Africa,[8] a view which was shared by the bishops of Proconsular Africa in their letter to Pope Innocent of 416.[9] If this was indeed the case, it is surprising that we hear so little of them during the Controversy, especially after the condemnation of Caelestius in 411 and Pelagius and Caelestius together in 417. Perhaps the African bishops panicked and saw Pelagians where they were not. There was a group at Rome sympathetic to Pelagius, as Aurelius of Carthage, Augustine, and their fellow-signatories recognized in their letter to Pope Innocent in 416[10] (though Innocent expressed ignorance of any Pelagian presence in the city),[11] and this group was sufficiently numerous to engage in open violence with its opponents in 418,[12] thus finally persuading the imperial government to intervene;[13] but rioting was as popular an activity in the Roman world as it would be in Boston, Massachusetts, and London, England, in the eighteenth century, and it may well be that many of those who indulged in violence were as much motivated by the excitement of the proceedings as by sympathy with Pelagian theology. The same may apply to the motives of those who assaulted Jerome's monastery at Bethlehem in 416. Jerome made enemies, and not a few persons might have been happy to join in an attack on him without being much concerned about his theology. Accordingly, we do not need to regard Jerusalem as a Pelagian stronghold. The writings of the Sicilian Anonymous and the statement of Augustine's correspondent, Hilary, that certain Syracusan Christians hold that a rich man could not enter the Kingdom of God unless he abandoned his wealth[14] – one of the Sicilian Anonymous's doctrines[15] – point to the existence of a Pelagian party in Sicily but give no indication of its strength. Again, there was a Pelagian group in the East, at Constantinople, which suffered from the attentions of the Patriarch Atticus,[16] but once more we have no information about its numerical strength.

It might be argued that the considerable quantity of Pelagian writing which has survived points to the existence of a reasonably large body of sympathizers, but this hardly amounts to proof. In the first place, the mass of Pelagian literature, though considerable, is not overwhelming. Some of it can be confidently assigned to individual authors, much remains of doubtful authorship, but the total number of Pelagian writers is not likely to have been large.

Furthermore, the fact that certain writings have been preserved tells us nothing about the readership which they enjoyed in their own day, and since a number of them are letters, their survival may well have been fortuitous. In short, there is nothing in the evidence available to us to suggest that Pelagianism was ever a mass movement like Donatism, or later movements like Nestorianism or Monophysitism. What really alarmed the African bishops, who were its earliest and most indefatigable opponents, was its theology, which went directly counter to their own. African concern, it may reasonably be suggested, arose from the conviction of their own rightness with regard to the doctrine of Original Sin, and a refusal to allow that there could ever be any compromise on this matter. Scholars today are wisely cautious about seeing heresies and schisms in the early Church as expressions of latent nationalism; but whatever the explanation, the ability of the African Catholic episcopate to stand together to defend what it believed to be the doctrine of the universal Church is both obvious and impressive.

Thus the struggle between the Pelagians and their opponents was essentially a literary – one might almost say, a pamphlet – war, were it not for the enormous size of the writings of the later contributors, notably Julian of Eclanum and Augustine, and it may be that the quantity of our source-material has helped to create the impression, at least in Western Christendom, that the Pelagian Controversy had an epic quality, comparable with the earlier struggle against Arianism. This seems to me to be untrue; and I would further utter a warning against any assumption, from the quantity of our documentation, that we can now reconstruct the people and the events of the Controversy with considerable exactitude. Such a supposition is too optimistic; and it remains true that the principal actors in the Controversy, on the Pelagian side, remain shadowy figures. Let us look at one or two, starting with Rufinus of Syria, the man who, according to Marius Mercator, first sowed the seeds of Pelagianism at Rome by corrupting Pelagius and using him as the agent for spreading heretical views which he was too astute to proclaim openly. Is he to be identified with the "Rufinus, a priest of the province of Palestine" who is alleged to be the author of the *Liber de Fide* by a colophon in St. Petersburg MS. Q.v.1.6, which is the sole existing witness to this anti-traducian work? And is he further to be identified with the priest Rufinus sent by Jerome from Bethlehem to Milan in 399, to give assistance at the trial of a certain Claudius, who was arraigned on a capital charge? I think that he may be; but there is a very large element of conjecture in this identification.[17] Again, let us consider

Pelagius. Apart from his Pauline commentaries, which are now generally accepted as genuine, and fragments quoted by Augustine, a question-mark hangs over the very large corpus of writings which have been attributed to him since the pioneering work of George de Plinval in the 1940s. Most people today seem to accept the arguments of Robert F. Evans, which identify a limited number of works as being by Pelagius himself - a list accepted by B. R. Rees in his recent volume of translations of Pelagian writings; but a recent, and very learned, work by three Italian scholars[18] expresses reservations about whether the *Letter to Celantia,* preserved among the works of Jerome but certainly not by him,[19] can safely be assigned to Pelagius. Again there is the treatise *On the hardening of Pharoah's heart*, discovered by Germain Morin and eventually published by Georges de Plinval, which some have wished to see as an answer to Augustine's two books *To Simplicianus on various questions* (396)[20] and which may be — but there is no proof. In short, much of the writing which has, from time to time, been ascribed to Pelagius is dubious; and the man himself, apart from a few moments of self-revelation, as in his vehement rejection of Augustine's petition: "Give what Thou commandest and command what Thou wilt" or his defiant question at the Synod of Jerusalem: "What is Augustine to me?",[21] displays few positive qualities and was certainly not the leader of the Pelagians once the battle began. His disciple, Caelestius, is a more impressive personality, the most effective man of action which the movement produced, but we have far too little material from his pen to evaluate him adequately. The writer whom John Morris called the Sicilian Briton, and I the Sicilian Anonymous, and B. R. Rees the Pelagian Anonymous, is a powerful writer with well-defined and remarkably radical views, which bring out the strongly ascetic tendency in Pelagianism; but we do not know who he was, and the writings which are attributed to him are attributed on stylistic and theological grounds, and if he played any active part in the controversy once it had broken out, we know nothing of it. Julian of Eclanum, is of course, familiar to us thanks to his own ready pen and the fact that Augustine preserved large portions of his writings in the *Opus Imperfectum*; but he only emerged as the active part of the Controversy drew to a close, and so only played a limited - but important - part in its events, as opposed to being a very sharp thorn in Augustine's flesh for the last decade of the saint's life.

With these reservations — and they are very considerable reservations — about our sources, which are usually established for us by others and which we are then all too often inclined to accept and to use without question, let us try to consider the thought-world and career of Pelagianism. I have already suggested that there is no reason to think that it was a mass movement. I have also maintained that it had no characteristic theology, other than a denial of any transmission of Original Sin, so that individual Pelagian writers show individual emphases in their thought. I would be inclined to regard Pelagius as being the theoretician of the movement, in that he, more than anyone else, tried to provide a general theological basis for its practical program. Julian of Eclanum is another theoretician, perhaps the ablest brain that Pelagianism produced; but he is more limited in scope than Pelagius, a polemicist rather than a constructive theologian.[22] Rufinus the Syrian, though he may be the inspirer of the movement, is a one-treatise man, who is at least as much concerned with denouncing Origen as with denying the transmission of Original Sin. The Sicilian Anonymous is the revivalist author of Pelagianism, enthusiastically denouncing riches and commending virginity. In his uncompromising asceticism he goes further than Pelagius, but his attitude reflects a very real tendency in Pelagianism: a rejection of any compromise in Christian living. The Pelagians were not monks; but their program, if it had been carried through uncompromisingly, would have turned the entire Christian Church into a monastery.

Let us now attempt to plot the outline of the history of Pelagianism. As a movement, it enjoyed a very short existence, between 408, when Pelagius first comes on to the stage, and 431, when it was condemned, in the person of Caelestius, by the Council of Ephesus, though its ghost was to haunt theologians for centuries. As regards its place of origin, there seems no reason to dispute the view that it arose in Rome and in aristocratic circles, largely female, to which Pelagius seems to have been a sort of lay spiritual director. Pelagius' own relationships suggest this interpretation, from his lost letter of 406 to Paulinus of Nola,[23] and his famous letter of 413 to Demetrias, the daughter of Anicia Faltonia Proba,[24] to his appeal, after his condemnation in 418, to Albina, Pinianus and Melania the younger.[25] Like his enemy Jerome before him, Pelagius had a liking for devout women of high rank, and they, equally, seem to have responded. At the same time, it would be unwise to overestimate the prestige enjoyed by Pelagius in Rome, outside the aristocratic circles which patronized him. In 416 Pope Innocent I expressed ignorance as to whether or not there were any Pelagians in the city,[26] though in 418-9 Augustine was to write at length to the presbyter Sixtus (a future pope), who was suspected of being too much inclined to Pelagian theology.[27] It may be that the great emigration of Roman aristocrats from 408 onwards, in the face of the threat to Rome of Alaric the Goth, effectively dissolved the Pelagian presence there.

Paradoxically, however, it was precisely this emigration which brought Pelagianism to the notice of the African bishops and so brought about the Pelagian Controversy. Indeed, but for Alaric Pelagianism, as we have come to understand it, might never have existed. As late as 412, when he embarked on the composition of the third book of *De Peccatorum Meritis et Remissione*, Augustine knew Pelagius only by repute, as a holy man of no small spiritual advancement, whose commentaries on the Pauline Epistles he had only recently read. Without laboring this piece of information, it at least implies that Pelagius' writings had not, at this time, achieved any particular fame outside his own circle except, perhaps, with the jealous Jerome, who may have had personal reasons for disliking Pelagius and his theology. Furthermore, it was not Pelagius who had provoked the attack on Pelagian doctrine in North Africa but his disciple Caelestius, who had been accused of teaching heresy by the Milanese deacon Paulinus, generally identified with the biographer of Saint Ambrose. I have long thought it probable that Caelestius' attitude to paedobaptism would have attracted attention in Africa, where the theology of baptism had played so important a part in the dispute with Donatism.[28] Caelestius, at his trial at Carthage, argued that the reason for infant baptism (a practice of which he approved) was not a matter of dogma, but admitted of a number of differing theological explanations. It was here, however, that he came up against African dogma, looking back to the teaching of Saint Cyprian, and was condemned. Significantly his personal opinion, so unacceptable to the Africans, proved to be no bar to his subsequent ordination at Ephesus.

The condemnation of Caelestius at Carthage apparently left the African bishops in a permanent state of concern about any denial of their theological expertise in general and of traducian doctrine in particular. However, they did not immediately launch an offensive against Pelagian teaching. Even Augustine, later to be the implacable opponent of anything Pelagian, contented himself with answering Pelagian doctrines brought to his attention, like that reported to him from Sicily by Hilary[29] and Pelagius' treatise *De Natura*, sent by Timasius and James.[30] With Pelagius himself he remained on civil terms, as is shown by his Letter 146 (413). But perhaps the best evidence of Augustine's desire to avoid an open breach with Pelagian theologians in revealed by his famous treatise, *On the grace of the New Testament* (Letter

140), written probably in the early months of 412, in response to an enquiry from a certain Honoratus regarding the meaning of five passages of Scripture. In his reply, Augustine added a sixth question of his own: *What is the grace of the New Testament?*, asked with Pelagianism in mind. In his work Augustine makes no reference to Pelagian denial of Original Sin or the need for infant baptism; rather, he is concerned with what he saw as the implications of Pelagian doctrine: a false self-sufficiency, resulting in a lack of humility. At its deepest level, Augustine's concern was with the sin of pride, which he believed, rightly or wrongly, to be the consequence of the train of reasoning initiated by Pelagius.

It was not, then, in Africa that a direct assault was first launched upon Pelagius himself, but in Palestine, for it was here that Jerome pursued a campaign which may have been of long standing, if we are to accept the suggestion that the unnamed monk who criticized the extreme views of Jerome's denunciation of Jovinian may have been Pelagius. Whether this is the case or not, there is substance in Robert F. Evans's suggestion that Jerome's *Dialogue against the Pelagians*, which we know from Orosius to have been in process of composition in July 415,[31] was inspired by Pelagius who had revived charges of Origenism, and undue disparagement of marriage.[32] It was, indeed, Jerome, rather than Augustine, who was the first opponent of Pelagius, albeit without naming him, and an explanation is clear: in Jerusalem Pelagius was an all-too-close neighbor of Jerome at Bethlehem and was supported by sympathetic elements of the Roman aristocracy, who like him, had preferred the safety of the East to the perils of life at Rome, threatened by the Goths. Augustine, in Africa, still at this time preoccupied by the attempt to bring the Donatists into unity and with the composition of the *De Civitate Dei*, to say nothing of smaller writings, like that against the Origenists and Priscillianists composed for Orosius, had far less motive than Jerome to embark upon a campaign against Pelagius, a man with a reputation for piety, as Augustine himself recognized, and who enjoyed the friendship of many of Augustine's friends. Perhaps by 415 Augustine's views were changing. In the letter to his friend Evodius, written at the end of 415, he referred to having recently written a large book "against the heresy of Pelagius,"[33] that is, the *De Natura et Gratia*. Nevertheless, in that work he was careful to attribute the erroneous opinions of Pelagius (whom he does not name) to a "burning zeal" (*zelo ardentissimo*) against the excuses of those who try to extenuate their sins by attributing them to the weakness of human nature and not to their own will.[34] Similarly, in the

De Perfectione Iustitiae Hominis, written at approximately the same time as the *De Natura et Gratia* and aimed at certain propositions attributed to Caelestius, Augustine was careful to say, with regard to the view that even before the coming of Christ there had been men free from actual, as opposed to Original, sin, that he dared not reprehend this view, although he was not able to defend it.[35] Among the charges leveled against Caelestius at his trial at Carthage in 411 was the allegation that even before the coming of Christ there had been sinless men – wholly sinless, that is to say, given Caelestius' denial of Original Sin. Augustine would not accept such a denial; but if the notion of sinlessness implied not giving consent to the lusts which Original Sin necessarily engendered, he was prepared to tolerate this view, even though he could not personally accept it. This particular doctrine was to be denounced by the pan-African Council of Carthage of May 1, 418, canons 6 and 7. In 415 Augustine was prepared to tolerate it as an opinion, while rejecting it personally.

Let us, at this point, consider the position of the Pelagian party – and the word party must, in this context be used with care, because it implies a degree of organized relationship which, so far as we can tell, was wholly lacking in the associates of Pelagius at this time – in the summer of 415, the point at which the campaign against Pelagian theology is set in motion by the behavior of Paul Orosius. Caelestius, condemned by a Carthaginian synod, has contrived to get himself ordained at Ephesus. Pelagius is at Jerusalem, in the congenial company of other Roman refugees and on good terms with the bishop, John, whose high opinion of him may not be wholly uninfluenced by the fact that he, too, has suffered from the attacks of Jerome during the Origenistic Controversy at the end of the fourth century. Furthermore, Jerome himself seems to have seen his own debate with Pelagius as being in part an extension of the earlier controversy; hence his interpretation of Pelagius' doctrine of *impecantia* (the view that a man is able to live without sin if he chooses) as being equivalent to the Stoic philosophical ideal of *apatheia* – freedom from passion.[36] Again, Jerome fastened on the deficiency of the Pelagian conception of grace, declaring that for Pelagius it was no more than free will and God's law.[37] Interestingly, however, although a believer in the guilt of Adam inherited by humanity, he made no reference to the issue of infant baptism until Orosius brought it to his notice, when he arrived in Bethlehem in the spring or early summer of 415, equipped with copies of Augustine's anti-Pelagian writing to that date, including the letter to Hilary

(Letter 157). Jerome had been first in the field in opposing Pelagius; but his activity had been essentially local, and he had not covered the whole range of Pelagian interest.

Such was the situation in the ecclesiastical world in the middle of 415. There was disagreement; there was suspicion; but there was no reason to expect the sequence of violent events which marked the three following years.

The initiator of the period of violence which was to come was Paul Orosius. He belongs to that category of individuals – John Wilkes Booth is another – whose influence on the course of history is out of all proportion to the time which they occupy the stage. To say that no one could have caused more trouble than Orosius in the Pelagian affair would be rash, give the talent of human beings to cause trouble. Let it suffice that his contribution was outstanding and may have been decisive. "Talented, opinionated, narrowly orthodox, impetuous"[38] – to these qualities ascribed to him by J. N. D. Kelly we may add another, which was to prove decisive: utter lack of tact. Orosius came to Bethlehem, according to his own account, to see Jerome. He was also the bearer of two long letters from Augustine, and had perhaps been asked to warn Jerome about the pernicious views of Rufinus the Syrian, the alleged inspirer of Pelagius and perhaps a monk from Jerome's monastery.[39] But Avitus of Braga, Orosius' fellow-countryman, says that Orosius was sent to Palestine by the African bishops, which may imply that he was deputed to make common cause with Jerome against the doctrines which had been condemned in Caelestius.[40] At all events, Orosius arrived in Bethlehem full of anti-Pelagian zeal. Invited to a diocesan synod at Jerusalem on July 30, 415 he behaved with astonishing arrogance, taking the line that the decisions of the synod of Carthage of 411 and the teaching of Jerome and Augustine were not open to discussion, but merely required endorsement by the Palestinian synod. His impertinence to Bishop John was amazing, reaching its high point in his celebrated retort to John, when the latter declared: "It is I who am the Augustine here," "If you are Augustine, follow his opinion!"[41] It was no wonder that Pelagius enjoyed the sympathy of the synod and that Orosius was only able to avert his acquittal by proposing that the matter, as a Latin affair, had best be referred to Innocent of Rome for his judgment. It was, however, the sequel to the Jerusalem synod which was decisive. When Orosius came to Jerusalem for the Feast of the Dedication of the Church of the Holy Sepulchre on September 12, he was publicly denounced by Bishop John as one who held that an individual could not avoid sin even with God's help. Nothing could have been further from Augustine's thought than such a doctrine of total corruption, but the fact that such a charge could be made at all was horrifying. The *débâcle* at Jerusalem in the summer of 415 was consummated by the fiasco at Diospolis in December, when Pelagius was exonerated from all the charges brought against him. The fact that he achieved his acquittal only by disowning Caelestius and by being economical with the truth regarding his own writings was not known to the African bishops in general and to Augustine in particular until some time afterwards. If Caelestius were now to make an appeal to Rome and if the Carthaginian decision of 411 were to be set aside, African theological rectitude would receive a disastrous blow and the Catholic faith – at least in the eyes of the Africans – would be imperiled.

So the African bishops arose, terrible as an army with banners, to crush one lay-theologian of the second rank and a maverick Roman aristocrat who, since his condemnation in 411, had been living an apparently blameless life at Ephesus, not giving offence to anybody. In their letter to Pope Innocent the bishops of Proconsular Africa declared that Pelagian error had many defenders, widely dispersed,[42] although they provided no evidence to support this assertion; while their colleagues from Numidia stated that, although Pelagius in Jerusalem was said to have deceived some hearers, the opposition to his views was far stronger.[43] Aurelius of Carthage, joined by Augustine, Alypius, Evodius and Possidius – all personal friends of the bishop of Hippo – declared that they had heard that Pelagius had some supporters in Rome[44] but went on to speak of many others who ensnared and made captive weak souls.[45] This letter, clearly influenced if not drafted by Augustine, provides in succinct form the doctrine which Pelagius and Caelestius are said to be attacking and is an excellent statement of Augustinian theology. What the Africans desired, however – no doubt sincerely – was that it should be forced on the Pelagians as the only acceptable form of orthodox doctrine.

What would have happened if Innocent had declined to fall in with these African proposals we cannot tell, though it is a reasonable guess that their rejection would have provoked a crisis far greater than than occasioned by the dispute between Saint Cyprian and Pope Stephen in the third century. The inflexible determination of the Africans was shown after Innocent's death when his successor, Zosimus, attempted to reopen the question, only to be met by a flat refusal. *Causa finita est* – "the matter is settled" – was their argument, and they did not hesitate to obtain the support of the secular arm for their contentions and, in the hour of victory, to issue a series of canons expressing African doctrine in its most extreme terms.[46] It would be going too far to regard the Pelagian affair as a case of deliberate empire-building on the part of the Africans; but their intolerance of any opinion other than their own and the ruthlessness of their methods cannot be denied.

It is curious that it is only after the condemnation of Pelagius and Caelestius in 418 that we begin to find evidence of some real support for their theology. This was provided by eighteen Italian bishops, of whom Julian of Eclanum is the leading spirit and the one antagonist who seems to have really shaken and irritated Augustine. The reason for this, apart from Augustine's understandable resentment that he, the great theological expert of the West, should be contradicted and insulted by a much younger man (and Julian's polemical style was undoubtedly offensive), lay in the fact that Julian was a really able controversialist, who chose the ground for debate very skillfully, by representing Augustine's understanding of sexual concupiscence as Manichaean, and thereby changing Pelagian tactics from a defensive to an offensive stance. Augustine and the Africans had called the Pelagians *inimici gratiae* – "enemies of grace"[47] – a charge which had a good deal of plausibility; it was very difficult to find confession of grace in Pelagian writing in any form other than grace of creation, illumination, and remission of sins in baptism, since their denial of any transmission of Original Sin postulated a self-sufficiency in man's created nature. Pelagius and Caelestius had behaved in a passive fashion in the face of such charges, defending themselves but not denouncing their accusers. Julian went on the offensive, attacking Augustine's preoccupation with sexual concupiscence as thc medium by which Original Sin was transmitted as being a species of Manichaean dualism, which regarded the flesh as inherently evil. Julian was able to point to the fact that Augustine was a former Manichee and suggest that he had never ceased to be one at heart – the Ethiopian cannot change his skin or the leopard his spots.[48] If for Augustine the Pelagians were *inimici gratiae*, for Julian and his supporters Augustine and his party were *illi Manichaei, quibus modo non communicamus* – "Manichees with whom we do not now communicate."[49] It was unfair, of course. Augustine had waged an implacable war with the Manichees from 388 onwards; but Julian did not intend to be fair. He wanted to win, and his tactics were very effective. In 415 John of Jerusalem had accused Orosius of holding that man could not be free from sin even with God's help.[50] Julian, whether consciously or unconsciously, had developed the accusation in the most damaging way, by associating Augustine's theology with the heresy which, more perhaps than any other, horrified the Fathers of the Church. It may well be that Augustine's virtual obsession with Julian sprang from embarrassment at the charges which Julian leveled. His Manichaean past was still haunting him, however strongly he anathematized it.

Unfortunately for Julian, impressive as his tactics were, they came too late. If he could only have intervened earlier, before the condemnation of Pelagianism, he might have affected the course of debate, but once Pelagianism had been proscribed by pope and emperor alike and the resources of the state directed to its suppression, no argument or eloquence on his part could avail to turn the clock back. It is significant that his writings survive in large measure only because Augustine adopted the technique, which he had previously employed when answering Faustus the Manichee, of reproducing long passages from Julian before giving his own reply. Augustine apart, we have effectively no knowledge of how influential Julian's writings were in his own lifetime. Undoubtedly they were read in some circles, but how large were these circles? There was certainly a Pelagian circle at Constantinople, which included the Pelagian bishop Florus, who found a copy of Mani's *Letter to Menoch* there and dispatched it to Julian, thereby providing him with what he regarded as decisive evidence that Manichaeism and Traducianism taught the same doctrine.[51] This group was persecuted and expelled by the Patriarch Atticus,[52] perhaps as a sequel to the Emperor Honorius' edict of June 9, 419, which threatened penal sanctions against Pelagians and instructed Bishop Aurelius of Carthage to make this decision generally known.[53] However, the most remarkable feature of the sequel to the condemnation of Pelagius and Caelestius and their supporters in 418 is a negative one: the absence of any strong reaction from the movement at large. It was not the Pelagians but the Massilians, the so-called Semi-Pelagians of Southern Gaul, who had no sympathy with Pelagius but who were horrified by the implications of Augustine's predestinarian theology, which seemed to take away all freedom from the individual, who constituted the most formidable opposition to the triumph of Augustinian deterministic theology.

Unlike Pelagius and Caelestius, John Cassian and his supporters were too famous, and too much respected, to be suppressed by strong-arm measures. Prosper of Aquitaine, Augustine's admirer, might see their teaching as no more than the remains of Pelagian depravity (*reliquiae Pelagianae pravitatis*),[54] but this was far from being a universal opinion. Thus Vincent, a Semi-Pelagian monk of the famous island monastery of Lérins, while dismissing both

Pelagius and Caelestius as introducers of impious novelty in his *Commonitorium*[55] and adding an even briefer reference to Julian of Eclanum,[56] nevertheless, significantly, omits the name of Augustine from a catalogue of defenders of Christian orthodoxy which includes names like Athanasius, Gregory of Nazianzus, Basil of Caesarea, Gregory of Nyssa, Cyprian of Carthage, an Ambrose of Milan, and in a short, but vicious paragraph, expresses a condemnation of a predestinarian heresy which looks uncommonly like the teaching of Augustine as seen by a Semi-Pelagian.[57]

Augustine's literary duel with Julian of Eclanum has provided material for theological discussion over the centuries; but there is no proof that it had more than a parochial interest during the last decade of his life. This, indeed, is the problem. After 418 effective opposition to predestinarian theology came from the Semi-Pelagians. Julian is the only impressive campaigner on the Pelagian side and Julian, interestingly, reflects the oriental, Greek outlook, which emphasized free-will and recoiled with horror from the rigor of Augustine's extreme predestinarian teaching. Cyril of Alexandria, a correspondent of Augustine, who forwarded to him a copy of the minutes of the Synod of Diospolis,[58] was later to use Pelagianism as a charge with which to smear Nestorius: Pelagianism (called by Cyril Caelestianism) and Nestorianism are one and the same, in that both ascribe man's salvation to his own action, since for Nestorius Christ is not the Son of God born of Mary but a man who was by his own choice united to the eternal Son of God[59] (hence Bishop Gore's famous *mot* that "the Nestorian Christ is the fitting savior of the Pelagian man").[60] The third Ecumenical Council of Ephesus of 431 included anathemas of Caelestius, now regarded as the leader of the Pelagian party, in its first and fourth canons, but these were probably intended more as a gesture to the West than as an expression of Cyril's opinions. As Lionel Wickham has put it: "If Nestorius was, in some sense as a pupil of Theodore [of Mopsuestia], anti-Augustinian, Cyril was certainly not an Augustinian",[61] and this judgment would seem to apply to the Eastern Orthodox Church to this day. Augustine is not much of a hero there.

But what of Pelagianism in the West? So far as I can see from the evidence, it was represented only by a small group of theological writers and a handful of their supporters. It was never a mass-movement. (I ignore the suggestion initiated by J. N. L. Myres, supported by John Morris and approved by Peter Salway in *The Oxford History of England* vol. I (1981), that Pelagianism was a movement against political corruption which exercised a powerful influence in Britain after the Roman withdrawal from the island, because I simply cannot believe it.) The Africans over-reacted against the movement after the failure of the prosecutions of Pelagius in Palestine in 415 because they saw their own theology in danger. In consequence they ascribed to Pelagius and Caelestius and their supporters an importance that they never in fact possessed, and this belief was sustained for centuries by the influence of Augustine's writings. Augustine, certainly, came to see Pelagianism as a deadly menace – "the proudest heresy of all" – and his criticism of its theology, whether we accept it or not, has played a decisive rôle in religious thought in Western Christendom. Peter Brown has said that "Pelagianism as we know it, that consistent body of ideas of momentous consequence, had come into existence; but in the mind of Augustine, not of Pelagius [in the winter of 411-412]."[62] I think that this date is too early, and would consider that Augustine's formal systematization of Pelagianism came to birth later, in the period 416-417, with Paul Orosius as midwife; but I accept Brown's view that historians and theologians have too long tended to form their image of Pelagianism by looking through Augustinian spectacles.

Notes

* The first of the two Otts Lectures for 1992, delivered at Davidson College, North Caroline, on March 25, 1992. The second lecture will be published in the next issue of *Augustinian Studies*.

1. *De Gratia Christi et de Peccato Originali* 1, 32,35; *CSEL* 42, 152.

2. *Confessionum libri XIII* 10, 29, 40; *CCSL* 27, 176; *De dono perseuerantiae* 20, 53; *PL* 45, 1026.

3. Nevertheless, both their denial of any transmission of Original Sin and their indignation at the excuses of sinners inevitably made them rigorist in their approach, with little inclination to accept the necessity of those 'daily light and trivial sins' from which, according to Augustine, life here on earth is never exempt (*Enchiridion ad Laurentium* 19, 71; *CCSL* 46, 88.

4. *De possibilitate non peccandi* 3, 2; *PLS* 1, 1460. Translated by B. R. Rees, *The Letters of Pelagius and his Followers* (Woodbridge: The Boydell Press 1991).

5. One may here note some psychological understanding on the part of the Pelagians, at least in the case of the Sicilian Anonymous.

6. Pelagius, *Epistula ad Celantiam* 28: "apostolicae doctrinae regula nec cum Ioviniano aequat continentiae opera nuptiarum nec cum Manicheo coniugia condemnat." *Inter* Jerome, *Epistula* 148; *CSEL* 56, 352.

7. *De Gratia Christi* 2, 3, 3; *CSEL* 42, 169.

8. *De Gestis Pelagii* 35, 62; *CSEL* 42, 116.

9. *Inter Aug*., *Epistula* 175, 4: "impietas, quae iam multos assertores habet per diuersa dispersos;" cf. 6: ". . . multi, qui eorum perhibentur esse uel fuisse discipuli, haec mala, quibus fundamenta Christianae fidei conantur euertere, quacumque possunt, adfirmare non cessant." *CSEL* 44, 658, 661-662.

10. Augustine, *Epistula* 177, 2; *CSEL* 44, 670.

11. *Inter Aug*., *Epistula* 183, 2; *CSEL* 44, 725-6.

12. Marius Mercator, *Chronicon*, s.a. 418. *MGH. Chronica Minora*, ed. T. Mommsen (Berlin 1892) i. p. 468.

13. See Honorius, *Rescript* of April 30, 418. *PL* 45, 126-7; 48, 39-86.

14. Augustine, *Epistula* 156; *CSEL* 44, 448.

15. *De Diuitiis* 18, 1-11; *PLS* 1, 1407-11; Tr. Rees, *The Letters of Pelagius* 200-05.

16. Celestine, *Epistula* 13, 1. 8; *PL* 50, 469B; 481B. See Gerald Bonner, "Some remarks on Letters 4* and 6*" in *Les lettres de Saint Augustin découvertes par Johannes Divjak: Communications présentées au Colloque des 20 et 21 sept. 1982* (Paris: Etudes Augustiniennes 1983), 161-2.

17. I made this suggestion in my Augustine Lecture, *Saint Augustine and Modern Research on Pelagianism* (Villanova: Villanova University Press 1972), 26-7. It remains no more than an hypothesis.

18. Rees, *op. cit.* (note 4 above). Writing in Washington, D.C., unable to remember the names of the scholars, and with my copy of their book in England, I shall have to give the reference with the text of the second lecture.

19. I accept the arguments of Robert. F. Evans, *Four Letters of Pelagius* (New York: The Seabury Press 1968).

20. See G. Martinetto, "Les premières reaction de Pelage", *Revue des Etudes Augustiniennes* (1971) 83-117. His attribution is accepted by Juan B. Valero, *Las bases antropologicas de Pelagio en su tratado de las Espositiones* (Madrid: Universidad Pontificia Comillas de Madrid 1980).

21. *De dono perseuerantiae* 20, 53; *PL* 45, 1026; Orosius, *Apologeticus Liber* 3; *CSEL* 5, 607.

22. This is not to deny Julian's originality as a polemicist. See Elizabeth A.Clark, "Vitiated seeds and holy vessels: Augustine's Manichaean past" in *Ascetic Piety and Women's Faith. Essays on Late Ancient Christianity* (Studies in Women and Religion v. 20 -- Lewiston, NY: The Edward Mellen Press 1986) 291-349.

23. See Augustine, *De Gratia Christi* 1, 35, 38; *CSEL* 42, 154.

24. *PL* 30, 15-45; 33, 1099-1120. Tr. by Rees, *op. cit.*, 35-70.

25. Augustine, *De Gratia Christi* 1, 1, 1; *CSEL* 42, 125.

26. Inter Aug., *Epistula* 183, 2; *CSEL* 44, 726.

27. Augustine, *Epistula* 194; *CSEL* 57, 176-214.

28. See Bonner, *op. cit.* (note 17 above) p. 36.

29. Inter Aug., *Epistula* 156; *CSEL* 44, 448-9; Augustine, *Epistula* 157; *CSEL* 44, 449-88.

30. *De natura et gratia* 1, 1; *CSEL* 60, 233.

31. Orosius, *Apologeticus Liber* 4, 6: ". . . et in libro, quem nunc scribit . . ." *CSEL* 5, 608.

32. Robert F. Evans, *Pelagius. Inquires and Reappraisals* (New York: The Seabury Press 1968) 6-25.

33. *Epistula* 169, 4, 13: "scripsi etiam grandem quendam librum aduersus Pelagii haeresim cogentibus nonnullis fratribus" *CSEL* 44, 621.

34. *De natura et gratia* 1, 1; *CSEL* 60, 233.

35. *De perfectione iustitiae hominis* 21, 44; *CSEL* 42, 48.

36. See Evans, *op. cit* (note 32 above) pp. 21-4.

37. Jerome, *Epistula* 133, 1-3; *CSEL* 56, 241-7; *Dialogus aduersus Pelagianos* 1, 1-5; *PL* 23, 495A-501B. See J. N. D. Kelly, *Jerome* (London: Duckworth 1975) 319.

38. Kelly, *op. cit.*, p. 317.

39. See J. A. Davids, *De Orosio et sancto Augustino Priscillianistarum et Origenistarum aduersariis: commentatio historica et philologica* (The Hague 1930) 23.

40. Avitus, *Epistula ad Palchonium*, *PL* 41, 805-06. See Davids, *op. cit.*, pp. 23-4.

41. Orosius, *Apologeticus Liber* 4; *CSEL* 5, 608.

42. See above, note 9.

43. Inter Aug., *Epistula* 176, 4; *CSEL* 44, 667.

44. Inter Aug., *Epistula* 177, 2; *CSEL* 44, 670.

45. *Ibid.*, 3; *CSEL* 44, 671.

46. See F. Floeri, "Le Pape Zosime et la doctrine augustienne du péché originel" in *Augustinus Magister* (Paris: Etudes Augustiniennes 1954), ii. pp. 755-61; G. Bonner, "Les origines africaines de la doctrine augustinienne sur la chute et le péché originel", *Augustinus* (1967) 102-03; Pier Franco Beatrice, *Tradux Peccati. Alle fonti della dottrina agostiniana del peccato originale* (Milan: Università Cattolica del Sacro Cuore 1978) 288-95; J. Patout Burns, "Augustine's role in the imperial action against Pelagius", *The Journal of Theological Studies*, NS 30 (1979) 67-83.

47. Augustine, *Epistula* 176, 2; *CSEL* 44, 664; *Contra duas epistulas Pelagianorum* 1, 1, 2; *CSEL* 60, 424.

48. *Opus imperfectum contra Iulianum* 4, 42; *PL* 45, 1361.

49. *Contra duas epistulas Pelagianorum* 1, 2, 4; *CSEL* 60, 425.

50. Orosius, *Apologeticus Liber* 7, 1-3; *CSEL* 5, 611.

51. *Opus imperfectum contra Iulianum* 3, 166. 187; *CSEL* 85, 469. 485-8.

52. Celestine, *Epistula* 13, 1. 8; *PL* 50, 469B. 481AB.

53. *Inter Aug.*, *Epistula* 201, 1-2; *CSEL* 57, 296-9.

54. Prosper, *Epistula ad Augustinum* 7; *PL* 51, 72C.

55. Vincent, *Commonitorium* 24, 8-9; *CCSL* 64, 181.

56. *Ibid.*, 28, 15; *CCSL* 64, 188-9.

57. *Ibid.*, 26, 8-9; *CCSL* 64, 185. On Gallic Opposition to Augustinian predestinarian theology, sce the papers by Ralph W. Mathisen. "For Specialists only; The Reception of Augustine and His Teachings in Fifth-Century Gaul" in *Presbyter Factus Sum*, edd. by Joseph T. Lienhard, Earl C. Muller and Roland J. Teske (*Collectanea Augustiniana*, edd. by Joseph C. Schnaubelt and Frederick van Fleteren, vol. II) Villanova, PA: 1992), 29-41 and Thomas A Smith, "Augustine in Two Gallic Controversies: Use or Abuse", *op. cit.*, pp. 43-55. Also Robert Markus, "The Legacy of Pelagius" in *The making of orthodoxy: Essays in honour of Henry Chadwick*, ed. by Rowan Williams (Cambridge University Press 1989), 214-34.

58. Augustine, *Epistula* 4*, 2; *CSEL* 88, 26-7. BA 46B, 108-10.

59. Photius, *Bibliotheca* 54; *PG* 103, 93C-97A. See Lionel Wickham, "Pelagianism in the East" in *The making of orthodoxy*, 204-05.

60. Charles Gore, "Our Lord's Human example", Church Quarterly Review 16 (1883) 98.

61. Wickham, *art. cit.* (note 59 above), p. 211.

62. P. Brown, *Augustine of Hippo: A Biography* (London: Faber 1967) 345.

VII

Augustine and Pelagianism*

In my previous lecture I offered you an interpretation of Pelagianism which regarded it as a literary movement, which has achieved a rather unhappy immortality by coming into conflict with the African bishops, who saw their dogma of Original Sin called into question by the conciliar decisions in Palestine in 415, which declared Pelagius to be orthodox. Alarmed by these developments, the Africans ruthlessly exerted all their considerable influence to crush Pelagius and his disciple, Caelestius, procuring their excommunication by Pope Innocent and refusing to consent to any reopening of the case by Innocent's successor, Zosimus. In this they succeeded so well that in the aftermath of the condemnations of 418 the real opposition came, not from the handful of Pelagian supporters and their indefatigable literary spokesman, Julian of Eclanum, but from the so-called Semi-Pelagian theologians of Southern Gaul, who were alarmed by the implications of Augustine's predestinarian theology, and who were too distinguished a group to be repressed by the methods which had been applied to the Pelagians. As a result of the influence exercised by Augustine's writings over Latin Christianity in the following centuries, a kind of heroic picture of the Pelagian Controversy was constructed, which seemed to be confirmed by the condemnation of Caelestius and his supporters at the Third Ecumenical Council of Ephesus in 431, though there is no particular reason to suppose that Cyril of Alexandria was much concerned with Pelagianism, except as another indictment to urge against Nestorius. In short, I sought to argue that the importance of Pelagianism as a movement, as opposed to its undoubted importance as a theological tendency, has been exaggerated by Church historians, both old and new, who have taken their estimate of it from the extreme opinions of Augustine and his African colleagues.

A criticism that could be levelled against my view, even by those who would be willing to give it a generally favorable reception, is that it underestimates the active — as opposed to the literary — role of Augustine in the Controversy and over-emphasizes the contribution of the African episcopate. I recognize the force of this argument, since nobody can ignore the part played by Augustine in pressing the campaign against Pelagius from the year 416 onwards. I think that he had good reason for his zeal, since the acquittal of Pelagius at Diospolis in 415 seemed to call into question, not only Augustine's personal theology but also his conviction, which had played so large a part in his arguments with the Donatists, that there was one Catholic faith, maintained from East to West by the undivided Church of Christ, and it was essential for him to have that conviction reaffirmed by the Roman see, the senior see of Christendom. Nevertheless, I remain persuaded that Augustine's African colleagues were not mere followers of their brilliant spokesman, but people with minds of their own and firmly-held beliefs about the rightness of African doctrine. The history of African Christianity, from the days of Cyprian to its fall to the Arab invaders in the seventh century, reveals a Church determined to maintain its own convictions against pope and emperor alike, not by disowning these authorities, but by insisting that they should recognize the correctness of African understanding of the faith. It has been suggested that the medieval Papacy only became possible because the African Church, the one Western local Church which had the prestige and the self-confidence to oppose Roman pretensions, had been destroyed by the Arabs. This has long seemed to me to be a very plausible hypothesis.

Nevertheless, even if one does not accept the view that Augustine was, from the first, the prime mover of the campaign against Pelagius, there can be no question of his importance in it, and this raises the question: What precisely was the effect upon him of the challenge of Pelagianism? One answer to this question was given by Martin Luther who, in his forthright way, suggested that the Pelagians "made a man of Augustine" who, but for them, would have been "a very dry and thin teacher."[1] Considering that the *Confessions* were written before Pelagius appeared on the scene of Augustine's life, and that the *De Trinitate* and the *De Civitate Dei*, although composed during the Controversy, were certainly not inspired by it, one can only say that Luther's opinion was a very personal one, reflecting the interests and preoccupations of the speaker. However, like many other sweeping generalizations, Luther's is not without an element of truth. The Pelagian Controversy had its effect upon Augustine, producing in him a theological hardening, pleasing to some in his own time and in later centuries, repulsive to others; and the hardening was of a different order from that produced by other controversies. It is an unhappy fact that Augustine, although never descending to the sort of controversial vituperation which disfigures the works of certain other patristic writers when disputing with theological opponents, tended as time wore on to become increasingly bitter. Thus, at the beginning of his anti-Donatist campaign, in the *Psalmus abecedarius*, composed in 394, he was to lament the alleged cruelties perpetrated upon the Donatists in 347, in the so-called Macarian persecution.[2] In his last anti-Donatist work, the *Contra Gaudentium* of 419-20, he had come to approve imperial coercion to bring the separatists back into the Catholic fold and could tell Gaudentius, the Donatist bishop of Thamugadi, who had threatened to burn himself and his congregation in his church, rather than give up that church to the Catholics, that it was better for a few abandoned people to perish, than for a multitude of souls, whose way to salvation they impeded, to burn with them in hell for ever.[3] But Augustine's hardening in the Pelagian Controversy went deeper. He became progressively more and more persuaded that the sovereignty of God had to be maintained against all human notions of love and justice. Julian of Eclanum observed that Augustine worshipped a God who was a *nascentium persecutor* — a tormentor of neonates.[4] Such an accusation cannot fairly be levelled against Augustine himself — the fate of unbaptized infants was a source of anguish for him; but he accepted the doctrine and expressed it in terrible language. Let me cite one example, taken from a letter of 418.

> God by His creation, has willed so many souls to be born who, He foreknew, would have no part in His grace, so that they might, by an incomparable multitude, outnumber those whom He has deigned to predestinate as children of promise in the glory of His kingdom, in order that it might be shown, by the very multitude of the reprobate, that the number of those who are most justly damned, whatever it may be, is of no concern with the righteous God; and that those who are redeemed from condemnation should thereby also understand that only damnation, which they see bestowed upon so large a part of humanity, was due to the whole lump, not only to those who, by the choice of an evil will have added many sins to the Original Sin, but also to so many little children who, being bound only by the chain of Original Sin, are snatched from this [mortal] light without the grace of the Mediator. Indeed, this whole lump would receive its debt of just damnation unless *the potter*, who is not only just but also merciful, should make some *vessels to honor*, according to grace (Rom. 9:21) and not according to what was due, while

> He relieves some little children, to whom no merits can be ascribed, and anticipates some adults, so that they may have some merits.[5]

This uncompromising declaration on Augustine's part shows that seven years of anti-Pelagian polemic had, indeed, in Luther's words, "made a man of him." During the next, and final, decade of his life, Augustine was to display an ever-increasing rigor, which justified John Calvin's claim: "If I wanted to weave a whole volume from Augustine, I could readily show my readers that I need no other language than his. But I do not want to burden them with wordiness."[6] If Calvin's assertion seems exaggerated, consider this passage from the *De Praedestinatione Sanctorum*, composed in 429, the year before Augustine's death.

> Let us therefore understand the calling by which the elect are made. They are not chosen because they have believed, but in order that they may believe. . . . And so they were chosen before the foundation of the world, by that predestination by which God fulfilled what He had preordained. *For those whom he had predestined, he also called*, by that calling according to His plan, and not therefore any others, but *those whom he called, he justified* (Rom. 8:30). Nor did He call any others but those whom he had predestined, called and justified, those also he glorified, by that end which has no end. God therefore chose the faithful; but in order that they might be faithful, not because they were already faithful.[7]

This passage well exemplifies the hardening in Augustine's pronouncements in the years following the condemnation of Pelagius and Caelestius. Many readers will find it distasteful, if not horrifying. Thus John Burnaby, one of the great exegetes of Augustine's theology of love, was moved to observe that "nearly all that Augustine wrote after his seventieth year [i.e. 423-424] is the work of a man whose energy has burnt itself out, whose love has grown cold," though he qualified this allegation by the admission that "not even in the *De Correptione et Gratia* [written in 426] is the Augustine of the *Confessions* altogether unrecognizable."[8] This is true; but it is true in a particular way, which Burnaby did not dwell upon. The fact is that the doctrines which Augustine maintained against the Pelagians, with all their implications, had been formulated long before Pelagianism came to Augustine's notice. Controversy constrained him to draw out the implications and to affirm them with a steadily increasing dogmatism, which admitted of no other understanding than his, a dogmatism which alarmed the Semi-Pelagian theologians of Marseilles, because it seemed to take from the individual any element of free choice and to leave him a puppet in the hands of his Creator, and their view is surely correct. Augustine never forgot the words of Romans 9:20-21: *Shall what is made say to the potter, Why hast thou made me thus? Does not the potter have power out of the same clay to make one vessel to honor and another for ignoble use?* It is a feature of Augustine's theological development that he came increasingly to emphasise the absolute power of God. It is true that he always insisted that this absolute power was not, as it might appear, exercised in an arbitrary and tyrannical way, and that at the Last Day the justice of God will be revealed, by which one soul is taken and another left; but in the meantime: *Does not the potter have power out of the same clay to make one vessel to honor and another for ignoble use?*

Let us endeavor to follow the development of Augustine's thought as it is revealed in the Pelagian Controversy.

It may reasonably be said that the foundation of Augustine's anti-Pelagian polemic is his belief in the need for baptism for all ages as a remedy for the guilt inherited from Adam, *in whom all sinned.* Augustine's first anti-Pelagian treatise, the *De Peccatorum Meritis et Remissione*, significantly, has for a subtitle: *De Baptismo Parvulorum.* The issue with Pelagian theology was one of principle, not practice. Caelestius, the man who initiated the debate in Africa, and Julian of Eclanum at later date, accepted the desirability of infant baptism, but denied that this had any particular theological implications. Augustine, and the other African bishops, insisted that it did. They could point to *Letter* 64 of their hero, St Cyprian, conveying the decision of an African council of sixty-six bishops, which probably met in the spring of 252.

> No one is denied access to baptism and grace. How much less reason is there then for denying it to an infant who, being newly born, can have committed no sins! The only thing that he has done is that, being born after the flesh as a descendant of Adam, he has contracted from that first birth the ancient contagion of death. And he is admitted to receive remission of his sins all the more readily in that what are being remitted to him are not his own sins but another's.[9]

Such was the doctrine of the African Church with which Augustine would have been familiar from the time of his return to Africa in 388. He may have learned it earlier, from the instruction of Ambrose, at Milan. (It is significant that the first attack on Caelestius in Africa for denying the need for infant baptism for the remission of sins came from the Milanese deacon, Paulinus.) In Augustine's case, however, the notion of an inherited sin is tied to another, and more terrible, theological conception: the idea of the *massa*, the lump of sin, to which all human beings adhere, because of their seminal participation in the Fall, and from which only a very small minority is liberated. The notion of the *massa* is not Augustine's invention. He inherited it, possibly from the unidentified theologian traditionally known as Ambrosiaster whom he calls Hilary; but for Augustine the notion had a more sinister connotation than it had for his predecessor, and this has caused some scholars — probably wrongly — to see in it a reflection of the *bôlos*, the lump of sinful, dark matter, from which, in the Manichaean theology, the imprisoned light-particles could not be set free, but were lost for ever.[10]

The doctrine of the *massa* first appears in Augustine's writings in Question 68 of the *De Diversis Quaestionibus LXXXIII*, published by him in 395/6, and must therefore have been formulated at some time before that date, probably when Augustine was presbyter of Hippo. To quote Question 68:

> For *just as we have borne the image of the earthly man* (I Cor. 15:49) let us now bear *the image of the heavenly man* (ibid.), *putting off the old man and putting on the new* (cf. Col. 3:9-10), so that no one may say to us, as to a vessel of clay, *Shall what is made say to its maker, Why hast thou made me thus*? (Rom.9:20) And in order that it may be made clear that these words are not said to a sanctified spirit but to fleshly clay, see what follows: *Does not the potter have power out of the same clay to make one vessel for honor and another of ignoble use?* (Rom.9:21) Therefore from the time that our nature sinned in paradise, we are formed by the same divine providence, not according to heaven, but according to earth, that is, not according to spirit, but according to the flesh by mortal generation, and we are now made from the same lump of slime, which is the lump of sin. Since therefore we lost our merit by sinning, and lacking God's mercy nothing is owed to sinners but eternal damnation, what does a man from this mass do, when he answers God back and says: *Why hast thou made me thus?*[11]

At about the time when Augustine was preparing *De Diversis Quaestionibus LXXXIII* for publication, or perhaps a little earlier — we cannot be more precise than this — he was completing the second and third books of his treatise *On Free Choice*, begun at Rome in 388. Of this work, Augustine specifically declares in the *Retractations* that it was directed against the Manichees, to discuss the question: *quid sit malum?* — what is evil? Augustine's concern was with the primal sin of Adam. If evil is not something positive, as the Manichees taught, but a non-entity, a negation, how did it come about that Adam, who was created by a good God, ever fell into sin? Augustine begins his enquiry from the orthodox Christian principle that God cannot be the source of evil: "We believe that everything that exists is created by the one God, and yet that God is not the cause of sin. The difficulty is: if sins go back to souls created by one God, and souls go back to God, how can we avoid tracing sins back to God?"[12] Augustine's answer is that sin arises from a movement in the soul which he calls *libido*, an evil form of *cupiditas* (desire).[13] *Libido* is, indeed, a blameworthy form of *cupiditas*.[14] In view of the importance which the word *libido* will subsequently have on Augustine's later works, whether as *libido dominandi*, the lust for rule which is so forcefully denounced in *The City of God*, or as *libido carnalis*, sexual lust, which is to figure so prominently in his later anti-Pelagian writings, it should be made clear that, in the *De Libero Arbitrio*, the word is not to be identified directly either with disordered sexuality (which did not exist before the Fall) or with lust for power and domination (which equally did not then exist). Essentially, *libido* is a desire for lower good things, good in themselves, but not supremely good, in preference to the Supreme Good, which is God (a theme which will become familiar in Augustine's later writings). In the *De Libero Arbitrio*, however, Augustine is not concerned with the consequences of Adam's sin, but with its cause. As he says in Book III: "It is more important to enquire in what state the first man was created than how his descendants have been propagated,"[15] and his opinion is, that Adam was created neither wise (*sapiens*) — for if he had been, he would not have fallen into sin — nor foolish (*stultus*) — for if he had been, God his creator would have been the cause of sin and not himself. Instead, Adam was created in a midway condition (*media adfectio*),[16] which could neither be called wisdom nor folly — the will is a certain midway good (*medium quoddam bonum*).[17] Free choice in Adam, Augustine was later to declare in the *De Spiritu et Littera*, was a *media vis*, a neutral power capable of being turned towards God for good or away from Him and so to sin.[18] Augustine never resolved the fundamental question of why this power, which was bestowed upon Adam by a good and loving Creator, should have led to sin rather than to obedience nor, in the *De Libero Arbitrio*, did he greatly care to do so.

> What need, then, is there to seek the origin of the motion, by which the will turns from the Unchangeable to a changeable good? We admit that it is a movement of the soul, that it is voluntary, and therefore culpable. All useful learning in this matter has its object and its value in teaching us to condemn this movement and to restrain it, and to turn our wills from falling into temporal pleasures to the enjoyment of the Eternal Good.[19]

The *De Libero Arbitrio* was destined to play an important role in the development of Augustine's view of Pelagianism, because a passage from it was quoted, together with those of other Christian authors, by

Pelagius in his work *De Natura*, in support of his own view that sin could be avoided, if an individual chose.

> Whatever is the cause of the will, if it cannot be avoided, there is no sin in yielding to it. If it can be resisted, then there must be no yielding and there will then be no sin. Or perhaps it may trick the unwary? Then care must be taken not to be tricked. Or is the trickery such that it cannot possibly be guarded against? In that case there is no sin, for who sins in committing what he cannot guard against? But since sin is committed, it therefore can be avoided.[20]

This quotation may well have been decisive in determining Augustine's later attitude to Pelagius; its citation seemed to imply that his own earlier theology had, in effect, been Pelagian. In fact, throughout the treatise *De Libero Arbitrio*, Augustine was discussing Adam's nature before the Fall and not as it exists today, in a vitiated state, among his descendants. Augustine had made this abundantly clear, in passages which he subsequently quoted in the *De Natura et Gratia*, written in 415 in reply to Pelagius' *De Natura*.

> There are two punishments for every sinful soul: ignorance and difficulty. Because of ignorance, error puts us to shame; because of difficulty, anguish afflicts us. But it is not the nature of man, as he was created, but rather the pain of man under condemnation to approve the false for the true, and not to be able to refrain from lustful action on account of the insistence and torturing anguish of the flesh.[21]

And again:

> Properly, we speak of nature in one way when referring to that nature in which man was first made guiltless as the first of his race, and in another way when we speak of that nature in which we are now born, condemned by the sentence passed upon Adam, ignorant and enslaved in the flesh, in the manner of which the Apostle says: We were by nature children of wrath, even as the rest (Eph.2:3).[22]

Given such specific declarations in the *De Libero Arbitrio*, it is difficult not to feel that Pelagius was either disingenuous, or at least grossly careless, in choosing quotations from Augustine to support his own position which Augustine did not hold. It is true that we have only Augustine's reference as evidence; but since Augustine's treatise was addressed to Timasius and James, the two former disciples of Pelagius who had brought the *De Natura* to Augustine's attention and asked for his comments, there seems every reason to assume the fundamental reliability of his evidence. The fact that Pelagius had cited the *De Libero Arbitrio* in support of his arguments would particularly concern Augustine, because he obviously thought well of the work. He had recommended its reading to Secundinus the Manichee in 405/6;[23] had defended its content in a letter addressed to Count Marcellinus in 412;[24] and had referred to its wide circulation in a letter to Jerome in 415.[25] In a letter to Paulinus of Nola, written in the middle of 417, he declared that it was Pelagius' *De Natura* which first opened his eyes to the dangers of Pelagian doctrine, which threatened to destroy any belief in the grace of God bestowed upon humanity through the one Mediator, Jesus Christ.[26] It is, of course, true that Pelagius, since he denied any transmission of Original Sin from Adam to his descendants, might have replied that what Augustine said about Adam's nature would be equally applicable to human nature today; but for Augustine such misrepresentation of his doctrine was more than misunderstanding: it was a perversion of his teaching which appeared to ascribe to him a theology which he held to be wholly wrong.

At the same time, it would be a mistake to suppose that the emphasis of the *De Libero Arbitrio*, completed at some time between 391 and 393, was exactly the same as that of Augustine's later anti-Pelagian writings. Because Augustine was dealing with the initial cause of sin in Adam, and not with its subsequent manifestations in the human race, and because when he wrote it there was no opposition of a Pelagian character to his assumptions, he did not, when he composed it, feel the same necessity to emphasis the need for grace as he did later.[27] But there was another consideration: in the period 391-395 Augustine's view on the overriding power of grace had still not fully developed. Evidence of this is to be found in his *Expositio in Epistulam ad Romanos*, composed in 394/5, in which he speaks of the *massa luti* — "the lump of slime" — from which the potter makes one vessel to honor and another to dishonor[28] and quotes Romans 9:20-21: *O man, who art thou, that repliest unto God?* But he also asserts the power of free choice, by which a person may believe and receive grace,[29] and speaks in a Semi-Pelagian fashion of grace being given as a reward for the faith which God foresees that an individual will have[30] — language which he was later to explain in the *Retractations:* "I had not yet sought diligently enough or discerned up to this time what is the nature of 'the election of grace,' concerning which the same Apostle says: *There is a remnant left selected out of grace* (Rom.11:5). This certainly is not grace if any merits precede it."[31] Augustine's thought in 395 is, indeed, very like the theology of the Semi-Pelagians of Marseilles, which he opposed some thirty years later.

A year after writing the *Expositio in Epistulam ad Romanos*, Augustine's attitude changed, with portentous consequences. Having been asked by his old pastor Simplicianus, the presbyter of Milan who succeeded St. Ambrose as bishop in 397, to explain certain passages of Scripture, Augustine suddenly came to comprehend, with an absolute clarity, what he believed to be the full significance of I Corinthians 4:7: *For who singles thee out? Or what hast thou that thou didst not receive? And if thou hast received it, why dost thou boast, as if it were not a gift?*[32] As an intellectual conversion, this illumination while writing to Simplicianus in 396 falls only a little short of that experience at Milan ten years before, for by it Augustine came to perceive that the elect are not chosen because they believe, but in order that they may believe. Put in another way, a conviction of God's absolute power took possession of Augustine's mind, and what he was to write subsequently in the later stages of the Pelagian Controversy represented a restatement, with increased emphasis and harshness, of the conclusions to which he had come in 396.

Augustine himself certainly did not underestimate the significance of his conversion, which marked for him the triumph of divine grace over human free choice, and acceptance of the absolute power of God over His creation, including human beings. At the end of his life, in the *De Dono Perseverantiae*, he cited the *Ad Simplicianum*, followed by the *Confessions*, as works which had opposed Pelagianism long before Pelagius had written.[33] One can see the *Confessions*, indeed, as the exemplification in Augustine's own career, up to his baptism, of the message of the illumination of 396. *What hast thou, that thou didst not receive? And if thou hast received it, why dost thou boast, as if it were not a gift?* "Give what thou dost command, and command what thou wilt." Is not this famous prayer effectively a practical application of the text of I Corinthians 4:7?[34]

I have, in my previous lecture,[35] spoken of the restraint exercised by Augustine in his early dealings with the Pelagians in the period 411-415: he sees them as brethren to be persuaded, rather then as heretics to be suppressed, even though their convictions went clean against his own. I have long been persuaded that the change in his attitude from fraternal remonstrance to implacable hostility, made clear when, after the condemnation of Pelagius, Albina, Pinianus and Melania attempted to approach him on Pelagius' behalf,[36] was not simply due to the fact that he had lost trust in Pelagius' honesty. Behind this obvious reaction we may, I suggest, see evidence of deep-seated alarm. The events of the year 415, notably the apparent endorsement of Pelagius' theology by the two Palestinian synods, seemed to call into question Augustine's assumption of the universality of Christian doctrine, including the African understanding of the doctrine of Original Sin. Although this initial impression was erroneous, as Augustine subsequently discovered by reading the minutes of the Synod of Diospolis, the fear persisted, and could be exorcised only by the formal confirmation of African — that is, Augustinian — theology by the Apostolic See. Hence the pressure on Pope Innocent in 416 and the unyielding opposition to Pope Zosimus, when he sought to reopen the case in 417. Furthermore, Augustine could not afford, for his own peace of mind, to tolerate any differences of opinion on the two great issues which were to preoccupy the last years of his life: the divine decree of predestination; and the problem of the transmission of Original Sin.

With regard to predestination, I have already quoted the terrifying letter of 418, in which Augustine declared that "by the very multitude of the reprobate" it is shown that "the number of those who are most justly damned, whatever it may be, is of no concern with the righteous God."[37] I have also quoted the assertion made at the end of his life in 429, in the *De Praedestinatione Sanctorum*, in which he declares that the elect "are not chosen because they have believed, but are chosen in order that they may believe."[38] One has only to compare these pronouncements with the language of his *Expositio in Epistulam ad Romanos* of 395 to see the change which has come over his thinking. Thus, in the Expositio, Augustine can quote Romans 9:20: *O man, who art thou who replies unto God?*[39] and speak of the *massa luti,* to which all pertain who are not brought to spiritual things;[40] but he can also say:

> For it is ours to believe and to will, but God's to give to those who believe and will the power of doing good through the Holy Spirit, through whom charity is poured into our hearts (Rom.5:5)[41]

and again:

> We cannot will if we are not called, and when, after the call, we have willed, our will and our course do not suffice, if God does not give strength to the runners and lead whither He calls. It is clear, therefore, that it is not *of him who wills or of him who runs but of God showing mercy* (Rom.9:16) that we do mercy[42]

both of which passages he sought to explain in the *Retractations,*[43] since he felt that each left a loophole for human initiative, however small. The conversion experience of 396 swept away all such scruples. We have freedom only because God gives us freedom, and we are saved, only because God wills us to be saved. The elect are not chosen because they have believed, but in order that they may believe.

It was this apparent denial of any possibility of human initiative in the response to the call of God which produced the reaction which is commonly, but misleadingly, called Semi-Pelagianism, and which may more accurately be described as a reassertion and defense of the same principles which Augustine had himself affirmed in his *Expositio in Epistulam ad Romanos* in 395.

> Man has it in his power by free choice to believe the Liberator and to receive grace, that with Him who now bestows it setting him free and aiding him, he need not sin, and thus he may cease to be under the Law, but rather with the Law or in the Law fulfil the Law by the love of God, which he could not do by the fear of God.[44]

This view had vanished, for Augustine, with the illumination of 396. Certain individuals, both in Africa and in Gaul, found his later theology, as expressed in the treatises *De Correptione et Gratia* and *De Dono Perseverantiae*, intolerable: it removed all freedom from man, so that he could not even respond to the Gospel, unless God gave him the power to do so, a power that was not simply free choice, but a specific and deliberate act of grace accorded to only the elect, who had been chosen by God without any regard to foreseen merit. The essence of the dispute between Augustine and the Semi-Pelagians turns on the beginning of faith (*initium fidei*). For the mature Augustine, this is solely the action of God. For the Semi-Pelagians, such an understanding was both too limited and too limiting. John Cassian of Marseilles, the most distinguished name among them, maintained that although God works in all men, it sometimes happens that the beginning of good works comes from individuals, as a result of the natural good which God has implanted in them in their creation — examples would be Zacchaeus the publican; the Penitent Thief; Abraham; and Cornelius, the centurion — while in other cases God's grace anticipates the human will — examples here would be Paul; Matthew; Peter; Andrew; and the rest of the Apostles.[45] Accordingly, divine grace is dispensed to humanity in various ways and according to the capacity of the individual.

The difference between the views of the Semi-Pelagians and Augustine might be explained as being due to their different pastoral experience: Cassian and the Massalians looked to the Egyptian Desert, where the monk waited upon God and needed to be reassured that, if God found even a tiny spark of faith, He would blow it into a flame, and the individual must therefore not lose heart if his prayers appeared to go unanswered; while Augustine, laboring in a parish with its usual quota of Laodicean souls, did not so easily assume that everyone of his flock was striving to make progress in the Christian life; but this explanation is too easy, and ignores the significance of the conversion of 396: *What hast thou, that thou didst not receive? And if thou hast received it, why dost thou boast, as if it were not a gift?* and the brutal words of the letter of 418: "The number of those who are most justly damned, whatever it may be, is of no concern with the righteous God."[46] Augustine believed that, since the Incarnation, with the particular and peculiar exception of the martyrs, there was no admission to the Kingdom of Heaven except by the reception of the sacrament of baptism, which Christ Himself had instituted. He was well aware that, in his day, the great majority of human beings went out of the world without receiving the sacrament. Accordingly, they were damned; though infants who had committed no personal sins would be afflicted with only the mildest penalties.[47] Augustine was, nevertheless, persuaded that there is no injustice in God.

> Likewise, as the Apostle says: *Not of him who wills nor of him who runs, but of showing mercy* (Rom.9:16). He also comes to the aid of some infants, although they do not even will or run, when He wishes to aid them, whom He chose in Christ before the foundation of the world. To these He gives grace graciously, that is, with no preceding merits on their part, either of faith or of good works. But He did not come to the assistance of those adults whom He did not will to aid, even when He foresaw that they would have believed His miracles, if they had been worked among them. In his foreknowledge He judged otherwise about them, secretly indeed, but justly, for there is no injustice in God for *inscrutable are his judgements and his ways* past finding out (Rom.11:33) and *all the ways of the Lord are mercy and truth* (Ps.24 [25]:10).[48]

Between such a view and that of the Semi-Pelagians there was no reconciliation. Augustine had no doubt about the harshness of his doctrine and recommended that it should be proclaimed discreetly;[49] but he never questioned its rightness —hence his attempts to explain away the words of I Timothy 2:4: *God willeth all men to be saved and to come to the knowledge of the truth* by declaring that "all" in this context means "many" or "all who are saved"[50] or "all, because no one is saved except those whom God wills to be saved." One may well believe that Augustine's sudden understanding of the significance of I Corinthians 4:7 when writing to Simplicianus had made him impervious to any argument pointing in another direction.

> And so let truth be expressed, especially when some disputed question demands it, and let those who are able, accept it, lest perhaps while it is passed over in silence because of those who cannot accept it, those who *can* accept truth as the means of avoiding falsehood will not only be defrauded of truth but will even be engulfed by falsity.[51]

Augustine had been accused by the Semi-Pelagians of teaching new and unsound doctrine[52] — a charge which he naturally denied. He recognized the pastoral difficulties raised by his theology — hence his suggestion that predestination should be preached discreetly, to avoid unsettling tender minds;[53] but his conviction of the truth of his position was absolute. It may be that his final position was an overreaction to Pelagian theology, as the Semi-Pelagians claimed; but it was nonetheless a logical development of the conclusions to which he had come more than thirty years before.

There is another example of the development of Augustine's opinions through controversy with Pelagianism: his emphasis upon sexual concupiscence in the transmission of Original Sin. This is a vast topic, has been much discussed in the past, and will probably continue to be much discussed, given the popularity of the study of sexuality and psychology in contemporary society, and it has implications for Augustine's social and moral teaching, with which I am not now concerned. We will here confine our discussion to the topic of sexual concupiscence in the debate with the Pelagians.

Let me begin by reminding you that Augustine has two words to describe sexual desire as experienced in our fallen world: *libido* and *concupiscentia.* Neither of them is limited to sexual desire, and *libido* in particular plays a major role in *The City of God* as *libido dominandi*, the lust for rule. There is a linguistic difference between them, in that *libido* is a classical word, while concupiscentia derives from the ecclesiastical vocabulary of the Latin Church.[54] We have seen that, in the *De Libero Arbitrio, libido* is the desire for a lower good thing, which drew Adam from his obedience to the command of God and so brought about the Fall.[55] In that context, *libido* is not sexual desire, but rather a self-assertive impulse on the part of the human soul — it is, indeed, a manifestation of *superbia,* pride, the head and fount of all sin and, by the just judgement of God, the pride which brought Adam to sin and fall becomes the punishment of the fallen human condition: the sexual instinct, which should have been the servant of the will, becomes a rebel against that will. The famous sixteenth chapter of Book XIV of *The City of God,* with its denunciation of orgasm because it overpowers the control of the mind, excellently expresses Augustine's mature view of human sexuality.

It is not, however, so much Augustine's view of the character of fallen sexual activity which is important here, but its corollary: Augustine's belief that the guilt inherited from Adam, "in whom we all were when we were all that one man,"[56] is passed to his descendants in the (for him) necessarily sinful concupiscence which accompanies the act of procreation. It was this view of concupiscence, which had been present in Augustine's outlook from the beginning of the Pelagian Controversy, which found expression and publicity in the two books, *On Marriage and Concupiscence,* addressed to Count Valerian in 418/9 and 419/20 respectively. These attracted the attention of the Pelagians, and especially of Julian of Eclanum, and provided an issue over which Augustine and Julian were to wrangle at tedious length during the last ten years of Augustine's life.

Julian of Eclanum is not a man to be easily evaluated. As a personality he is not endearing — an aristocrat, he adopted the superior tone of a cultured patrician talking down to a country parson. Estimates of his theological ability vary (for myself, I dislike him, but consider him to have an able intellect). He certainly had powers of initiative and leadership; considerable learning; and the ability, as a controversialist, to see the weak point in the adversary's argument and so to fight his battles on ground of his own choosing and on issues where his opponent was most vulnerable. These were, in Augustine's case, the doctrine of Original Sin and its consequences, which seemed to make God unjust[57] — by what equity can an infant be damned, who has committed no sin other than that of having been born? — and the origin of evil — if God is seen as the author of evil He is, by Julian's reckoning, no different from the Prince of Darkness, the Evil Principle of the Manichees. In short, the Augustinian view seemed to Julian to turn Manichaean Dualism into a Monotheism with a self-contradictory God who is both good and evil.[58] Traducianism — the transmission of Original Sin by physical generation — is simply a new form of Manichaeism, the Manichaeism which Augustine had allegedly renounced, after having professed it for a decade in his youth.[59]

Augustine provided Julian with an opening in 418/9 by writing the first book of the *De Nuptiis et Concupiscentia* in which, in his own words, he "defended the good of marriage to prevent the belief that marriage is vitiated by the concupiscence of the flesh" and showed that "conjugal chastity makes good use of the evil of lust (*malo libidinis*) for the procreation of children."[60] In this work, Augustine did not affirm anything more than he had previously said about the element of concupiscence in Christian marriage; but he said it here specifically, in a treatise addressed to Valerian, the Count of Africa, a high official who was strongly anti-Pelagian. Julian saw his opportunity. He identified Augustine's teaching with that of Mani — an excellent controversial tactic, but one which ensured that there could be no question of any reconciliation between the two controversialists. Once again Augustine's orthodoxy, which meant so much to him, was impugned, and in a manner which, so far as he was concerned, utterly misrepresented his way of thinking.

It is possible, even easy, when reading Julian's criticisms of Augustine, to see him as a reasonable man who tried to bring an element of common sense into the Pelagian debate, as when, for example, he countered Augustine's argument that the general human desire for privacy when engaging in sexual intercourse is proof of a sense of shame induced by concupiscence, by observing that, equally, we do not care to relieve ourselves in public — an example of modesty which has nothing to do with concupiscence.[61] It would, however, be unwise to suppose from this that Julian's outlook was "modern" in a way that Augustine's was not. Julian was a man of his time, influenced alike by Stoic and Aristotelian philosophical principles and by the Christianity of the day. His thought was based on certain fairly simple assumptions: that God cannot be unjust or the author of evil; that while man possesses a material body, in common with the animals, he is distinguished from them by the God-given faculty of reason, whereby he can recognize moral principles; and that the mature human being is endowed with the power of free choice, a quality which cannot be nullified or weakened by any previous action. As a Pelagian Julian naturally rejected any suggestion that Adam's primal sin passed to his descendants, and he goes to considerable trouble to argue that the word "all" (*omnes*) in Romans 5:18 is to be understood in the sense of "many" — if, he says, we speak of a solitary schoolmaster in a certain city and say that he teaches all the inhabitants, we mean by that all who study, and not all who live there.[62] Again, he explains (correctly) the phrase of Romans 5:12: *in quo omnes peccaverunt*, which Augustine misunderstood, as meaning "in that all sinned" — that is, by imitation — and not "in whom all sinned" — that is, in Adam — as Augustine wished to understand it.[63] Given such views, it naturally followed for Julian that infants did not, and could not, share in Adam's sin; and since they were unable to exercise a free choice of the will, they clearly were unable to sin, since Julian, in defining sin, borrowed Augustine's own definition in his anti-Manichaean treatise *On the Two Souls*, composed in 392: "Sin is the will to admit or to maintain what justice forbids and from which one is free to abstain."[64] But Julian went further. He pointed out that the Apostle had said that the free grace of Christ had abounded for many more that the sin of Adam had been able to destroy (Rom. 5:15).[65] Accordingly, he altogether rejected Augustine's view of the damnation of the greater part of the human race.

One might say, allowing for the distortion imposed by any literary quotation, however apposite, that Julian's attitude is

> God's in His heaven, all's right with the world,

in contrast to Augustine's:

> Oh yet we trust that somehow good will be the final end of ill.

Augustine's reaction to Julian's assaults was defensive, but completely confident. He had absolute assurance of his own understanding of Scripture as a justification of his own opinions (a confidence which, it may be observed, he shared with Julian) and saw himself supported by a host of famous Christian theologians: Irenaeus of Lyons; Cyprian of Carthage; Reticius of Autun; Olympius of Spain; Hilary of Poitiers; Ambrose of Milan; Gregory of Nazianzus; Innocent of Rome; John Chrysostom; Basil of Caesaria; and (of course) Jerome.[66] Particularly he appealed to Ambrose of Milan, "whom I reverence as a father, for in Christ Jesus he begot me through the Gospel, and from this servant of Christ I received the laver of regeneration,"[67] as a guarantor of his orthodoxy and right belief; but even without this formidable cloud of witnesses (not all of whom, incidentally, were as favorable to his opinions as he believed), it is all but impossible to believe that Augustine would have been swayed by Julian's arguments. Between him and Julian a great and unbridgeable gulf had been fixed.

If one considers Augustine's role in the Pelagian Controversy, it is difficult not to be impressed by his overwhelming energy. Between 411 and his death in 430, treatises flowed, at his dictation, from the pens of his amanuenses, even when, at the end of his life, he was fighting a war on two fronts maintaining, against the Semi-Pelagians, the absolute decree of God over human initiative, and defending, against Julian, his own understanding of the transmission of Adam's sin and denying that there could be any injustice in the apparently undeserved fate of unbaptized infants. Nevertheless, in all this productivity, Augustine was essentially re-stating the arguments which he had employed at the very beginning of the controversy in the *De Peccatorum Meritis et Remissione;* and these arguments in turn derived from the theological conclusions which he had reached in 396 when answering the questions of Simplicianus. But these conclusions would appear from Augustine's subsequent explanations to have been not so much the result of a course of reasoning and argument as of a sudden illumination, which may have resembled the illumination which came to him at Milan about the nature of evil, as a result of the ascents of the mind brought about by reading the Neoplatonists. We do not have sufficient evidence available to test this hypothesis, but it is to be observed that in the *De Praedestinatione Sanctorum,* composed in 429, at the end of his life, Augustine states that God revealed the truth to him when writing to Simplicianus. It may be that Augustine's unyielding obduracy in the last decades of his life is to be explained by an interior conviction, brought about by a conversion experience, against which no counter-argument, however distinguished its source, could hope to prevail.

Notes

* The second Otts Lecture, delivered at Davidson College, North Carolina, on March 26, 1992. The first Lecture was printed in *Augustinian Studies* 23 (1992), 33-51. Please note that the reference that was not included in the first lecture (p. 38 note 18) is *La coppia nei Padri.* Introduzione, traduzione e note di Giulia Sfameni Gasparro, Caesare Magazzù, Concetta Aloe Spada. Milan: Edizione Paoline 1991, pp. 135-6, 364-66. In my lecture, referring to this work from memory, I suggested that they called into question the Pelagian authorship of the *Letter to Celantia.* This was incorrect. What they said was that most scholars would attribute the letter to Pelagius, but this hypothesis could be overturned by later investigations. It might be well to quote them: "Nonostante che — é bene sottolinearlo — le consonanze tematiche o stilistiche lascino sempre un margine di ipoteticità che altre fortunate scoperte potreberro fugare completamente, si può ritenere tuttavia con buona dose di verosimiglianza che la *Lettera a Celanzia* appartengna a Pelagio" (pp. 365-6).

1. Luther, *Tischreden (D. Martin Luthers Werke,* Weimer 1883), IV, 56: "Augustinus nihil acriter de fide scribit, nisi cum contra Pelagianos scribit: *sie haben* Augustinum *auffgeweckt und zum manne gemacht;*" V, 414-5: "Augustinus, *wenn er die Pelagianer nit het wider sich gehabt, so wers ein ser* aridus *und* tenuis doctor *worden.*"

2. Psalmus abecedarius, lines 157-8: "Nolite nobis iam, fratres, tempus Macarii imputare/ Si crudeles erant illi, et nobis displicent valde." *CSEL* 51, 9.

3. *Contra Gaudentium* 1,22,25. *CSEL* 53,224.

4. *Opus imperfectum contra Iulianum* 1,48: IUL. (4). *CSEL* 85,38.

5. Augustine, *Epistula* 190,3,12. *CSEL* 57,146-7.

6. *Institutio Christianae Religionis,* edd. P. Barth & W. Wiesel, *Iohannis Calvini Opera Selecta*3 (Munich 1931), 389. Translated by Ford W. Battles, *Calvin: Institutes of the Christian Religion* (The Library of Christian Classics Vol. XXI) (Philadelphia: The Westminster Press 1961), 942.

7. *De Praedestinatione Sanctorum* 17,34 *PL* 44,985; 986 (My translation).

8. Burnaby, *Amor Dei. A study in the religion of Saint Augustine* (London 1936), 231.

9. Cyprian, *Epistula* 64,5.2. *CSEL* 2,720-21. Translated by G.W. Clarke, *The Letters of St Cyprian of Carthage*. Vol. III (Ancient Christian Writers Vol. 46) (New York/Mahwah, N.J. 1986), 112.

10. The originator of this suggestion seems to have been Ernesto Buonaiuti, *La genesi della dottrina agostinian intorno al peccato originale* (Rome 1916), repeated in the "The genesis of St. Augustine's idea of Original Sin," *Harvard Theological Review* 10 (1917), 159-75. Augustine cites Ambrosiaster under the name of Hilary in *Contra duas epistulas Pelagianorum* 4,4,7 (*CSEL* 60,528), composed in 420/421, but seems to have known him earlier; see N. Cipriani, "Un' altra traccia dell' Ambrosiaster in Agostino (*De pecc.mer.remiss.* 2,36,58-59)", *Augustinus* 24 (1984), 515-25. Augustine could have derived his doctrine of the *massa damnata* and its implications from Ambrosiaster; but it could equally well have been inspired by African tradition and St Ambrose, and the Ambrosian influence would seem more likely, given Augustine's personal contact with, and deep veneration for, the great Bishop of Milan. See P.F. Beatrice, *Tradux Peccati, Alle fonti della dottrina agostiniana del peccato originale* (Milan 1978), 159 ff. On the *bôlos*, see Buonaiuti, "Manichaeism and Augustine's idea of *massa damnationis*," *Harvard Theological Review* 20 (1927), 117-27.

11. *De diversis Quaestionibus LXXXIII*, q.68,2,3. CCSL 44A, 176-7 (My translation).

12 *De Libero Arbitrio* 1,2,4. *CCSL* 29,213. Translated by Mark Pontifex, *St. Augustine. The Problem of Free Choice* (Ancient Christian Writers Vol. 22) (Westminster, MA./London 1955), 38.

13. *Ibid.* 1,4,9. *CCSL* 29,215.

14. See the note by Pontifex, *op. cit.* note 12, pp.239-40.

15. *De Libero Arbitrio* 3,24,71. *CCSL* 29,317. Pontifex, p.212.

16. *Ibid.*, Pontifex, pp.212-3.

17. *Ibid.*, 2,19,53. *CCSL* 29,272. Pontifex, p.134.

18. *De Spiritu et Littera* 33,58. *CSEL* 60,216.

19. *De Libero Arbitrio* 3,1,2. *CCSL* 29,276. Translation by John H.S. Burleigh, *Augustine: Earlier Writings* (The Library of Christian Classics Vol.VI) Philadelphia: The Westminster Press 1953), 171.

20. *Ibid.*, 3,18,50. *CCSL* 29,304. Quoted by Pelagius in *De Natura*. See *De Natura et Gratia* 67,80. *CSEL* 60,293. Cf. *Retractationes* I,9 [8]. *CCSL* 57,25-6 (My translation).

21. *Ibid.*, 3,18,50. *CCSL* 29,306; *De Natura et Gratia* 67,81. *CSEL* 60,296 (My translation).

22. *Ibid.*, 3,19,54. *CCSL* 29,307; *De Natura et Gratia* 67,81. *CSEL* 60,296 (My translation).

23. *Contra Secundinum* 11. *CSEL* 25 (2),923.

24. Augustine, *Epistula* 143,5. *CSEL* 44,255.

25. Augustine, *Epistula* 166,3,7. *CSEL* 44,555-6.

26. Augustine, *Epistula* 186,1,1. *CSEL* 57,45-6. Cf. *Retractationes* II, 42 [68]. *CCSL* 57, 124.

27. Cf. *Retractationes* I,9 [8], 4: "... quamvis et in his libris, qui non contra illos [sc. Pelagianos] omnino, quippe illi nondum erant, sed contra Manichaeos conscripti sunt de libero arbitrio, non omnimodo de ista dei gratia reticuimus, quam nefanda impietate conantur auferre." *CCSL* 57,26.

28. *Expositio in Epistulam ad Romanos* 54 (62),18-19. *CSEL* 84,38-9.

29. *Ibid.*, 37 (44),3. *CSEL* 84,19.

30. *Ibid.*, 54 (62),9. *CSEL* 84,37.

31. *Retractationes* I,23 [22],2. *CCSL* 57,68-9.

32. *Ibid.*, 2,1 [27]. *CCSL* 57,89-90.

33. *De Dono Perseverantiae* 20,52-53; 21,55. *PL* 45,1026; 1027.

34. *De diversis Quaestionibus ad Simplicianum* 1,2,9. *CCSL* 44,34; *Confessionum Libri XIII,* 10,29,40. *CCSL* 27,176; cf. *De Spiritu et Littera* 13,22. *CSEL* 60,175-6.

35. See *Augustinian Studies* 23 (1992), 40-42.

36. *De Gratia Christi et de Peccato Originali* 1,35,38-37,41. *CSEL* 42,154-6.

37. See p. 29 above and note 5.

38. See pp. 30 above and note 7.

39. *Expositio in Epistula ad Romanos* 54 (62),18. *CSEL* 84,38.

40. *Ibid.*, 19. *CSEL* 84,39.

41. *Ibid.*, 53 (61),7. *CSEL* 84,36 (My translation).

42. *Ibid.*, 54 (62),3. *CSEL* 84,36 (My translation).

43. *Retractationes* 1,23 [22],3. *CCSL* 57,69-70

44. *Expositio in Epistula ad Romanos* 37 (44),3. *CSEL* 84,19 (My translation).

45. Cassian, *Collationes* 13,11; 14 and 15. *CSEL* 13,375-8; 384-90.

46. Augustine, *Epistula* 190,3,12. *CSEL* 57,146-7.

47. Augustine, *Epistula* 184A,1,2. *CSEL* 44,732-3; *Enchiridion* 23,93. *CCSL* 46,99.

48. *De Dono Perseuerantiae* 11,25. *PL* 45,1007 (My translation).

49. *Ibid.,* 22,58-62. *PL* 45,1029-31.

50. *Contra Iulianum* 4,8,44. *PL* 44,760; *Enchiridion* 27,103. *CCSL* 46,104-06; *De Correptione et Gratia* 15,47. *PL* 44,945.

51. *De Dono Perseuerantiae* 16,40. *PL* 45,1017 (My translation).

52. *Inter Augustini Epistulae* 225,2; 226,2. *CSEL* 57,455-6; 469-70.

53. See quotation from *De Dono Perseuerantiae* 16, 40 (note 51 above).

54. See G. Bonner, "*Libido* and *concupiscentia* in St. Augustine, "*Studia Patristica VI*, ed. F.L. Cross (Texte und Untersuchungen zur altchristlichen Literatur Bd 81) (Berlin: Akademie Verlag 1962), 303-14; *Saint Augustine of Hippo. Life and Controversies*[2] (Norwich 1986), 398-401.

55. See pp. 33 above.

56. *De Civitate Dei* 13,14. *CCSL* 48,395-6.

57. *Opus imperfectum* 1,67 (5): "Non potest autem deus nisi iustus et pius esse, quod est deus meus Iesus Christus." *CSEL* 85,68.

58. *Ibid.*, 3,172-177. *CSEL* 85,473-8.

59. *Ibid.*, 6,18. *PL* 45,1535-6. For a discussion of the debate between Julian and Augustine, see Elizabeth A. Clark, "Vitiated seeds and holy vessels: Augustine's Manichean past" in *Ascetic piety and woman's faith. Essays on late ancient Christianity* (Studies in Women and Religion Vol.20), Lewiston: New York 1986, 291-349.

60. *Retractationes* 2,53 [79]. *CCSL* 57.131.

61. *Opus imperfectum* 4,37. *PL* 45,1356-7.

62. *Ibid.*, 2,135;144. *CSEL* 85,174.

63. *Ibid.*, 2,174. *CSEL* 85,174.

64. *De Duabus Animabus* 15. *CSEL* 25 (1),70; *Opus imperfectum* 1,44. *CSEL* 85,31.

65. *Opus imperfectum* 2,85; 96-98. *CSEL* 85,222-3; 228-30.

66. *Contra Iulianum* 2,10,33; 37; 3,17,32;. *PL* 44,697; 709; 719.

67. *Ibid.*, 1,3,10. *PL* 44,645.

VIII

'Working the Earth of the Heart'. The Messalian Controversy in History, Texts, and Language to AD 431
By Columba Stewart OSB. (Oxford Theological Monographs.) pp. xi + 340. Oxford: Clarendon Press, 1991

The Messalian movement and its opponents provide one of the most interesting and obscure debates in the patristic age. As Columba Stewart observes, 'the historian's appraisal of such conflicts, difficult in any case, becomes especially awkward when a controversy is ancient, when the disputants are of uncertain identity, and when documentary evidence is wanting' (pp. 2–3). This has not, of course, prevented scholars from making a good deal of the limited evidence – Pier Franco Beatrice, for example, in his *Tradux Peccati: alle fonti della dottrina agostiniana del peccato originale* (1978), placed the Messalians, with Augustine, in a common descent from the encratite doctrine of the gnostic theologian Julius Cassianus; but long before Beatrice, there had been much scholarly discussion regarding an alleged Messalian influence on the famous ascetic homilies ascribed to Macarius of Egypt, which some historians of doctrine have seen as either a Messalian document, or an orthodox composition corrupted by the Messalian belief in a demonic infestation of the fallen human soul, which can only be kept at bay and eventually conquered by constant prayer. Consideration of the Pseudo-Macarian writings is one of the concerns of Stewart's study: 'These rich and colourful texts certainly deserve study in their own right, not simply through the narrow lens of the Messalian controversy' (p. 9). However, the Messalian movement is important in itself, inasmuch as it is an element of an ascetic tendency, common alike in East and West in the patristic age, which powerfully influenced the climate of spirituality in the early and medieval Church, and helped to create in Christianity that powerful strain of hostility to sexuality, on occasion coming close to Manichaeism, which has aroused so much opposition among progressively minded Christians in recent times.

The starting point for any investigation of Messalianism must, obviously, be the evidence of the available documentation, whose nature, stemming as it does from hostile sources, means that it is necessary to reconstruct the history of the controversy rather than that of the rather nebulous movement. The evidence, provided by authors like Ephraem, Epiphanius (who 'is clearly puzzled by the Messalians, for he comments in the *Panarion* that they have "neither beginning nor end, neither head nor root, but are completely unstable and deceptive"'), Theodoret, Photius, Severus of Antioch and John Damascene, indicates that

Messalianism was a Syrian movement, particularly strong in Mesopotamia, which moved northwards and westwards into Armenia, Lycaonia and Pamphylia, and was eventually condemned by a Council at Constantinople in 426, by the imperial edict against heresy of 428, and by the Third Ecumenical Council of Ephesus in 431. Descriptions of Messalian doctrines by Theodoret, Timothy of Constantinople and John of Damascus (printed in appendix 2, pp. 244–79), exhibit a considerable measure of agreement, and show the Messalians as maintaining that continuous prayer alone, and not baptism, can destroy the root of sin in fallen man; that Satan and the demons continue to infest the baptised; and that the goal of prayer is *apatheia*, a state achieved by participation in the Holy Spirit. Such doctrinal points can be related to themes in the writings of Ps.-Macarius, though none can be regarded as 'a representative précis' of his teaching (p. 68). Stewart suggests that the explanation of the resemblances between Messalian teaching and that of Ps.-Macarius is that both draw upon a common heritage of Syriac Christian tradition, and that Ps.-Macarius was 'interpreting and translating aspects of the Syriac traditions for a Greek-speaking audience' (p. 69). He therefore carries out a detailed examination of three words in Ps.-Macarius' vocabulary: *plerophoria* (confidence or experience); *aisthesis* (feeling or sensation); and *peira* (experience), collating them with Syriac writings like the Peshitta and the *Liber graduum* and coming to the conclusion that 'in the writings of Ps.-Macarius one sees the emergence into a Greek-speaking environment of language and imagery rooted in the Semitic earth of Syriac Christianity' (p. 169). Whether Ps.-Macarius himself was bilingual, 'bringing Syriac idioms to bear directly on his work', or whether he was influenced by 'a teacher or a group of Christians who themselves had some connection with Syriac Christianity' (p. 237), cannot be established. The important fact is, that while it is generally accepted that the Greek language influenced Syriac theology, it would also appear that Syriac exercised a certain influence on Greek theological language and imagery. Stewart shares the opinion, commonly held among patristic scholars, that not a little of theological controversy in the patristic period turned upon misunderstandings of vocabulary: 'Had they lived in another age, with major research libraries, dictionaries, and concordances available to them, they might have worked it all out. Such is the task of today's ecumenical dialogue, and of the scholarship upon which it is founded' (p. 238). In the case of Ps.-Macarius, he was condemned as a result of misunderstanding.

'*Working the Earth of the Heart*' is an immensely learned and fascinating contribution to patristic studies, particularly for its recognition of the way in which one theological tradition could act upon another, without necessarily being acceptable in its new environment. Furthermore, such influence may have wholly undesigned and unexpected consequences. One detail which Stewart has recorded has important implications for students of Latin theology. He points out that Jerome attributes the doctrine of *apatheia* both to the Messalians and to Pelagius (*Dialogus adversus Pelagianos*, PL xxiii. 517) (pp. 41–2); he records that baptism, according to the Messalians, cannot remove the root of sin, just as a razor can only shave the surface of the skin (pp. 60, 248–9); but he does not notice that this last assertion, attributed by Theodoret to the Messalians (*Haereticarum fabularum compendium* 4. 11, PG lxxxiii. 429B) was anticipated by Julian of Eclanum, though by him applied to Augustine's teaching on original sin (Aug., *C. duas Epp. Pel.* i. 13. 26, CSEL lx. 445). Thus we have the curious fact that, while Jerome saw Pelagianism as a sort of Messalianism, Pelagians like

Julian saw anti-Pelagianism as being doctrinally Messalian; and this in turn helps to elucidate the failure of Orosius' attack on Pelagius at the Synod at Jerusalem in 415: Augustine's theology, as presented by Orosius, could well have appeared as a species of Messalianism to a Greek clerical assembly, since it seemed to imply that fallen human beings are so deeply tainted by Adam's legacy that they cannot be free from sin, even with the help of divine grace. Thus an Eastern heresy may well have affected the judgement of Greek divines on a Western theological issue.

Of the interest and value of Columba Stewart's study there can be no question, particularly with regard to his emphasis on the Syriac contribution to patristic theology. No scholar who wishes to acquire a comprehensive understanding of the teachings of the Fathers can today afford to ignore the Semitic contribution. Even more important, however, is Stewart's demonstration of the interaction between the traditions of East Syria and Greek Christianity. Syriac theological writing is not a matter for a minority of specialists. It is relevant to any understanding of early Christian theology.

IX

Saint Cuthbert - Soul Friend

A major difficulty which confronts anyone seeking to evaluate St. Cuthbert, as a man and as a saint, is the fact that he wrote nothing. Other saints have left treatises and letters, and Augustine of Hippo has, in addition, provided an autobiography of his earlier years which constitutes a major work of spirituality in its own right. Bede's autobiography, which concludes his *Ecclesiastical History*, is a mere sketch – a *Who's Who* entry; but Bede has the gift of transmitting his personality through his writings in such a way as to produce a sense of familiarity, even of intimacy, in the reader. Nothing of this nature is available for understanding Cuthbert. Instead we have four biographical descriptions, none of them over-long. All these biographies are written in the hagiographical tradition, in which the sanctity of the subject is taken for granted. The evidence of it is provided, both in his lifetime and posthumously from the grave, largely in the form of miracles which, whether true or not, tend to produce a stereotyped form which obscures the personality of the individual and subsumes him within a particular type of sanctity. Behind the lives of Cuthbert are the famous and influential life of St. Martin of Tours by Sulpicius Severus[1], and the still more famous and influential life of St. Antony the First Hermit, traditionally ascribed to St. Athanasius and available in Northumbria in the Latin translation of Evagrius of Antioch. The anonymous monk of Lindisfarne who wrote the earliest life of Cuthbert had no hesitation in borrowing part of the wording of his first two chapters from these two lives, and to make his account of Cuthbert's life conform to that of Antony, as did Bede | likewise, in his later versions. Again, Bede does not hesitate to conform the cure effected by the dying Cuthbert on Walhstod to a similar death-bed healing described in Possidius' life of Augustine. The aim of both biographers is to set Cuthbert in a tradition of sanctity; but one cannot avoid the question: have they, in so doing, obscured the man, in order to establish the saint?

p.23

p.24

Must we then despair of knowing anything about Cuthbert as a human being and accept him simply as an idealized type, whose cultus, although doubtless encouraged sincerely by his admirers, has removed most

1 The life of St. Martin of Tours by Sulpicius Severus is translated by F.R. Hoare, *The Western Fathers* (London, 1954).

of the historical from his personality, so that our admiration, if any, must be for a symbol rather than for a man? I suggest that this is too pessimistic an approach: our sources, though unquestionably stylized, can be regarded as historical, as well as theological, documents, and the historian can hope to obtain concrete information from them which will enable him to build up a convincing picture of Cuthbert as a man, for a number of reasons. Let us consider these reasons in turn.

The four accounts we possess of Cuthbert's life, work and miracles have a good deal in common (see above, p.9). Their foundation is the Anonymous Life, which no doubt represents the Lindisfarne tradition less than twenty years after Cuthbert's death in 687. The author was able to draw upon the recollections of a number of people who had known Cuthbert, like the priest Plecgils; the nun Kenswith, who had been Cuthbert's foster-mother and survived him; and Prior Aethilwald of Melrose (*VA* II.3,7; IV.4). It was this account which provided Bede with the basic material for his Verse Life, in which he omitted many details given by the Anonymous, but also added some material of his own, like the incident of the rafts which were being swept out to sea | but were turned back at the intercession of Cuthbert (*VM* 3). In composing the Prose Life Bede had the advantage of the reminiscences of Abbot Herefrith, who had known Cuthbert at Melrose (*VP* 8), and who was to provide Bede with the moving description of the saint's last days which constitutes a particular ornament of the Prose Life. Finally, in the *Ecclesiastical History*, which contains the shortest of all our notices of Cuthbert's life, Bede felt able to speak, albeit indirectly, about the reason for the expulsion in 661 of Cuthbert and his companions from the monastery at Ripon, presented to Abbot Eata, subsequently Bishop of Lindisfarne and then of Hexham, by Alhfrith, sub-king of Deira under his father, King Oswiu. Under the influence of St. Wilfrid Ahlfrith later became a fanatical supporter of the Roman fashion of calculating the date of Easter, while Eata and his monks remained faithful to the Irish system, which they had inherited from Iona. In the Prose Life Bede merely remarks: 'All the ways of this world are as fickle and unstable as a sudden storm at sea. Eata and Cuthbert and all the rest were thrown out of Ripon and the monastery they had built given over to other monks' (*VP* 8). In the *Ecclesiastical History* (*HE* III.25; cf. V.19) he says that Alhfrith had

p.25

> rightly preferred [the] teaching [of Wilfrid] to all the traditions of the Irish and had therefore given him a monastery of forty hides in the place called Ripon. He had presented the site, a short time before, to those who followed Irish ways; but because when given the choice they preferred to renounce the site rather than change their customs, he gave it to one who was worthy of the place both by his doctrine and his way of life.

From the historical point of view this supplementary information is of enormous interest, because it provides a fact about Cuthbert which is not mentioned in any of the Lives: before the Synod of Whitby in 664 he was, as might be expected of one | trained in the tradition of St. Aidan of Lindisfarne, an adherent of the Irish compustistical tradition for establishing the date of Easter. By the time the Lindisfarne Anonymous and Bede came to write about him, his Irish sympathies were too delicate a matter to be mentioned openly; but Bede has contrived to convey them, indirectly, to readers with understanding.

p.26

The motive for Cuthbert's expulsion from Ripon, small in itself but having portentous implications, is an example of how our materials, even if written in a hagiographical tradition, can nevertheless supply historical detail of the greatest value to the modern biographer. But this is not the only sort of detail which can be gleaned from the four biographies; for their authors, even though they wished to place their hero in a succession which looked back to Martin of Tours and Antony of Egypt, did not necessarily do so at the cost of destroying his personality. Thus the Lindisfarne Anonymous, wishing to describe the manner of Cuthbert's life on the Inner Farne, writes (*VA* III.7):

> At all hours he was happy and joyful, neither wearing a sad expression at the remembrance of a sin nor being elated by the loud praises of those who marvelled at his manner of life. His conversation, seasoned with salt, consoled the sad, instructed the ignorant, appeased the angry; for he persuaded them all to put nothing before the love of Christ. And he placed before the eyes of all the greatness of future benefits and the mercy of God, and revealed the favours already bestowed, namely that God spared not His own Son but delivered Him up for the salvation of us all.

Now the greatest part of this description is taken from the Evagrian translation of the life of Antony, but with one significant alteration. In the first sentence, where the author of the *Life of Antony* had written that Antony 'never through the excess of hilarity broke into laughter', the Lindisfarne Anonymous declared of Cuthbert that 'at all hours he was happy and joyful'. Given the tendency in monastic asceticism at all | times to discourage undue cheerfulness - the Benedictine Rule, after all, tells the monk 'not to love much or excessive laughter' - one may reasonably suppose that the Lindisfarne Anonymous made his emendation deliberately, to record a characteristic feature of Cuthbert's temperament: he was always cheerful.

p.27

We have, then, reasons for thinking that our biographical material relating to Cuthbert may be regarded as containing details which are historically reliable; and there are other considerations to support this view. There is, first, the subjective impression made upon the reader by a particular episode, whether small or great. As an example of the former I would refer to the incident at the dinner with the Abbess Aelfflaed, when Cuthbert became suddenly aware that one of her servants would die the following day, and in his emotion dropped his knife, replying, when the abbess asked the reason, with the light-hearted question: 'Can I eat all day? I must rest sometimes' (*VP* 34) - words which, to me at least, create the impression of having been actually spoken by the saint. Of a larger episode I would cite the account given by the priest Tydi of how Cuthbert, as a bishop, came to an unidentified village called *Medilwong* during a time of pestilence and asked if there were anyone sick, whom he might visit and bless. Tydi pointed to a woman standing by, weeping, and holding a dying child in her arms, who had already lost one son from the plague and was now awaiting the death of the other. Cuthbert immediately approached and blessed and kissed the child, saying to the mother: 'Do not cry, woman. Your son will be saved and no other member of your family who is still alive will die of the plague' (*VA* IV.6). I find this incident convincing, even to the prophecy. According p.28 | to the author of the Anonymous Life the woman and her son were still alive at the time of his writing, and could bear witness to its truth; but even without them I would find Cuthbert's language, with its combination of consolation and reassurance, carrying conviction. Theological discussion of the nature of the prophecy apart, I am prepared to accept that in Cuthbert we find a kind of psychic intuition of future events.

There is, however, a further and paradoxical reason for regarding the lives of Cuthbert as being historically reliable, and that is precisely *because* they stand in a hagiographical tradition. If a man lives within a tradition - not necessarily religious; it may be military or academic - he will commonly deliberately conform his life and actions to that tradition, and one may therefore appeal to the tradition as evidence of what he would have done in particular circumstances. Now it seems clear that behind Cuthbert there is an ascetic tradition, inherited from the Irish but ultimately looking back to the origins of Christian monasticism in the Egyptian desert. We see this in the life of Cuthbert, particularly in the tension between the life lived in community and the desire for the seclusion of the hermitage. We find this tension three centuries earlier in John Cassian's story of Abba John the Short[2] who, after spending thirty years in a monastery, retired to the desert to become a hermit from whence, twenty years later, he returned to community life, believing himself to be unworthy and incapable of following the higher way. The career of Cuthbert resembles, if it does not

2 John Cassian's account of John the Short is translated by Owen Chadwick, *Western Asceticism* (Library of Christian Classics, vol.12, 1958), pp.280-1.

parallel, the life of John. He too tried his vocation in community and then turned to elected solitude, from whence he was drawn - reluctantly, in the best desert tradition - to be made a bishop. I do not know whether we can take as an original the words | which Bede ascribes to Cuthbert in the Prose Life - Bede was, after all, a cenobite and familiar with the rule of St. Benedict, which regards the cenobites as the strongest form of monks - but if genuine they admirably express the tensions of the monastic vocation (*VP* 22):

p.29

> He was also accustomed very frequently to bid the brethren not to wonder at his way of life, as though it were specially exalted because he despised worldly things and preferred to live alone. 'But', he said, 'the life of monks ought rightly to be admired, for they are in all things subject to the commands of the abbot and govern all their times of watching, praying, fasting and working by his judgement; and I have known many of those who, both in purity of heart and in loftiness of prophetic grace, far exceed me in my weakness. Among these is the venerable servant of Christ Boisil, a man to be named with all honour, who formerly in his old age, when I was but a youth, brought me up in the monastery of Melrose and amid his instructions predicted with prophetic truth all the things which were to happen to me.

There is, however, another and more interesting comparison than that between Cuthbert and John the Short. Some years ago I was struck by the resemblance between the career of Cuthbert and that of a great Russian saint of more recent times: St. Seraphim of Sarov[3], who was born in 1759, professed at the Sarov monastery in 1793 and died at the beginning of 1833. Like Cuthbert Seraphim spent several years as a hermit, living in the forest, from whence ill health and the command of his superior constrained him to return to his monastery in 1810. Five years later, after a vision of the Virgin Mary, he began to be what the Russians call a *starets* (an elder, equivalent to the *geron* of the Egyptian desert) and the old Irish a soul-friend (*ammchara* - a much happier term than the English 'spiritual director'), drawing crowds of people to the Sarov monastery, seeking his advice, encouragement and consolation. The parallel with Cuthbert on the Inner Farne, where he was visited by people even from the remoter parts of Britain, is striking. So, too, is the manner in which | both saints prepare for death: Seraphim selecting his place of burial and meditating before a coffin placed at the entrance of his cell; Cuthbert indicating to Herefrith the stone coffin, the gift of Abbot Cudda, which was hidden under the turf on the north side of his oratory (*VP* 37); and, in the end, both depart this life, fortified by the communion of the Body and Blood of Christ.

p.30

The parallel between the lives and deaths of Cuthbert and Seraphim is striking; but what must be emphasised is that neither Seraphim, who

3 On St. Seraphim of Sarov, see G. Bonner, '"The Holy Spirit Within": St. Cuthbert as a Western Orthodox Saint,' *Sobornost*, new series 1:1 (1979), 7-22.

lived more than eleven centuries after, nor the friends who recorded his career, could have had any notion of the life of the English Cuthbert: the two lives resemble one another because they were lived in the tradition of monastic asceticism ultimately derived from Egypt. Both saints looked, consciously or unconsciously, to St. Antony as the pattern of their way of life. Accordingly, when we find details in the life of Cuthbert which seem to draw upon the life of Antony, we should not too readily conclude that Bede or the Lindisfarne author have borrowed from the one to make a traditional and acceptable setting for the other. We may, or we may not, accept the possibility that either Antony or Cuthbert actually fought with demons; it is not necessary to assume that Cuthbert is said to have done so simply because this was said of Antony.

It is in the light of these considerations that we can examine the evidence provided by the various lives of Cuthbert available to us and see to what extent we can safely attempt to reconstruct Cuthbert's career, and what lessons we can draw from it which may be relevant to Christian living today. Can Cuthbert be a soul-friend to those who live in the last decades of the twentieth century? |

p.31

I begin with what is essentially an historical problem, but which does have a bearing on Cuthbert's career as a bishop: his social position. In view of the aristocratic character of church government in early Christian Northumbria, it would seem natural to assume that Cuthbert was himself a member of the ruling class, and this is confirmed by the fact that he had a foster-mother, Kenswith (it is the upper classes who have nannies; peasants have to nurse their own children) (*VA* II.7; *VP* 14); that he rode a horse, bore arms (*VP 6*); and, according to the Lindisfarne Anonymous, went on campaign before he turned to the religious life (*VA* I.7). Against this is to be set the statement by the Anonymous, which is repeated by Bede, that when Cuthbert saw the vision of the soul of St. Aidan ascending into heaven, he was keeping his lord's flocks in the company of other shepherds (*VA* I.5; cf. *VM* 4 and *VP* 4) - a statement which has persuaded some readers that he must have been of peasant extraction; a nobleman may farm his estate himself and be respected, but the work of a shepherd is more honoured in a religious than in a social context. One might simply decline to accept this information on the ground of inherent improbability, but this is too easy. My own solution would be to regard Cuthbert as being of free, but not unduly elevated, social origins. He could serve in the war-band of some aristocrat, and to that extent was socially acceptable; but he might, on occasion, be called upon to undertake duties which were not normally those of an officer and a gentleman. I would place him then among the country gentry of his native Northumbria.[4]

This point having been made - and I do not claim that it is a definitive solution of the problem - we may turn to the character of Cuthbert's career; and here it is noteworthy that |the influences on his early religious life p.32 were those of Irish Christianity, which gave so much to the devotional life of early England. He was converted to religion by a vision of the soul of St. Aidan ascending into heaven. This led him to try his vocation at Melrose under the guidance of the Irish monk Boisil. Inevitably, he accepted the Irish method of calculating the date of Easter, and was evicted with his brethren from Ripon in 661 for refusing to abandon it. In his austerities - notably in standing up to his armpits in the sea throughout the night, praying (*VA* II.3) - he is in the Irish tradition, as he is in his relationship with the animal world - though here the Irish inherited a trait that was common enough in the Desert Fathers. The Irish influence on Cuthbert goes very deep; I have sometimes wondered whether the skin boots, which he wore all the year round on the Inner Farne and which made a thick callus on his skin (*VP* 18), may not have been identical with the pampooties with which J.M. Synge[5] was provided, at the end of the nineteenth century, on the Aran Islands, when the rocks were tearing his Dublin-made shoes to pieces. Synge describes them as:

> a piece of raw cowskin, with the hair outside, laced over the toes and round the heel with two ends of fishing-line that work round and are tied above the instep. In the evening, when they are taken off, they are placed in a basin of water, as the rough hide cuts the foot and stocking if it is allowed to harden. For the same reason the people often step into the surf during the day, so that their feet are continually moist.

As a bishop Cuthbert adopted St. Aidan's Irish practice of travelling around his diocese on foot; and he may have maintained the dignity of his episcopal office, assuming as I have done that he was not by birth of a rank to command immediate obedience, in virtue of the power so terribly displayed by St. Cedd - himself an Englishman trained by the Irish - when he cursed King Sigeberht of the East Saxons, and prophesied his death, for consorting with | a nobleman whom Cedd had excommunicated for matrimonial p.33 offences (*HE* III.22). The Irish Christian bishop is not simply an ecclesiastical nobleman; he has something of the druid's powers[6], as well as those displayed by St. Peter, when he pronounced sentence of death on Ananias and his wife.

---

4 Charles Thomas, *The Early Christian Archaeology of North Britain* (Oxford University Press, 1971), p.5, independently reached the conclusion that Cuthbert was 'middle class'.

5 J.M. Synge's description is in *The Aran Islands*, published in 1907 and reprinted in the World Classics series, pp.177-8.

6 On the saints as inheriting 'the prophetic and visionary powers of the druids', see K. Hughes and A. Hamlin, *The Modern Traveller to the Early Irish Church* (London, 1977), p.6, and also I. Finlay, *Columba* (London, 1979), ch.1.

Cuthbert entered Melrose in 651, when he was aged about seventeen. He went there, according to Bede, rather than to Lindisfarne because he was attracted by the reputation of Boisil (*VP* 6), who was a lover of the gospel of John (*VP* 8) - the most spiritual of the gospels, according to Augustine of Hippo - and who also, like Cuthbert, had a prophetical instinct, which enabled him from the first to appreciate the quality of the postulant who had come to him. It could well be that Boisil's admiration played its part in determining the course of Cuthbert's future - the recognition by one holy man of another was not lightly to be disregarded. From Boisil Cuthbert learned the duty of going out from the monastery to preach the gospel (*VP* 9), his enthusiasm on occasion taking him far into the depths of Pictland (*VA* II.4). We may gather from this that he had a great pastoral concern for the Pictish peoples, and the late Julian Brown once suggested to me that Cuthbert's concern for Ecgfrith's Pictish expedition, which ended so disastrously at *Nechtanesmere*, may have been less due to care for the king than for his intended Pictish victims (*VA* IV.8; *VP* 27; *HE IV.26[24]*). At all events, Cuthbert seems, from the first, to have understood that the religious life involved pastoral obligations; and this conviction remained, even in his hermitage on the Inner Farne. The servant of God may not be indifferent to the needs of others.

The episode of the expulsion from Ripon, where Cuthbert was guestmaster (*VP* 7), cannot have failed to make an impression. It | must have come as a shock to discover that a Christian king could first give a monastic foundation to servants of God like Eata and his monks and then take it back and bestow it on others because of their loyalty to their own tradition regarding the calculation of the date of Easter. It is possible that it was at Ripon that Cuthbert first became aware of the Paschal Controversy: the strength of the Romanising party in Northumbria was in the south, in Deira, where Paulinus had preached and James the Deacon still maintained the Roman order at Catterick. Melrose, in the far north, would be in a region where the Irish influence of Iona would be dominant and disputes about it unknown. Clearly, at that time, Cuthbert would have felt bound to maintain the Irish tradition, which was that of Lindisfarne and Iona. Equally clearly, as events were to show, he was not so bound to it as to join the band of English and Irish supporters who left Northumbria for Ireland with Bishop Colman after the decision of the Synod of Whitby. What the Ripon experience may well have suggested to him was the need for agreement about religious practice in a particular ecclesiastical province; and this may explain those controversial words, allegedly uttered when he was dying, condemning those who departed from the unity of Catholic faith by diversity of practice as regards the celebration of Easter (*VP* 39).

p.34

From Ripon Cuthbert returned to Melrose, there to succeed Boisil as prior on the latter's death. Here he continued Boisil's practice of pastoral care, sometimes absenting himself from the monastery for as long as a month, in order to visit the more inaccessible villages (*VP* 9). From Melrose he was transferred to be prior of Lindisfarne by Abbot Eata (*VP* 16), perhaps when Eata had been made abbot there at the request of | Bishop Colman, after the latter resigned the see as a result of the decision of the Synod of Whitby in favour of the Roman Easter (*HE* III.26). However, a sentence of the Lindisfarne Anonymous implies that this summons came after Eata had been made bishop of Lindisfarne late in 664, in succession to Colman's short-lived successor Tuda, and that it arrived to find that Cuthbert had 'fled from worldly glory and sailed away privately and secretly' (*VA* III.1). This would seem to imply that Cuthbert was already trying to live as a hermit at this time; but it might also be interpreted as an attempt on Cuthbert's part to resist translation to Lindisfarne, which would presumably have been regarded as advancement in the eyes of the world. What seems to be clear is that Eata regarded him as the man who would, by precept and example alike, inspire the Lindisfarne community to the strictest observance of monastic living. According to the Lindisfarne Anonymous, it was Cuthbert who was responsible for arranging the monastic rule of Lindisfarne which was observed in the Anonymous's own day together with that of St. Benedict (*VA* III.1). Bede says that he continued the corporal works of mercy for which he had been distinguished at Melrose (*VP* 16).

p.35

Cuthbert had, then, during his period as prior of Lindisfarne, made a reputation as a holy man, a wonder-worker; and it is not surprising that his fame attracted great numbers of penitents and pilgrims when he was installed as a hermit on the Inner Farne. This decision to follow an eremitical way of life is not in any way surprising in Cuthbert's day. The idea of solitude, with its opportunities both to seek God in extended prayer and to battle in His service against the demonic hosts which frequent deserts and other lonely places, long remained the crown of the monastic life, preferably to be undertaken by the | monk who had been prepared by long residence in a community. As late as the eleventh century both Lanfranc of Bec[7] and St. Anselm had seriously considered such a life; and we have a local example of the prestige which could accrue from it in the career of Godric of Finchale. But Cuthbert's reputation did not permit him to live in solitude, and there is no reason to question the large numbers who came to him, not only locally but also, according to Bede, 'from remoter parts of Britain, attracted by the reports of his miracles' (*VP* 22).

p.36

On Lanfranc, see M. Gibson, *Lanfranc of Bec* (Oxford, 1976), p.25.

These words of Bede may explain the reason for Cuthbert's election to a bishopric in 685: his reputation as a holy man. In 1971 Peter Brown published an article, which has had great influence on subsequent discussion, on the rise and function of the holy man in Late Antiquity (*Journal of Roman Studies*, vol. 61 (1971), pp. 80-01). Brown notes four qualities of the holy man: he carried the burden of making a distant, transcendent God relevant to the particularity of human needs; he was a professional in a world of religious amateurs - he had opened his whole life to the grace of God; he was an allayer of anxiety: 'Caught between a bottomless God and an archaic system of public penance, laymen flocked to the holy man to know whether there was anything at all that they could do in their small way'; and finally, he was the oracle - what Brown calls the *décisionnaire universel* - of his local community: 'His judgement decided how Christian ethics might be applied.' All these characteristics would appear to hold true of Cuthbert, so far as we can interpret our information. His importance in his society was due to himself, to his character as a man of God, quite independently of his social position. The power ascribed to the Christian ascetic in the fifth and sixth centuries remained potent in the seventh | and eighth.

p.37

This consideration may explain the choice of Cuthbert as a bishop in 685. On the face of things, he was not an obvious candidate. He was not, like Wilfrid, a courtier - when Princess Aelfflaed conferred with him in 684 it was because she wanted to learn about the fate of her brother, King Ecgfrith, and not to indulge in social chit-chat (*VA* III:6; *VP* 24). No doubt she knew of her brother's intentions regarding the Picts and may have been anxious for his safety, and for the safety of Northumbria, if things went wrong. It was also clear that Ecgfrith himself was well aware of Cuthbert's reputation, since both the Lindisfarne Anonymous and Bede say that at the time of her visit Aelfflaed knew that he intended to make Cuthbert a bishop. On the other hand, the church which appointed him included Archbishop Theodore of Canterbury (*VA* IV.1; *VP* 24), the forceful prelate who had compelled St. Chad to ride a horse, in the belief that he would the better discharge his episcopal commitments by riding than by going on foot. It may safely be assumed that Theodore would have required evidence of some qualities other than mere noble birth in a candidate for the episcopate; and there already existed an excellent precedent for choosing an ascetic as bishop in the famous case of Martin of Tours, the ex-soldier turned hermit, whose disreputable appearance at the time of his election displeased some of the aristocratic Gallo-Roman episcopate.

Cuthbert, like others before him, attempted to decline episcopal orders and had to be constrained to accept consecration (*VA* IV.1), after which, it appears, he fled back to the Inner Farne, and was only persuaded to come back by the command of Eata, to whom Cuthbert would have felt the obedience due to an abbot, and who instructed Cuthbert to come to confer with him at | Melrose, after which Cuthbert gave way (*VP* 25). A point worth noting is that Cuthbert was not originally chosen for the see of Lindisfarne. Bede is quite specific on this (*HE* IV.28[26]):

p.38

> Cuthbert was first of all elected to the bishopric of the church of Hexham in the place of Tunberht, who had been deposed from the episcopate; but because Cuthbert preferred to rule over the church of Lindisfarne in which he had lived, it was arranged that Eata should return to the church at Hexham to which he had been originally consecrated and Cuthbert was to undertake the government of the church of Lindisfarne.

The explanation of this curious arrangement lies in the plans of Archbishop Theodore for the reorganisation of the administration of England by an increase in the number of dioceses. Eata had become bishop of Lindisfarne in 664. In 678, when Wilfrid was driven out of his see and succeeded at York by Bosa, Eata became the bishop of the Bernicians, reigning with his seat at Lindisfarne and Hexham alike. In 681 the see was divided, with Tunberht, former abbot of Gilling, becoming bishop of Hexham. Four years later Tunberht was deposed from his office, perhaps for offending King Ecgfrith, and it was to replace him that Cuthbert was chosen for consecration. Cuthbert, however, was reluctant to go as far afield as Hexham, and Eata agreed to an exchange, with himself resuming Hexham, and leaving Lindisfarne to Cuthbert. No doubt this arrangement was the result of Cuthbert's visit to Melrose to confer with Eata.

Cuthbert's reign as bishop was destined to be short - less than two years. He was, we may suspect, already in poor health and suffering from the tuberculosis which eventually killed him; but once he became bishop, his ministry resumed the form which it had taken at Melrose and Lindisfarne, with long journeying which took him as far afield as Carlisle and into mountainous and wild regions, where he had to camp out, since there was no building in which to shelter (*VP* 28, 32). Even when | the consciousness of his approaching death made him determine to resign his office, Cuthbert would not depart without having first carried out a diocesan visitation in order to encourage his flock (*VP* 34). Before his consecration he had told the royal abbess Aelfflaed that he would only last for two years - perhaps a prophecy, perhaps a realistic appreciation of his physical resources.

p.39

Cuthbert's last days have been recorded by Bede from the personal narration of Abbot Herefrith, and are among the most moving descriptions of a Christian end, fit to be compared with the account of Bede's own death by his disciple, the future Abbot Cuthbert of Wearmouth-Jarrow. There is, however, a dramatic contrast between these two ends: Bede's calm and confident preparations, surrounded by his friends; and Cuthbert's lonely vigil, assaulted by the hosts of darkness, and assuaging his hunger and thirst by sucking an onion (a well-known method of relieving thirst). At the last there was peace; and the dying bishop was able to cure a sufferer from dysentery 'after the example of the most holy and reverend father and bishop, Aurelius Augustinus' (*VP* 38). At the end, we are told, Cuthbert exhorted his hearers to show charity to other Christians, 'but [to] have no communion with those who depart from the unity of the catholic peace, either in not celebrating Easter at the right time or in evil living' (*VP* 39). Some scholars have been unable to accept these words, seeing in them an echo from the life of Antony the First Hermit, and argue that an attack upon the Irish use was something to which Cuthbert, the pupil of Boisil and the heir of Aidan and Iona, would never have given his support. Such a view is possible; but it may be that Cuthbert's denunciation was aimed, not at all followers of the Irish practice, but rather at | elements which had remained in Northumbria after the departure of Colman and his sympathisers, and now constituted a source of division within the English Church. The memory of the expulsion from Ripon and the breach in ecclesiastical unity which it signified may well have had its effect.

p.40

The end came on 20 March 667. In Herefrith's words (*VP* 39):

> He passed a quiet day in the expectation of future bliss until the evening; and he also continued quietly in prayer through a night of watching. But when the accustomed time of nightly prayer arrived, he received from me the sacraments of salvation and fortified himself for his death, which he knew had now come, by the communion of the Lord's body and blood; and raising his eyes to heaven and stretching out his hands aloft, he sent forth his spirit in the very act of praising God to the joys of the heavenly kingdom.

The body was taken to Lindisfarne and there buried on the right-hand side of the altar. Miracles were worked at the tomb. Eleven years later the grave was opened and the body found intact. This provided unquestionable demonstration of Cuthbert's sanctity and established him as the great saint of the northern church, giving him an influence which is still to be felt, even after the passage and vicissitudes of many centuries.

On 18 July 1883 Joseph Barber Lightfoot, bishop of Durham preached at the millenary festival of the parish church of Chester-le-Street and put the question: 'What was it that won for Cuthbert the ascendancy and fame which no Churchman north of the Humber has surpassed or ever rivalled?' Lightfoot recognised that Cuthbert was not a great writer like Bede. He was not a first preacher [i.e. of the Gospel in Northumbria] like Aidan; he erected no magnificent building [like Benedict Biscop and Wilfrid]. He was not martyred for his faith or for his church [like Thomas Becket]. His episcopate was exceptionally short, and undistinguished by any event of signal importance. Whence then this transcendent position which he long occupied, and still to a certain extent maintains? |

Lightfoot observed that there were fortuitous elements in Cuthbert's dominance: p.41

He owed something doubtless to what men call accident. He was on the winning side in the controversy between the Roman and English (*sic*) observances of Easter. Moreover, the strange vicissitudes which attended his dead body, served to emphasise the man in a remarkable way.[8]

But these things, Lightfoot recognised, were not enough: 'these are only the buttresses of a great reputation. The foundations of the reverence entertained for Cuthbert must be sought elsewhere', and Lightfoot found them in the words of St. Paul: *Not I, but Christ liveth in me* (Gal. 2:20). No one can fairly accuse Bishop Lightfoot of being deficient in historical insight (even though, like other historians, his judgement could sometimes be swayed by sectarian sympathies, as was demonstrated in his evaluation of St. Aidan) and it is of interest that he should have chosen that particular text from Galatians to explain Cuthbert; for in a certain way those words epitomize the thought underlying the lives of the monk of Lindisfarne and the Venerable Bede. In the last analysis, however much they may appear to extol the virtues of their hero, the medieval lives of the saints are about the grace of God, working through the actions of His servants. So the *Life of Antony*, which exercised such a powerful literary influence on the various lives of Cuthbert, when it comes to describe Antony's earliest triumph over the demon, says: 'This was the first victory of Antony over the devil, or rather, it was the power of the saviour in Antony.' This notion determines the account given by the Lindisfarne Anonymous and Bede of Cuthbert's life: he is from the first a chosen vessel, whose destiny is predicted even when a boy by a tiny child, and prophesied by the Venerable Boisil, when he first comes to Melrose. At the last, too, his bodily afflictions are ordained | by the providence of God (*VP* 37): p.42

For in order that Almighty God might, by chastisement, purify His servant from all blemish of worldly weakness, and in order that He might show his adversaries that they that they could avail nothing against the strength of his faith, [God] wished to test him by bodily pain and by a still fiercer contest with the ancient foe, cutting him off from mankind for that space of time.

For Lightfoot's sermon, see J.B. Lightfoot, *Leaders in the Northern Church: Sermons preached in the diocese of Durham* (London, 1891).

We can see here the contrast between the Christian view of the saint and the pagan ideal of the hero in the society and culture from which Cuthbert and his biographers came. The hero trusts in his own efforts; though he may be aided by the gods he is, in the last event, his own saviour. The Christian saint relies upon Christ; and because the pagan hero relies upon himself, his career must end in defeat and death. The Christian saint dies too; but for him death is only the gate of life, opened by Christ, who has already won the battle and now gives His servants strength to enjoy the fruits which His victory has gained. In the *Life of Antony* (ch.9) we are told that, after a particularly savage assault, the demons vanished and Antony beheld a great light in his cell.

> Straightaway Antony recognised the presence of the Lord, and drawing a deep sigh from the depth of his heart he spoke to the light which had appeared to him, saying: 'Where were You, good Jesus, where were You? Why were You not here at the beginning to heal my wounds?' And a voice came to him saying: 'Antony, I was here; but I waited to see your struggle; but now, because you did not cease to play the man in fighting, I will always aid you and make you to be known in all the world.'

Not I, but Christ liveth in me. If St. Cuthbert continues to be a spiritual guide in the present age, it is not his miracles, not his asceticism, not even his pastoral devotion which commend him, but rather the self-offering and devotion to God which made him a burning and a shining light in his own generation.

X

The Christian Life in the Thought of the Venerable Bede*

'There is no period in the history of Britain or of the English Church for which Bede is antiquated; in every generation he speaks familiarly'—W. P. KER.

IN the month of November 734, only six months before his death, the Venerable Bede composed a letter to his friend and disciple Egbert, Archbishop of York.[1] It might have been thought that Bede, writing at the close of a life spent almost entirely in the cloister and distinguished by a scholarship which far exceeded that of any other man of his generation, would in this letter have dwelt upon the transience of the present world and on the Vision of God, which he so ardently longed to see, and to which he refers, so often and so eloquently, in his writings. Instead, he addressed to the recently-consecrated archbishop what amounted to a programme of reform for the Northumbrian Church. With the aid of Christ, the king of virtues, Egbert was exhorted to see that the Gospel was preached to the people of Northumbria, and himself provide an example of Christian living.[2] More frequent episcopal visitation was necessary—many villages and hamlets in remote and inaccessible places never saw the bishop for years on end, though the episcopal dues were rigorously exacted.[3] There were not enough bishops to cope with the requirements of the Church. The intention of Pope Gregory I at the very beginning of the English conversion to create twelve northern dioceses had never been carried out. To meet this lack, Archbishop Egbert was urged to seek the support of King Ceolwulf in selecting suitable monasteries to become episcopal sees, and consecrate bishops for them. After this it would be easy to apply to Rome to recognise the metropolitical status of the see of York.[4] Fraudulent monasteries which, in Bede's opinion, were only a device to enable slothful and dishonourable men to avoid their secular obligations, were to be suppressed.[5] The laity were in need of proper instruction in the faith, to be taught the Lord's Prayer and the Apostles Creed in their own language,[6] and to be encouraged to communicate more frequently.[7] Bede ended his letter with renewed, and very earnest, denunciations of clerical avarice—a vice which was, in his opinion, a besetting sin of his age and of his people.[8]

The *Letter to Egbert* has been called the swan-song of the Venerable Bede,[9] and it is remarkable that, at the end of his career, we should find Bede so much concerned

* The Cathedral Lecture for 1970 delivered in Durham Cathedral on 20th February 1970.

[1] *Epistola ad Ecgbertum Episcopum* (ed. Plummer, *Venerabilis Bedae Opera Historica,* Oxford, 1896, i. 405–23).

[2] Ibid., 4: 'In hoc namque officium a Domino electus, in hoc consecratus es, ut verbum evangelizes virtute multa, praebente tibi auxilium ipso Rege virtutum Domino nostro Iesu Christo' (Plummer, p. 408).

[3] Ibid., 7: 'Audivimus enim et fama est, quia multae villae ac viculi nostrae gentis in montibus sint inaccessis ac saltibus dumosis positi, ubi numquam multis transeuntibus annis sit visus antistes, qui ibidem aliquid ministerii aut gratiae caelestis exhibuerit; quorum tamen non unus quidem a tributis antistiti reddendis esse possit immunis' (Plummer, p. 410). On these remote villages and hamlets see Rosalind Hill, 'Christianity and geography in early Northumbria,' *Studies in Church History,* Vol. III, ed. G. J. Cuming, Leiden, 1966, 126–39.

[4] Ibid., 9 (Plummer, pp. 412–13). Not all bishops would welcome such division, which inevitably diminished their status. See E. W. Watson, 'The Age of Bede,' *Bede, His Life, Times and Writings,* ed. A. Hamilton Thompson, Oxford, 1935, 56–58.

[5] Ibid., 11–13 (Plummer, pp. 414–18). On this, see the comments of A. Hamilton Thompson, 'Northumbrian monasticism,' *BLTW,* 86 ff.

[6] Ibid., 5 (Plummer, pp. 408–09).

[7] Ibid., 15 (Plummer, pp. 418–19).

[8] Ibid., 16, 17 (Plummer, pp. 419–23).

[9] John Smith, *Historiae ecclesiasticae gentis Anglorum Libri quinque auctore Venerabili Baeda* . . . cura et studio Johannis Smith, Cambridge, 1772, 309 *n*: '. . . ita ut haec epistola habeatur tanquam Baedae cygnea cantio.'

with the state of the Church outside his cloister. In this, if not perhaps in much else, Bede resembles St. Bernard five centuries later. Bernard sought to direct the whole Western Church from Clairvaux. Bede, more modest, confined himself to Northumbria. In the *Ecclesiastical History,* completed in 731 three years before the *Letter to Egbert* was written, Bede had celebrated, with a pride which is free from disparagement of other peoples (except the British, whose refusal to work for the conversion of the heathen Saxons was never forgiven them), the achievements of the English nation, from its conversion to his own days—'favourable times of peace and prosperity'.[10] Now, however, Bede considered that the situation required him to sound a note of alarm. As a doctor of the Church—and this was what he deemed himself to be, thereby anticipating the verdict of later ages—it was his duty to enquire diligently into the state of religion in his time and point the way to necessary reforms.[11]

Bede's concern with the Church of his own day is easily understood. It was not simply that, as a religious withdrawn from the world, he had that clear view which sometimes comes from detachment, or even because he had an historian's interest in contemporary affairs. Both these factors no doubt helped to inspire Bede to write to Egbert as he did; but besides these there was the whole tradition of Northumbrian monasticism, deriving from the twin influences of the Latin and Celtic churches. The earliest Irish missionaries had been monks, while the Roman mission, if not exclusively monastic in composition,[12] had been planned and led by professed religious. Indeed, all Bede's heroes had been monks, engaged in active pastoral work. Of Gregory the Great, the Apostle of the English nation, who had regretted the loss of the peace of the cloister necessarily occasioned by assuming the government of the Roman Church, Bede was moved to observe: 'We need not believe, however, that he had lost any of his monastic perfection by reason of his pastoral cares. It would appear that he profited more by his efforts over the conversion of many than he had done from the quiet retirement of his way of life.'[13] Moreover, Bede has left us unforgettable pictures of monks engaged in active works: St. Aidan travelling round Northumbria, preaching and exhorting, accompanied by companions whom he required, whether clerical or lay, to study the Scriptures or to memorise the psalms;[14] Boisil, and St. Cuthbert after him, preaching the Word to the villages around Melrose Abbey;[15] St Chad, as bishop of Lichfield, faithful to the Irish tradition that a bishop in his pastoral visits should go on foot, being forcibly lifted into the saddle by Archbishop Theodore who, with a zeal for efficiency worthy of a later age, argued that Chad would get more work done if he rode a horse;[16] Benedict Biscop, journeying to and from Rome with books and treasures for his foundations of Wearmouth and Jarrow[17]—all these examples show that the tradition of monasticism with which Bede was familiar involved pastoral work as well as contemplation. Indeed, in one of his sermons in which he contrasts the active and the contemplative lives, Bede remarks that very few come to the contemplative life, and those the more exaltedly who come after the perfection of pious action.[18]

[10] Bede, *HE* V, 23: 'qua adridente pace ac serenitate temporum . . .' (tr. Colgrave).

[11] *In Ezram et Neemian* III: 'Sic et doctorum est spiritalium saepius noctu surgere ac sollerti indagine statum sanctae ecclesiae quiescentibus ceteris inspicere ut vigilanter inquirant qualiter ea quae vitiorum bellis in illa sordidata sive deiecta sunt castigando emendment et erigant.' *CC* cxix A, 343. 187–91.

[12] See Hamilton Thompson, 'Northumbrian monasticism,' *BLTW,* 70.

[13] *HE* II, 1 (tr. Colgrave, p. 125).

[14] *HE* III, 5.

[15] *Vita Cuthberti,* 9; quoted *HE* IV, 25 [27].

[16] *HE* IV, 3.

[17] *Historia Abbatum auctore Baeda,* 6, 9 (ed. Plummer, pp. 368–70, 373).

[18] *Hom.* I, 9: 'Possumus autem mystice in his quae Petro et Johanni a domino praedicta atque in eis sunt gesta duas ecclesiae vitas quibus in praesenti exercetur activam scilicet et contemplativam designatas accipere quarum activa communis populo Dei via vivendi est; ad contemplativam vero perpauci et hoc sublimiores quique post perfectionem piae actionis ascendunt.' *CC* cxxii, 64. 145–51.

Bede's career and writings suggest that, so far as he was concerned, he regarded himself as remaining in the active life all his life long;[19] and it is perhaps significant that he is at some pains to point out that the active life—self-discipline, feeding the hungry, clothing the naked, sheltering the homeless, succouring the needy and the like—is not only the business of monks in the cloister but is open to all the people of God.[20] Monks were, apparently, regarded as being the natural dispensers of charity.

To carry conviction, a man's teaching about how life should be lived must be demonstrated in himself. With this principle, Bede would wholeheartedly have agreed, for no Christian thinker is more insistent on the principle that faith without works is dead.[21] 'The mere confession of faith,' he declares, 'is in no way at all sufficient for salvation where testimony of good works is lacking; but neither are just works of any avail without simplicity of faith and love.'[22] Archbishop Egbert was reminded that a bishop's duties involved both action and teaching (*operatio et doctrina*) for, says Bede, 'neither of these virtues can be rightly discharged without the other, if either the bishop who leads a good life neglects the duty of teaching or the good teacher neglects to put his teaching into proper practice. But he who performs both offices faithfully is in truth that servant who may await the coming of the Lord with confidence, hoping speedily to hear: *Well done, good and faithful servant . . . . Enter into the joy of thy Lord.*'[23] Judged by such standards, what are we to say of Bede's own life?

In the first place, we may mention a point which is easily overlooked: Bede's religious vocation was not, initially, of his own choosing but was imposed upon him by the kinsmen who placed him in his monastery at the age of seven.[24] We are apt to think of Bede as a monk by nature, and so he probably was; but the fact remains that his decision was, in effect, made for him by others when he was still a child. Thus, he is an admirable example of one who chose to abide in the state to which God called him. Again, it is to be noted that with all his brilliant talents, Bede never (so far as we know) held any important office at Jarrow, and remained all his life in priest's orders. It may be, of course, that he lacked the powers of administration which were as essential to a bishop in the Eighth century as at other times; and it is very likely that, like other scholars, he would not have desired elevation to the episcopate; but, when all is said and done, it seems a fair deduction from the course of his career to suppose that if he had wanted a bishopric he could have had one, and the reason why he remained in a comparatively humble position all his life was his humility—the virtue which he consistently commends in all his work. It is worth remarking that his one explicit citation from the Benedictine Rule, which comes in his commentary on Ezra and

[19] Ibid.: 'Activa quippe vita est studiosum Christi famulum iustis insistere laboribus et prius quidem se ipsum ab hoc saeculo immaculatum custodire mentem manum linguam ac membra corporis cetera ab omni inquinamento culpae temptantis continere ac divinis perpetuo subiugare servitiis; deinde etiam proximi necessitatibus iuxta vires succurrere. . . . Contemplativa autem vita est cum longo quis bonae actionis exercitio edoctus diutinae orationis dulcedine instructus crebra lacrimarum conpunctione adsuefactus a cunctis mundi negotiis vacare et in sola dilectione oculum mentis intendere didicerit gaudiumque perpetuae beatitudinis quod in futura percepturus est vita etiam in praesenti coeperit ardenter desiderando praegustare et aliquando etiam quantum mortalibus fas est in excessu mentis speculando sublimiter.' *CC* cxxii, 64. 151–57, 163–71. In view of the fact that Bede was still teaching and translating on his death-bed, his whole life would appear, on his own terms, to have been an active one.

[20] Ibid.: 'Namque activa non solis in coenobio monachis sed et cuncto ut diximus populo Dei generaliter ingredienda proponitur.' *CC* cxxii, 65. 175–76.

[21] *De Templo* I: '. . . neque fides sine operibus neque sine fide Deo possunt opera bona placere.' *CC* cxix A, 190. 1715–16.

[22] *Exp. in I Ep. Ioh.*: 'Nequaquam . . . sola fidei confessio sufficit ad salutem, cui bonorum operum attestatio deest. Sed nec operum rectitudo sine fidei et dilectionis simplicitate prodest.' *PL* xciii, 87 B.

[23] *Ep. ad Ecgbert. Ep.*, 2 (Plummer, p. 406).

[24] *HE* V, 24.

Nehemiah, is taken from Chapter 7, which deals with the twelve degrees of humility by which we arrive at the perfect love of God.[25]

It is therefore abundantly clear that Bede loyally accepted both the monastic vocation which was not initially of his own choosing and the principles of the religious life. Bede's devotion to the Divine Office—a devotion which lies at the heart of Benedictine spirituality—is expressed in the words quoted by Alcuin in a well-known passage in which Bede explained why he would never absent himself from the choir-office: 'I know that the angels visit the canonical hours and the assemblies of the brethren. Will they not say: "Where is Bede? Why does he not come to the devotions laid down for the brethren?"'[26] That Bede should actually have uttered such words is very likely, in view of the awe with which he elsewhere speaks of the presence of angels at the service of the Church and especially at the celebration of the Eucharist;[27] and it is to be noticed that even here he only echoes the Benedictine Rule: 'Let us therefore consider how we ought to behave ourselves in the presence of God and His angels, and so assist at the Divine Office that our mind and voice may accord together.'[28]

Prayer however, although central to the religious—and, indeed, to the Christian—life, is not the sole activity of that life while it is lived upon earth. Bede makes this clear when he emphasises the need to prepare the way to contemplation by action, by the performance of works of charity. The form which the active life took for Bede is clear enough: scholarship and teaching. 'I have spent all my life in this monastery,' he wrote at the end of the *Ecclesiastical History,* 'applying myself entirely to the study of the Scriptures; and amid the observance of the discipline of the Rule and the daily task of singing in the church, it has always been my delight to learn or to teach or to write.'[29] Even during his last illness he continued to teach his pupils daily,[30] and the description of how death overtook him, still at work on his translation of the Gospel of St. John, is one of the unforgettable incidents of English history.[31] No one reading Bede's writings can fail to note the importance which he assigns to what he calls the Doctors of the Church, understanding by this term, not only the great patristic theologians like Augustine and Gregory, but teachers like the members of the Roman

[25] *In Ez. et Neem.* III. *CC* cxix A, 350. 466–351. 473 (citing Bened., *Reg.,* 7. *CSEL* lxxv, 40–41.

[26] Alcuin, *Ep.* 16. *MGH Epp.* iv, 443.

[27] *In Luc.* VI: 'Quo modo autem posito in sepulchro corpore salvatoris angeli adstetisse leguntur ita etiam celebrandis eiusdem sacratissimi corporis mysteriis tempore consecrationis adsistere sunt credendi. . . . Et nos autem exemplo devotarum Deo feminarum quoties ecclesiam intramus mysteriis caelestibus appropinquamus sive propter angelicae praesentiam virtutis seu propter reverentiam sacrae oblationis cum omni humilitate et timore debemus ingredi.' *CC* cxx. 411. 1926–29, 1936–38—412 .1939–40; *Hom.* II, 10: 'Maxime tamen angelici nobis spiritus adesse credendi sunt cum divinis specialiter mancipamur obsequiis, id est cum ecclesiam ingressi vel lectionibus sacris aurem accommodamus vel psalmodiae operam damus vel orationi incumbimus vel etiam missarum sollemnia celebramus.' *CC* cxxii, 249. 97–101.

[28] Bened., *Reg.,* 19. 6. 7. *CSEL* lxxv, 75.

[29] *HE* V, 24 (tr. Colgrave, p. 567).

[30] *De Obitu Bedae*: ' . . . usque ad diem Ascensionis dominicae, id est septimo kalendas Iunii vitam ducebat, et nobis suis discipulis cotidie lectiones dabat' (ed. Colgrave & Mynors, p. 580).

[31] Colgrave (*Bede's Ecclesiastical History,* ed. Colgrave & Mynors, 1969, p. xxi) asserts that Bede *finished* his translation of the Fourth Gospel on his death-bed; but the text of the *De Obitu Bedae* merely says that he was translating on as far as *Sed quid haec inter tantos* (John 6:9) (Colgrave & Mynors p. 582). C. E. Whiting's suggestion that this is an interpolation in the St. Gall MS. ('The life of the Venerable Bede,' *BLTW* p. 34), presumably made because the Insular Version of the *De Obitu* merely reads: 'evangelium vero sancti Iohannis in nostram linguam ad utilitatem ecclesie convertit' (ed. E. van Kirk Dobbie, *The manuscripts of Caedmon's hymn and Bede's Death Song,* New York, 1937, 123) is not supported by the Tenth-century Hague MS. 70. H. 7 (printed by N. R. Ker, *Medium Ævum* viii (1939), 40–44) used by Colgrave & Mynors as their text.

mission;[32] St. Columba of Iona;[33] and the Irish mission to Northumbria.[34] Indeed, he is willing to apply it to ordinary priests and catechists[35]—to anyone, indeed, who is concerned with instructing the faithful in the rudiments of the faith. Thus when in 653 King Sigberct of the East Saxons asked King Osuiu of Northumbria for 'doctors' to convert and baptise his people he was sent St. Cedd and an unnamed priest.[36] Now in this sense Bede could, in his own lifetime, legitimately think of himself as a doctor, and regard teaching as a form of Christian activity which may fairly be compared with almsgiving,[36a] and which operates to the same end: the fulfilment of the law of love. 'The joy of the doctors,' he says, 'is made full when by preaching they lead many to the society of Holy Church and of Him by whom the Church is strengthened and guarded, God the Father and His Son, Jesus Christ.'[37] Certainly Bede spared no effort to communicate his own learning to others, and he was as willing to provide unlettered priests with English versions of the Lord's Prayer and the Apostles Creed[38] as to compose a commentary on the Gospel of St. Luke in six books for Bishop Acca of Hexham.

We may therefore claim that Bede in his own career admirably displayed that combination of doctrine and action which he held to be the mark of right Christian living. Two problems however confront us when we turn to Bede for information on the Christian life, one minor, the other more serious. The lesser problem is this: can we properly talk of any specifically Bedan teaching on the Christian life, when much of his writing consists of the reproduction, often verbatim, of the works of his predecessors, notably of course the four great doctors of the Latin Church: Ambrose, Jerome, Augustine and Gregory?

This is undoubtedly a problem; and the difficulty is not diminished by the fact that even today, despite the labours of editors whose names include Plummer, Laistner, Jones, Colgrave and Hurst, there are still many of Bede's works which lack any critical edition and in which unacknowledged quotations from another author may lurk, all unsuspected by the unwary reader. Indeed, even the modern editor may nod from time to time and

[32] *HE* I, 26: 'didicerat enim a doctoribus auctoribusque suae salutis'; Ibid., II, 14: '. . . ipsi doctori et antistiti.'

[33] *HE* III, 4: 'iuxta exemplum primi doctoris illius.'

[34] *HE* III, 26: 'Tota enim fuit tunc sollicitudo doctoribus illis Deo serviendi, non saeculo.'

[35] *De Templo* II: 'ostia domus templi doctores sunt sancti ac sacerdotes qui instruendo baptizando dominici corporis et sanguinis mysteria communicando prima nobis ecclesiae praesentis limina pandunt.' *CC* cxix A, 232. 1583–86.

[36] *HE* III, 22: 'Igitur rex Sigberct . . . temporalis sui regni sedem repetiit, postulans ab Osuiu rege, ut aliquos sibi doctores daret, qui gentem suam ad fidem Christi converterent . . . At ille . . . clamavit ad se virum Dei Cedd, et dato illi socio altero quodam presbytero, misit praedicare verbum genti Orientalium Saxonum.'

[36a] *In Luc.* V: 'Si autem hi qui praebent elemosinam de iniquo mammona faciunt sibi amicos a quibus in aeterna tabernacula recipiantur, quanto magis hi qui spiritales largiuntur epulas qui dant conservis cibaria in tempore suo certissima debent spe summae retributionis erigi.' *CC* cxx, 298. 111–16. Cf. *De Muliere forti: 'Manum suam aperuit inopi, et palmas suas extendit ad pauperem.* Quod et de operibus eleemosynarum quae generaliter fiunt in pauperes accipi potest, sed melius de verbo Dei quod indumentum salutis animabus confert, intelligitur,' *PL* xci, 1046 D. Sister Mary T. A. Carroll, in her excellent book, *The Venerable Bede: His spiritual teachings* (Catholic University of America. Studies in Medieval History, N.S. Vol. 9, 1946), which I did not have available when I prepared this lecture, remarks (pp. 257–58): 'Lofty as was Bede's appreciation of [the monastic] state of life, he valued still more his life as a priest, and his writings turn frequently to the duties of the clergy.' This comment, which seems to be anticipated by Plummer (i. p. lxxviii–xix): '. . . the very model of the saintly scholar-priest,' probably supplies the key to the pastoral concern of Bede's life and writings.

[37] *In Ep. I Ioh. Exp.*: 'Gaudium doctorum fit plenum, cum multos praedicando ad sanctae Ecclesiae societatem, atque ad eius per quem Ecclesia roboratur et crescit, Dei Patris et Filii eius Iesu Christi societatem perducunt.' *PL* xciii, 87 A.

[38] *Ep. ad Ecgbert. Ep.*, 5 (Plummer, p. 409).

fail to identify a quotation.[39] However, from the point of view of the interpretation of Bede's teaching one may, I suggest, reasonably assume that if he quotes from another author he adopts his views, unless he makes a specific declaration to the contrary. Furthermore, Bede is by no means a mere reproducer of other men's views, and the present exposition is based, so far as may be, on Bede's own words and not on those which he cites from others.

The second, and more serious, problem is this: how far can the teaching of Bede, a professed religious writing in Latin for the benefit of educated readers (who would, of course, be overwhelmingly clerical), be regarded as applicable to the life of the ordinary layman? In one sense, of course, this is no more than the problem which confronts any student of the spirituality of the Latin West in the early Middle Ages. The Latin Fathers, at an earlier date, had had the advantage of preaching to congregations of ordinary people in their own tongue, and we can accordingly distil a great deal of simple pastoral instruction from their sermons. Bede, on the other hand, wrote in an academic language unintelligible to the majority of his fellow-countrymen; and although we know that he was prepared to put his learning at the disposal of the simple and unlettered, we have no vernacular writings from his pen as we have, for example, from a later English writer like Ælfric. To say that there were no laymen in Bede's day who could have read his works with profit is an exaggeration; the scholarly King Ceolwulf of Northumbria, to whom Bede dedicated the *Ecclesiastical History,* is an example to the contrary. Nevertheless, the number of learned laymen could, at best, have been very small indeed.

In spite of this, the fact that the Northumbrian tradition of the monastic life had in the past necessarily involved a good deal of pastoral activity would in itself have encouraged Bede, in writing his commentaries on Scripture and his other theological works, not to neglect teaching which would be relevant to the life of the laity. Inevitably, in view of his religious profession and his patristic authorities, his treatment of certain topics is, from the ordinary Christian's point of view, not very helpful. Thus Bede can maintain the dignity of marriage by pointing out that, if there had been any sin in matrimony, our Lord would never have attended the wedding at Cana in Galilee,[40] and he is even prepared to defend the frequent reception of communion by married persons in certain circumstances;[41] but his real enthusiasm is reserved for the life of dedicated virginity, and his unconcealed admiration for Queen Ethelthryth's refusal to lead a normal married life with her husband King Egfrid[42] can hardly have been very helpful to more ordinary persons, even in his own day, and is, indeed, in marked contrast with the attitude of St. Augustine of Hippo, one of Bede's masters who, although not less fervent than Bede in his admiration of continence, strongly deprecated any attempt by one spouse to live in that state against the wishes of the other.[43] However, we must

[39] e.g. even Plummer missed the Gregorian citation in *HE* II, 1: 'crebris viscerum doloribus cruciabatur' (Greg., *Moralia, Ep. Missoria,* 5. *PL* lxxv, 515), which is supplied by Colgrave & Mynors, p. 129*n*[1]. Dom Hurst has overlooked quotations from Cyprian (*De Unitate,* 4 in Bede, *Hom.* II, 22 [*CC* cxxii, 347. 205–09]—an important piece of evidence for our knowledge of the history of the Cyprianic text in England, see Maurice Bévenot, *The tradition of manuscripts,* Oxford, 1961, 53, 89*n*[7]) and Augustine (*In Ioh. Evang. Tr.* 120, 2 in *De Templo* I [*CC* cxix A, 166. 764–67]).

[40] *Hom.* I, 14: 'Si enim thoro immaculato et nuptiis debita castitate celebratis culpa inesset, nequaquam dominus ad has venire nequaquam eas signorum suorum initiis consecrare voluisset.' *CC* cxxii, 95. 6–9.

[41] *Ep. ad Ecgbert. Ep.,* 15: 'Ipsi etiam coniugati, si quis sibi mensuram continentiae ostendat, et virtutem castitatis insinuet, idem et licenter possint, et libenter facere velint' (Plummer, p. 419).

[42] *HE* IV, 17 [19], 18 [20].

[43] Aug., *Ep.* 262, 2: 'Omitto enim, quod ipsam continentiam illo nondum volente non secundum sanam doctrinam te suscepisse cognovi, neque enim corporis tui debito fraudandus fuit, priusquam ad illud bonum, quod superat pudicitiam coniugalem, tuae voluntati voluntas quoque eius accederet.' *CSEL* lvii, 622. 3–7.

recognize that, in his outlook, Bede is very much a man of his age, seing as he does an almost magical quality in virginity, which preserved the body of Ethelthryth from corruption after death, just as the body of St. John the beloved disciple and lover of virginity had been similarly preserved at an earlier date.[44]

Nevertheless, when allowance has been made for this particular predilcction of Bede—a predilection which would after all have been shared by every serious theologian of his day and of the patristic age before him—there are many passages in his works which suggest that what he says is not addressed solely to professed religious, but is intended to be a guide to men and women living in the world. For example, Bede is careful to explain that the dominical injunction to forsake all and follow Him is addressed only to those who follow the monastic life, and he recognizes that there are other Christians who may rightly retain their possessions and from them minister to the poor.[45] Commenting on Christ's words *Woe to you that are rich, for ye have received your consolation* (Luke 6:25) he remarks that what will exclude a man from the kingdom of heaven is not riches in themselves, but the desire to seek consolation in them. It is not riches but the love of riches which is at fault,[46] and Bede recalls with approval the generosity of King Oswald, when he commanded that his Easter dinner should be given to the poor and the silver dish on which it was served broken up and distributed among them.[47] Again, Bede's discussion of Christ's words: *Give to every one that asketh of thee, and of him that taketh away thy goods ask them not again* (Luke 6:30) seems to be generally more applicable to laymen than to monks. 'Our Lord is speaking about clothing, homes, farms, livestock and generally, about all sorts of wealth; but it is a very big question whether what He says also applies to slaves, for a Christian should not own a slave like a horse or a piece of silver, even though it can happen that a horse commands a higher price than a slave, and a gold or silver object a very much larger sum still. If however you think that a slave will be more honestly and piously educated and governed by you as his lord than by the man who wants to take him away, I do not know if anyone would dare to say that you ought to despise the slave and part with him as you would a garment.'[48] The *Commentary on Luke,* in which this passage occurs, was dedicated to Bishop Acca of Hexham, whose episcopal household would no doubt include slaves or persons of lowly status who might be coveted by other men; but the principles which Bede lays down would, one may hope, be more generally applicable to a layman than to a cleric.

Furthermore, Bede is not unmindful of the place of the laity in the Church. In one of his sermons, when discussing the verse from Luke: *And all that heard it wondered at the things which were spoken by the shepherds* (2:18) he sees this as having an allegorical meaning and says: 'The shepherds did not conceal in silence the hidden mysteries which they had learned from God but declared them to whomsoever they could. This was because the spiritual shepherds of the Church are chiefly ordained to this end: to preach the mysteries of the Word of God, and to show the wonderful things they have learned in Scripture to the admiration of their hearers. But by shepherds we must here understand not only bishops, priests and deacons or even monastic superiors; but all the faithful, however small their house may be, are rightly called shepherds, insofar

[44] *Hom.* I, 9: 'Et hoc virgini [sc. Iohanni evangelistae] privilegium recte servabatur ut ad scrutanda verbi incorruptibilis sacramenta incorrupto ipse non solum corde sed et corpore proderet.' *CC* cxxii, 66. 247–67. 249.

[45] Ibid., I, 13: 'Unde notandum quod duo sunt ordines electorum in iudicio futuri, unus iudicantium cum domino de quibus hoc loco commemorat qui reliquerunt omnia et secuti sunt illum, alius iudicatorum a domino qui non quidem omnia sua pariter reliquerunt sed de his tamen quae habebant cotidianas dare elemosinas pauperibus Christi curabant.' *CC* cxxii, 89. 41–90. 47.

[46] *In Luc.* II: 'Ubi notandum quod non tam divitiae quam divitiarum amor in culpa est.' *CC* cxx, 141. 1606–07.

[47] *HE* III, 6.

[48] *In Luc.* II. *CC* cxx, 144. 1740–51.

as they rule over that house with watchful care.'[49] Again he declares: 'The name of priest is not ascribed in Scripture to the ministers of the altar alone, that is bishops and priests, but to all who are distinguished by eminence of conduct and sound doctrine, who while they offer their bodies a *living sacrifice holy and pleasing to God* exercise a sacerdotal ministry, though in a spiritual fashion. For the Apostle Peter did not address himself to bishops and priests alone but to all the Church of God when he said: *You are an elect race, a royal priesthood, a holy nation, a people for God's own possession.*'[50]

We are therefore, I would maintain, justified in holding that Bede's writings can rightly be regarded as providing a picture of the Christian life which is applicable not only to monks in the cloister or secular priests but to all the faithful, irrespective of their place in the Church or state of life.

What, at the outset, is Bede's doctrine of man? Fundamentally, it is the teaching derived from St. Augustine, that all mankind fell in Adam and, from the mass of perdition so formed, some individuals are elected, by the inscrutable but wholly just judgement of God, to salvation in Christ.[51] This is Augustine's doctrine, and it is also Bede's, but with one significant modification, made possible by the famous decision of the Council of Orange of 529 which, using language which was borrowed in large measure from Augustine's writings, nevertheless declared it to be Catholic belief that all the baptized, with the aid and co-operation of Christ, can and, if they labour faithfully, ought to fulfil the things which pertain to salvation.[52] Accordingly, Bede teaches that, while baptism is indeed absolutely necessary to salvation,[53] no one need fear that he may be predestined to wrath and so despair of pardon on account of the magnitude of his sins. 'Let no one,' says Bede, 'through despair withdraw his mind from seeking pardon on account of the quality or quantity of his sins, nor let the sight of the foulness of his wounds or the extremity of his spiritual sickness hold anyone back from seeking salvation.'[54] This does not mean that we can indulge in a careless confidence in the mercy of God. 'Let none despair of salvation because, great as are the sicknesses of sin which weigh men down, the almighty physician has come to save. But let every man remember that the same Son of God who came in meekness to save will come again in strictness to judge.'[55] Bede is the last Christian teacher to make light of serious

[49] *Hom.* I, 7. *CC* cxxii, 49. 98–108.

[50] *De Temp.* II. *CC* cxix A, 194. 82–91.

[51] *In Ep. I Ioh. Exp.*: '. . . mors est animae amittere Deum. Unde constat, quod in anima mortui omnes in hanc lucem nascimur, trahentes ex Adam originale peccatum, sed Christi gratia fidelibus regenerando agitur, ut in anima vivere possint. . . . Et frustra nititur Pelagius affirmare quod parvuli recens editi non opus habeant gratia baptismatis renasci, quia tam mundi nascantur ab omni sorde peccati, quam fuit mundus in paradiso conditus Adam, nullam scilicet ex illo trahentes originalis culpae maculam, in nullo existentes rei donec propria sponte peccare incipiant.' *PL* xciii, 102 D, 119 C; *In Ez. et Neem.*, I: 'Laetantur et neophiti gratia sui redemptoris se esse collectos dolent se cum toto genere humano in primo parente perisse et quasi corrupto ab hostibus templo Dei statu videlicet corporis et animae immortalis in Babylonem . . . se fuisse transmigratos.' *CC* cxix A, 281. 1586–91.

[52] 'Hoc etiam secundum fidem catholicam credimus, quod post acceptam per baptismum gratiam omnes baptizati, Christo auxiliante et cooperante, quae ad salutem animae pertinent, possint et debeant, si fideliter laborare voluerint, adimplere.' H. Denzinger, *Enchiridion Symbolorum* (31st ed., 1960), no. 200.

[53] *De Tab.*, III: '. . . [ecclesia] . . . in qua nullus est absque peccato etiam si unius diei fuerit vita eius super terram nullus qui non ex peccato praevaricationis Adae carnaliter natus necesse habeat in Christo renasci et spiritus eius igne mundari . . . aqua baptismatis . . . cuius lavacro necesse est purgentur omnes qui ecclesiae ianuas ingrediuntur.' *CC* cxix A, 133. 1567–70, 136. 1683–85.

[54] *Hom.*, II, 14: 'Neque rursus quispiam considerata peccatorum suorum qualitate seu quantitate a petenda venia mentem desperando revocet. Neminem visa suorum putredo vulnerum sui magnitudo languoris a quaerenda salute retrahat.' *CC* cxxii, 273. 43–47.

[55] *In Ep. I Ioh. Exp.*: 'Nemo de salute desperet, quia etsi magni sunt morbi scelerum qui deprimunt, omnipotens medicus venit qui salvet. Tamen meminerit quisque quia idem Filius Dei qui venit mitis ut salvaret, venturus est districtus ut iudicet.' *PL* xciii, 110 B. Cf. Aug., *In Ep. Ioh. ad Parthos Tr.* 8, 13. *PL* xxxv, 2043.

sin incurred after baptism.[56] It must be expiated by stern penance,[57] and there is always the fearful possibility of the sinner becoming hardened in despair, as happened in the case of an unhappy monk known personally to Bede, who refused the viaticum on his death-bed, and for whom no one ventured to say masses or even to pray;[58] but Bede recognizes—again following St. Augustine—that as long as they are in the body, even the saints of God, and much less the majority of Christians, cannot hope to make their pilgrimage through this present world without committing from time to time at least some venial sins.[59] This is not a matter for despair; but what is essential is that the baptized Christian should use his freedom, restored in baptism, to perform works of charity. 'Remission of past sins is not enough if a man does not henceforth take pains to press forward with good works.'[60] No writer is more insistent than Bede that both faith *and* works are necessary to salvation;[61] though equally, no writer is more anxious to anticipate and reject any suggestion of Pelagianism in this insistence on good works. Thus, commenting on the words in the First Epistle of St. John: *Every one that has this hope set on him sanctifies himself* (3:3), Bede writes: 'It must not be imagined that because it is said about a man that he *sanctifies himself* this gives any support to Pelagianism, as if anyone could sanctify himself through free will without divine aid. But the man who has hope in the Lord sanctifies himself, so far as he is able, by striving and by vehemently demanding His grace in all things, Who says: *Without Me you can do nothing* and by saying to Him: *Be Thou my helper, forsake me not.*'[62]

[56] *In Ez. et Neem.* II: 'Facile . . . est conversum quemque ad fidem agnitionemque veritatis abrenuntiare diabolo et confiteri Deum vivum et verum sacramenta Christi percipere hisque initiatum in remissionem omnium peccatorum templum eius effici atque acceptam vitae innocentiam comitante eius gratia servare; sed multi laboris est eum qui accepta fidei sacramenta peccando contemnit pristinam recipere dignitatem quia non huic facilis emundatio per aquam baptismi denuo dari potest sed infectum scelus longo paenitentiae labore largis lacrimarum fluentis districtiore continentiae sudore eluendum est.' *CC* cxix A, 305. 694–704.

[57] Ibid., III: '. . . si post ablutionem sacri fontis diabolo seducente ad peccata relabimur et virtutum moenia nostrarum hostis victor igne vitiorum deicit, gravioribus necesse est orationis adflictionis vigiliarum elemosinarum et vitae artioris studiis ea quae perdidimus bonorum operum aedificia reparemus.' *CC* cxix A, 359. 794–99.

[58] HE V, 14.

[59] *Hom.* I, 24: ' . . . quia quod omnibus patet nemo est qui sine corruptione ac dolore vivere possit super terram, quod omnibus sapientibus patet licet haeretici contradicant nemo est qui sine adtactu alicuius peccati vivere possit super terram.' *CC* ccxxii, 173. 131–34; *In Ep. I Ioh. Exp.*: 'Sacramentum . . . dominicae passionis et praeterita nobis omnia in baptismo pariter peccata laxavit, et quidquid quotidiana fragilitate post baptismum commisimus, eiusdem nostri Redemptoris nobis gratia dimittit.' *PL* xciii, 87 D. Cf. Aug., *Enchiridion* xix, 71: 'De quotidianis autem brevibus levibusque peccatis, sine quibus haec vita non ducitur, quotidiana fidelium oratio satisfacit.' *PL* xl, 265.

[60] *De Temp.* II: ' . . . non sufficit praeteritorum remissio peccatorum, si non quisque bonis deinceps insistere studuerit operibus.' *CC* cxix A, 207. 634–208. 636.

[61] Ibid., I: 'neque fides sine operibus neque sine fide Deo possunt opera bona placere.' *CC* cxix A, 190. 1715–16; *In Ep. I Ioh. Exp.*: 'Nequaquam . . . sola fidei confessio sufficit ad salutem cui bonorum operum attestatio deest. Sed nec operum rectitudo sine fidei et dilectionis simplicitate prodest.' *PL* xciii, 87 B.

[62] *In Ep. I Ioh. Exp. PL* xciii, 100 A. Cf. *De Tab.* II: 'Sic etenim sic per omnia necesse est ut nequaquam obduremus corda nostra neque obseramus more Pelagianorum adversus gratiam Dei sed diligenter aperiamus ea et quasi plurimis simul patefactis ianuis seduli deprecemur ut per omnia quae inchoamus vel agere desideramus bona quasi per singula victimarum eius frusta sua nos misericordia illustrare et in amorem ipse suum accendere dignetur.' *CC* cxix A, 82. 1591–97. For the absolute necessity of divine grace for all our actions, see *De Tab.* I: 'Et nos primitias bonorum nostrorum domino tollimus quando, si quid boni agimus, totum hoc divinae gratiae tribuimus veraciter et intimo ex corde profitentes quod ne initium quidem bonae actionis aut cogitationis aliquod nisi a domino possumus habere mala vero nostra semper a nobis ipsis diabolo instigante et coepta et consummata nec nisi domino donante laxanda esse fatemur.' *CC* cxix A, 10. 214–21. Cf. *In Luc.* I. *CC* cxx, 62. 1710–14.

The reception of baptism, then, liberates man from the sin and weakness which he has contracted in Adam and leaves him free, under divine grace, to perform works worthy of the Christian profession. But it does more: it incorporates the baptized person into the Church,[63] which is the Body of Christ.[64] Bede's theology of the Church comes, like so much else in his teaching, from St. Augustine, though (perhaps fortunately) it lacks the subtlety which made Augustinian ecclesiology so fruitful a field for academic enquiry and controversy. Thus Bede identifies the Church with the City of God, 'which partly pursues her pilgrim way upon earth, far from the Lord, and partly already reigns with the Lord in heaven, and after the end of this age, being made perfect, will reign with Him for ever.'[65] Her members comprise both angels and men;[66] she is indeed Jacob's ladder, which reaches from earth to heaven.[67] The foundations of the Church are upon the holy hills, that is, the solidity of the faith of the Apostles and Prophets.[68] Her unity is a unity of love—love of God and of His elect,[69] and to depart from that unity is to lose the salvation bestowed in the reception of the Church's sacraments.[70] Bede, it may be noted, had read St. Cyprian to good effect.[71]

Nevertheless, this insistence on union with the Church as an essential part of the Christian life does not, in the mind of Bede, imply something formal or mechanical. Bede regarded the acceptance of the Church's dogmas as being obligatory for all her children and the famous occasion in 708 when he was himself charged with holding heretical opinions by persons whom he describes, with unwonted asperity, as 'boors carousing in their cups'[72] was a terrible shock, which he never forgot and which provoked him to write a crushing rejoinder. But for Bede the essence of Christian unity is something altogether deeper and more spiritual than mere conformity. It is fellowship—a fellowship which, like the Church herself, extends beyond the bounds of space and time. 'By the wonderful grace of the divine dispensation it comes about,' he says, 'that we *on whom the ends of the age have come,* may with sincere affection also love those who were faithful at the very beginning of the age, and receive them in the

[63] *In Ez. et Neem.* III: '. . . talis est aedificatio spiritalis quae in animarum salute geritur ut in baptismate renati per fidem et confessionem sanctae trinitatis absque ullo nostro labore per gratiam Dei civitas ac domus eius efficiamur.' *CC* cxix A, 359. 791–94. Cf. *In Ep. I Ioh. Exp. PL* xciii, 86 C D.

[64] *In Luc.* III: '. . . nemo nisi baptizatus nisi corpori Christi adunatus ecclesiam intrabit.' *CC* cxx, 224. 2272–73. *Hom.* II, 1: '. . . corpus eius quod est ecclesia.' *CC* cxxii, 189. 206.

[65] *Hom.* II, 1: '. . . ecclesia partim in terris peregrinatur a domino partim cum domino regnat in caelis.' *CC* cxxii, 190. 235–36.

[66] *In Ez. et Neem.* II: '. . . ecclesiam totam, hoc est congregationem omnium electorum et angelorum et hominum.' *CC* cxix A, 300. 492–93.

[67] *Hom.* I, 17. CC cxxii, 126. 279–127. 284.

[68] *Hom.* II, 1: 'fundamenta ecclesiae in soliditate fidei apostolorum et prophetarum.' *CC* cxxii, 186. 73–74.

[69] *De Tab.* II: 'Neque aliter quisquam potest veraciter ad ecclesiae membra pertingere nisi integro corde et eum per quem aedificatur et eos in quibus aedificatur ecclesia, hoc est Deum et electos eius, amare didicerit.' *CC* cxix A, 44. 112–15.

[70] *Hom.* I, 23: 'qui in unitate catholica Christi mysteriis inbuitur sanus fit a quocumque peccatorum languore detenebatur, quisque autem ab unitate discrepat salutem quae ab uno est consequi non valet.' *CC* cxxii, 163. 57–60; *De Tab.* III: 'Ceterum si quis loquatur linguis, si quis facultates pauperibus omnes distribuat, si quis tradat corpus suum ut ardeat, si unitatem catholicae caritatis non habuerit nihil illi prodest.' *CC* cxix A, 105. 472–74.

[71] *Hom.* II, 22: 'Quod enim Petro dictum est, *pasce oves meas,* omnibus utique dictum est. Hoc namque erant ceteri apostoli quod fuit Petrus, sed primatus Petro datur et unitas ecclesiae commendetur. Pastores sunt omnes, sed grex unus ostenditur qui ab apostolis omnibus tunc unanima consensione pascebatur et deinceps a successoribus communi cura pascitur quorum plurimi conditorem suum morte omnes autem vita sua clarificare probantur.' *CC* cxxii, 347. 204–11. The citation is from Cyprian, *De Unitate,* 4. See above, *n*[39].

[72] *Ep. ad Pleguinum,* 1: '. . . me audires a lascivientibus rusticis inter hereticos per pocula decantari' (ed. C. W. Jones, *Bedae Opera de Temporibus* [Medieval Academy of America, Cambridge, Mass.], 1943, 307. 5, 6).

bosom of our affection no less than those who live with us at present, and we may believe that we too can be received by them through the embrace of charity.'[73] And again: 'In this universal company of the just, different individuals succeed one another in turn and the lesser members rejoice to cleave to the footsteps of their greater predecessors and to their sayings and writings, so that they do not, through their own inadequacy, fall into error.'[74] Bede draws attention to the fact that the petitions of the Lord's Prayer are in the plural number: we pray for all Christians who have the same Father in heaven;[75] and he also observes that if we cannot imitate the holiness of life of the saints, we ought at least to make it our own by rejoicing with them and venerating them,[76] for great saints and lesser Christians will, in the resurrection, rejoice together in the common reward of eternal life.[77]

The Christian life is therefore to be lived in the fellowship of the Catholic Church, to which we are admitted when our guilt, inherited from Adam, is washed away by the water of baptism. Bede is, however, aware that the fellowship of the Church does not destroy the responsibility of the individual, to which we may now turn our attention.

For Bede, as we have seen, the Church is a stranger and sojourner in the present world, and the same holds true for her individual members. Man, by his very nature as a created being, is incapable of eternal happiness or stability except by participation in God, Who alone is stable, immutable and good.[78] It is therefore essential that the Christian should not put his trust in this unstable world, understanding by 'the world', as Bede had learned from Augustine,[79] the men who love this world,[80] turning from the Creator to the creature.[81] Between the world and the Church there is implacable hostility.[82] So Bede, commenting on I John 2:15: *If any man love the world, the love of the Father is not in him,* writes: 'Let no one lie to himself. One heart does not contain two loves so much at variance with one another. Whence indeed the Lord says: *No man can serve two masters,* and again: *You cannot serve God and mammon.* For just as the love of the Father is the fount and origin of all the virtues, so love of the world is the root and fount of all the vices.'[83] Bede, like St. Paul, longed *to be*

[73] *De Tab.* II. *CC* cxix A, 62. 801–06.

[74] *De Temp.* II. *CC* cxix A, 204. 483–86.

[75] *In Ez. et Neem.* II: 'dominum precemur iuxta ipsum dominicae orationis exemplum in qua sibi nemo specialiter panem cotidianum dari vel peccata dimitti vel se specialiter a temptatione et malo liberari sed potius pro omnibus qui eundem habent patrem in caelo orare iubetur.' *CC* cxix A, 302. 567–72.

[76] Ibid., III: '*Benedixit autem populus viris qui se sponte obtulerunt ut habitarent in Hierusalem.* Et nos sublimen vitam electorum quam sequi imitando non possumus congaudendo ac venerando nostram facere debemus.' *CC* cxix A, 375. 1426–29.

[77] Ibid.: '[In] tempore resurrectionis non solum illi qui vel evangelizando verbum vel fortiter in operibus fidei persistendo ecclesiam aedificaverant fructum sui magni laboris accipiunt magnum sed et infirmiores quique eiusdem fidei consortes una eandem cum eis vitae aeternae perceptione laetantur.' *CC* cxix A, 385. 1824–29.

[78] *In Luc.* III: 'nihil est per semet ipsum stabile nihil immutabile nihil bonum nisi deitas sola. Omnes vero creaturae ut beatitudinem aeternitatis vel immutabilitatis obtineant non hoc per suam naturam sed per creatoris sui participationem et gratiam consequuntur.' *CC* cxx, 230. 2510–15.

[79] *In Ep. I Ioh.: 'Nolite mirari, fratres, si odit vos mundus* (iii. 13). Mundum dilectores mundi dicit. Nec mirandum quod qui amant mundum fratrem a mundi amore separatum, et coelestibus tantum desideriis intentum, amare non possunt.' *PL* xciii, 102 C. Cf. Aug., *In Ep. Ioh. ad Parthos, Tr.* 5, 9. *PL* xxxv, 2017.

[80] *Hom.* II, 17: 'Mundum autem appellat homines mundi huius amori deditos sicut e contra sancti qui caelestium desiderio flagrant caeli recte vocantur.' *CC* cxxii, 302. 58–303. 61.

[81] Ibid., I, 8: 'Mundum . . . hos loco dicit homines mundi amore deceptos atque inhaerando creaturae ab agnoscenda creatoris sui maiestate reflexos.' *CC* cxxii, 56. 157–59.

[82] *In Ep. I Ioh.* (iii. 13). Cited above, *n*[79].

[83] Ibid.: 'Nemo sibi mentiatur. Unum cor duos tam sibi adversarios amores non capit. Unde et Dominus ait: *Nemo potest duobus dominis servire;* et iterum: *Non potestis Deo servire et mammonae.* Sicut enim charitas Patris fons est omnium et origo virtutum, ita dilectio mundi cunctorum est radix et fons vitiorum.' *PL* xciii, 92C.

dissolved and to be with Christ, to pass from the 'night of this present world'[84] into the fulness of light in the Kingdom of God. Thus, for him, a truly Christian death can never be an occasion for mourning but, rather, a re-enactment of the *Nunc dimittis* of Simeon. 'Happy indeed shall that man see the death of his flesh who has first striven to see the Lord's Christ with the eyes of his heart by having his conversation in the heavenly Jerusalem and by frequenting the threshold of the temple of God, that is by following the holy examples of the saints in whom the Lord dwells, and by sighing with the Psalmist: *One thing have I sought of the Lord which I will require: that I may dwell in the house of the Lord all the days of my life, that I may see the will of the Lord.*'[85] No one can read the Ecclesiastical History without observing the loving detail with which Bede describes the deaths of his holy men and women—a detail which is free from any morbidity, though there is in his descriptions a pathos which can sometimes move the reader to tears. Bede does not, of course, ignore that other aspect of death: the dreadful judgement-seat of Christ before which we must all appear. He says, indeed, that we ought not to celebrate our earthly birthdays or at any time indulge in carnal pleasures but rather anticipate the day of our death with tears and prayers and frequent fasting,[86] and on his own death-bed he quoted, in his own English tongue, a solemn poem on the last dread journey.[87] But he also quoted the words of St. Ambrose: 'I have not so lived as to be ashamed to live among you; yet neither do I fear to die, for we have a loving Lord.'[88]

But how is the individual Christian, living within the fellowship of the Church and nourished by the sacraments—and this, as we have seen, Bede takes for granted—to prepare himself for the Christian death by leading a Christian life? The answer is, by the practice of the virtue of humility to which must be added the performance of good works. 'After the rudiments of the faith, after laying the foundations of humility in ourselves by following the example of holier men, a wall of good works must be raised on high, like courses of stones laid one upon another, by walking and advancing from virtue to virtue.'[89] Bede repeatedly dwells on the beauty of humility, which was displayed by Christ in His own person when He was born in a stable[90] and when He sat in the Temple questioning the doctors.[91] It was indeed fitting that the human race, which had perished by the sickness of pride, should be healed by the medicine of humility.[92] 'The Lord our maker and redeemer, wishing to heal the wounds of our pride has enjoined us to take the way of humility.'[93] Accordingly, we should take care

[84] *De Tab.* III: '*Et usque mane luceat coram domino* [*Ex.* xxvii. 21]. Cum enim transacta nocte saeculi huius mane futuri saeculi claruerit de quo dicit propheta, *Mane adstabo tibi et videbo* [Ps. v. 5], non iam ultra lucerna librorum indigebimus apparante et illustrante nos vera luce mundi de quo dicit propheta: *Vobis autem timentibus nomen orietur sol iustitiae* [Mal. iv. 2].' *CC* cxix A, 95. 88–93. Cf. *In Apoc.* I (ii. 28). *PL* xciii, 140 B C.

[85] *In Luc.* I. *CC* cxx, 66. 1838–45.

[86] *Hom.* II, 23: 'Non enim festis diem nostri natalis in memoriam revocare non ullum tempus inlecebris indulgere carnalibus sed diem potius exitus nostri debemus lacrimis et precibus et crebris praevenire ieiuniis.' *CC* cxxii, 351. 92–352. 95.

[87] *Ep. Cuthberti de obitu Bedae* in *Bede's Ecclesiastical History* ed. Colgrave & Mynors, pp. 582, 583.

[88] Ibid., quoting Paulinus, *Vita Ambrosii,* 45. *PL* xiv, 43 A. The words also appealed to St. Augustine (Possidius, *Vita Augustini,* 27).

[89] *De Temp.* I. *CC* cxix A, 156. 356–62.

[90] *Hom.* I, 6: 'Ille quem caelum et caeli caelorum non capiunt parvi praesepis angustia continetur ut amplitudinem nobis supernarum sedium tribueret.' *CC* cxxii, 41. 175–77.

[91] *In Luc.* I: 'Quasi fons sapientiae doctorum medius sedet sed quasi exemplar humilitatis audire prius et interrogare doctores quam instruere quaerit indoctos. Ne etenim parvuli a senioribus erubescant discere et ipse ob aetatis humanae congruentiam hominibus auscultare non erubescit Deus.' *CC* cxx, 72. 2087–91.

[92] *Hom.* I, 17: 'Nam quia peste superbiae adtactum genus humanum perierat decebat ut medicamentum humilitatis quo sanaretur prima mox incipientis salutis tempora praetenderent.' *CC* cxxii, 21. 3–6.

[93] *Hom.* II, 21. CC cxxii, 335. 1–6.

that whatever good we do should be ascribed to the Lord, while at the same time recognizing that our evil actions are our own, though inspired by the devil.[94] The steps of the ladder whereby we ascend to heaven (as Bede had learned from St. Benedict) are the degrees of humility.[95]

It is then on the foundation of humility that the edifice of good works is raised. The task is not an easy one, but requires effort and struggle.[96] It is, for example, of no avail to come to hear the Word of God and then immediately turn away to worldly matters.[97] We ought, rather, while we live upon earth to try to imitate the life of the angels in heaven. 'They love God and their neighbours, imitate this; they help the wretched—not angels, who are all happy, but men—imitate this; they are humble, mild and peaceful among themselves, they obey God's command, imitate this, so far as you can; they neither speak, perform or think anything evil, idle or unjust, they devote themselves unweariedly with tongue and mind to the praise of God, do you imitate this, so far as you can.'[98] To do this, to live the angelic life so far as may be while on earth, requires discipline of body as well as of the mind by fasting, vigils, and prayers,[99] by means of which the flesh is disciplined and boasting quelled; and by almsgiving, by which avarice is vanquished.[100] Almsgiving, as Bede points out, does not consist simply in supplying physical needs, but also in giving spiritual help and guidance according to our ability.[101] The advance to virtue will not be without its reverses and Christians will, from time to time, fall into sin, for which they must ask God's pardon in their prayers[102] or, if the sin be a grave one, receive absolution from a priest.[103]

Bede, although he hates sin, nevertheless recognizes that, under God, it may sometimes operate to the eventual salvation of the sinner. Just as the Babylonian captivity helped bring the Jews to a state of penitence, so it sometimes happens that a man who has previously lived a careless life but without committing any serious sin may, by a sudden grievous lapse, be brought to a consciousness of his negligence to a new and more careful frame of mind.[104] Something similar may occur in the life of the Church

[94] *De Tab.* I (cited above, *n*[62]).

[95] See above, *n*[25].

[96] *Hom.* I, 1: 'populus fidelium non statim post baptisma caelestis patriae potest gaudia subire sed primo longis virtutum exercendus agonibus ac deinde perpetuis supernae beatitudinis est donandus muneribus.' *CC* cxxii, 3. 52–55. Cf. *Hom.* I, 24. *CC* cxxii, 170. 1–9.

[97] *Hom.* II, 11: 'Quid enim prodest ad audiendum verbum Dei convenire et expleto auditu ad inania mox et saecularia conloquia vel acta converti?' *CC* cxxii, 258. 196–98.

[98] *De Tab.* I. *CC* cxix A, 13. 308–14.

[99] *Hom.* II, 16: '. . . per macerationem carnis adversarii spiritalis machinas evitare et ad angelorum debeamus pervenire consortium.' *CC* cxxii, 296. 223–25. Cf. *De Tab.* I. *CC* cxix A, 84. 1675–83.

[100] *In Luc.* I: 'Qui cum alibi praeciperat ne iustitiam nostram coram hominibus faciamus in eiusdem definitione ieiunium tantum elemosinam atque orationem subiunxit triplici scilicet hostis telo totidem arma defensionis opponens ut ieiunio concupiscentia carnis elemosinis avaritia precibus iactantia pellatur meritorum.' *CC* cxx, 99. 3164–69.

[101] *In Ep. I Ioh.* (iii. 18): *'Filioli mei, non diligamus verbo, neque lingua,* etc. *Opere,* videlicet, ut cum frater aut soror nudi sunt, et indigent victu quotidiano, demus eis quae necessaria sunt corpori. Similiter cum spiritualibus donis eis egere conspicimus, praestemus eorum necessitati quae possumus.' *PL* xciii, 103 D. *De Temp.* I *CC* cxix A, 151. 184–92.

[102] *Hom.* II, 14: 'Ipse [sc. Christus] levioribus cotidianisque nostris erratibus sine quibus haec vita transigi non potest cotidiana confessionis et intercessionis mutuae medicamenta concessit.' *CC* cxxii, 273. 57–274. 59. The reference to daily venial sins is an echo of Augustine, *Enchiridion,* xix,71.

[103] *In Ez. et Neem.* II: 'per sacerdotum necesse est manus diluantur in baptismo et consecrentur domino quicumque ad consortium sanctae ecclesiae pertingere desiderant, per sacerdotum aeque officium debent reconciliari sanctae ecclesiae paenitendo qui ab eius societate peccando recesserant et in servitium diaboli qui in captivitatem Babylonii regis in peccatis perseverando deciderant.' *CC* cxix A, 321. 1344–50.

[104] Ibid., I: '. . . multis qui in pace ecclesiae neglegenter vixerant subito errasse et in flagitia aliqua cecidisse profuit dum post casum paenitendo erecti vigilantius domino servire coeperunt et qui pigri ac desides in innocentia stare videbantur per accidentem sibi ruinam

—the fall of one of its members may act as a warning to many others, the rise of heresies may encourage Christian theologians to produce great works which would otherwise have remained unwritten.[105] Bede notes that a similar conversion may occur without any sin supervening; a slothful Christian may suddenly be moved by the words of his teachers or the Scriptures to a more enthusiastic way of life.[106]

Altogether, Bede's discussion of the details of the Christian life is marked by shrewdness and spiritual insight. For example, however highly he may prize virginity, he recognizes that unless it is supplemented by the performance of good works it is of no value—the physical integrity of the foolish virgins was no advantage to them when the Bridegroom came since they lacked the light of internal purity, the chastity of the heart.[107] Again, Bede observes that a man can easily denounce homicide while remaining unaware of the more serious evil of hatred festering within himself; or accuse his neighbour of fornication without recognzing that he is himself puffed up with pride in his own chastity; or condemn a drunkard without seeing that he himself is consumed with envy.[108] Many, he remarks, have learned to turn the other cheek without having learned how to love the man who strikes them.[109] Again, with regard to wealth, Bede quotes with approval the comment of St. Jerome, that when Christ said: *You cannot serve God and mammon,* He did not condemn the possession of riches but enslavement to them; one should own wealth as a master, not be its servant.[110] He remarks that Dives was not left in hell because he had been rich, but because he had not been merciful and humble, while Lazarus was not received into Abraham's bosom because he had been poor but because he had been humble and innocent.[111] The essential characteristic of holy poverty is not the lack of possession but contempt of visible things, which makes Christ's poor despicable in the eyes of the world. The rich, on the other hand, as those who set their riches above Christ.[112]

ammoniti sunt sollertius erga sui custodiam contra omnes antiqui hostis insidias accingi.' *CC* cxix A, 278. 1495–1500.

[105] Ibid., III: 'Sic etenim saepe sancta ecclesia ex detrimentis suis maiora recipit incrementa cum uno per incuriam lapso in peccatum plures exemplo eius territi ad persistendum in castitate fidei fiunt cautiores, saepe idem ipsi qui peccaverunt maiores post actam paenitentiam bonorum operum fructus ferre incipiunt quam ante incursum peccati ferre consuerant.' *CC* cxix A, 377. 1517–23.

[106] Ibid., II: 'Quod eodem nunc ordine in sancta ecclesia geritur dum hi qui malignorum vel hominum vel spirituum insidiis retardati tepidores erga opus bonum aliquamdiu permanserant repente verbis sive doctorum fidelium seu divinarum scripturarum correcti in tantum bonis studiis fervere incipiunt ut nullis temptationum valeant machinis vinci atque a proposito suae intentionis revocari.' *CC* xcix A, 290. 83–90.

[107] *De Tab.* III: 'Sic nimirum sic castimonia carnis saepe non nullis castimoniam cordis adimit cum tanto segnius bonis insistere operibus curant quanto minus perspiciunt quia nil castimoniae custodia absque aliorum augmento bonorum valeat quae tamen adiunctis bonis actibus magnam habenti gloriam conquirit. Denique virginibus stultis nil castitas profuit carnis quibus veniente sponso lumen defuit internae puritatis.' *CC* xcix A, 120. 1050–57.

[108] *Hom.* I, 25: '. . . et prius quam peccantem proximum corripiamus et postquam debitae castigationis illi ministerium reddiderimus nos ipsos digna humilitatis investigatione perpendamus ne forte aut eisdem quae in illis reprehendimus aut aliis quibuslibet simus facinoribus inretiti. Evenit enim saepe ut qui verbi gratia homicidam publice peccantem iudicant peius odiorum malum quo ipsi in secreta depopulantur non sentiant; qui fornicatorem accusant pestem superbiae qua ipsi de sua castitate extolluntur ignorent; qui ebriosum condemnant virus invidiae quo exeduntur ipsi non videant.' *CC* cxxii, 180. 97–181. 106.

[109] *In Luc.* II: 'Multi autem alteram maximillam praebere noverunt diligere vero illum a quo feriuntur ignorant.' *CC* cxx, 144. 1717–18.

[110] Ibid., V (quoting Hieron., *In Mat.* I, cap. vi. *PL* xxvi, 45 A). *CC* cxx, 300. 162–65.

[111] *In Ep. Iac. Exp.*: 'Sed non ideo divitem [Abraham] reliquit quia dives erat, quod et ipse fuerat, sed quia misericors et humilis, quod ipse fuerat, esse despexerat.' *PL* xciii, 13 B.

[112] Ibid.: '*Nonne Deus eligit pauperes in hoc mundo, divites in fide, et haeredes regni quod promisit diligentibus se? Pauperes* vocat humiles, et qui per contemptum rerum visibilium, fide autem invisibilium divitiarum mundo huic despicabiles parent . . . [Divites] nimirum qui divitias suas Christo praeponunt.' *PL* xciii, 18 D, 19 A, B.

Shrewd Christian common sense is shown by Bede's comment of incautious swearing. It is better to break an oath and endure the guilt of perjury than to observe it when it seems clear that some far worse crime will result, as happened when King Herod kept his promise to the daughter of Herodias and was thereby driven to murder John the Baptist.[113] Again, Christ's injunction: *Give to everyone that asketh,* is not meant to be observed literally when the gift will be to the disadvantage of the recipient. If a man asks for money to enable him to oppress the innocent or to go to a brothel he should be refused—though in refusing one should make clear the grounds of denial. In this way one should indeed *give to everyone that asketh,* but not necessarily what he asks.[114] A charitable reproof may be the best gift one can give a man.

The Christian life must be nourished by prayer, for Christ Himself did not only pray for mankind while He was upon earth but now, being ascended into heaven and sitting on the right hand of the Father, continues to intercede for us and, dwelling in the hearts of His elect through faith, stirs them up to pray.[115] Thus all prayer becomes a communal activity—in the Lord's Prayer no one specifically prays for himself, but for all.[116] Prayer, together with the preaching and exhortation of the doctors, is the one support of the Church against all her enemies.[117] For the individual, it is a way of expressing penitence for past sins and of imploring the divine mercy and aid.[118] But prayer is more than intercession, either for others or for oneself—it is the natural action of the Christian man. Thus Bede, when commenting upon Christ's visit to the temple, following His triumphant entry into Jerusalem, says: 'So we too when we come to any town or village in which there is a house of prayer dedicated to God, ought first to turn aside to this and, when we have commended ourselves to God in prayer, then go about the worldly business for which we came.'[119] There is a simplicity about these words, perhaps deriving from St. Benedict's well-known instructions with regard to the monastic church: 'If anyone desire to pray in private, let him go in quietly and pray.'[120]

As regards the manner of our prayer, Bede emphasises that it must involve an intention of the mind and not simply a recitation of words. 'Some people go into church

[113] *Hom.* II, 23: 'At si aliquid forte incautius nos iurasse contigerit quod observatum scilicet peiorem vergat in exitum libere illud consilio salubriore mutandum noverimus ac magis instante necessitate peierandum nobis quam pro vitando periurio in aliud crimen gravius esse divertendum. . . . Iuravit Herodes dare saltatrici quodcumque postulasset ab eo et ne peiurus diceretur a convivis ipsum convivium sanguine polluit dum prophetae mortem saltationis fecit praemium.' *CC* cxxii, 352. 110–15, 120–23.

[114] *In Luc.* II: *'Omni autem petenti de tribue. Omni petenti,* inquit, non "omnia petenti," ut id des quod dare honeste et iuste potes. Quid si enim pecuniam petat qua innocentem conetur opprimere? Quid si postremo stuprum petat? Sed ne multa persequar quae sunt innumerabilia id profecto dandum est quod nec tibi nec alteri noceat quantum sciri aut credi ab homine potest et cui iuste negaveris quod petit indicanda est ipsa iustitia ut non eum inanem dimittas. Ita *omni petenti* tribues quamvis non semper id quod petit tribues et aliquando melius aliquid tribues cum petentem iniusta correxeris.' *CC* cxx, 144. 1730–39.

[115] *De Tab.* III: *'Deprecabitur* autem *super cornua* altaris [cf. Ex. xxx. 10] quia et ipse [sc. Christus] non solum inter homines conversatus pro hominibus oravit verum etiam nunc ad dexteram patris in caelestibus sedens interpellat pro nobis et in cordibus electorum per fidem inhabitans dum eos ad deprecandum excitat recte ipse deprecari narratur.' *CC* cxix A, 132. 1536–41.

[116] *In Ez. et Neem.* II, cited above, *n*[75].

[117] Ibid., III: *'Et oravimus Deum nostrum et posuimus custodes super murum die et nocte contra eos.* Hoc est unicum adversus hostes universos ecclesiae suffugium, oratio videlicet ad Deum et industria doctorum qui die noctuque in lege eius meditantes corda fidelium contra insidias diaboli ac militum eius praedicando consolando exhortando praemuniant.' *CC* cxix A, 357. 723–28.

[118] *Hom.* I, 22: 'Ideoque necesse est talis ut reatum suum cognoverit mox ad preces lacrimasque confugiat sanctorum crebras intercessiones et auxilia quaerat qui pro animae eius salute rogantes domino dicant, precamur domine *miserator et misericors patiens et multae miserationis* dimitte eam quia clamat post nos dimitte reatum et dona gratiam quia nostrum intimo affectu quaerit pronus suffragium.' *CC* cxxii, 159. 118–25.

[119] *In Marc.* III. *CC* cxx, 575. 1298–1303 (tr. by Plummer, i. p. xiii).

[120] Bened., *Reg.*, 52. 4. *CSEL* lxxv, 122.

and prolong their prayer with many words but, turning their thoughts elsewhere in their heart, cannot even recall what they have said, praying with their mouths indeed but wandering afar in their minds and losing all fruit of prayer, thinking their prayer will be heard by God which they themselves who offered it do not hear.'[121] Bede is, however, fully aware of the practical difficulties of keeping the mind fixed in prayer, and of the hosts of wandering, idle and impure thoughts which so often assail it, and he accordingly recommends that we should, at all times, try to exercise a discipline over our thoughts, and particularly devote ourselves to the reading of the Scriptures.[122]

As we should expect, Bede insists that prayer is only real when it is matched by our actions. 'These truly call upon the Lord who do not in their lives contradict the words of their prayer; who, when they are about to offer Him their prayers, first strive to fulfil His commands, who when they are about to say: *Forgive us our debts as we forgive our debtors* have already fulfilled His injunction: *Whenever you stand praying, forgive, if you have aught against anyone, that your Father also which is in heaven may forgive you your trespasses.*'[123] And again: 'We cannot otherwise fulfil that apostolic precept *pray without ceasing* unless by God's grace we so direct all our acts, words, thoughts and indeed our very silences that each and every one of these is tempered by regard of His fear, so that all may be rendered profitable to our salvation.'[124]

With personal prayer must go the corporate worship of the Church, which is expressed above all in the celebration of the Eucharist in which Christ daily '*takes away the sins of the world* and washes out from our daily sins in His blood; when the memory of His blessed passion is repeated at the altar; when by the ineffable sanctification of the Spirit the creatures of bread and wine are changed into the sacrament of His Body and Blood, not being delivered into the hands of faithless men to be hurt and slain but being received by the mouths of the faithful for salvation.'[125] Bede regretted the neglect of communion by the laity of his day, and ascribed it to lack of proper teaching. Even devout laymen communicated only at Christmas, Epiphany, and Easter, and in Bede's opinion there were many of the laity who, 'without any scruple of controversy,' might safely communicate every Sunday and on Saints' Days as well.[126]

But life below, with its good works, its prayers, and even with its nourishment by the sacraments, is only a shadow of reality, a preparation for the future, for the glory of the resurrection 'when all the elect are refreshed with the flesh of the Lamb without spot, our God and Lord, no longer believing in sacrament but beholding in reality and truth.'[127] 'The whole life of the elect with one and the same faith and charity directs its course to heaven and attains to one and the same end: The Vision of God.'[128] For Bede, the characteristic quality of eternal blessedness will be the contemplation of the beauty of God, no longer hidden beneath forms and signs but revealed to His saints for ever. This is his understanding of the text of Revelation: *Blessed are they which are bidden to the marriage feast of the Lamb* (19:9). 'Those therefore who come to the refreshment of heavenly contemplation when the time of this present life is ended are

[121] *Hom.* I, 22. *CC* cxxii, 160. 145–50.

[122] Ibid.: 'Multum . . . iuvat orationis puritas si in omni loco vel tempore nos ab actibus temperemus inlicitis si semper ab otiosis sermocinationibus auditum pariter castigemus et linguam si in lege domini ambulare et testimonia eius adsuecamus toto corde scrutare.' *CC* cxxi, 160. 163–67. Cf. *In Marc.* I. *CC* cxx, 454. 659–72; *In Luc.* II. *CC* cxx, 120. 789–803.

[123] *Hom.* II, 14. *CC* cxxii, 274. 73–81.

[124] Ibid., II, 22. *CC* cxxii, 344. 94–345. 99.

[125] Ibid., I, 15. *CC* cxxii, 106. 22–28.

[126] *Ep ad Ecgbert. Ep.*, 15 (Plummer, p. 419).

[127] *In Ez. et Neem.* II: 'immolatio paschae gloriam insinuet resurrectionis cum omnes electi carne agni immaculati, id est Dei et domini nostri, non amplius in sacramento credentes sed in re ipsa ac veritate videntes reficiuntur.' *CC* cxix A, 306. 737–40.

[128] *De Tab.* II: 'omnis electorum vita una eademque fide et caritate ad caelestia tendit in unum eundemque finem divinae visionis pervenit.' *CC* cxix A, 67. 991–93.

assuredly called to the marriage feast of the Lamb.'[129] This is why the contemplative life must be reckoned higher than the active, necessary as they both are in the present world, for the contemplative life 'is not destined to be ended by death like the active, but after death will be fulfilled more perfectly by the coming of the Lord. For active labour ends with death, receiving after death its eternal reward.'[130] And what is this eternal reward? It is the state 'in which our nature will be eternally conjoined to the Vision of God.'[131] This is the 'solemn festivity' where 'all evils being done away, our whole life will consist in the vision and praise of God. . . . For when we have earned our entrance into our fatherland, the land of the living and the gift of the heavenly kingdom which the Lord has promised us, then as we have known Him perfectly so also we shall be able to praise Him perfectly, according to that word of the Psalmist: *And in His temple all shall do Him honour.*'[132] 'In that supernal country where the eyes of the saints behold Christ the King in His beauty the grace of divine and fraternal love shines throughout. . . . love alone reigns.'[133] To this country of eternal light we must go by the darkness of the transitory passage of death;[134] but this darkness had no terrors for Bede, for he looked for the rising of the day-star Jesus Christ 'Who, when the night of this world is ended, promises and reveals to His saints the eternal light of life.'[135]

[129] *In Apoc.* III: 'Qui ergo, finito praesentis vitae tempore, ad refectionem supernae contemplationis veniunt, profecto ad coenam Agni vocantur.' *PL* xciii, 188 D. Cf. *Hom.* I, 19. *CC* cxxii, 134. 13–18.

[130] *Hom.* I, 9: ' . . . statum contemplativae virtutis . . . quae non per mortem finienda ut activa sed post mortem est perfectius domino veniente complenda. Activus namque labor cum morte deficit mercedem post mortem accepturus aeternam.' *CC* cxxii, 65. 189–92.

[131] *De Temp.* II: ' . . . merces aeterna . . . in qua nostra natura in aeternum divinae visioni coniungitur.' *CC* cxix A, 227. 1373–74.

[132] *Hom.* II, 16. *CC* cxxii, 294. 155–56, 296. 208–13.

[133] *De Temp.* I: 'in superna illa patria ubi regem Christum in decore suo vident oculi sanctorum sola caritatis divinae ac fraternae gratia per omnia fulget . . . in superna patria sola caritas regnat.' *CC* cxix A, 176. 1175–77, 178. 1255.

[134] *De Tab.* II: ' . . . Quasi enim occidit ei sol qui ab hac temporali luce per tenebras transitoriae mortis ad gaudia lucis et vitae transmigrat aeternae, quasi occidit omni ecclesiae sol in occidente ut verius in oriente tenebris transeuntibus oriatur cum finita in adventu domini vita saeculi praesentis mox verum saeculi futuri mane iustis ac vera dies aeternitatis apparebit.' *CC* cxix A, 65. 933–39.

[135] *In Apoc.* I: 'Christus est stella matutina qui, nocte saeculi transacta, lucem vitae sanctis promittit et pandit aeternam.' *PL* xciii, 140 B, C.

XI

Bede and medieval civilization

The mortal remains of the Venerable Bede rest today in the cathedral church of Christ and Blessed Mary the Virgin, Durham. They were brought there in the early eleventh century by one Ælfred Westou, priest and sacrist of Durham and an enthusiastic amateur of that characteristically medieval form of devotion expressed in the acquisition, by fair means or foul, of the relics of the saints to the greater glory of God. The removal of Bede's remains to Durham, involving as it did considerable preliminary planning and solitary nocturnal vigil before the final successful snatch, was one of his more brilliant coups, upon which he seems especially to have preened himself. The bones were first kept in the coffin of St Cuthbert, being subsequently removed to a reliquary near the saint's tomb. In 1370 they were placed in the Galilee Chapel, where they now lie under a plain table-tomb of blue marble, made in 1542 after the medieval shrine had been defaced. Bede himself would certainly have preferred that his body should have been left in its grave among his brethren at Jarrow, there to await the coming of Christ which he so ardently desired to see; but if a removal had to be made, we need not doubt that he would have been content to lie at Durham, near but not too near the shrine of St Cuthbert, the great saint and patron of the north, under a modest tombstone, so much more in keeping with his nature than the earlier and richer shrine, despoiled by the commissioners of Henry VIII.

Bede in his writings gives many accounts of miraculous happenings; but no cult of miracles was associated with his name. Rather, there was a spontaneous recognition of his quality, expressed in St Boniface's phrase: 'a candle of the church'. In him may be seen an outstanding example of that flowering of Christian culture in Northumbria produced by the encounter between the Irish tradition of Iona and Lindisfarne and the Latin order of Wearmouth and Jarrow in the seventh and eighth centuries. This flowering is an astonishing phenomenon, inviting exaggerated comparisons with Periclean Athens or the renaissance of the twelfth century in western Europe. But when all qualifications have been made and all proportions duly guarded, there remains an extraordinary cultural achievement, accomplished within a few generations from the time of the conversion to Christianity. Works of art like the Codex Amiatinus and the Lindisfarne Gospels and the Ruthwell and

Bewcastle crosses; vernacular poems like those of Cædmon and *The Dream of the Rood*; and Latin compositions like the anonymous lives of Gregory the Great and Cuthbert and Eddius Stephanus's biography of Wilfrid – all these are a testimony to a genius latent in the Northumbrians and brought into being by the inspiration of Christianity. To these must be added the work of Bede. Bede cannot, of course, be regarded simply as a Northumbrian, nor even as an English, figure. He is a European, writing in the international – or supranational – tradition of the Fathers of the Church; but even in this he may be said to exemplify Northumbrian tradition. After all, the uncial hand of the Codex Amiatinus and the inhabited vine-scroll ornamentation of the Ruthwell cross are themselves a reminder of continental associations.

The character of Bede – 'vir maxime doctus et minime superbus' as William of Malmesbury called him[1] – presents something of an historical anomaly. Our biographical information is scanty in the extreme, so that our knowledge of his personality has to be formed from his writings – and Bede is one of the least egotistical of authors. Yet in a strange fashion Bede reveals himself through his pages, disarming criticism and making his reader feel that he knows the writer as a man.[2] One may indeed believe that it is Bede himself, as well as his writings, who has attracted many of the scholars who have studied them. In Charles Plummer, one of the greatest of Bede's editors, whose personal life in no small measure resembled that of his author,[3] Sir Roger Mynors has noted 'qualities of heart as well as head',[4] and one may observe similar qualities in more recent students of Bede, like Max Ludwig Wolfram Laistner and Bertram Colgrave.

There is an historical cliché to the effect that St Augustine of Hippo resembles a man standing on the frontiers of two worlds: the ancient world that was passing away, and the medieval world that was coming into being. In a certain sense the same is true of Bede. In the circumstances of his life he was a man of the early Middle Ages, as surely as Augustine was a man of the later Roman Empire; but as a Christian teacher – and this would seem, from the circumstance of Bede's life and from his own words[5] to have been his own view of his vocation – he stood in an unbroken tradition, descending from the Fathers of the Church. Indeed, as everyone knows who attempts to work on the text of Bede's scriptural commentaries, he has so thoroughly assimilated

1 William of Malmesbury, *De Gestis Regum Anglorum*, ed. W. Stubbs, Rolls Series (1887–9) I, I.

2 W. P. Ker, *The Dark Ages* (Edinburgh and London, 1923): 'The reputation of Bede seems always to have been exempt from the common rationalist criticism, and this although his books are full of the things a Voltairian student objects to' (pp. 141–2).

3 See the memoir by P. S. A[llen], 'Charles Plummer 1851–1927', *Proc. of the Brit. Acad.* 15 (1929), 463–76 (pub. sep. 1931): 'The keynote of his life was to take as little as possible for himself in order to have the more to give to others' (p. 466).

4 *Bede's Ecclesiastical History*, ed. B. Colgrave and R. A. B. Mynors (Oxford, 1969), p. lxxiii.

5 *HE* v. 24.

the patristic idiom and the patristic fashion of thought that it is often difficult to decide whether he is quoting from another author or expressing himself in his own words. There is no question here of conscious plagiarism, for Bede, more than most medieval authors, is anxious to acknowledge his indebtedness to others.[1] Rather, he regarded his commentaries as elementary text-books for those unable or unwilling to read more distinguished authors and his own contributions as little more than glosses on what had already been said authoritatively by those greater than he. A good example of this is provided by his treatment of the verse: '[Ishmael] shall be a wild man, his hand against all and the hands of all against him; and he shall pitch his tents over against all his brethren' (Genesis XVI.12). To explain this passage, Bede first quotes Jerome, without naming him: 'He declares that his seed will dwell in the wilderness – that is, the wandering Saracens with no fixed abode, who harry all the peoples dwelling on the borders of the desert and are assailed by them.'[2] Bede then adds his own observation: 'But these things are of the past. For now is *his hand against all and the hands of all against him* to such a degree that they oppress with their domination the whole of Africa throughout its length and hold the greatest part of Asia too, and some part of Europe, hateful and hostile to all.'[3] In this comment Bede makes no mention of the period of more than three centuries which had elapsed between Jerome's day and his own. He does not question the identification of the Saracens with the descendants of Ishmael, or with the Arab invaders of Syria, Egypt and Spain. He accepts the tradition and merely brings it up to date.[4]

Bede's sense of writing within the patristic tradition is exemplified in another way, in his detestation of heresy and schism. He denounces the 'Arian madness' which corrupted the whole world and even invaded Britain[5] and sees it prefigured in the Pale Horse of the Apocalypse;[6] declares that the precepts and promises of Holy Scripture overturn both the Adoptionism of the Photinians and the Dualism of the Manichees;[7] and warns his readers that Donatists and all others who separate themselves from the unity of the Catholic Church will have their place with the goats at the left hand of Christ on the Day of Judgement.[8] The menace of Pelagianism is recognized and its teaching

[1] See E. F. Sutcliffe, 'Quotations in the Venerable Bede's Commentary on St Mark', *Biblica* 7 (1926), 428–39 and M. L. W. Laistner, 'Source-Marks in Bede Manuscripts', *JTS* 34 (1933), 350–4.

[2] Hieronymus, *Hebraicae Questiones in Libro Geneseos* XVI. 12, ed. P. Antin, Corpus Christianorum Series Latina 72, 21, lines 1–4.

[3] Bede, *Libri Quatuor in Principium Genesis* IV (XVI. 12), ed. C. W. Jones, CCSL 118A, 201, lines 250–6.

[4] On this, see R. W. Southern, *Western Views of Islam in the Middle Ages* (Cambridge, Mass., 1962), pp. 16–18; but note the qualification by C. W. Jones, CCSL 118A, ix, n. 19.

[5] *HE* I. 8.

[6] Bede, *Explanatio Apocalypsis* VI. 7, ed. Migne, Patrologia Latina 93, col. 147 C and D.

[7] Bede, *In Cantica Canticorum Allegorica Expositio* VI (PL 91, col. 1205 A and B).

[8] *In Cant.* V (PL 91, col. 1183 B); cf. *In Primam Epistolam S. Iohannis* (PL 93, col. 90 A and B).

denounced.[1] Julian of Eclanum, the ablest of the Pelagian apologists, had written a commentary on the Songs of Songs which was apparently still extant in Bede's time and Bede, when writing his own commentary explaining the canticle as an allegory of Christ and his church, devoted the first book to a refutation of Julian's teaching.[2] This concern with doctrinal error of the past seems to the modern reader somewhat surprising. Pelagianism, it is true, is often said to be a heresy to which the English are prone and Pelagian writings were still in circulation in Bede's day; but none of Bede's contemporaries was likely ever to see a Manichee,[3] while Donatism had never had much appeal outside Roman Africa and by Bede's day was as dead as Arianism. But such considerations probably never entered Bede's mind. For him the faith of the Fathers was as his own and their enemies were to be regarded as his.

It is, therefore, difficult to exaggerate the extent of patristic influence on Bede and misleading to confine it to the Latin tradition or even to those among the Greek Fathers whose works we know to have existed in Latin translation. Two examples of occasions on which Bede draws on an unexpected Greek tradition are provided by his sermon on the Decollation of St John Baptist. In this, Bede remarks that we ought not to celebrate our birthdays with feasts or at any time indulge in carnal delights but rather anticipate the day of our death with tears, prayers, and frequent fastings.[4] This rather depressing exhortation appears at first sight to be no more than a typical expression of claustral asceticism, and when a patristic source is discovered it comes as no surprise to find that Bede's immediate inspiration appears to be St Jerome who, with characteristic erudition, points out that the only persons recorded in scripture as having celebrated their birthdays were Pharaoh, who hanged his butler, and Herod, who beheaded John the Baptist.[5] But behind Jerome, and the source upon which he drew, is Origen;[6] and Bede here stands in a tradition of thought going back to the great Alexandrian exegete of the third century. Whether Bede had actually read Origen's homily for himself is not clear. It was available in Latin translation, and we know that the Latin version of another of Origen's homilies in the same series was used by Bede in his commentary on Samuel.[7] More than this we cannot say.

[1] Bede, *In Ep. I Ioh.* (PL 93, cols. 88B, 98B and C and 100A).

[2] Bede, *In Cant.* I (PL 91, cols. 1065 C-77B).

[3] I assume the virtual extinction of Manichaeism in western Europe between the end of Roman rule and its reintroduction from the east in the eleventh century; see Steven Runciman, *The Medieval Manichee* (Cambridge, 1955), p. 118.

[4] Bede, *Homeliarum Evangelii Libri II* II. 23, ed. D. Hurst, CCSL 122, 351, lines 92–5.

[5] Hieronymus, *Commentariorum in Evangelium Matthei Libri Quatuor* II (XIV. 7) (PL 26, col. 97 B and C).

[6] Origen, *In Leviticum Homilia* VIII. 3, ed. W. A. Baehrens, Die Griechischen Christlichen Schriftsteller, Origenes Werke VI, 396, line 20–397, line 4.

[7] Bede, *In Primam Partem Samuhelis Libri IIII* I (I Reg. IV. 18; CCSL 119, 45, lines 1420–3), citing Origen, *In Lev. Hom.* II. 2–4 (GCS, Origenes Werke VI, 292, line 4–296, line 22).

The second example is even more interesting. In the same sermon Bede refers to Herod's fatal promise to the daughter of Herodias, remarking that if we perceive that the performance of an incautious oath will entail a greater crime than its violation we should not hesitate to perjure ourselves and so avoid committing the worse offence – a piece of advice which directly contradicted the ethical assumptions of Bede's society, in which oath-breaking was one of the most shameful crimes that a man could commit.[1] Now in this case, as in the preceding instance, Bede's obvious source of inspiration is Jerome who, however, merely says that he will not excuse Herod for keeping his oath, since if the girl had demanded the murder of his father or mother he would certainly have refused.[2] It is Origen, in his commentary on Matthew, who says that the guilt of oath-keeping which led to the killing of the prophet was greater than the guilt of oath-breaking would have been.[3] Had Bede read Origen on Matthew? No Latin translation survives and the problem arises: is it possible that Bede had actually read the original Greek? Dom Hurst appears to think that he may have done so, judging from the reference in his edition of Bede's sermons.[4] I am not fully convinced of either Bede's ability or the availability of a Greek manuscript. Perhaps we should assume a Latin translation which has perished, or some reference in a florilegium? The problem remains; but the essential point is that Bede was drawing on a tradition which looks back to the third-century school of Alexandria. Dom Leclercq has emphasized the importance of the influence of Origen in determining the character of biblical exegesis in the west during the Middle Ages.[5] These examples, in indicating Bede's utilization of the past, also reveal his anticipation of the future.

It is not necessary to labour the theme of Bede's devotion to the Fathers, in view of his declared desire to walk 'iuxta vestigia patrum'.[6] Nevertheless, it should be added that his attitude to patristic authority was in no way servile, and he was prepared to disregard patristic exegesis if it seemed to him unreasonable. Thus, in discussing why Cain's offering was rejected by God and Abel's accepted, he is concerned to defend the calling of the husbandman, and to see Cain's sin, not in his offering but in the mind in which he made the offering: 'Cain was not rejected on account of the humble nature of his offering, seeing that he offered to God from his habitual livelihood. It was rather on

[1] I am grateful to Mr Christopher Ball of Lincoln College, Oxford, for pointing this out to me.

[2] Hieron., *In Matt.* II (XIV. 7) (PL 26, col. 97 C).

[3] Origen, *Matthäuserklärung* X. 22, ed. E. Klostermann, GCS, Origenes Werke X, 30, lines 20–3).

[4] Bede, *Hom.* II. 23 (CCSL 122, 352, lines 108–15).

[5] *The West from the Fathers to the Reformation, The Cambridge History of the Bible* II, ed. G. W. H. Lampe (Cambridge, 1969), pp. 194–6.

[6] Bede, *Expositio Actuum Apostolorum*, ed. M. L. W. Laistner (Cambridge, Mass., 1939), p. 3, line 9; *In Regum Librum XXX Quaestiones, Prolog.* (CCSL 119, 293, line 23); and *In Cant.* VII (PL 91, col. 1223 A).

account of the impious mind of the man who offered that he was rejected together with his gifts by him who searches all hearts.'[1] The significance of this exegesis lies in the fact that it ignores the view of Ambrose, whose treatise *De Cain et Abel* Bede had used in composing his commentary, that Abel's sacrifice was preferred to Cain's because it consisted of living animals and not insensate vegetables.[2] Ambrose was, for Bede, a great authority. He had, indeed, for a time been deterred from writing his own commentary on Luke because of the existence of Ambrose's;[3] but when the need arose, he was prepared to maintain his own opinion.

Indeed, when full justice has been done to the influence of the Fathers upon Bede, it remains true that his life was lived in another world than theirs, and that his learning and culture, however profound, were not those of a man of the later Roman Empire but of the Middle Ages. Bede's very scholarship is of a different character from that of Ambrose, Jerome and Augustine and, more important, his outlook is different. One obvious distinction is, of course, that they were all Latin speakers by birth, while Bede was not. For him Latin could never have the flavour and nuances of a mother tongue. This may explain why his Latin verses have never aroused much enthusiasm, even in the kindest critics[4] – few men can hope to write poetry in a foreign tongue.[5] Nevertheless, as we shall see, there are reasons for not laying too much stress on the alien character of Bede's Latin. Rather, the essential difference between Bede's Latin culture and that of the Fathers is that Bede had no foundation of classical literature such as they enjoyed. M. L. W. Laistner in a brilliant paper drew attention to Bede's limitations, and demonstrated how many of his citations from the classical authors were probably at second-hand, in contrast to those from Christian poets.[6] Here is the great cultural change; and if we are to understand Bede, we must try to discover how it came about.

Some clue to the problem is provided by Dom Jean Leclercq in a beautiful and learned study of monastic culture in the west during the early Middle

[1] Bede, *In Gen.* IV (IV. 3–4; CCSL 118A, 74, lines 42–6 and 49–52).

[2] Ambrose, *De Cain et Abel,* IV, IV. 3–4 (PL 14, col. 337B).

[3] Acca, *Epistola ad Bedam, apud* Bede, *In Lucae Evangelium Expositio* (CCSL 120, 5, lines 5–18).

[4] Helen Waddell, *The Wandering Scholars,* 7th ed. (London, 1934): 'He is a greater critic than craftsman; there are cadences in his prose lovelier than anything in his poetry' (pp. 38–9); and F. J. E. Raby, *A History of Christian-Latin Poetry,* 2nd ed. (Oxford, 1953): 'His was not a poetic nature' (p. 146).

[5] A fact of which Bede was aware. See his remark on Cædmon's hymn: 'Neque enim possunt carmina, quamvis optime composita, ex alia in aliam linguam ad verbum sine detrimento sui decoris ac dignitatis transferri' (*HE* IV. 24).

[6] M. L. W. Laistner, 'Bede as a Classical and a Patristic Scholar', *TRHS* 4th ser. 16 (1933), 69–94, repr. *The Intellectual Heritage of the Early Middle Ages: Selected Essays by M. L. W. Laistner,* ed. Chester G. Starr (Ithaca, N.Y., 1957), pp. 93–116 (to which all references are made); see esp. pp. 95–9.

Ages[1] which, although concentrating upon the period from the Caroline reform to the rise of Scholasticism, also throws light on the earlier period from the lifetime of St Benedict onwards and makes several references to Bede. Reading this work one is constantly carried into the world of Wearmouth and Jarrow. First, Leclercq emphasizes the significance of the Benedictine tradition in early medieval western monasticism.[2] Here, at first sight, some difficulty appears to arise. Was Bede in fact a Benedictine? We have been warned not to give too much credence to the belief that Wearmouth and Jarrow were centres of Benedictine monasticism or that Bede, from his earliest profession, was a Benedictine monk. 'Although the influence of the Benedictine Rule may have been considerable, especially as the eighth century advanced, the composite or mixed rule was probably characteristic of much of Anglo-Saxon monasticism during Bede's lifetime'[3]– such is the judgement of one expert. For our purposes, however, the question is not whether the rule occupied 'a preponderant though not an exclusive position'[4] in Benedict Biscop's foundations, but rather to what degree Bede's mind and thought were shaped by it. It is generally agreed that there is only one direct citation from the Rule in Bede – that from ch. 7 in the commentary on Ezra and Nehemiah;[5] but Dom Justin McCann has identified two unmistakable citations in the *History of the Abbots*[6] and to these may be added the 'dura et aspera' of ch. 58, cited in the commentary on the First Epistle of John,[7] while the 'compunctione lacrimarum' of ch. 20 is quoted in Bede's sermon on St John the Evangelist and echoed in the *De Tabernaculo*.[8] There is, indeed, an opportunity for a

[1] J. Leclercq, *The Love of Learning and the Desire for God: a Study of Monastic Culture*, trans. C. Misrahi (New York, 1962).

[2] *Ibid.* pp. 19ff.

[3] Peter Hunter Blair, *The World of Bede* (London, 1970), pp. 197 and 199.

[4] Justin McCann, *Saint Benedict* (London, 1938), p. 233. Dom McCann notes that not only were abbatial elections governed by the Rule (Bede, *Historia Abbatum*, §§11 and 16, ed. C. Plummer, *Venerabilis Baedae Opera Historica* (Oxford, 1896) I, 375 and 381; and *Vita Ceolfridi auctore Anonymo*, §16, ed. Plummer, *Bede* I, 393) but also Bede, *Hist. Abbat.* contains unacknowledged borrowings from the Rule: 'vero regi militans' (§1 (Plummer, *Bede*, p. 365) from *Benedicti Regula, Prolog.*, 3, ed. R. Hanslik, Corpus Scriptorum Ecclesiasticorum Latinorum 75, 2) and 'in pistrino, in orto, in coquina' (§8 (Plummer, *Bede*, p. 371) from *Reg.* XLVI. 1 (CSEL 75, 112–13)).

[5] Bede, *In Ezram et Neemiam Libri III* III (CCSL 119A, 350, line 466–351, line 473); *Reg.* VII. 6 and 7 (CSEL 75, 40–1).

[6] See above, n. 4.

[7] Bede, *In Ep. I Ioh.*: 'Quae enim natura dura sunt et aspera, spes coelestium praemiorum et amor Christi facit esse levia' (PL 93, col. 113 C); *Reg.* LVIII. 8: 'Praedicentur ei omnia dura et aspera, per quae itur ad deum' (CSEL 75, 134).

[8] Bede, *Hom.* I. 9: 'Contemplativa autem vita est cum longo quis bonae actionis exercitio edoctus diutinae orationis dulcedine instructus crebra lacrimarum conpunctione adsuefactus a cunctis mundi negotiis vacare et in sola dilectione oculum intendere didicerit' (CCSL 122, 64, lines 163–7), and *De Tabernaculo* III: 'Duobus namque modis lacrimarum et compunctionis status distinguitur' (CCSL 119 A, 137, lines 1700–2); *Reg.* XX. 3: 'Et non in multiloquio, sed in puritate cordis et conpunctione lacrimarum nos exaudiri sciamus' (CSEL 75, 75). It is, however, to be noted that this expression is to be found in Cassian, *Collationes*, IX. 28 (CSEL 13, 274, line 18), which was available in Bede's library, and cannot therefore constitute a decisive argument.

detailed study of the influence of the Rule on the thought of Bede by some competent scholar. For the present we need only observe that Bede was plainly within the Benedictine tradition in the broad sense of the term, and it is easy to imagine him thoroughly at home in the company of Benedictine scholars like Jean Mabillon and Bernard de Montfaucon. Now the attitude of the Rule to monastic scholarship, as interpreted by Dom Leclercq, is that while a knowledge of letters is regarded as being necessary and normally part of a monk's life, such knowledge forms no part of his vocation, his ideal, or of his monastery's ideal. For the monk the only values are those of eternal life, the only evil sin.[1] Any approach to Bede as a scholar must be conditioned by this view. His concern with the study of scripture – the aspect of his work which most impressed his contemporaries – was determined by pastoral rather than academic considerations. Bede is a literary artist by nature rather than by intention.

Reading Leclercq's study one is made aware how remarkably Bede's writings fit into the pattern of monastic culture as there described. Besides the bible and the Rule, those twin bases of early western monasticism, Leclercq points to St Gregory as the great doctor of monastic spirituality[2] – and we remember Bede's devotion to the greatest of popes. He speaks of the desire for celestial contemplation as being characteristic of the medieval religious life[3] – and we recall how often the theme of contemplation appears in Bede's writings. He tells of the importance of the Song of Songs as an influence on the theology of the medieval cloister[4] – and Bede's commentary comes to mind. He refers to the debt owed by medieval monasticism to Latin patristic tradition[5] – and we recall Bede's frequent quotation from Ambrose, Jerome and Augustine. He speaks of the importance of history as a monastic literary genre[6] – and one remembers that the *Ecclesiastical History* is, in a sense, Bede's crowning achievement. In all these details, and in many others, Bede is wholly within the monastic culture described by Dom Leclercq.

It is in the light of these considerations that we can discuss the problem of how, and why, Bede differs from his predecessors the Latin Fathers. It has been remarked above that his Latin differed from theirs in being an acquired tongue and one that was not, like theirs, formed by a profound study of the pagan classics. Nevertheless, there are two considerations which suggest that too much stress should not be laid on the alien character of Bede's Latinity. First, the position of Wearmouth and Jarrow in Northumbrian monasticism was peculiar, in that they represented a sophisticated and cosmopolitan community constantly in touch with the outside world in general, and with Rome and Italy in particular. In such a society the study and use of

[1] Leclercq, *Love of Learning*, p. 31. [2] *Ibid.* pp. 33–43. [3] *Ibid.* pp. 57–75.
[4] *Ibid.* pp. 90–3. [5] *Ibid.* pp. 103–5. [6] *Ibid.* pp. 156–60.

Latin was more than a mere liturgical, or even theological, exercise; and the presence of an Italian like John the Archchanter, brought to Northumbria to ensure the correct singing of the Roman chant, would require the use of Latin for the purpose of oral communication. The Latinity of Wearmouth and Jarrow was therefore influenced by the living tradition of the Roman church. But there is another, deeper reason why Bede's Latin should not be regarded as a foreign language, as we commonly use the term today. For a man like Bede, as for Alcuin, Anselm and Bernard of Clairvaux, Latin was not a foreign tongue at all; it was the tongue of the church. Dom Leclercq[1] refers to the question raised by Wolfram von den Steinen in his book *Notker der Dichter und seine geistige Welt* as to why Notker wrote his famous sequences in Latin and not in his German mother-tongue, to which von den Steinen replies that for Notker and for others like him – among whom he specifically mentions Bede – there was no choice. Their native language was inadequate to express their thoughts.[2] Latin was the language of the bible, the liturgy, and of Christian culture; and there was no other literary culture available to Bede in Northumbria.

Thus Bede learned Latin in order to be a monk and a priest. He learned it accurately enough from the standard grammars and, inevitably, read Vergil; but once he was trained it was to the study of the bible and the Fathers that he directed his attention. He had, of course, a number of stock quotations from classical authors at second hand, which he was prepared to employ for the purposes of literary embellishment or illustration;[3] but he had little inclination to add to this store and even less opportunity, in view of the resources available to him in the library of Wearmouth and Jarrow.

One of the most valuable of the many contributions made by the late Max Laistner to Bedan studies was the famous article on the library of the Venerable Bede.[4] Lacking as we do any contemporary catalogue of the library of Benedict Biscop's foundations, it is possible to estimate its resources only by reference to citations, either avowed or unacknowledged, in Bede's writings, and here Laistner's pioneering work is of fundamental importance. In the very nature of things it could not be definitive, and since its publication some additional works have been identified. For example, it would seem that we can add St Cyprian's *De Unitate Ecclesiae* and his fifty-sixth letter to Laistner's list, together with Jerome's Letter 22.[5] Furthermore, as we have seen, Bede may have

1 *Ibid.* p. 57.

2 Steinen, *Notker der Dichter und seine geistige Welt* (Berne, 1948) I, 76–80, esp. 79–80.

3 Ruby Davis, 'Bede's Early Reading', *Speculum* 8 (1933), 179–95 and Laistner, 'Bede as a Classical and a Patristic Scholar', pp. 93–8.

4 'The Library of the Venerable Bede', *Bede: his Life, Times and Writings*, ed. A. H. Hamilton Thompson (Oxford, 1935), pp. 237–66; repr. *Intellectual Heritage of the Early Middle Ages*, pp. 117–49.

5 Bede, *Hom.* II. 22 (CCSL 122, 347, lines 205–9) citing Cyprian, *De Unitate*, 4 (on which see Maurice

had access to Origen's commentary on Matthew, either in the original Greek or in Latin translation. Further research will no doubt add more volumes to the total, though it is difficult to believe that Laistner's list will be enormously enlarged, so thoroughly did he do his work. It is, of course, impossible to be certain that any particular citation is necessarily given by Bede at first hand; but when due allowance has been made for intermediate sources, we are entitled to use Laistner's list with some confidence.

Now from this list it appears that the authors used by Bede are predominantly ecclesiastical, with the writings of the greater Latin Fathers being most abundant. Furthermore, the titles of the works identified lend support to Leclercq's view that monastic readers primarily looked in the Fathers for what would be most helpful in leading the monastic life.[1] Overwhelmingly, Bede's library consists of commentaries on scripture, patristic treatises, or secular works like Pliny's *Natural History*, which would be of value in biblical exegesis. The standard grammaraians are there of course – Donatus, Charisius, Diomedes, Pompeius and the rest – but their function is to train men to read the bible and * the Fathers; and if Vergil is present – and no one could have kept him out – he is balanced and indeed overwhelmed by Christian poets like Ambrose, Prudentius, Paulinus, Sedulius and Arator. This is understandable; Benedict Biscop and Ceolfrith had not faced laborious and dangerous journeys to Rome to build up a classical institute. As a result, Bede's is a theological library, designed for a monastery inspired by the spirit of the Benedictine Rule rather than by the principles for study laid down by Cassiodorus for his monastery at Vivarium in the middle of the sixth century;[2] for Cassiodorus, although a sincere Christian, made far greater provision for the liberal arts in his programme of monastic studies than did St Benedict. In the second book of the *Institutes* Cassiodorus provides for a course of study which anticipates the later medieval *trivium* and *quadrivium*: first grammar, rhetoric, and dialectic; then arithmetic, music, geometry and astronomy. There is no hint in Bede of any such programme.[3] He knows Cassiodorus indeed; but he knows him as the former senator suddenly transformed into a teacher of the church and the

Bévenot, *The Tradition of Manuscripts* (Oxford, 1961), pp. 53 and 89, n. 7); and *In Apoc.* II. 9: 'sicut Beatus Cyprianus sub Deciana contigisse conquestus: "volentibus," inquit, "mori non permittebatur occidi"' (PL 93, col. 158 B) citing Cyprianus, *Epistulae*, LVI. 2; 'maxime cum cupientibus mori non permitteretur occidi' (CSEL 3(2), 649, line 20). I am indebted to Fr Bévenot for this reference.

[1] Leclercq, *Love of Learning*, p. 104. His remark that Augustine's 'polemics against the Manichaeans or the Neoplatonists had lost all timeliness for the medieval monks and therefore did not claim their attention' is only partly true of Wearmouth and Jarrow, since there were a number of Augustine's anti-Manichaean treatises in Bede's library. It is however significant that they were all concerned with scriptural exegesis and not with a direct attack on Manichaean doctrines.

[2] *Ibid.* pp. 28–31.

[3] See Pierre Riché, *Éducation et Culture dans l'Occident Barbare, 6e–8e Siècle*, Patristica Sorbonensia 4 (Paris, 1962), 434 ff.

author of a commentary on the psalms and not as an educational theorist.[1]

It may therefore be said that the cultural activities of Wearmouth and Jarrow were, in the last resort, determined by utilitarian motives; the highest utilitarianism, it is true – the salvation of souls – but utilitarian nevertheless. In the long run this utilitarianism was to have important cultural consequences, as is clearly seen by G. P. Fedotov, in his classic study *The Russian Religious Mind,* when he comes to discuss the problem of why there was no flowering of culture in medieval Russia as there was in France, Germany and England, finding the answer, rather unexpectedly, in the fact that in the ninth century the Slavs received the bible and the liturgy in Slavonic translations, to which were later added some works of theological and scientific content. As a result, there was no intellectual stimulus for the Slavs similar to that supplied in the west by the study of Latin, and the Slavonic bible and liturgy, priceless endowment as they undoubtedly were for Russia's spiritual life, were also an ambiguous gift, in that the Russian intellect was for a long time stunted by the absence of external occasions for exercise. On the other hand, says Fedotov:

> The western barbarians, before they were able to think their own thoughts and to speak their own words – about 1100 AD – had been sitting for five or six centuries on the school bench, struggling with the foreign Latin language, learning by heart the Latin Bible and the Latin grammar with Virgil as the introduction to the Bible. Men of the dark ages had no independent interest in culture. They were interested only in the salvation of their souls. But Latin gave them the key to salvation. As the language of the Church, Latin was a sacred tongue and everything written in it became invested with a sacred halo. Hence the popularity of Ovid in medieval monasteries, and the Latin versifying of Irish saints, such as Columban, who in their severe asceticism and primitive rudeness of life did not yield to the anchorites of Egypt and Syria. For the Irish the *Trivium* and *Quadrivium* were the way to the Latin Bible.[2]

Fedotov's judgement agrees very well with the estimate which has just been attempted of the character of study at Wearmouth and Jarrow, and it may be remarked in passing that, in the light of what he says about the effect of a vernacular literature on medieval Russia, it may be counted fortunate that the development of an Old English literature went hand-in-hand with, and not to the exclusion of, the study of the universal Latin. Bede, we know, was familiar with the poems of his own English tongue, and enthusiastically praised the poetry of his fellow-countryman Cædmon, and it is certainly a matter for regret that no examples of his own vernacular writing survive;[3]

[1] Bede, *In Ez. et Neem.* II (CCSL 119A, 295, lines 283–5).

[2] Fedotov, *The Russian Religious Mind* (New York, 1960), p. 39. For a more reserved comment on Irish classical studies see Riché, *Education et Culture*, pp. 371–83.

[3] I can see no safe grounds for regarding the Death Song as Bede's own composition. Only a small and late group of the manuscripts of the *Epistola de Obitu Bedae* assigns the poem to Bede himself, and so the evidence for his authorship is at best weak. See Colgrave and Mynors, p. 580, n. 4.

but we may be thankful that his legacy to posterity was written in the international language of the medieval west.

The monastic and utilitarian character of the library available to Bede explains the character of his work. His great contribution to computistical studies – a contribution of such importance that as late as 1537 it was possible to publish his writings for their practical, and not for their historical, value[1] – was inspired by the practical issues of his day. This does not mean that Bede was lacking in scientific curiosity. A modern historian of science has said of the *De Temporum Ratione* that 'it contains the basic elements of natural science', pointing out that Bede, in his discussion of tides, was the first writer to enunciate the principle known as 'the establishment of a port';[2] but while computistical arithmetic, astronomy and cosmography engaged Bede's attention, he was not concerned with the more abstract discipline of geometry.[3]

Furthermore, the nature of Bede's education and the character of the literature available to him helps to shed some light on his attitude to the pagan classics. Notoriously, he is hostile, more hostile than his master, Gregory the Great. An often cited example is his comparison of those who leave the heights of the word of God to listen to worldly fables and the teachings of the demons to the men of Israel who went down to the Philistines unarmed to have their agricultural implements sharpened (I Samuel XIII.20), and another is his identification of the honey which Jonathan ate, in ignorance of his father's orders (I Samuel XIV.27), with pagan literature.[4] These are in marked contrast to Gregory, who considered both passages as furnishing a justification for secular studies.[5] It should however be observed that when Bede comes to expound the significance of the episode of Jonathan, the great warrior who climbed the rocky crag and smote the Philistine, he wishes to use it as an example of how a teacher of the church may be led astray by the enticements of pagan literature, citing the famous story of how St Jerome was scourged in a vision before the judgement seat of God for having been a Ciceronian rather than a Christian.[6] Bede's object, however, is less to condemn pagan literature

[1] The Cologne ed. of Noviomagus, 1537. See C. W. Jones, *Bedae Pseudepigrapha: Scientific Writings Falsely Attributed to Bede* (Ithaca, N.Y., 1939), pp. 1 and 7.

[2] A. C. Crombie, *Augustine to Galileo,* 2nd ed. (London, 1969) I, 41.

[3] Riché, *Éducation et Culture*, pp. 434–6.

[4] Bede, *In I Samuhelem* II (I *Reg.* XIII. 20 (CCSL 119, 112, lines 1853–9) and XIV. 27 (*ibid.* p. 120, lines 2169–96)).

[5] Gregory, *In Librum Primum Regum,* ed. P. Verbraken, CCSL 144, 470–2.

[6] Bede, *In I Samuhelem* II (I *Reg.* XIV. 27): 'Ionathan igitur qui prius scopulorum dentes et ictus devicerat ensium qui hostis audacia compressa suis victoriae salutisque praebuerat improvisa subito blandientis gastrimargiae culpa consternitur. Et nobiles saepe magistri ecclesiae magnorumque victores certaminum ardentiore quam decet oblectatione libros gentilium lectitantes culpam quam non praevidere contrahebant adeo ut quidam eorum se pro hoc ipso scribat in visione castigatum obiectumque sibi a domino inter verbera ferientia quod non christianus sed Ciceronianus potius esset habendus' (CCSL 119, 120, lines 2170–9); Hieronymus, *Epistulae,* XXII. 30, ed. I. Hilberg, CSEL 54, 189–91.

than to demonstrate that even great Christian saints continue to be tempted to small sins in order that they may be reminded that their virtues are a gift of God.[1] Pagan eloquence may legitimately be employed to support and sweeten authority;[2] and Bede is aware that neither Moses nor Daniel nor St Paul utterly eschewed pagan learnings or letters.[3] Bede's recognition that the reading of the pagan classics may be of value is clear, if grudging, and was in full accord with the teaching of the Fathers of the Church. Like them, however, he was in his heart doubtful about the reading of the pagan authors by a Christian; and his basic hesitation and suspicion could only be confirmed by the fact that he was unable to take the vision of Jerome other than seriously. Indeed, from the theological viewpoint it taught an unquestionable truth. The demands of Christ are absolute, and if a concern for Cicero leads a man to neglect them, then Cicero must be rejected as giving occasion for sin.

There is, however, one important difference between Bede and the Fathers. For them, the temptation offered by the pagan classics was a very real one. As children their minds had been formed by Vergil and Cicero, Plautus and Terence, and however hard they might try they could never entirely break the spell. Bede's education, on the other hand, had been a progress from the grammarians directly to the bible, without any intervening stage of concentrated literary study. Indeed, apart from Vergil and Pliny, his classical reading seems to have been slight, and his learning mostly from other men's quotations. In describing the dangers of the classics he was denouncing a peril to which he had never been exposed. And this held true, not only in respect of the danger of distraction from the heavenly to the temporal, but also in respect of a reversion to paganism. For the Fathers the classics were, in a very obvious fashion, a temptation to apostasy. For Bede and his age they could never be that. The classical deities might be demons, masquerading as gods; but fundamentally they were literary fictions, without any power to move to adoration. The paganism of Bede's world was German heathenism, not the literary paganism of classical antiquity. This fact may help to explain the revival of classical studies in the Carolingian period. They were no longer, in themselves, a danger to a man's soul.

We have, then, suggested a way in which Bede, although inspired by and thinking within the tradition of the Fathers, nevertheless inhabits another intellectual world from theirs, even within the confines of his monastery of Jarrow. The world of Bede is a monastic world, his culture a monastic culture, designed to bring men to heaven. Of course, the Fathers were equally

[1] *Ibid.*: 'Sed et auditorum fidelium non pauci magna virtutum gratia pollentes minoribus vitiis temptari non desinunt quod divina geri dispensatione non latet ut qui minora certamina per se superare nequeunt in magnis quae habent non sibi aliquid tribuere sed solo patri luminum gratias agere discant' (CCSL 119, 120, lines 2179–84).

[2] *Ibid.* (lines 2186–94).

[3] *Ibid.* (XIV. 28–9; CCSL 119, 121, lines 2209–16).

concerned to bring men to heaven, and many of them were monks; but the majority of them received their education not in the cloister but in the secular schools. Thus Bede's world, although not a narrow one, was narrower than theirs.

But Bede's world differs from that of the Fathers in another way which is more difficult to describe. Put briefly and misleadingly, it is a world in which Christianity has triumphed. Clearly, in the most literal sense of the words this statement is untrue, for the Fathers, after the legal suppression of paganism had begun in earnest at the end of the fourth century, were accustomed to think of themselves as living in Christian times, while the age of Bede was a harsh and barbarous one, as appears all too clearly in the atrocities of nominally * Christian kings like Cædwalla of Wessex on the Isle of Wight or Egbert of Northumbria in Ireland;[1] while across the Channel, in the Low Countries and Germany, paganism flourished and the work of the English mission to the continent, begun in Bede's lifetime, was ultimately to be accomplished only by the ruthless extirpation of heathenism wherever the Frankish armies got the upper hand. Yet in spite of this, and in spite of the alarm for the future of Northumbria expressed at the end of the *Ecclesiastical History* and the *Letter to Egbert*, there is in Bede a note of optimism. The night of infidelity has been dispersed by the Sun of Righteousness,[2] and now Christ and his bride the church go forth to the vineyards: '*In the morning,* therefore, he says, *let us go forth to the vineyards*, as though he should say openly: Because the night of ancient unbelief has passed, because the light of the bright gospel already begins to appear, *let us*, I pray, *go forth to the vineyards*, that is, let us labour in establishing churches for God throughout the world.'[3]

It is in the spirit of this passage that we should, I think, understand St Boniface's famous reference to Bede as a candle of the church in the letter sent to Archbishop Egbert of York in 746–7, asking him to send copies of Bede's scriptural commentaries.[4] It is easy when we read it today to impose our own preconceptions upon it, and to think of Bede's life shining with a small but clear flame in a waste of great darkness, the early Middle Ages; but such a romantic image was surely far from Boniface's thought. Rather, our image

[1] Bede, *HE* IV. 16 [14] and 26 [24].

[2] Bede, *In Cant.* II: 'Sicut enim tenebras noctis, sic etiam recte per austeritatem hiemis et imbrium, tempestas exprimitur infidelitatis, quae totum orbem usque ad tempus regebat Dominicae incarnationis. At ubi Sol iustitiae mundo illuxit, abscedente mox ac depulsa prisca brumalis infidelitatis perfidia, flores apparuerunt in terra, quia initia iam nascentis Ecclesiae in sanctorum fideli ac pia devotione claruerunt' (PL 91, col. 1110 C and D).

[3] *Ibid.* IV (col. 1202A).

[4] Boniface, *Ep.* 91, ed. M. Tangl, *Die Briefe des heiligen Bonifatius und Lullus,* Monumenta Germaniae Historica, Epistolae Selectae I, 207, line 17; cf. *Ep.* 75 *ibid.* p. 158, lines 8–11) and 76: 'quem nuper in domo Dei apud vos vice candellae ecclesiasticae scientia scripturarum fulsisse audivimus' (*ibid.* p. 159, lines 13 and 14).

should be of some great basilica ablaze with brightness, with the great candles of the apostles and the saints and the lesser lights of humbler Christians, all afire with the love of God; and among them Bede, shining with a light hardly less than that of the apostles, a great candle in the house of God. What we somewhat condescendingly call the Dark Ages did not necessarily seem so dark to those who lived in them. Rather, they seemed the age of the triumph of Christ and his church.

Such an interpretation of the mood of the age will explain certain features of Bede's thought which are otherwise puzzling. Let us consider first the *Ecclesiastical History*. It has been observed of this work:

No single term will describe Bede's book. It includes a great deal of material quoted from papal and episcopal letters, *concilia*, epigraphic and verbal accounts; it ignores and thus condemns to oblivion, the greater part of the history of the period with which it deals, yet it repeats in detail the lives of monks who took no part in the public affairs of their day ... As an *ecclesiastical* history – and no event without ecclesiastical relevance is mentioned in the book – Bede's work is an adjunct to scriptural study, that study which he elsewhere described as his life's occupation.[1]

With all this we may agree, except the first sentence. The work is, as Bede says, an ecclesiastical history, composed in the tradition of Eusebius of Caesarea, whom Bede knew in the Latin version of Rufinus. Eusebius was aware, when he embarked upon his *History*, that he was in effect creating a new type of historiography, unknown to the pagan,[2] and the novelty of his enterprise is reflected by his lengthy citations from his authorities. Professor Momigliano, in an important article, has drawn attention to this particular feature of Christian history, destined to make a peculiar contribution to the technique of scientific historiography, though without actually abolishing the style of the classical historians. 'We have learnt', he says, 'to check our references from Eusebius ...'[3] – though we have contrived to secularize him by the use of footnotes. Bede, in the *Ecclesiastical History*, followed the Eusebian tradition. Where he differs from Eusebius is not in his method but in his ability to exploit his materials – Sir Frank Stenton's comment that 'in an age when little was attempted beyond the registration of fact, he had reached the conception of history'[4] is not likely to be applied to the Father of Church History. Yet so far as the philosophy which underlies their work is concerned, Eusebius and Bede are in agreement. Both saw ecclesiastical history as a

[1] W. F. Bolton, *A History of Anglo-Latin Literature* (Princeton, New Jersey, 1967) I, 171 and 172.

[2] Eusebius, *Ecclesiastica Historia*, I.i.5 (GCS, Eusebius Werke II (1), 8, lines 17–21). On this see Arnaldo Momigliano, 'Pagan and Christian Historiography in the Forth Century A.D.', *The Conflict between Paganism and Christianity in the Fourth Century*, ed. A. Momigliano (Oxford, 1963), p. 90.

[3] *Ibid.* p. 99.

[4] Stenton, *Anglo-Saxon England*, 2nd ed. (Oxford, 1947), p. 187.

struggle between the new nation, the Christians, and the devil.[1] Both wrote to record the victory of the church: Eusebius in the conversion of Constantine, Bede in the conversion of the English. The difference between them – a difference fraught with portentous consequences – is that while Eusebius took for his field the Roman Empire, Bede confined his to a particular race within a limited locality. In so doing he was, of course, only following a trail already blazed by Gregory of Tours and Cassiodorus in his lost work on Gothic history; but the very fact that he did is significant. Here, as in his biblical commentaries, Bede stands in the tradition of the Fathers but points the way to another age.

Let us consider another aspect of this idea of the triumph of Christianity. Perhaps the most significant, and certainly the most distinctive, contrast between the culture of Bede and that of the Fathers – and one which also helps to explain his attitude to the pagan classics – is to be found in the fact that he had at his disposal a corpus of Christian poetry, as distinct from the literature of theological works composed according to the rules of literary composition, which he shared with the Fathers. In this respect the two treatises *De Arte Metrica* and *De Schematibus et Tropis*, regarded by Bede as constituting a single treatise and dated by Laistner to 701 or 702,[2] are instructive. In the *De Arte Metrica* not only are Bede's examples taken overwhelmingly from Christian poets – this, after all, was determined by the resources of his library – but when he lists the three types of poetry, dramatic, narrative, and mixed, he gives examples both from pagan authors and from the Old Testament. Vergil's ninth eclogue is matched by the Song of Songs; to the *Georgics* and the *De Rerum Natura* of Lucretius are opposed Proverbs and Ecclesiastes; the *Odyssey* and the *Aeneid* have the book of Job as their Christian equivalent. *Apud nos* – 'our authors' – is Bede's theme.[3] The Christians have their own literature and do not need the pagans any more. Similarly in the *De Schematibus et Tropis* Bede observes that Holy Scripture surpasses all other writings, not only by authority, because it is divine, or by utility, because it leads to eternal life, 'sed et antiquitate et ipsa positione dicendi' – by age and style.[4] We have come a long way from the days when Jerome found the language of the prophets barbarous, or the young Augustine, excited to the pursuit of philosophy by reading the *Hortensius*, found himself repelled by the style of the bible, so inferior to that of Cicero.[5] Some three centuries before Bede's lifetime

1 Momigliano, 'Pagan and Christian Historiography', p. 90.
2 Laistener, *A Hand-List of Bede Manuscripts* (Ithaca, N.Y., 1943), pp. 131–2.
3 Bede, *De Arte Metrica,* 25, ed. H. Keil, *Grammatici Latini* VII (Leipzig, 1880), 259–60.
4 Bede, *De Schematis et Tropis* (PL 90, col. 175 B).
5 Hieron., *Ep.* XXII. 30: 'si . . . prophetam legere coepissem, sermo horrebat incultus' (CSEL 54, 189, lines 17–18); and Augustine, *Confessiones,* III. 9 (CSEL 33, 50, lines 4–14). Both these works were apparently available to Bede.

Bede and medieval civilization

Augustine of Hippo had produced, in the *De Doctrina Christiana*, a theory of a Christian culture in which the scriptures would take the place of the pagan classics and secular studies would be pursued insofar as they provided material for the Christian exegete. At about the same time Prudentius, the first great Christian poet, and Paulinus of Nola were beginning to provide the church with a corpus of poetry in addition to the liturgical hymns which had already been composed by Hilary of Poitiers and Ambrose of Milan, and Prudentius and Paulinus would be supplemented by the works of Sedulius, Arator and Venantius Fortunatus, all known to Bede. The question whether these writers were, in respect of literary quality, the peers of the great pagan poets is for our purposes irrelevant. So far as Bede was concerned, both the resources of his library and his own writings represent the embodiment of the programme of study proposed by Augustine, even to the extent of his warning expressed – ironically enough in a phrase of Terence! – against any excessive pursuit of learning beyond the bounds of the church of Christ: 'Ne quid nimis!'[1] Thus Bede's attitude to the classics was not simply determined by the consideration that they might be harmful; rather they had, in a certain sense, become unnecessary, in view of the existence of a specifically Christian literature. This particular assumption of Bede was not shared by the scholars of the Caroline renaissance, who decided that Christian writings alone could not provide the norms of the Latinity which they desired. Few will doubt that they were right in their decision; but Bede's position, granting his premises, was unassailable, and most of us, it may be added, would be well content if we could emulate Bede's Latin style, formed as it was on the grammarians and the Fathers.

We have hitherto considered Bede as a writer who is a key figure in the transmission of patristic tradition and who also modifies that tradition and adapts it to the conditions of his own age. In this respect no one could have been better fitted to be one of the great teachers of the early Middle Ages, in which his influence was immense, as is demonstrated in the most obvious way by the great quantity of manuscripts of his writings which have survived.[2] A few examples of the range of his influence may be given, without any claim to be comprehensive. His *De Arte Metrica* was still in use at the cathedral school of Fulbert of Chartres in the eleventh century,[3] while the *De Temporum Ratione* (described by a leading modern authority as being still 'the best introduction to the ecclesiastical calendar')[4] was, as we have seen, published in the sixteenth century for practical, and not historical, reasons. Again, the

[1] Augustine, *De Doctrina Christiana*, II. XXXIX 58 (CSEL 80, 74, line 12). On all this, see H.-I. Marrou *Saint Augustin et la Fin de la Culture Antique*, 4th ed. (Paris, 1958) and esp. pt 3, ch. 3: 'La Formation de l'Intellectuel Chrétien'.

[2] For which see Laistner, *Hand-List*.

[3] See H. O. Taylor, *The Medieval Mind*, 4th ed. (London, 1925) I, 300.

[4] C. W. Jones, *Bedae Opera de Temporibus* (Cambridge, Mass., 1943), p. 4.

Ecclesiastical History enjoyed a popularity which was not confined to England[1] where, in the twelfth century, it was to be a source of inspiration to the historian William of Malmesbury.[2] Yet again, Bede's biblical commentaries, the part of his work which his contemporaries most highly valued, enjoyed a remarkable renaissance of popularity during the fifteenth century, if the number of manuscript copies which have survived is any indication.[3] We are not here concerned to give a description of the diffusion of Bede's writings[4] or to give a detailed account of his influence in any particular field. Rather, if we are to regard Bede as an outstanding representative of early medieval culture and a teacher who exercised a decisive influence on the development of the civilization of the Middle Ages, it would be well to conclude this paper by a consideration of what he did not contribute, to note his deficiencies as well as his achievements, and to establish what was lacking in the Christian culture of Northumbria, of which he was the outstanding representative, which later thinkers and scholars would have to supply.

In the *Ecclesiastical History* when he comes to describe the Council of Hatfield of 679, Bede gives part of its confession of faith, declaring its adhesion to the doctrine of the first five ecumenical councils and of the council 'which was held in the city of Rome in the time of the blessed Pope Martin, in the eighth indiction, in the ninth year of the reign of the most religious Emperor Constantine',[5] that is, the Lateran Synod of 649, convened by Pope Martin I under the influence of St Maximus the Confessor, who was probably present at it, to condemn the Monothelite heresy. Now Bede in his writings makes very little mention of Monothelitism, and none at all of St Maximus, one of the greatest of the later Greek theologians, who had lived in exile in the west, at Carthage from 632 onwards, and then at Rome from about 646 until about 655. It seems curious that Bede should know nothing about this great theologian and catholic Confessor, whose teaching was later to influence the thought of St Bernard,[6] but such is apparently the case. Now if one turns from the thought of Bede to that of Maximus, one enters another world,[7] the sophisticated world of Greek patristic theology in which all the resources of Greek philosophy and Christian experience were applied to the solution of the mystery of the union of the two natures, divine and human, in Christ. To this world, Bede is a stranger. This is not to say that he was intellectually inferior to Maximus – one cannot fairly compare the biblical scholar and historian with the dogmatic

1 Laistner, *Hand-List,* p. 94.

2 *De Gest. Reg. Angl.,* ed. Stubbs I, I and 59.

3 Laistner, *Hand-List,* p. 7.

4 For which, see Dorothy Whitelock, *After Bede,* Jarrow Lecture 1960.

5 Bede, *HE* IV. 17 [15].

6 See E. Gilson, *The Mystical Theology of St Bernard,* trans. A. H. C. Downes (London, 1940), pp. 25 ff.

7 See the excellent study by Lars Thunberg, *Microcosm and Mediator: the Theological Anthropology of Maximus the Confessor* (Lund, 1965).

and philosophical theologian – but rather, that there was a department of Christian theology which was unfamiliar to Bede as it would not be, for example, to St Anselm at a later date.

How did this come about? Here again, an examination of Bede's library as established by Laistner is revealing, always allowing for the omissions and errors of such a reconstruction. If one looks at the titles of the works available to Bede, one is struck by the absence of books of philosophical theology or of a metaphysical content. Bede did not, apparently, have access to Augustine's early philosophical writings, the *Contra Academicos*, the *De Beata Vita* or the *De Ordine*, nor did he have the *De Trinitate*, perhaps the greatest of Augustine's * theological works, nor any of the treatises of the fourth-century Latin Christian Platonist Marius Victorinus. Again, he did not have a copy of Chalcidius's commentary on part of the *Timaeus*, one of the very few Platonic sources available in the Latin west in the early Middle Ages, or of a work like that of Apuleius, *De Deo Socratis*. One can understand the absence of such works from a monastic library; but what is surprising is the lack of any work of Boethius, either the *Consolatio* – an omission so remarkable as to cause Laistner to remark upon it in his article on Bede's library[1] – or of the theological tractates and translations.

The implications of this deficiency in his library are clear: Bede was deprived, through no fault of his own, of precisely the sort of works needed by a Latin divine to whom the writings of the Greek Fathers were not available, if he aspired to be in any sense of the term a dogmatic theologian. To suggest that, had such works been available, Bede would have produced great works on dogmatic theology would be wholly unwarranted; and in any case such an achievement, however admirable and desirable in itself, would have been of less value to the church of his day in England or on the continent of Europe than what he actually achieved. The process by which the barbarian kingdoms, established after the ending of Roman rule in the west, were turned into the civilized states of the Middle Ages was a gradual one, requiring several centuries of diligent scholarship to prepare the way for the renaissance of the twelfth century. To that renaissance Bede contributed much; but there are some things – its philosophy and its humanism – in which he had no share. The cultural achievement of Northumbria was a limited one, the work of a small élite of monks and clerics and a few cultured laymen within a restricted field, and it was within that field that Bede made his great contribution to medieval civilization. Bede was, without question, a great intellect, a great teacher, and a great Christian; but it is important in any evaluation of his work to maintain a sense of proportion. Bede served later generations as a

[1] Laistner, 'The Library of the Venerable Bede', p. 264.

commentator, a grammarian, an historiographer and a computist. This is his achievement, and it is enough to establish his greatness.

Yet having said this, it does not seem enough; for a man's performance is, after all, dependent upon his opportunities, and when all reservations have been made it is astonishing that Bede, a 'grandchild of pagans' and a 'child of barbarians'[1] should have become a Doctor of the Church and provide, in Plummer's words, 'the very model of the saintly scholar-priest'.[2] In attempting to determine the place of Bede in medieval civilization, it would be well to remember the words of Fedotov previously quoted, that 'the western barbarians, before they were able to think their own thought and to speak their own words . . . had been sitting for five or six centuries on the school bench'. It is a measure of his greatness that for more than three of those centuries they sat under the instruction of the Venerable Bede.

[1] Leclercq, *Love of Learning*, p. 45.

[2] Plummer, *Bede* I, lxxviii–lxxix.

Corrigenda

p. 84, l. 12, for Egbert, please read: Ecgfrith.

XII

SAINT BEDE IN THE TRADITION OF WESTERN APOCALYPTIC COMMENTARY

In taking as my subject St Bede as a commentator on the Book of Revelation, I am aware that I am dealing with an aspect of his work which does not, generally, excite much interest. Posterity regards Bede primarily as the historian of the English Church, and justifiably so. Nevertheless, we would do well to remind ourselves of two facts. First, that although Bede is the greatest English ecclesiastical historian, his *Ecclesiastical History* was read, not only in its homeland but on the mainland of Europe as well, as may be seen from the large number of surviving manuscripts of European origin.[1] Secondly, although today we consider Bede to have been first and foremost an ecclesiastical historian, it does not follow that his own age shared our opinion or that it was mistaken in not doing so. The values of one age differ from those of another, and if the Middle Ages thought of Bede as being above all else a teacher of Christian doctrine and an expositor of the Word of God, it is not for us to regard this as evidence of a lack of critical standards. 'Later generations', says Sir Frank Stenton, 'considering the long series of Bede's commentaries, placed him in the succession of the great Fathers of the Church. He himself would certainly have wished to be remembered by these works of exposition.'[2] It is this consideration which has determined my choice of subject, and I ask you to join me this evening in thinking of Bede as a European rather than as an English figure, and as writing within an established tradition of exegesis, to which he made his own contribution, but without enjoying the rather solitary preëminence which he has obtained as an historian. I hope that this enquiry will show how much Bede was an inheritor of the general tradition of western Christian thought, even though he never, so far as we know, left England and rarely stirred from the vicinity of Jarrow. *

To do this I am going to discuss Bede's commentary of the Apocalypse, and here I must warn you of a difficulty which at present confronts any student of Bede's theological writings: the unsatisfactory character of our available texts. For most of these we have to rely upon the labours of the Rev. Dr. J. A. Giles, an indefatigable but undiscriminating editor, in whom energy was not tempered with discretion. In a review of another of Giles' ventures – his edition of the correspondence of Thomas Becket – the English historian E. A. Freeman observed, with the devastating candour of the Victorian reviewer: 'We suppose we must allow the praises of zeal and research to a man who has edited, translated, and written more books than any other living English scholar. But really we can give him no other praise,' and he went on to emphasise his point by remarking: 'The Letters [of Becket] of course are invaluable; at least they will be when anyone shall be found to edit them decently.'[3] It would be unkind to apply Freeman's verdict to Giles' edition of Bede without qualification. His edition – at least so far as the commentary on the Apocalypse is concerned – is sufficient for practical purposes. Unfortunately, for any detailed study of the text it is unsatisfactory, not only because it lacks any reference to original manuscripts, but also because no attempt is made to indicate the sources used by Bede, which would help us to estimate both the range of his reading and his personal contribution to the commentary. Giles' edition appeared in 1844.[4] It was reprinted by the Abbé Migne in 1850 in the *Patrologia Latina*,[5] and no one familiar with Migne's editorial practice will suppose that Giles' text underwent any particular improvement at his hands. The Migne edition, which is in effect Giles', is the text most readily available today, and it is high time it was replaced. As long ago as 1912 Alexander Souter, in the preface to the first edition of a small but valuable book on the Text and Canon of the New Testament, expressed a desire to 'allure some Churchmen from the fascinating pursuit of liturgiology, and some Nonconformists from the equally if not more fascinating pursuit of speculative theology, to the study . . . of the abundant manuscript materials which exist for the writing of the history of the Latin Bible. Why, for instance,' asked Souter, 'should we still lack a scientific edition of the biblical commentaries of our countryman, the Venerable Bede? The materials exist in abundance and are of superlative quality.'[6] Unhappily, Souter's invitation went unheeded, and in 1964 my predecessor in these Lectures, Dom Paul Meyvaert, was compelled to observe: ' . . . we lack in particular fully annotated editions of Bede's works, especially of the Scriptural commentaries, listing all the known sources from which he borrowed, and therefore showing us in what sections Bede is most at his own.'[7] This neglect of Bede is a reproach to English scholarship, and one cannot help feeling that if he had been a native of certain other European countries, a commission would long ago have been established for the publication of Bede's works as a whole, instead of leaving matters to the efforts of individual scholars. [Since this lecture was delivered, I have learned that a critical edition of Bede's commentary is being prepared by Professor H. F. D. Sparks of Oriel College, Oxford, for the series *Corpus Christianorum*.] *

To turn now to our immediate theme. Bede's commentary on the Apocalypse stands a little apart from his other Biblical commentaries, in that it deals with a book which has a peculiar place in the history of western biblical criticism. The Revelation of St. John the Divine is generally regarded as one of the most mysterious books of the New Testament. A series of majestic and terrible visions reveals the ending of the world, the coming of the Antichrist and his overthrow, the Last Judgement, and the final peace of the New Jerusalem. The confident and authoritative tone of Revelation, not to speak of the fierce note of exultation which informs it, have long been an embarrassment to some Christians and no doubt partly account for the reluctance shown in certain sections of the early Church to receive it into the Canon of Scripture, although nobody went quite so far as the late Professor A. N. Whitehead, who wanted to remove it from the Bible and replace it by the oration on the Athenian dead, which Thucydides puts into the mouth of Pericles, and which Whitehead considered more edifying reading. Whitehead's objection to the Apocalypse was inspired by the 'barbaric elements which have been retained to the undoing of Christian intuition.'[8] No doubt many educated Christians in the early Church felt much the same, although they would not have expressed themselves in such words. Fortunately for posterity, the intellectual and practical problems raised by Revelation could be resolved by the method of allegorical interpretation associated with Origen and Alexandrian Christian thought. However, even when this treatment had been applied, the problem of the authorship remained, and a good textual critic like Dionysius of Alexandria could point out that the Greek style of the Apocalypse was not that of the Gospel and First Epistle of St. John, whom some claimed as its author.[9] With its apostolic authority doubtful, and the general tone reminiscent of a certain type of apocryphal literature like the Apocalypse of Peter,[10] the Book of Revelation was accepted by Eastern Christians only after hesitations and heart-searching, and to this day the Greek Orthodox Church while receiving it into the Canon of Scripture, does not employ it for liturgical purposes.

In the West it was otherwise. The fact that western Christians read the Apocalypse in Latin translation prevented them from entertaining doubts about the Johannine authorship.[11] Furthermore, there seems to have been in Latin Christianity – at least in North Africa, the cradle and nurse of Latin theology – a stern, enthusiastic element, to which the visions of the Apocalypse made an immense appeal. Finally, in the Fourth century, African Christianity produced in Tyconius a theologian capable of directing the course of Latin Apocalyptic commentary for eight centuries, by developing a method of typological exegesis which long remained the standard form.

The measure of Tyconius' achievement is better appreciated if it is remembered that he was not the first in the field. That distinction belongs to Victorinus, bishop of Poetovio (the modern Pettau), who was martyred under Diocletian in 304. Victorinus was apparently of Greek origins, with only a limited command of Latin.[12] He was one of the last orthodox exponents of the millenarianist belief in a literal thousand-year reign of Christ upon earth before the Judgement, and his commentary was coloured by his convictions. Because of this, St. Jerome subsequently carried out a revision of Victorinus, removing his more extreme millenarianistic passages and replacing them with various additions, some of which he borrowed from Tyconius.[13] It would appear that Bede had at his disposal a copy of Jerome's revision of Victorinus when he wrote his commentary on the Apocalypse, but it does not appear to have influenced his own interpretation to any great degree. This is not surprising for, despite the support of Jerome's authority, the work of Victorinus had little influence upon Latin Apocalyptic commentary in the Middle Ages, when compared with that exercised by Tyconius.

This remarkable man was a native of North Africa and a member of the Donatist Church – the powerful, schismatic group which had broken with the Catholic Church on the question of the validity of sacraments administered by *traditores* – clerics who had surrendered copies of the Scriptures to the pagan authorities during the persecution of the early Fourth century. The dates of Tyconius' life are uncertain; he was writing in the last two decades of the Fourth century.[14] He was by far the most original and interesting mind which Donatism produced, and thanks to the admiration of St. Augustine of Hippo, he exercised great influence on the theology of many Catholic writers to whom his ecclesiastical views were profoundly repulsive. The essence of Tyconius' genius was two-fold. First he was one of those theologians – St. Ambrose was another – who helped to adapt the allegorical method of interpreting Scripture, so popular in the East, to the service of western theology. Secondly, he was able to develop the Donatist doctrine of the two churches – the true Church of God, visibly present in themselves, and the Church of the false Christians, the *traditores*, which they conceived the Catholics to be – into something more profound and more subtle: the doctrine of the two Cities, the City of God, the Elect, and the City of the Devil, the Reprobate.[15] The importance of Tyconius' teaching lay in his view of the Church. Unlike most Donatists, he held that a separation of good and evil was impossible in this world; the Church Militant is, and must be, a mixed body, which contains both saints and sinners, who will be visibly distinguished only at the Last Judgement. One might suppose that such an outlook would have led Tyconius to leave the Donatists and join the Catholics, and St. Augustine thought him mad not to have done so.[16] What Tyconius had in mind, however, was less to question the propriety of separating from deliberate and open sinners, such as he conceived the *traditores* to have been, as to reject the Donatist idea of the infection incurred by association with sinners, which led the Donatists to hold that overseas churches in communion with the Catholics of Africa had become partners in their original act of *traditio* and must therefore be rejected. Logically, no doubt, Augustine was right, and Tyconius' views ought to have led him to the Catholic Church; but he is not the only thinker to decline to be governed by a rigorous logic. The originality of his doctrine caused Tyconius to be rejected and excommunicated by the Donatist Church, but he never, apparently, became a Catholic.

It is these two elements in the thought of Tyconius: his allegorical interpretation of Scripture, and his conception of the two supernatural Cities of God and Satan, which determined the form of his commentary on Revelation in which, in the words of the Fifth-century ecclesiastical writer Gennadius, he understood 'nothing carnally but everything spiritually.'[17] An example of his technique is provided by his treatment of Rev. xii. 4 – the vision of the great red dragon whose tail *drew the third part of the stars of heaven, and did cast them to the earth* – a vision which is commonly understood to imply that a third part of the angelic host participated in Lucifer's rebellion and shared his fall. Tyconius, 'in his fashion,' says Bede, regarded the third part of the stars that fell as signifying the fall of false brethren within the Church, while of the remaining two-thirds one part is the true Church and the other her open enemies.[18]

I have called Tyconius' method of exegesis allegorical, but it is in fact better described as typological, since Tyconius interpreted the visions of the Apocalypse within a fixed pattern of thought – the struggle of the true Church, the City of God, against the City of the Devil, whose members include both open enemies of the Church without and false friends within. A similar principle governs Tyconius' seven rules for understanding Holy Scripture, which are quoted by Bede (who got them second-hand from St. Augustine) in his commentary on the Apocalypse. Particularly important are Tyconius' first rule, *Of the Lord and His Body*, which explains that Scripture often speaks of Christ the Head by referring to His Body, the Church, and *vice versa*, and the seventh, *Of the devil and his body*, which declares that the devil is often mentioned, not in himself but in the mass of his sinful followers.[19] Tyconius understands the Book of Revelation not so much as prophecy of the End of the World than as an image of the history of the Church in the World, in other words, not eschatologically but as theology of history.[20] This is not to imply that Tyconius did not believe in the immediate Second Coming of the Lord – on the contrary, he apparently considered that it was soon to be expected[21] – but he did not allow this belief to condition his treatment of the Apocalypse, with the result that the millenarianistic tendencies which had appeared in the commentary of Victorinus disappeared from subsequent Latin Apocalyptic commentary. The objection to Millenarianism lay not so much in its literal acceptance of the account of a thousand-year reign of Christ with His saints on earth – St. Augustine of Hippo, who denounced Millenarianism, does not object to the idea as such, which he had himself once held – as in the materialistic notion of the character of that reign of the saints which it encouraged.[22] The merit of Tyconius was that his exegesis made such crude literalism impossible, while at the same time leaving intact the sense of an immediate expectation of the end of the world, which was to haunt the Middle Ages. This sense of immediacy, although rejected by St. Augustine in the Fifth Century,[23] reappears in the Sixth in the thought of St. Gregory the Great, faced with the horrors of the Lombardic invasion of Italy,[24] and finds expression in the letter which he sent in 601 to King Ethelbert of Kent, which Bede reproduced in the *Ecclesiastical History*.[25] Bede himself shared Gregory's belief regarding the imminence of the Second Coming, and while he accepted St. Augustine's view that one cannot determine the day and the hour, he was quite certain that the end of time was close at hand.[26] We shall return to this aspect of his thought later.

The success of Tyconius as a commentator was immense. For eight hundred years his method of interpretation dominated all commentary on the Book of Revelation. His success is the more remarkable when we remember that Tyconius was not an orthodox writer but a schismatic, separated from the Catholic Church. Because of his Donatism he might well have been expected to fall into oblivion after his death, and his continuing influence was largely due to the recommendations of St. Augustine, who greatly admired his writings, and Cassiodorus, who was more reserved in his estimate.[27] Augustine, however, was unstinting in his praise, and paid Tyconius the compliment of transcribing a considerable portion of his Rules for understanding Scripture into his work, the *De Doctrina Christiana*,[28] from which Bede, in turn, incorporated them into his commentary on the Apocalypse.[29]

In view of the esteem which Tyconius enjoyed and the influence which he exercised upon succeeding generations, it is curious that (so far as is known) no manuscript of his commentary has survived. It appears from the oldest catalogue of the library of the famous Swiss monastery of St. Gall that a copy was to be found there in the Ninth century,[30] but this is the last clue that we have. There are, it is true, in the Biblioteca Nazionale at Turin some fragments of a commentary on the Apocalypse from the Italian monastery of Bobbio, presented by the Coptic scholar Amadeo Peyron, and first published in 1897 by the Benedictines of Monte Cassino, under the title *Tyconii Afri Fragmenta Commentarii in Apocalypsim.* [31] However, this attribution to Tyconius (which is not to be found in the Fragments themselves) presents many difficulties, since there occur in the Fragments theological statements which are directly contrary to Tyconius' principles. A suggestion has been made by the late Francesco Lo Bue, whose edition of the Fragments appeared in 1963,[32] that these discordant statements may perhaps be interpolations, made in the Catholic interest to adapt Tyconius' popular commentary for orthodox use. This suggestion is a pure hypothesis, and Lo Bue frankly admitted that he could not bring forward any argument amounting to proof. However, whether or not Lo Bue's theory is accepted, it is clear that the Turin Fragments have Tyconian affinities, and collation with Bede's commentary on the Apocalypse shows that the two documents agree exactly in a number of passages. The fact that Bede used a copy of Tyconius when compiling his own commentary strongly suggests that the passages which he has in common with the Turin Fragments are indeed of Tyconian origin.

One fact is to be recorded regarding the Turin Fragments which is significant for determining their place in the tradition of Western Apocalyptic commentary. Amadeo Peyron who, as has been said, presented the Fragments to the Biblioteca Nazionale of Turin, assigned the writing to the Thirteenth century. This dating was accepted by Lo Bue, who rather curiously described the hand as being 'book-gothic.'[33] In fact it is nothing of the kind, being a caroline minuscule hand of the first half of the Tenth century, which Professor Bernhard Bischoff assigns to upper Italy[34] – a locality which agrees very well with the known Bobbio provenance of the Fragments. In this context, however, it is relevant to recall that there was a copy of Tyconius at St. Gall in the Ninth century, and that close historic ties existed between Bobbio and St. Gall.[35] In fact, the correct dating of the Fragments enables us to place them in their proper context in the tradition of Latin Apocalyptic commentary: they were copied within the period of the intellectual dominance of Tyconius, namely from the Fourth to the Twelfth century, and more specifically just after two centuries of pronounced interest in the Book of Revelation, represented in the writings of Bede and Ambrosius Autpertus in the Eighth century and the Carolingian theologians in the Ninth.

Let us now consider briefly the transmission of the Tyconian tradition from Tyconius to Bede. We have already seen that St. Jerome, disliking the Millenarianism of the commentary of Victorinus, had redrafted it, and in so doing made use of Tyconius. However, the Victorine–Hieronymian commentary does not lie in the main stream of the Tyconian tradition. For this we must look to two groups of theologians, one writing in the Sixth and the other in the Eighth century.

The middle of the Sixth century saw the production of three commentaries on the Apocalypse, written in Gaul, Spain, and North Africa respectively. The first of these was the work of St. Caesarius, bishop of Arles (d. 542), and was destined to have a curious history. Caesarius of Arles, one of the outstanding preachers of the early Church, was an admirer of St. Augustine, from whose works he drew not only inspiration but also material, and it is therefore neither inappropriate nor surprising that a group of his homilies on the Apocalypse, nineteen in number, have come down to us under the name of Augustine. That Caesarius was the real author of these pseudo-Augustinian homilies was demonstrated in the Eighteenth century by the Abbé J.B. Morel (d. 1772), a fine scholar whose abilities never received the recognition they deserved. Morel's researches passed unnoticed, and it was left to the late Dom Germain Morin finally to affirm the Caesarian authorship of the homilies and to edit them critically in his edition of Caesarius' works.[36] For our purposes, the importance of Caesarius' commentary lies in the fact that it drew heavily upon Tyconius.

The second Sixth-century commentary is that of Apringius, bishop of Pax Julia (the modern Béja in Portugal), written at some time between 531 and 548. This work, which survives today in one manuscript at Copenhagen, published by Dom Férotin in 1900,[37] made use of the Victorinus-Jerome commentary, and was in its turn utilised by Beatus of Liebana for his commentary compiled in the Eighth century. It is not, however, of great significance for the Bedan scholar.

Far more important is the third of our Sixth-century commentators, Primasius, bishop of Hadrumetum (the modern Sousse, in Tunisia), who died in 552. Primasius, who was much used by Bede, tells his readers that he based his work in the first place upon the writings of St. Augustine, to which he added whatever he could discover in Tyconius congruent with true doctrine, acting on the principle (in his own elegant phraseology) that a precious jewel which has fallen on a dung-heap ought to be picked up and treated with the respect due to its value.[38] Because of his influence on Bede, and through Bede on the early Middle Ages, the commentary of Primasius is of great importance, and it is unfortunate that we still lack a critical edition, although I am glad to say that the Rev. A. W. Adams, Dean of Divinity of Magdalen College, Oxford, has almost completed one. *

The earliest known manuscript of Primasius (Oxford, Bodleian Library Douce MS. 140) is assigned by Professor Lowe to the Seventh or Eighth century, and described as being 'written certainly in some centre with Insular traditions and probably in England, as script, corrections, and manner of pricking show,'[39] and most of the other manuscripts come from monasteries founded by English or Irish monks. In the circumstances, it is not surprising that we should find Bede using Primasius or that the earliest manuscript should probably be of English origin. Unfortunately the Migne edition of Primasius, which is the text most readily available for the purposes of comparison with Bede, seems to be based on an apparently mutilated text, resembling that of a Ninth-century manuscript from Corbie, now at Paris (B.N. MS. 13390).[40] A collation of the text of Bede's commentary with that of Primasius as given in the Migne edition (*PL* lxviii, 793 D-936 D) makes it clear that Bede transcribed a considerable part of his commentary *verbatim* from Primasius, but it is not possible to establish from this the type of text which he used. For this we must await the publication of Mr. Adams' edition.

Victorinus of Pettau as revised by Jerome; Tyconius; Caesarius of Arles; Apringius of Béja; and Primasius of Hadrumetum – these are the commentators on the Apocalypse who wrote before Bede and were available as his guides. In fact, he seems to have used only Victorinus-Jerome, Tyconius and Primasius. Nevertheless, in discussing Bede's sources we cannot ignore the commentary of Caesarius, since although not consulted by Bede, it can be used, because of its direct quotations from Tyconius, to identify the same quotations in Bede's commentary. The process is laborious, but rewarding.

Before looking more closely at Bede's commentary, we must mention two commentators who wrote after him, but who are relevant to our enquiry on account of their value as witnesses to the text of Tyconius. The first is the Italian abbot Ambrosius Autpertus (d. 778/779), who produced a commentary of enormous length, based principally upon Primasius, but with reference to all the other available commentators. His work is available only in an edition published at Lyons in 1677.[41] The second author is the Spaniard Beatus of Liebana, whose commentary was written about 786. Beatus was a writer of very little originality, who contented himself with reproducing lengthy quotations from the writings of his predecessors, among them Tyconius, for whose text he is generally reckoned our best source.[42] The commentary of Beatus enjoyed great popularity in Spain, where it inspired a famous group of illuminated manuscripts, of which more than twenty have survived, to the delight of the art historian.[43]

We may now turn to Bede's own commentary. This is probably the earliest of his commentaries on Scripture, and seems to have been written between 703 and 709. It is dedicated to Hwaetberct, who succeeded Ceolfrid as Abbot of Wearmouth and Jarrow in 716, to whom Bede also dedicated the *De Temporum Ratione*, and who was called by his brethren Eusebius, on account of his piety.[44] The work, Bede says, was deliberately kept short from consideration of the national inertia of the English who – at least in Bede's experience – could not be troubled to read long books.[45] Whether because of its brevity or from some other cause, Bede's commentary proved popular. Professor Laistner has listed no fewer than 73 manuscripts,[46] and although his list is not wholly reliable, having at least one manuscript wrongly ascribed to Bede,[47] there can be no doubt that the total number surviving is very considerable.

Since the commentary on the Apocalypse is probably to be dated between 703 and 709, it is therefore one of Bede's earlier works, written when he was in his thirties. It is characterised by a dependence on earlier writers from whom, in fact, Bede reproduced considerable sections word for word. Thus, in the preface, when he quotes the seven Rules of Tyconius for understanding the Scriptures, Bede takes the appropriate passages from St. Augustine's *De Doctrina Christiana*, amounting to more than 550 words.[48] Again, in a discussion regarding the sealing of the twelve tribes of Israel (Rev. vii. 5 – 8) Bede, in a passage of 550 words, takes some 390 directly from Primasius.[49] These are two extreme cases, but quotations of passages of 50 – 60 words are common enough,[50] and there can be no question of the extent to which Bede reproduces from his authorities, frequently (though not invariably) without acknowledgement. Bede is not to be blamed for this method of composition, which is familiar to every reader of the earlier pages of the *Ecclesiastical History*, and which he makes no attempt to deny. As he says in a letter to his friend Acca, his extracts are made for the poor and unlearned, who have neither the money to own a large library nor the learning to use one if they had.[51] Indeed, as Dom Meyvaert has observed, Bede generally shows more sense of literary proprietorship than many medieval writers.[52]

Furthermore, although Bede borrowed from others, he fitted what he took into a plan which was his own. He is no mere anthologist. It may well be, as Professor Laistner says, that 'the commentary on the Apocalypse probably contains far less of Bede's ideas than do some of his later works,' and it is certain that 'in expounding the last book of the New Testament canon, which lent itself so particularly to allegorical interpretation, he had had many predecessors,'[53] but the attentive reader will find in the commentary passages which, one feels, only Bede would have written. One such passage must surely be the exposition of Rev. ii. 28: *And I will give him the morning star.* Victorinus, followed by Jerome, had understood the morning star to mean the first resurrection (Rev. xx. 5, 6). Tyconius – or so I assume, for the explanation is found alike in the Turin Fragments, Apringius, Primasius and Bede himself (Apringius and Primasius in addition mention the explanation of Victorinus-Jerome that the morning star is the first resurrection) – had understood the morning star to be Christ. Bede accepts the Tyconian exegesis, but his comment upon it is his own. 'Christ is the morning star who, when the night of this world is ended, promises and discloses to the saints the eternal light of life.'[54] Or consider the comment on Rev. xix. 9: *Blessed are they which are bidden to the marriage supper of the Lamb.* 'Those therefore who come to the refreshment of heavenly contemplation, when the time of this present life is ended, are assuredly called to the marriage feast of the Lamb.'[55] Both these passages in turn recall – to me at least – the account given many years later in the *Ecclesiastical History* of the words of the young nun, dying of the plague at Barking Abbey in 664, who saw her cell full of heavenly light: 'I know you think I speak deliriously, but understand that this is not so, for I tell you truly that I see such a light that your lamp seems to me in every way to be but darkness . . . . Burn then your lamp as long as you will, but know that it is not for me, for my light will come to me when the dawn breaks.'[56]

One may regret that passages of this nature rarely occur in Bede's commentary on the Apocalypse, and that he is frequently content to employ the words of other men. Nevertheless, even this practice has its advantages, since it enables us to estimate the extent of Bede's reading and, in consequence, the contents of the library which Benedict Biscop had built up at Monkwearmouth and Jarrow, the fruit of his many visits to the Continent. The subject has already been discussed by Professor Laistner in a masterly essay,[57] to which I will add only a few points of detail.

Bede's commentary, as we have already seen, draws upon three earlier commentators: Victorinus-Jerome, Tyconius, and Primasius. Besides these, Bede used certain works of Augustine: the *De Doctrina Christiana*,[58] the *De Civitate Dei* (which had also been used by Primasius, but Bede consulted it independently),[59] the *De Sancta Virginitate*, [60] and the *Tractates on the Gospel of St. John*.[61] Of the works of St. Gregory the Great, his favourite writer, Bede quotes from the *Homilies on Ezekiel*[62] and the *Moralia in Job*.[63] Of St. Jerome's writings he cites a passage from the commentary on Daniel,[64] and apparently refers to the commentary on Isaiah.[65] He also has a * quotation from St. Cyprian which I have not identified,[66] and appears to quote from, and certainly used, Isidore of Seville's *Etymologiae*.[67] He also had at his disposal, as Miss Rosemary Cramp observed last year, Rufinus' Latin version of the *Ecclesiastical History* of Eusebius of Caesarea,[68] from which he obtained his reference to Clement of Alexandria's account of the origin of the Nicolaitans (Rev. ii. 15).[69] From the same source he presumably obtained his quotation of the famous saying of St. Ignatius: 'I am the wheat of God and I am ground by the teeth of beasts that I may be made pure bread.'[70] A reference to Dionysius of Alexandria also comes from Rufinus.[71]

These sources of Bede's Commentary are only those which can be identified directly from his text and there is no doubt that he had other books available when he went to work. The long excursus on the precious stones which adorn the foundations of the wall of the New Jerusalem (Rev. xxi. 19, 20)[72] seems to be based on some treatise on gems which I have not identified. Professor Laistner suggests that this was Pliny,[73] but my own feeling is that the author was a Christian writer. One obvious candidate is the old Latin version of St. Epiphanius' treatise on gems, but collation does not confirm this identification.

There can, however, be no doubt that Bede's main guides in composing his commentary were Primasius and Tyconius, supported by Victorinus-Jerome and the passages in Book XX of St. Augustine's *De Civitate Dei* which deal with the Last Judgement. If we consider only the quantity of material incorporated into his text, Bede would appear to have been most greatly influenced by Primasius. On the other hand, Primasius is only named once in Bede's commentary,[74] while Tyconius is named no less than ten times. This fact led Professor Laistner to suggest that Bede specifically acknowledged every one of his borrowings from Tyconius' commentary,[75] but I believe that this is not the case and that there is in fact a considerable quantity of unacknowledged Tyconian quotation in Bede. Some of this can be identified by collation with other commentators indebted to Tyconius, like Beatus, Caesarius, and the Tyconian Fragments of Turin, while other passages may be provisionally identified as being by Tyconius because of their agreement with his characteristic theology.[76] By these tests the number of apparently Tyconian citations in Bede becomes so considerable as to imply that Bede had a very genuine admiration for Tyconius' writings. Naturally, he deplored his Donatism; but unlike Primasius he spoke of Tyconius himself with respect[77] and admitted that he had followed the pattern of his commentary in his own work.[78] For this reason I would suggest that Bede's qualitative debt to Tyconius is greater than his quantitative debt to Primasius and regard him as reasserting the Tyconian tradition in Apocalyptic commentary.[79]

We must, however, qualify this statement. Bede took from Tyconius his typological interpretation of the Apocalypse, but he nevertheless held firmly to the principle which he had learned from St. Augustine: that allegorical interpretation cannot be permitted to nullify the literal understanding of the text. We see this principle maintained in Bede's explanation of Rev. xx. 13: *And the sea gave up the dead which were in it, and death and Hades gave up the dead which were in them.* Tyconius had apparently understood by 'the dead of the sea' those who, being dead by reason of their sins, were physically alive at the Last Judgement in the stormy sea of this present world and declared (in one of the passages which Bede gives *verbatim*): 'The peoples whom He will here find living are the dead of the sea. *And death and Hades gave up their dead.* These are the buried nations.' Bede, however, takes care, in giving Tyconius' exegesis, to warn the reader in advance: 'This passage can be taken literally as meaning that all the bodies which the flood has swallowed up or the sea monster devoured will be resurrected.'[80]

Furthermore, we must remember what has already been said: that Bede, following his master Gregory the Great, had constantly in mind the thought of death and of the Last Judgement.[81] Indeed, the representation of the Judgement must have been familiar to his eyes, since he records in his *History of the Abbots* that among the treasures brought back by Benedict Biscop from his fifth visit to Rome were pictures of the Virgin Mary and the twelve Apostles, and of scenes from the Gospels and from the Apocalypse of St. John, all of which were exhibited in Monkwearmouth church so that, according to Bede, 'all those who entered the church even though ignorant of letters, wherever they turned their gaze might contemplate, even though only in an image, the beloved aspect of Christ and of His saints; or might with more vigilant mind recall the grace of the Incarnation; or else having before their eyes the great danger of the final testing, might remember to try themselves more strictly.'[82] The character of these Apocalypse paintings constitutes a fascinating problem for the art historian, which unfortunately cannot be discussed here. I will only say that from references which Professor Julian Brown has generously communicated to me, it would seem that it may be possible to form some valid impression of the style and character of these Apocalypse paintings in Monkwearmouth church.

Bede then always recognised the validity of the literal acceptance of the text of Holy Scripture and never allowed the allegorical interpretation of the Book of Revelation to diminish his sense imminence of the Second Coming and the awful character of the Last Judgement. These two qualifications made, we may recognise the degree to which he incorporated Tyconius into his text, both in the spirit and in the letter. This is in flat contradiction to the method of Primasius who handled Tyconius (as it were) with the tongs, as an alien and schismatic. Primasius cannot be blamed for this – he wrote at a time when Donatism was still a live issue, and human memories are long and often bitter. Bede, for whom Donatism was a long-dead issue, could afford to take a more detached view of Tyconius' merits. However, whatever the explanation, Bede drew upon Tyconius, and one of the primary desiderata in the study of Bede's commentary is to identify the passages which may be Tyconian in origin.

The method of doing this is fairly simple, though somewhat tedious. It consists of comparing the text of Bede with other authors who are known to have used Tyconius or who appear (as in the case of the Turin Fragments) to be dependent upon him, and to distinguish those passages where they and Bede are in verbal agreement. Such passages may be assumed to have a common ancestor, namely Tyconius. If of course exact verbal agreement is to be found between Bede and more than one of the other authors, the case for identification is correspondingly strengthened. In this context, fruitful results are afforded by the collation of Bede with Caesarius of Arles, Beatus of Liebana, and with the Fragments of Turin. These three sources agree with one another and with Bede surprisingly often – a fact which would seem to substantiate the view that the Fragments derive, directly or indirectly, from the original Tyconian text. The origin of the Turin Fragments is obscure, but one may safely say that no results derived from comparison with Bede in any way invalidate Lo Bue's hypothesis that they represent part of Tyconius' commentary adapted for Catholic use. Furthermore, the fact that on occasion the totality of a passage in Bede can be made up from partial quotations in the text of Caesarius, Beatus and the Fragments, goes far to suggest that Bede regularly reproduced substantial passages from Tyconius' commentary which he was using.

The result of these processes of collation, then, is to confirm the influence of Tyconius' on Bede and to disprove the suggestion of

Professor Laistner that the only occasions when Bede cites Tyconius are those on which he specifically mentions him by name. On the contrary, it appears that Bede frequently quoted Tyconius without acknowledgement, and it would seem that the passages where he mentions him by name are those in which Tyconius' view is either unconventional (as in his explanation of Rev. v. 6 that the Lamb which is slain is the Church),[83] or when he speaks, '*more suo*,' from a Donatist standpoint. On such occasions, one may assume, Bede considered Tyconius' explanation worthy of consideration, but felt it desirable to disclaim any personal responsibility for the views expressed by giving the name of the author. In the case of Primasius this necessity did not arise and, in any case, Bede was well aware that a great deal of his commentary had been taken, without acknowledgement, from the work of abler men. Indeed, on two occasions Bede deliberately quotes Augustine by name in passages where Primasius had given no reference.[84] The only occasion when Bede actually names Primasius is in his discussion of the significance of the number of the Beast (Rev. xiii. 18),[85] where he has already given (this time without acknowledgment) an explanation which he apparently found in Victorinus-Jerome,[86] only in order to complete the interpretations of his predecessors by one of his own: that six hundred and sixty-six is a number of perfection, being the number of talents of gold which came to Solomon annually (I Kings x. 14), which Antichrist usurps to himself through his overweening pride. 'What therefore was lawfully owed to the king as a gift and duly paid, the seducer and tyrant presumes to demand for himself.'[87] Bede would seem to have valued Primasius rather as a quarry for material than as a guide to understanding.

It would seem, then, that Bede is both a disciple of Tyconius as an interpreter of the Book of Revelation and also a valuable source from which the Tyconian commentary may be reconstructed, so far as this is possible with our limited materials. In fact, the provision of a critical edition of Bede's Commentary on the Apocalypse will be of value in two related, but nevertheless independent fields of scholarship. In the first place, it will help to supply what every student of Bede earnestly desires: a modern edition of his works, based upon a critical study of the manuscripts, and giving references to all sources employed by Bede, so that we can see what is original in his work and what derivatory. In the second place, such a critical edition will fill a gap in the material employed by the historian of doctrine and medieval culture in tracing the course of the development of the Tyconian tradition of apocalyptic commentary. With critical editions of Primasius and Bede to hand, to reinforce those of Beatus, Caesarius and the Fragments of Turin, it will finally be possible to proceed to the task of reconstructing, so far as may be, the original commentary of Tyconius, by a process of text-collation and the identification of Tyconian passages on theological grounds. When this is done, the material for a major study of Latin Apocalyptic commentary in the early Middle Ages will be available, which will be of interest, not only to theologians, but to students of medieval culture and psychology.

It seems desirable, in concluding this lecture, to speak briefly of the development of the Tyconian tradition in which Bede stands in the centuries which followed his lifetime, down to the Twelfth century, when the typological interpretation which had characterised it began to be superseded by a renewed emphasis on eschatology.[88] The characteristic of the Apocalypse commentaries which followed those of Bede and Aurelius Autpertus was a lack of originality. The scholars of the Carolingian epoch concerned themselves with the construction of a good biblical text whose exegesis was to be based on the Bible itself and the authority of the Fathers of the Church – a tradition which seems to have gone more or less undisputed until Peter Abelard, that *enfant terrible* of the Twelfth century, arose to challenge the arbitrary use of patristic authority in determining theological difficulties. However, from the Ninth to the Twelfth century the authority of tradition prevailed, and theologians based their works upon the writings of their greater predecessors. In the field of Apocalypse commentary there were above all Bede and Ambrosius Autpertus. Of the two, Ambrosius Autpertus' vast commentary offered more material for later writers, and the highly influential commentaries associated with Auxerre, which go under the name of Haimo, drew upon him.[89] The commentary of Bruno, bishop of Segni, written perhaps about 1080/82,[90] seems to indicate a return to Bede, but the extent to which Bruno used him is controversial.[91] In one way, however, Bruno certainly represents a return to Bede, and that is in his acceptance of Bede's division of the text of the Apocalypse. Bede had considered the Book of Revelation as falling into seven sections, namely (1) the letters to the Seven Churches (i. 1 – iii. 22); (2) the Lamb and the seven seals (iv. 1 – viii. 1); (3) the seven angels with their trumpets (viii. 2 – xi. 18); (4) the Woman and the Dragon (xi. 19 – xiv. 20); (5) the seven last plagues (xv. 1 – xvii. 18); (6) the damnation of the Great Harlot (xviii. 1 – xx. 15); and (7) the New Jerusalem (xxi. 1 – xxii. 21).[92] Bede's system had been discarded by 'Haimo' in favour of another system of seven divisions constructed from a ten-division system employed by Ambrosius Autpertus. Bruno, however, reverted to Bede's system of division, which became the standard form for the glossators of the Twelfth century.[93] In terms of his influence upon later writers, it may be held that one of the most important aspects of Bede's work was his discovery of the fundamental significance of the number seven in the construction of the Apocalypse.

A second important legacy from Bede to medieval theology, mentioned in his commentary on the Apocalypse[94] but more fully described in the *De Temporum Ratione*, written in 725,[95] is the doctrine of the Six Ages of the world.[96] This conception, inherited from St. Augustine[97] through Isidore of Seville,[98] saw human history divided into six periods: (1) from Adam to Noah; (2) from Noah to Abraham; (3) from Abraham to David; (4) from David to the Exile; (5) from the Exile to the Incarnation; (6) from the Incarnation to the end of time. The seventh age is the eternal Sabbath of the New Jerusalem, to which there will be no ending. We now live in the sixth age, initiated by the birth of Christ, which will be ended only by the coming of

Antichrist. The significance of this Augustinian division is that it constitutes a further obstacle to any millenarianist doctrine of the thousand-year reign of the saints with Christ. The end of the sixth age, as Bede says, is more obscure than those of the others.[99] We do not know the times and the seasons.

Such was the pattern of the Tyconian tradition of Apocalyptic commentary, among whose exponents Bede is to be numbered, and which dominated western scriptural exegesis from the Fourth century until the Twelfth, when it gave way to another, more eschatological type of interpretation, more in keeping with the apocalyptic atmosphere of the mid-Twelfth century, whose introduction is commonly associated with the name of Joachim of Flora (d. 1202). The older system had served its purpose and today remains a subject of study by the historian rather than a guide to the interpreter of Scripture. Nevertheless, a system which commanded the admiration of Augustine of Hippo and Bede of Jarrow deserves our respect, especially when we recall that it gave significance to a difficult work like the Apocalypse at a time when materials for critical analysis in the manner of modern scholarship were not available. And, let us add, in the hands of a scholar and saint like Bede, the Tyconian system could offer opportunity for moving men's hearts and arousing in them that love of Almighty God, Father, Son, and Holy Ghost, to which all study of Holy Scriptures should ultimately tend.

NOTES

1 M. L. W. Laistner, *A Hand-List of Bede Manuscripts*, New York: Columbia University Press, 1943, p. 94.

2 F. M. Stenton, *Anglo-Saxon England*, 2nd ed., Oxford, 1947, p. 185.

3 E. A. Freeman, 'Saint Thomas of Canterbury and his Biographers,' *National Review*, April 1860, reprinted in *Historical Essays*, London, 1871, pp. 86, 94.

4 *Venerabilis Bedae Commentaria in Scripturas sacras*, ed. J. A. Giles, vol. vi, London, 1844.

5 Migne, *PL* xciii.

6 Alexander Souter, *The Text and Canon of the New Testament*, 2nd ed. revised by C. S. C. Williams, London, 1954, p. vii.

7 Paul Meyvaert, *Bede and Gregory the Great* (Jarrow Lecture 1964), pp. 14, 15.

8 A. N. Whitehead, *Adventures of Ideas*, Cambridge, 1933, p. 218.

9 Dionysius *apud* Eusebius, *HE* VII, 25. 9 – 27. *CGS: Eusebius Werke*, 2er Bd., 2er Teil (1908), pp. 692–700.

10 See E. Hennecke, *New Testament Apocrypha*, ed. by W. Schneemelcher, E. T. by R. McL. Wilson, Vol. II, London, 1965, pp. 663–83.

11 Tertullian, although fluent in Greek, has no doubt as to the Johannine authorship of Revelation, e.g. *De Praescr. Haer.*, 33: 'Ioannes vero in Apocalypsi idolothyta edentes et stupra committentes iubet castigare.' *PL* ii, 46 B.

12 Hier., *De Vir. Illus.*, 74: 'Victorinus, Petavionensis episcopus, non aeque latine ut graece noverat.' *PL* xxiii, 719 C.

13 See Pierre de Labriolle, *Histoire de la littérature latine chrétienne*, 3rd ed. by G. Bardy, Paris, 1947, i. p. 320.

14 Gennadius, *De Script. Ecclesiast.*, 18: 'Floruit hic vir aetate qua iam memoratus Ruffinus, Theodosio et filio eius regnantibus.' *PL* lviii. 1072.

15 Tyconius *apud* Beatus (ed. Sanders, p. 575): 'Hae duae civitates una mundo et una desiderat servire Christo; una in hoc mundo regnum cupit tenere, et una ab hoc mundo fugere; una tristatur, altera laetatur; una flagellat, altera flagellatur; una occidit, altera occiditur; una ut iustificetur adhuc, altera ut impie agat adhuc. hae utraeque ita laborant in unum, una ut habeat unde coronetur, altera ut habeat unde damnetur;' *apud* Bede (*PL* xciii, 185 A): 'Duae sunt enim in mundo civitates: una de abysso, altera de coelestibus oriens.' See T. Hahn, *Tyconius Studien* (Studien zur Geschichte der Theologie und Kirche), Leipzig, 1900, pp. 25, 29.

16 Aug., *De Doct. Christ.*, III, xxx, 42: 'Tichonius quidam qui contra Donatistas invictissime scripsit, cum fuerit donatista, et illic invenitur absurdissimi cordis, ubi eos non omni ex parte relinquere voluit.' *CSEL* lxxx, 104.

17 Gennadius, *De Script. Eccles.*, 18: 'Exposuit et Apocalypsin Iohannis ex integro nihil in ea carnale, sed totum intelligens spiritale.' *PL* lviii. 1071.

18 Bede, *Expl. Apoc.*, Lib. II: 'Tychonius more suo tertiam partem stellarum quae cecidit falsos fratres interpretatur, quod altera tertia Ecclesia sit, et hostes forinseci tertia.' *PL* xciii, 166 C.

19 Ibid., *Praef. PL* xciii, 131 B, 132 D.

20 See Wilhelm Kamlah, *Apokalypse und Geschichtstheologie* (Historische Studien, Heft 285), Berlin, 1935, pp. 57 ff.

21 Ibid., p. 71.

22 Aug., *De Civ. Dei*, XX, vii. *CSEL* xl (2), 440, 441.

23 Aug., *Ep.* 199 *ad Hesychium. CSEL* lvii, 243–92. Cf. *De Civ. Dei*, XX, v.

24 Raoul Manselli, *La "Lectura super Apocalipsim" di Pietro di Giovanni Olivi: Ricerce sull' escatologismo medioevale* (Istituto storico italiano per il Medio Evo: Studi storici, Fasc. 19–21), Rome, 1955, pp. 5–16.

25 Bede, *HE* I, xxxii (ed. Plummer, p. 69).

26 Bede, *In Samuel Prophetam*, IV, viii: '. . . appropinquante mundi termino.' *PL* xci, 704 B. Cf. Manselli, op. cit., p. 19.

27 Cassiodorus, *Institutiones*, I, 9. 3 (ed. Mynors, p. 33).

28 Aug., *De Doct. Christ.*, III, xxxi, 44 – xxxvii, 55. *CSEL* lxxx, 106 – 117.

29 Bede, *Expl. Apoc., Praef. PL* xciii, 131, 132.

30 It was no. 224. See C. Becker, *Catalogi bibliothecarum antiquarum*, Bonn, 1885, p. 48: 'Explanatio tichonii donatistae in Apocalypsim vol. I vetus.'

31 *Spicelegium Casinense*, III, 1. Montecassino, 1897, pp. 261–331: *Tyconii Afri Fragmenta Commentarii in Apocalypsim.*

32 Francesco Lo Bue, *The Turin Fragments of Tyconius' Commentary on Revelation* . . . prepared for the press by G. G. Willis (Texts and Studies, N.S., Vol. VII), Cambridge, 1963, pp. 35–38.

33 Ibid., p. 3.

34 In a letter to the author of 22 December 1963: '. . . your doubt about Peyron's dating and Lo Bue's "book-gothic"is only too well justified – the script is pure caroline minuscule. So far as the plates (which seem to be well chosen) illustrate it, there is no sign of admitting those majuscule elements which by and by became reestablished within the minuscule; nor is there any appearance of stylistic symptoms which, even in Italy, essentially transform the script before the 11th century: breaking of the shaft, stiffness, development of sharp initial and final tags, etc. By such aspects must the script be judged since it is, in my opinion, North Italian. Similarly we must consider whether the script, owing to the contrary tendency, possibly lacks specifically caroline characteristics,

through a weak formlessness which also appears in Italy in the 10th century. This is not the case either.

'It must therefore be asked to what period of carolingian writing this MS. can be assigned and what distinctive qualities determine the period. I should consider that these rather plain forms, each taken by itself, can already be expected in the 3rd/4th quarter of the 9th century, even in the relatively upright type of writing seen in the MS., and that these could appear up to the middle of the 10th century. However, what makes me prefer the *first half of the 10th century* as opposed to the end of the 9th is 1) the narrow spacing of the lines, which is more frequent in the 10th century than previously and is not perhaps conditioned by economic factors alone; 2) in the top lines of fol. 5 (Pl. II) the letters are more widely spaced (same hand?). Their placing suggests to me a peculiar lack of elasticity – a symptom of lateness.'

35 Lo Bue, op. cit., p. 5.

36 Germain Morin, 'Le commentaire homilétique de S. Césaire sur l'Apocalypse,' *Revue Bénédictine* xlv (1933), pp. 43–61; *S. Caesarii Opera Omnia*, ed. G. Morin, Vol. II (Maredsous, 1942), pp. 209–77: *Expositio de Apocalypsi S. Iohannis.*

37 *Apringius de Béja: Son commentaire de l'Apocalypse*, ed. Marius Férotin, Paris, 1900.

38 Primasius, *Commentarius super Apocalypsim B. Iohannis Libri V*, *Praef. PL* lxviii, 793 C.

39 E. A. Lowe, *Codices Latini Antiquiores*, Vol. II (Oxford, 1935), p. 33, no. 337.

40 See A. C. Clarke, *The Descent of Manuscripts*, Oxford, 1918, pp. 105–23.

41 *Ambrosii Autperti in Apocalypsim Commentarium* (Bibl. Patr. et antiquor. Script. Ecclesiasticorum, Tom. XXIII), Lyons, 1677, pp. 403–639.

42 Hahn, *Tyconius Studien*, p. vii: '. . . Dabei steht mir fest: den ursprünglichen Kommentar des Tyconius finden wir nur bei Beatus.'

43 See Wilhelm Neuss, *Die Apokalypse des hl. Johannes in der altspanischen und altchristlichen Bibel-Illustration* (Spanische Forschungen der Görresgesellschaft 2-3), Münster, Westphalia, 1951; André Grabar & Carl Nordenfalk, *Early Medieval Painting*, Lausanne: Skira Books, 1957, pp. 161–75.

44 Bede, *In Samuel Prophetam*, IV *Praef. PL* xci, 663 D.

45 Bede, *In Apoc. Expl.*, *Praef. PL* xciii, 134 A.

46 Laistner, *A Handlist of Bede Manuscripts*, p. 25.

47 London, British Museum, MS. Harley 223.

48 Aug., *De Doct. Christ.*, III, xxxi, 44 – xxxvii, 55. *CSEL* lxxx, 106–17 cited by Bede, *PL* xciii, 131 C – 132 D.

49 Bede, *PL* xciii, 151 B: 'Propterea Nephthalim succedit' – 152 C: 'millium summam colligi' citing Primasius, *PL* 847 B – 848 A, 848 B – 849 A.

50 e.g. Bede, *PL* xciii, 191 D: 'Tunc solvetur . . . fuerit omnipotens' = Aug., *De Civ. Dei*, XX, viii. *CSEL* xl (2), 445 = Primasius, *PL* lxviii, 916 A (Bede acknowledges the source of the Augustinian quotation); Bede, 191 A: 'Subauditur . . . certaverunt' = Primasius, 916 D, 917 A; Bede, 194 C D: 'Isto fiet ordine . . . qua Deus eam fecit' = Primasius, 921 B C D (cf. Aug., *dCD* XX, xvi. *CSEL* xl (2).

51 Bede, *Hex.*, *Ep. ad Accam. PL* cxi, 11 A B.

52 Meyvaert, *Bede and Gregory the Great*, p. 15.

53 Laistner, 'The Library of the Venerable Bede,' in *Bede: His Life, Times and Writings*, ed. Hamilton Thompson, Oxford, 1935, p. 252.

54 Victorinus-Jerome: 'primam resurrectionem scilicet promisit. stella enim matutina noctem fugat et lucem adnuntiat, id est diei initium.' *CSEL* xlix, 38, 39; Turin Fragments: 'Christus est stella matutina.' Ed. Lo Bue, p. 58; Apringius: '*Et dabo illi stellam matutinam*, id est Dominum Ihesum Christum, quem numquam suscepit vesper, sed lux semper aeterna est, et ipse semper in

luce est. Item aliter "stellam matutinam" primam resurrectionem repromittit; stellam matutinam quae noctem fugat, et lucem adnuntiat.' Ed. Férotin, p. 21; Primasius: 'Stellam natutinam, et Christum intelligi, et resurrectionem primam convenit accipi, quia et ille apparents errorum tenebras repulit, et resurrectione properante, mundanae noctis tenebrae fugabuntur. Haec enim stella sicut noctis finem, sic diei praebere videtur initium.' *PL* lxviii, 809 B C; Bede: 'Christus est stella matutina, qui, nocte saeculi transacta, lucem vitae sanctis promittit et pandit aeternam.' *PL* xciii, 140 B C.

55 'Qui ergo, finito praesentis vitae tempore, ad refectionem supernae contemplationis veniunt, profecto ad coenam Agni vocantur.' *PL* xciii, 188 D.

56 Bede, *HE* IV, 8. Ed. Plummer, i. p. 221.

57 Laistner, 'Library of the Venerable Bede.' See above, *n*[53].

58 See above *n*[48]; also Bede, *PL* xciii, 175 C.

59 Ang., *dCD* XX, ix: 'Quae sit porro bestia . . . "in manu" propter operationem' *CSEL* xl (2), 452 = Primasius: 'Quae sit porro bestia . . . in manu propter operationem' *PL* lxviii, 917 A B = Bede: 'Bestiam sanctus Augustinus impiam civitatem, imaginem vero eius simulationem eius (avis [*sic!*] ed. Giles), fallaci imagine Christianos, characterem autem notam criminis interpretatur, quam adorari, et subiici ei, et consentiri, dicit' *PL* xciii, 175 C. Bede, unlike Primasius, acknowledges the Augustinian source of his quotation. Other citations are *dCD* XX, viii (Primasius 916 A B), Bede 191 D; *dCD* XX, x (Primasius 918 A), Bede 192 C; *dCD* XX, xiv (Primasius 920 A), Bede, 193 C; *dCD* XX, xvi (Primasius 921 C D), Bede, 194 C D.

60 Aug., *De Sancta Virginitate*, xxvii, 27. *CSEL* xli, 263, 264; Bede, xciii, 173 D.

61 Aug., *In Iohannem Tr.* 36, 5. *PL* xxxv, 1665, 1666; Bede, 144 A B.

62 Greg., *Hom. in Ezech.*, I, vii, 20. *PL* lxxvi, 862 D; Bede, 143 A.

63 Greg., *Mor. in Iob, Lib.* II. *PL* lxxv, 559 D – 560 A; Bede, 146 C.

64 Hier., *Com. in Danielem*, 12. *PL* xxv, 579 B; Bede, 134 C.

65 Hier., *Com. in Isai.*, VI, xiii. *PL* xxiv, 208 A.B.; Bede, 176 C.

66 Bede: 'Sicut beatus Cyprianus sub Deciana contigisse tempestate conquestus: "Volentibus, inquit, mori, non permittebatur occidi." ' *PL* xciii, 158 B.

67 Isidore, *Etymol.*, XVI, vii. *PL* lxxxii, 571 A B; Bede, 198 C.

68 Rosemary Cramp, *Early Northumbrian Sculpture* (Jarrow Lecture 1965), p. 5.

69 Rufinus, *HE* III, 29. 1–4. *CGS: Eusebius' Werke*, 2er Bd., 1er Teil (1903), pp. 261, 263; Bede, 138 D. The original account is Clement, *Stromateis*, III, iv, 25. *PG* viii, 1129–32.

70 Rufinus, *HE* III, 36. 12. *CGS*, p. 279; Bede, 187 B. Bede's phrase: 'beatus Ignatius *fertur* dixisse' would seem to exclude any possibility of knowledge of the original Ignatian source (*Ad Rom.*, 4).

71 Rufinus, *HE* VII, 25.

72 Bede, 197 B – 203 B.

73 Laistner, 'Library of the Venerable Bede,' p. 243.

74 Bede, 172 C.

75 Laistner, art. cit., p. 253.

76 e.g. Bede, 185 A: 'Duae sunt enim in mundo civitates: una de abysso, altera de coelestibus oriens.' See above, *n*[15].

77 Bede, 131 B: 'Septem quoque regulas Tychonii, viri inter suos eruditissimi . . . '

78 Bede, 132 D, 133 A B.

79 Cf. Kamlah, *Apokalypse und Geschichtstheologie*, p. 12: 'Beda unternimmt die Arbeit des Primasius noch einmal, er gibt in Ergebnis einen neuen verkirchlichten Tyconius.'

80 Bede, 194 A. The Tyconian citation is confirmed by Beatus (ed. Sanders, p. 615) and Caesarius (ed. Morin, pp. 270, 271). Cf. the comment of Augustine, *dCD* XX, xv: 'Hos ergo mortuos exhibuit mare, qui in eo erant, id est, exhibuit homines hoc saeculum, quicumque in eo erant, quia nondum obierant.' *CSEL* xl (2), 463.

81 See the comments of Plummer in his edition of Bede, *HE*, i. pp. lxvi, lxvii.

82 *Hist. Abbat. auctore Baeda*, 6 in Bede, *HE*, ed. Plummer, i. pp. 369, 370.

83 Bede, 145 D: 'Idem Dominus qui Agnus est innocenter moriendo, leo quoque factus est mortem fortiter evincendo. Tychonius agnum Ecclesiam dicit, quae in Christo accepit omnem potestatem.'

84 Bede, 175 C (*dCD* XX, ix), Primasius 917 A; Bede 191 D (*dCD* XX, viii), Primasius 916 A.

85 Bede, 172 C (Primasius 884 A B).

86 Bede, 172 B (Victorinus-Jerome *CSEL* xlix, 125).

87 Bede, 172 C D.

88 See Kamlah, op. cit., pp. 12 – 53.

89 Ibid., pp. 14, 15. Commentaries in *PL* cxvii, 937 C – 1220 D under the name of Haimo of Halberstadt.

90 *PL* clxv, 605 A – 736 C.

91 Kamlah, op. cit., p. 17 *n*[36].

92 Bede, 130 D – 131 B.

93 Kamlah, op. cit., pp. 20 – 22.

94 Bede, 138 A; 165 A; 191 C; 199 D.

95 Bede, *De Temporum Ratione*, 10 (ed. Jones, pp. 201, 202).

96 See Plummer in his edition of Bede, *HE* i. pp. xli, xlii; Manselli, *La "Lectura super Apocalypsim" di Pietro di Giovanni Olivi*, pp. 17 – 19.

97 Aug., *dCD* XXII, xxx. *CSEL* xl (2), 669–70.

98 Isid., *Etymologiae*, V, xxxviii, xxxix. *PL* lxxxii, 223 A – 228 D.

99 Bede, *dTR*, 10: 'Huius sextae aetatis vespera caeteris obscurior in antichristi est persecutione ventura' (ed. Jones, p. 202).

APPENDIX

THE IDENTIFICATION OF THE TYCONIAN PASSAGES IN BEDE'S COMMENTARY

If, when collating the text of Bede's commentary on the Apocalypse with other writers who have made use of Tyconius independently, exact verbal agreement can be found, it may reasonably be assumed that the particular passage represents a verbatim Tyconian citation. Such collation has been made between Bede and the Turin Fragments, Caesarius of Arles (the pseudo-Augustinian homilies), and Beatus of Liebana (since there is no reason to think that Bede had access to the Turin Fragments or to Caesarius, or that Beatus used Bede) and the result has been very rewarding. Exact verbal agreement frequently occurs and, on occasion, two or more of the other commentators each supplies part of a quotation which appears as a whole in Bede. It therefore appears that Bede treated Tyconius as he did Primasius, reproducing whole sections word for word, and one may fairly assume that there is more Tyconian material in Bede than can he revealed by collation. At all events, even when working upon the text by the method of collation, a considerable portion of Tyconius can apparently be recovered. The results of the collation are given below (*Tyconian passages in italics*).

EDITIONS USED

Apringius	*Apringius de Béja: son commentaire de l'Apocalypse*, ed. M. Férotin, Paris, 1900.
Beatus	*Beati in Apocalypsim Libri* XII, ed. H. A. Sanders (Papers and Monographs of the American Academy in Rome, Vol. VII), 1930.
Bede	*Bedae Explanatio Apocalypsis. PL* xciii, cols. 129 – 206.
Caesarius	*Expositio de Apocalypsi S. Iohannis*, ed. G. Morin, *S. Caesarii Opera Omnia*, Vol. II (Maredsous, 1942), pp. 209 – 77.
Primasius	*Primasii Commentariorum super Apocalypsim B. Iohannis Libri V. PL* lxviii, cols. 793 – 936.
Tyconius (T)	*The Turin Fragments of Tyconius' Commentary on Revelation* (Texts and Studies, N.S., Vol. VII), ed. Francesco Lo Bue, Cambridge, 1963.

Col. 135 A	ECCE VENIT CVM NVBIBVS, etc. *Qui* iudicandus primo *venit occultus*, tunc iudicaturus *veniet manifestus*. Beatus 53 Cf Primasius 798 D
136 B	CAPVT AVTEM EIVS ET CAPILLI ERANT CANDIDI, etc. Antiquitas et immortalitas maiestatis *in capite candor ostenditur*. Beatus 71
136 C	ET HABEBAT IN DEXTERA SVA STELLAS SEPTEM. *In dextera Christi est spiritalis Ecclesia*. ASTITIT, inquit, REGINA A DEXTRIS TVIS IN VESTITV DEAVRATO. *Cui astanti ad dexteram dicit: 'Venite, benedicti Patris mei, percipite regnum.'* Caesarius 213 Beatus 76
138 B	ET HABEBITIS TRIBVLATIONEM DIEBVS DECEM. *Totum tempus* significat, in quo Decalogi sunt necessaria mandata. Caesarius 217 Beatus 188
139 A	ET DABO ILLI CALCVLVM CANDIDVM. *Id est, corpus nunc baptismo candidatum*. Caesarius 217 Beatus 200
139 C	ET SEDVCERE SERVOS MEOS, FORNICARI, etc. *Utique sub Christi nomine fornicationem et idolatriam spiritalem docebat. Nam quomodo aperte idolorum culturam doceret, quae in Ecclesia prophetam se dicebat?* T 49, 50

140 A QVI NON COGNOVERVNT ALTITVDINES SATANAE, etc. Sic et *qui operantur iniquitatem, non cognoscunt Deum, licet ipsum praedicent.* Hoc modo et *Deus, licet omnes noverit, non cognoverit operarios iniquitatis.*
T 55 Beatus 213

140 B QVI ENIM VICERIT FALSA, ET MEA IVSSA CVSTODIERIT, etc. *In Christo habet Ecclesia hanc potestatem* tanquam corpus in capite.
T 57 Caesarius 218 cf Primasius 809 B
ET DABO ILLI STELLAM MATVTINAM. *Christus est stella matutina.*
T 58 Beatus 99 (cf Beatus 215 Apringius 21: id est, Dominum Iesum Christum, quem numquam suscepit vesper, sed lux sempiterna est, et ipse semper in luce est).

141 A HAEC DICIT SANCTVS ET VERVS QVI HABET CLAVEM DAVID. *Id est regiam potestatem.*
T 63 Caesarius 218 Beatus 213 cf Primasius 810 A
QVIA MODICAM HABES VIRTVTEM, etc. Causam ostendit, quod ideo haec dona promereatur Ecclesia, quia non in suis viribus, sed in regis Christi gratia confidit, *laus*que *est protegentis Dei et devotionis Ecclesiae quod modicae fidei aperiatur ostium vincendi, et quod modica virtus fide roboretur.*
T 64 Caesarius 218 Beatus 235

141 B ECCE DABO DE SYNAGOGA SATANAE, QVI DICVNT SE IVDAEOS ESSE ET NON SVNT. Hoc omni *Ecclesiae tunc promisit, quia non Philadelphiae tantum crediderint ex Synagoga Iudaeorum, sicut in Actibus Apostolorum invenimus*
T 65

141 C ECCE VENIO CITO. TENE, QVOD HABES, etc. Ne tolerando lassescas. Cito enim auxiliabor, ne forte, te deficiente, alius tibi decretam accipiat mercedem. *Sic sanctorum numerum*, qui apud Deum fixus est, *impossibile est* zizaniorum *crescentium perfidia breviari. Si enim corona alteri tradatur amissa*, non vacat *locus eius* qui quod tenebat amisit.
T 70, 69

141 D ET NOMEN MEVM NOVVM. Hoc *est nomen Christianum*, non quod novum sit istud Filio Dei, qui hanc habuit claritatem antequam mundus fieret, *sed novum Filio hominis qui* fuit *mortuus et resurrexit et sedet ad dexteram Dei.*
T 73, 74

142 B ÆMVLARE ERGO ET POENITENTIAM AGE. *Ostendit fuisse*, illic, *qui aemulandi sequendique fuissent.*
T 77

142 D POST HAEC VIDI, ET ECCE OSTIVM APERTVM IN CAELO. *Descriptis Ecclesiae operibus, quae* et qualis *futura* esset, recapitulat *a Christi nativitate, eadem aliter* dicturus. *Totum enim tempus Ecclesiae* variis in hoc libro *figuris repetit.*
T 79, 80

145 C ET NEMO POTERAT IN CAELO, NEQVE IN TERRA, etc. *Neque angelus*, neque ullus iustorum etiam carnis vinculo absolutus mysteria divinae legis revelare vel investigare potuerunt, neque respicere illum, id est, *contemplari splendorem gratiae Novi Testamenti.*
Caesarius 222 Beatus 326

147 A ET EXIVIT ALIVS EQVVS RVFVS. *Contra vitricem vincentemque Ecclesiam exiit equus rufus, id est, populus sinister, ex sessore suo diabolo sanguinolentus. Quamvis* legerimus apud *Zachariam equum Domini* refum; *sed ille suo sangine* rufo, *hic alieno.*
Caesarius 224 Beatus 335

149 A — ET REGES TERRAE ET PRINCIPES ET TRIBVNI. *Reges potentes homines accipimus. Ex omni enim gradu et conditione* vult intelligi. *Caeterum, qui tunc reges praeter unum persecutorem, 'absconderunt se in speluncis et in petris montium.'*
Caesarius 227, 228 Beatus 354 cf Primasius 840 B

155 A — Alia editio habet *Super aram*
T 86 (and cf. 23 *n*[1])
ET DATA SVNT ILLI INCENSA MVLTA, etc. De *orationibus sanctorum obtulerit incensa. Ipsi enim* delegavit *Ecclesia preces suas.*
T 88 Beatus 408

155 C — ET SEPTEM ANGELI, QVI HABENT SEPTEM TVBAS, PARAVERVNT SE VT TVBA CANERENT. *Ecclesia,* septiformi spiritu inflammata, *se ad praedicandum* fiducialiter *praeparavit.*
T 90 Caesarius 230 Beatus 409 cf Primasius 657 A

155 D — ET FACTA EST GRANDO ET IGNIS, MIXTA SANGVINE, etc. . . . Hunc versum Tychonius sic exponit: *'facta est ira Dei, quae haberet in se multorum necem.'*
Caesarius 230 Beatus 409, 410

156 A — Tychonius de tertia parte sic in hoc loco inquit. Tertiam hostes intestinos dicit. Caeterum quidquid praeter Ecclesiam est, tertia pars dicta est, et Ecclesia tertia, quae contra geminum malum pugnet.
Cf T 91 Caesarius 230 Beatus 230 Primasius 857

156 C — ET MORTVA EST TERTIA PARS EORVM, QVAE HABEBANT ANIMAS IN MARI. Quas habent animas dixit, *ut ostenderet vivos spiritaliter mortuos.*
Caesarius 230 Beatus 416 cf Primasius 858 A

156 C — ET TERTIA PARS NAVIVM INTERIIT. Alia editio dicendo *'et tertiam partem navium corruperunt'* significat quod tertia, quae mortua est, aliam *tertiam,* id est, *succedentem sibi,* occiderit noxia traditione, et inutilis imitatione doctrinae.
Beatus 416 cf Caesarius 230 Primasius 858 A

156 D - 157 A — ET DIEI NON LVCERET PARS TERTIA, ET NOCTIS SIMILITER. Alia editio sic habet: *'Et diei tertia pars appareret et noctis similiter.'* Id est, *ad hoc percussa est ut* appareret tertia pars diei et tertia noctis, quae Christi et quae *diaboli.* Ad hoc, inquam, percussa est, id est, suis *voluntatibus tradita, ut, redundantibus et insolescentibus peccatis,* in *suo tempore revelaretur.*
T 96, 97 Caesarius 230, 231 cf Beatus 419 Primasius 859 B

158 C — ET SVPER CAPITA EARVM TANQVAM CORONAE SIMILES AVRO. *Seniores viginti quatuor, qui sunt Ecclesia, coronas aureas habent. Isti autem similes auro* falsos sibi fingentes de victoria stulta triumphos.
T 107 Beatus 427, 428 Caesarius 233

159 B — *Euphrates enim,* qui *fluvius est Babyloniae,* mundani regni potentiam et persecutorum indicat undas.
T 114, 115 Beatus 430 cf Primasius 860 B

160 A — ET DE ORE IPSORVM PROCEDIT IGNIS ET FVMVS ET SVLPHVR. *Ostendit* quod *pro fumo hyacinthum dixerat. Non autem perspicue ista exeunt* de *ore ipsorum, sed* noxia praedicatione poenam sibi suisque generant auditoribus.
T 120 Beatus 433 cf Primasius 862 B
POTESTAS ENIM EQVORVM IN ORE, ET IN CAVDIS EORVM. *Id est in sermone et officio:* propheta enim docens mendacium, ipse est cauda.
T 121 Beatus 434

160 B — ET CAETERI HOMINES QVI NON SVNT OCCISI IN HIS PLAGIS, etc. Quia falsos Christianos et hereticos descripserat, nunc, ut corpus omne diaboli circumscribat, gentilium quoque commemorat errorem, quibus nihil prodest *his plagis non* occidi, *cum constet eos* in gentili tunc quoque *perdurare malitia. Neque enim in illa persecutione cogentur gentiles supradictis consentire sed in sua incredulitate morientur.*
T 123 Beatus 434, 436

161 B — Quod utrumque apud Danielem uno versiculo comprehenditur, cui per angelum dicitur: *Signa librum et claude sermonenm usque ad tempus* statutum.
T 133 Beatus 441

161 D — ET DIXIT MIHI: ACCIPE LIBRVM, ET DEVORA ILLVM. *Id est, insere tuis visceribus et describe in latitudine cordis* tui. ET FACIET AMARICARI VENTREM TVVM, etc. *Cum perceperis, oblectaberis divini eloquii dulcedine, sed amaritudinem senties, cum praedicare et operari coeperis quod intellexeris.*
T 137, 138 Caesarius 238 Beatus 442, 443.

162 A, B — SVRGE ET METIRE TEMPLVM DEI ET ALTARE. SVRGE dixit, *non* quia *haec Iohannes sedibundus audiebat*, sed quia hoc verbo excitantur corda singulorum evangelicam Scripturam actusque metiri. Ibi enim quantum singuli proficiant, quantumque regulae divinae concordent, inveniunt. ET ADORANTES IN EO. *Quia non omnes qui videntur*, in eo *adorant*, sicut qui confessus fuerit in me.
T 140 Caesarius 238 Beatus 443

162 C — SACCIS AMICTI. *Id est, in exomologesi constituti.*
T 144 Caesarius 239 Beatus 446

162 D — HI SVNT DVAE OLIVAE, etc. Ecclesia duorum Testamentorum lumine radiata, Domini semper iussis assistit *Nam* et *propheta Zacharias unum candelabrum vidit septiforme, et has duas olivas, id est testamenta, infundere oleum candelabro. Haec est Ecclesia cum oleo suo indificiente, quod eam facit in lumine orbis ardere.* ET SI QVIS EOS VOLVIT NOCERE, IGNIS EXIET DE ORE ILLORVM, etc. *Si quis Ecclesiam laedit*, eiusdam laesionis reciprocante iudicio *igne* consumitur condemnatus.
T 146, 148 Caesarius 239 Beatus 446, 447 cf Primasius 867 A, B

163 B — ET CVM FINIERINT TESTIMONIVM SVVM, BESTIA, etc. *Aperte ostendit omnia haec ante novissimam persecutionem fieri* dicendo '*Cum finierint testimonium suum,*' *utique illud quod perhibent usque ad revelationem bestiae*, quae cordibus emersura est impiorum.
T 152, 153 Caesarius 239 cf. Primasius 867 D

163 B, C — ET VINCET EOS ET OCCIDET ILLOS. *Vincet in eis qui succuberint, occidet in eis qui* pro Christi nomine laudabili patientia fuerint interempti. Aut si *spiritaliter* vincet et occidet, *partem testium* accipiemus. *Sicut in Evangelio Dominus* dicit: '*Tradent vos in pressuram et occident vos.*' *Quod Lucas evangelista* pro parte dictum insinuat *dicens:* '*Occident ex vobis.*'
T 153, 154 Caesarius 239 Beatus 449 cf Primasius 867 D – 868 A

163 D – 164 B — ET CORPORA NON SINENT PONI IN MONVMENTIS. *Votum eorum dixit et impugnationem. Non* quod *valeant ne sit Ecclesia in memoriam. Sicut: 'Nec vos intratis, nec alios sinitis intrare,' cum intrent, illis impugnantibus. Faciunt* autem perspicue *de vivorum occisorumque corporibus, quia nec vivos sinent celebrando in memoriam colligi, nec occisos in memoriam recitari, nec eorum corpora in memoriam Dei testium sepeliri.* ET HABITANTES TERRAM GAVDEBANT SVPER EOS. *Quoties affliguntur iusti, exsultant iniusti et epulantur*, sicut, dum superbit impius,

incenditur pauper. QVONIAM HI DVO PROPHETAE CRVCIAVERVNT EOS. *Propter plagas quibus propter testamenta Dei humanum genus urgetur, etiam visus ipse iustorum gravat iniustos. Sicut ipsi dicunt: 'Gravis est nobis etiam ad videndum'* ET POST TRES DIES ET DIMIDIVM, SPIRITVS VITAE A DEO etc. *Hucusque angelus futurum narravit, et* nunc *inducit factum quod futurum audit*, regno Antichristi perdito, sanctos resurrexisse in gloriam. ET TIMOR MAGNVS CECIDIT SVPER EOS QVI VIDERVNT EOS. *De omnibus vivis dixit, quia et* iusti superstites *pertimescent in resurrectione dormientium.* ET ASCENDERVNT IN CAELVM IN NVBE. *Hoc est quod Apostolus dixit: 'Rapiemur in nubibus obviam* Domino *in aera.'* ET VIDERVNT ILLOS INIMICI EORVM. *Hic separavit iniustos ab* his *quos in commune dixerat timuisse.* ET ILLA HORA FACTVS EST TERRAE MOTVS MAGNVS, etc. Incumbente terrore iudicii, omnis diaboli civitas super arenam condita cum omnibus aedificationibus suis corruet. *Et denarius et spetenarius numerus est perfectus. Quod si non esset, a parte totum intelligendum* erat.
T 158, 159, 160, 161, 163, 166, 164, 167–68 Caesarius 240
Beatus 450–53 cf Primasius 868 B – 870 C

165 C

ET FACTA SVNT FVLGVRA ET VOCES, etc. *Haec omnia virtutes sunt coruscationis et praedicationis, et bellorum Ecclesiae.*
T 177 Caesarius 241 Beatus 457 cf Primasius 872 B, C

166 B

ET ECCE DRACO MAGNVS RVFVS, etc. Diabolus saevitia cruentus contra Ecclesiam potentia terreni regni armatur. *In septem enim capitibus omnes reges* suos *et in decem cornibus* omne regnum *dicit.*
Caesarius 242 Beatus 462 cf T 182

166 D

ET PEPERIT PVERVM MASCVLVM. *Semper Ecclesia*, dracone licet adversante, *Christum parit. Masculum autem dicit victorem* diaboli qui feminam vicerat. *
Caesarius 242 T 158

168 D

ET IRATVS EST DRACO IN MVLIEREM, etc. Videns *non posse continuari persecutiones quod ore sanctae* terrae avertantur, magis se armavit mysterio facinoris insistere, quo possit iugiter insidiari.
Caesarius 244 Primasius 878 B

169 A

ET STETIT SVPER ARENAM MARIS. *Id est, super multitudinem populi*, quem proiicit ventus a facie terrae.
Caesarius 244 Beatus 471

169 B

ET BESTIA QVAM VIDI, SIMILIS ERAT PARDO, etc. *Pardo, propter varietatem gentium; urso, propter malitiam et vesaniam; leoni, propter virtutem corporis et linguae superbiam* simulatur.
Caesarius 248 Beatus 475, 476 Primasius 878 D

170 A

ET DATVM EST ILLI BELLVM FACERE CVM SANCTIS, etc. *A toto partem. Quae vinci potest*, cum violentia temporis, si fieri potest, etiam electi quatientur. Ut condemnentur Iudaei, qui, non credens veritati, susceperunt mendacium. ET ADORAVERVNT EAM OMNES QVI HABITANT TERRAM. *Omnes dixit, sed habitantes terram.*
Caesarius 246 Beatus 480

170 D

ET VIDI ALIAM BESTIAM ASCENDENTEM DE TERRA. Aliam dixit de officio. Alias una est. *Quod est* autem *mare, hoc* teste Daniele, *est terra.* Cui quatuor bestias ascendere de mari cernenti per angelum dicitur: 'Hae quatuor bestiae magnae, quatuor regna consurgent de terra'.
Caesarius 246

172 A	HABERE CHARACTEREM IN DEXTERA MANV AVT IN FRONTIBVS. Character est mysterium iniquitatis, quod *hypocritae sub nomine Christi in opere* et professione accipiunt. Caesarius 246 Beatus 494
173 A	HABENTIA NOMEN EIVS ET NOMEN PATRIS SCRIPTVM IN FRONTIBVS SVIS. Ostendit *quae sit imitatio notae in fronte* corporis bestiae, *dum Deum et Christum dicit scriptos in frontibus Ecclesiae.* Caesarius 248 Beatus 510
174 B	Hanc visionem Tychonius non de virginibus specialiter, sed de tota generaliter interpretatur Ecclesia, quam despondit Apostolus 'uni viro virginem castam exhibere Christo,' ita concludens: '*Non dixit, Non fuit in ore eorum mendacium, sed non est inventum. Sicut Apostolus dicit: "Et haec quidem fuistis aliquando, sed lavati estis." Et iniquitas iniusti non nocebit ei; qua die conversus fuerit ab iniquitate sua, et poterit esse virgo, et dolus in ore eius non inveniri.* Caesarius 248 Beatus 511
177 B	ET EXIIT SANGVIS DE LACV, etc. Exiit *ultio usque ad rectores populorum. Usque enim ad diabolum et eius angelos novissimo certamine* exiit *ultio sanguinis* sanctorum *effusi.* Caesarius 249 Beatus 524 cf Primasius 890 B
178 A	PER STADIA MILLE SEXCENTA. *Id est, per* omnes *quatuor mundi partes. Quaternitas enim est conquaternata, sicut in quatuor faciebus quadriformibus et rotis. Quater enim quadringenteni, mille sexcenti.* Caesarius 249 Beatus 524 Primasius 890 C
178 D	ET VNVM EX QVATVOR ANIMALIBVS DEDIT SEPTEM ANGELIS, etc. *Istae sunt phialae quas cum odoribus ferunt animalia et seniores, qui sunt Ecclesia, qui et septem angeli.* Caesarius 250 Beatus 530
181D – 182 D	Hactenus sub plagarum nomine persecutio novissima describitur, quas Tychonius omnes a contrario vult intelligi. Plaga est, inquiens, insanabilis, et ira magna accipere potestatem peccandi maxime in sanctos, nec corripi adhuc maiore ira Dei. Proventus enim beatudinis malorum mors est, sicut e contrario tormenta et humiliatio Ecclesiae claritas est. Nam ipso tempore illaesus erit omnis populus impius ab omni plaga corporis, quasi qui acceperit totam saeviendi potestatem. Nec opus erit tunc adimpletione peccatorum, et irae consummatione aliquem malorum flagellari, et a furore compesci. *Recapitulat ab eadem persecutione* ruinam describens impiae civitatis. Caesarius 253 Beatus 551.
183 A	HABENTEM CAPITA SEPTEM ET CORNVA DECEM. *Id est, habentem reges mundi et regna,* quorum et Domino gloriam in monte monstravit. Caesarius 256 Beatus 558
183 A, B	ET INAVRATA AVRO ET LAPIDE PRETIOSO ET MARGARITIS. *Id est omnibus illecebris simulatae veritatis. Quid sit denique intra hanc pulchritudinem, exponit, dicens* HABENS POCVLVM AVREVM, etc. *Aureum* poculum *plenum immunditiarum hypocrisis est, quia* hypocritae *foris quidem parent hominibus quasi iusti, intus autem pleni sunt omni* spurcitia. Caesarius 256 Beatus 558
183 B, C	ET VIDI MVLIEREM EBRIAM DE SANGVINE SANCTORVM, etc. *Unum est corpus adversum intus ac foris: quod licet videatur loco separatum, in commune tamen, unitate spiritus operatur. Sic pronepotes pravorum sensu Zechariam lapidasse accusantur, cum ipsi non fecerint.* Caesarius 257 Beatus 559

185 A — *Duae* sunt enim in *mundo civitates:* una de abysso, altera de coelestibus oriens.
cf Beatus 575: 'hae duae civitates una mundo, et una desiderat servire Christo; una in hoc mundo regnum cupit tenere, et una ab hoc mundo fugere; una tristatur, altera laetatur; una flagellat, altera flagellatur; una occidit, altera occiditur; una ut iustificetur adhuc, altera ut impie agat adhuc. hae utraeque ita laborant in unum, una ut habeat unde coronetur, altera ut habeat unde damnetur.'

185 C — REDDITE ILLI SICVT IPSA REDDIDIT VOBIS. *De Ecclesia enim exeunt in mundum plagae visibiles et invisibiles.*
Caesarius 262 Beatus 581

186 A — LONGE STANTES PROPTER TIMOREM TORMENTORVM EIVS. *Longe stantes non corpore, sed animo, dum unusquisque sibi timet, quod alterum per calumnias et potentiam pati videt.* DICENTES: VAE, VAE, CIVITAS ILLA MAGNA BABYLON, etc. *Spiritus dicit nomen civitatis; verum illi mundum plangunt exiguo admodum tempore* poena *interceptum, omnemque industriam labefactatam cessare.*
Caesarius 262, 263 Beatus 582

186 B — Iumentorum porro et mancipiorum vocabulo caetera humanitatis auxilia perire quaeruntur; *duplici genera,* ut dixi, *quod deficiant ista mundo moriente,* vel quod miseri superstites eorum interitum qui mundi gaudia morte relinquerunt quasi suae civitatis ruinas deplorent. qui et ideo, metu poenae similis, longe stare dicuntur.
Beatus 582

186 C, D — QVAE AMICTA ERAT BYSSINO ET PVRPVRA ET COCO. *Nunquid civitas* amicitur *bysso aut purpura, et non homines? Ipsi itaque* se *plangunt, dum supradictis exspoliantur.* ET OMNIS GVBERNATOR ET NAVTAE LONGE STETERVNT, etc. *Nunquid omnes* mare navigantes adesse *poterunt ut videant incendium civitatis? Sed omnes saeculi cultores et operarios dicit timere sibi, videntes spei suae ruinam* DICENTES: QVAE EST SIMILIS CIVITATI HVIC MAGNAE? Id est, *non posse* mundum in *integrum restitui.*
Caesarius 263 Beatus 583

187 C — ET IN EA SANGVIS PROPHETARVM ET SANCTORVM INVENTVS EST, est. *Nunquid eadem civitas occidit apostolos, quae et prophetas, aut omnes* sanctos? *Sed haec est civitas quam Cain fratris sui sanguine fundavit, et vocavit* nomine *filii sui Enoch, id est, posteritatis* suae omnis. Nam septem generationes descriptae sunt *Cain. In* cuius *civitatis aedificium 'funditur omnis sanguis iustus a sanguine Abel iusti usque ad sanguinem Zachariae,' id est, populi et sacerdotis.*
Caesarius 266 Beatus 585 cf Aug., *De Civ. Dei*, XV, xvii cf Primasius 901 A

187 D — POST HAEC AVDIVI QVASI VOCEM MAGNAM TVBARVM MVLTARVM IN CAELO DICENTIVM: ALLELVIA, etc. *Haec* nunc ex parte dicit *Ecclesia*; tunc autem perfecte *cum discessio facta fuerit, et cum apertius vindicata.*
Caesarius 268 Beatus 587

188 A — ET FVMVS EIVS ASCENDIT IN SAECVLA SAECVLORVM. ASCENDIT dixit, *non ascendet. Semper* autem *in perditionem vadit Babylon,* et iam *crematur in parte, sicut Ierusalem transit in paradisum, Domino manifestante in paupere et divite.*
Caesarius 268

188 C — ET DATVM EST ILLI, VT COOPERIAT SE BYSSINO SPLENDENTE CANDIDO. *Datum est* illi *factis suis indui.*
Caesarius 269

189 B — ET IN CAPITE EIVS DIADEMATA MVLTA. In quo faciemus virtutem, *in* ipso *multitudo* sanctorum *coronatum* dicitur habere decorem. HABENS NOMEN SCRIPTUM QVOD NEMO NOVIT NISI IPSE. Nisi *ipse*, sit, quia *in illo est omnis Ecclesia.*
Caesarius 264

189 D — ET EXERCITVS QVI SVNT IN CAELO, SEQVEBANTVR EVM IN EQVIS ALBIS. *Id est, Ecclesia in corporibus candidis* imitabatur *eum*, quae propter agonem certaminis sui iure nomen accipit exercitus.
Caesarius 264 Beatus 592

190 A, B — ET IPSE CALCAT TORCVLAR VINI FVRORIS ET IRAE DEI OMNIPOTENTIS. *Calcat* enim *nunc* quoque, *donec extra civitatem calcet*. ET HABET IN VESTIMENTO ET IN FEMORE SVO SCRIPTVM: REX REGVM ET DOMINVS DOMINANTIVM. *Hoc est nomen quod nemo superborum cognoscit.* Ecclesiae autem non atramento sed spiritu Dei vivi, in tabulis scilicet cordis inscribitur. Femore *autem posteritas* seminis designatur. Unde et *Abraham, ne posteritas eius alienigenis misceretur, inter se* servumque suum tertium [*leg.* certum] *testimonium femur adhibuit.*
Caesarius 264 Beatus 593 cf Primasius 913 A

190 B, C — ET VIDI VNVM ANGELVM STANTEM IN SOLE, etc. *Id est, praedicationem in Ecclesia*, quae quanto magis premitur, tanto lucet clarius, et liberius intonat.
Caesarius 265 cf Primasius 913 B

191 A — Hanc coenam Tychonius sic exponit: '*Omni tempore comedit Ecclesia carnes inimicorum suorum*, dum comeditur *ab eis*, satiabitur *autem in resurrectione de eorum carnali opere vindicata.*'
Beatus 598

191 D — ET VIDI SEDES, ET SEDERVNT SVPER EAS, etc. Quid in istis mille annis quibus diabolus ligatus est agatur indicat. Ecclesia enim, quae sedebit, *in Christo super duodecim thronos ad iudicandum iam* sedet, *iudicans*, quae a suo rege meruit audire: 'Quaecunque ligaveris super terram, erunt ligata et in caelo.'
Beatus 603

192 B, C — HAEC EST, *inquit*, RESVRRECTIO PRIMA. *Utique qua resurgimus per baptismum, sicut Apostolus dicit: 'Si consurrexistis cum Christo, quae sursum sunt quaerite.' Sicut enim prima mors in hac vita est per peccata*, cum anima quae peccaverit ipsa morietur, *ita et prima resurrectio in hac vita est per remissionem peccatorum.* BEATVS ET SANCTVS, etc. *Id est, qui servaverit quod renatus est.*
Caesarius 269 Beatus 605

192 C — ET REGNABVNT CVM CHRISTO MILLE ANNIS. *Retulit Spiritus, cum haec scriberet, regnaturam Ecclesiam mille annos, id est, usque ad finem mundi. De perpetuo* enim *regno manifestum est.* ET CVM CONSVMMATI FVERINT MILLE ANNI, etc. Consummatos *dixit a toto partem, nam sic solvetur ut supersint anni tres et menses sex novissimi certaminis. Sed praeter hunc tropum recte dicitur finitum tempus. Non enim computandae sunt tam* exiguae *reliquiae*, cum septingenti et quot Deus voluerit anni hora ab apostolo appellati sint.
Caesarius 269, 270 Beatus 605, 606

193 D — ET IVDICATI SVNT MORTVI EX HIS, etc. *Id est, ex Testamentis iudicati sunt secundum quod ex eis fecerunt aut non fecerunt.*
Caesarius 270 Beatus 615

194 A	Quod Tychonius sic exponit: '*Gentes quas hic inveniet vivos, ipsi sunt mortui maris.* ET MORS ET INFERNVS DEDERVNT MORTVOS SVOS, *ipsae sunt gentes sepultae*'. Caesarius, 270, 271 Beatus 616
195 D – 196 A	LVMEN EIVS SIMILI LAPIDI PRETIOSO. *Lapis pretiosus Christus est,* qui ait: 'Claritatem quam dedisti mihi, dedi eis.' Caesarius 273 Beatus 623
203 C	ET CIVITAS NON EGET SOLE NEQVE LVNA VT LVCEANT IN EA. *Quia non lumine aut elementis mundi regitur Ecclesia, sed Christo aeterno sole* deduci *per mundi tenebras.* Caesarius 274

Corrigenda

p. 12, l. 14, please read: ... sense of the imminence.

p. 25, col. 166D, l. 3, please read: *qui feminam vicerat.*

XIII

Bede's Ecclesiastical History of the English People. A Historical Commentary
By J.M. Wallace-Hadrill. (Oxford Medieval Texts.) pp. xxxv + 299. Oxford: Clarendon Press, 1988

EVER since its publication in 1896, Charles Plummer's edition of the historical writings of Bede has been recognized as one of the major achievements of English nineteenth-century scholarship, worthy to be compared, in the range and sweep of its learning, with Lightfoot's *Apostolic Fathers*. Sir Roger Mynors has observed of the text established by Plummer for the *Ecclesiastical History* that it 'can fairly be described as final'. Equally, the notes with which he furnished his edition show a breadth of reading, particularly of patristic and medieval authors, which has never been surpassed and rarely rivalled, and for nearly a century scholars have turned for information to Plummer's Bede with a confidence only matched by their admiration. Nevertheless, the passage of time and the labours of more recent historians have inevitably rendered some of Plummer's comments obsolete and qualified others in the light of a greater knowledge of the world in which Bede lived and wrote. In this field, as in so many others, the past half-century has seen an unparalleled multiplication of information, which it was desirable to concentrate in a single volume. Accordingly, the editors of the Oxford Medieval Texts series invited J. M. Wallace-Hadrill to prepare a commentary to the edition and translation of the *Ecclesiastical History* by Bertram Colgrave and Sir Roger Mynors in 1969. The choice was a wise one, for Wallace-Hadrill was an expert on Frankish Gaul, an area which Bede was apt to neglect in his desire to link the English Church as far as possible with Rome (for instances of Bede's admiration of *Romanitas*, both secular and sacred, see pp. 18, 124–5, 158, 191, 193–4). Unhappily, Wallace-Hadrill died before the final revision of his commentary, which has been seen through the press, in accordance with his wishes, by Thomas Charles-Edwards. To him, and to Patrick Wormald, we owe a collection of addenda (pp. 207–43) which amplifies—and, in a few cases, corrects—Wallace-Hadrill's notes. Whether this arrangement is

[Journal of Theological Studies, NS, Vol. 40, Pt. 2, October 1989]

necessarily the best, so far as the user of the commentary is concerned, is controversial. A commentary reflects the personality of the commentator, and Wallace-Hadrill, no less than Plummer, had a highly personal style, which deserved preservation. On the other hand, a commentary is also an instrument of study, and it is tiresome, to say the least, to have to turn repeatedly to the end of the book in order to discover the latest available contribution to the topic discussed. In the circumstances it might have been better to have integrated the addenda with the text, if necessary indicating their character by enclosing them in square brackets, or by some other typographical device.

This reservation made, how does Wallace-Hadrill's commentary compare with Plummer's? It should be made clear that it does not wholly supersede it, nor does it set out to do so. Plummer's references to patristic and medieval authors were so profuse (and sometimes, it must be admitted, largely irrelevant to the matter in hand) that a commentary which incorporated them all would be unwieldy. Accordingly, the student of the *Ecclesiastical History* will continue to consult Plummer with advantage. To give one example: the drastic intervention of St Peter to deter Archbishop Laurence from abandoning Kent after the death of King Æthelbert (*HE* ii. 6). We can agree with Wallace-Hadrill that 'it is St Peter who saves the day' (p. 62), but it is to Plummer that we must turn for information about such supernatural flagellation, as illustrated by the case of Natalius, scourged all night by angels to bring him back to orthodoxy (Eusebius, *HE* v. 28)—an incident which may have helped to shape the tradition about Laurence—and Jerome's famous beating for being a Ciceronian rather than a Christian (*Ep.* 22, 30). Not that Wallace-Hadrill fails to pay tribute to his great predecessor. For example, he comments on ii. 10: *uiro glorioso . . . Dei*: 'There are possible corruptions or unexpected difficulties in the text which Plummer did not miss. I follow Colgrave and Mynors here' (p. 69).

What then does Wallace-Hadrill offer as distinct from Plummer? In the first place, he provides a number of corrections to the translations in the Colgrave and Mynors edition. These are generally minor, but a few are important, as the correction of the rendering of *quadragies octies LXXV* to '3600 miles' instead of Colgrave's 4,875 (i. 1) or the translation of *ad mediterranea* as 'the Midlands' instead of 'the marchlands' (i. 21), or again the correction of Colgrave's misunderstanding of *ibidem* as meaning 'in England' and not 'in Ireland' in iii. 27. However, the number of such corrections is relatively small.

On a wider field, an important feature of Wallace-Hadrill's

commentary is the degree to which it demonstrates that the title, *The Ecclesiastical History*, means what it says. Bede as a historiographer is a true heir of Eusebius of Caesarea, and incorporates into his text only those items of secular history which contribute to the understanding of Church affairs. Thus, of the final paragraph of iv. 26[24] (*Quo uidelicet anno . . . liberaret*), Wallace-Hadrill notes: 'This is one of the few passages in *HE* that have no immediate bearing on ecclesiastical history. Bede has the annalistic record or king-list before him and decides to include this entry' (p. 170). Again, with regard to the Mercian rebellion against Oswiu (iii. 24), he observes: 'Bede clearly approves of the Mercian rebellion. . . . He accepts the blood-right of Penda's kin to rule and welcomes the loyalty of the Mercians to that kin. However, the more significant consequence for Bede is that they could now freely serve Christ, "uero regi", under Wulfhere his vicar' (p. 124). This concept of *ecclesiastical* history explains the significance of miracles in Bede's work. King Sebbi of the East Saxons (iv. 11) appears 'not because something needed to be said of the East Saxons but because the Barking *libellus* recounted two miracles associated with his death as a monk' (p. 147). Yet, in the case of the saintly East Anglian king, Sigeberht, Wallace-Hadrill points out: 'Bede records no miracle associated with him; it was enough that he had chosen the monastic life despite his obvious success as king; and of this Bede strongly approves' (p. 111). It is this religious motive which explains the famous *uerax historicus* of iii. 17: '. . . the "uerax historicus" will benefit his readers by frankly ("simpliciter") rebuking error and praising virtue' (p. 110). Indeed, 'one imagines that Bede's first question to a new West Saxon acquaintance would not have been: "Can you explain the succession-problems of Wessex?" but: "Do you know any good miracle-stories?"' (p. 187). Accordingly, Ethelwald the hermit's miracle, which opens Book V—a book which 'looks less well structured than the others'—'may not be a chance piece of flotsam but a vital clue to an understanding of [Bede's] purpose' (p. 174). In short, 'Bede omits what does not contribute to the picture of the pope [Gregory I (ii. 1)] he wished to present to his readers; and that picture is a piece of hagiography, and not biography in our sense' (p. 50).

A third characteristic of Wallace-Hadrill's commentary is a concern with Bede's sources: where did he get his information? Plummer, in his edition of *HE*, indicated direct quotations by printing them in italic type (a device unfortunately abandoned by Colgrave and Mynors). Wallace-Hadrill attempts more generally to suggest Bede's possible sources, and the result is both interesting and rewarding. As might be expected, Canterbury is by far the principal source for Books I and II ('with Book III one can feel Bede moving into a more familiar world' [p. 86]), but even in the later books, Canterbury remains important. So it is noted of v. 11: *postulans ut . . . archiepiscopus ordinaretur* that 'the precision of Bede's statement suggests that his informant might have been Canterbury rather than Bishop Acca' (p. 184)—who is elsewhere described as the man 'to whom, with Albinus [of St Augustine's, Canterbury], *HE* owed most' (p. 195). The range of Bede's informants is extraordinary, and by its very diversity illustrates Stenton's observations that 'the quality which makes [Bede's] work great is . . . his astonishing power of co-ordinating the fragments of information which came to him through tradition, the relation of friends, or documentary evidence. In an age when little was attempted beyond the registration of fact, he had reached the conception of history.' Stenton's judgement is borne out by Wallace-Hadrill's comment on iv. 12 (*Quartus . . . antistes Leutherius fuit*): 'It is difficult to spot the heart of this chapter, which looks like a ragbag based on materials derived from several sources that must include Winchester and Canterbury. . . . [It] is a deft survey of episcopal succession over comparatively few years in which Archbishop Theodore was the moving force.' But there follows an inevitable qualification: 'The amount of secular history included by Bede is precisely what is needed to explain episcopal flux, and no more' (p. 148). Furthermore, even on the ecclesiastical side, the character of *HE* is inevitably determined by the availability of material. 'I agree with [D.P.] Kirby . . . that "Chad's conspicuous position in the *HE* results simply from the fact that Bede was in touch with Lastingham" ' (p. 140). The limitations in source-material are a factor to be borne in mind in evaluating the *HE*. Columbanus, the great missionary, is named but once (ii. 4). The monastery at Breedon in Leicestershire is in a similar case (v. 23). 'That Breedon, a comparatively recent foundation from Peterborough, should have produced an archbishop of Canterbury is some measure of the standing of a monastery about which Bede has nothing more to say. I take it that Bede's list of contemporary bishops came from Canterbury' (p. 199). But the most conspicuous absentee from Bede's pages is surely St Boniface, the Apostle of Germany. Bede knew about the Hiberno-Northumbrian mission to the Continent—Egbert (see pp. 94, 181), Willibrord, and the two Hewalds, perhaps through Bishop Acca (p. 182); but he makes no reference to the great missionary and martyr, presumably because an appropriate Wessex source was not available to him.

It might be expected that archaeology would be one of the fields of learning illuminating *HE* which has particularly advanced since Plummer's day, and such has been the case through the labours of scholars such as Leslie Alcock, Rupert Bruce-Mitford, Martin Biddle, Rosemary Cramp, Brian Hope-Taylor, and Charles Thomas; but the total effect for the understanding of *HE* is rather disappointing, to the reviewer at least. The excavations at Yeavering (the Adgefrin of ii. 14) are of real significance (pp. 74–5); individual items such as the comb sent by Pope Boniface to Queen Æthelburh (ii. 11) and the bronze drinking-cups provided by King Edwin for the use of travellers (ii. 16) have been studied by Peter Lasko (p. 70) and Rosemary Cramp (p. 80) respectively; but many sites mentioned by Bede still retain their secrets: 'Recent excavations at York Minister have not revealed the site of Edwin's church, first of wood and later of stone' (p. 73). At times the interpretation of archaeological evidence is contradictory. On p. 148 we are told that 'it was clearly a mark of distinction to be buried in a stone sarcophagus', whereas on p. 177 D. A. Bullough is quoted as declaring that 'coffin burial is not in itself evidence of superior social standing' (though a stone-coffin was clearly an acceptable gift, as witnessed by the sarcophagus presented to St Cuthbert by Abbot Cudda (*Bede's Prose Life*, 37)).

A reviewer is inevitably tempted to add his widow's mite to Wallace-Hadrill's treasury. The statement that 'Lindisfarne also produced books [like Wearmouth-Jarrow]' on p. 130 is an almost breathtaking understatement, and there could have been reference to the researches of palaeographers and art-historians such as E. A Lowe, Bernhard Bischoff, Rupert Bruce-Mitford, Janet Backhouse, and—especially—Julian Brown (George Henderson's study *From Durrow to Kells* (1987) appeared too late for inclusion in the bibliography). The note on the Council of Hatfield (iv. 17[15]) (pp. 157–8) fails to observe that the passage in the synodical letter: 'secundum sanctos patres . . . gloriae et honoris' (386. 2–6 Colgrave and Mynors) is a citation, with some explanatory amplifications, from Canon 1 of the Lateran Council of 649 (Denzinger[31] no. 254). Bede then continues: 'Et post multa huiusmodi, quae ad rectae fidei confessionem pertinebant . . .' What were these *multa huiusmodi*? We know from Bede again that John the Archchanter was present at Hatfield and had brought with him the record of the Lateran Council of 649: 'Nam et synodum beati papae Martini centum quinque episcoporum consensu non multo ante Romae celebratum, contra eos maxime qui unam in Christo operationem et uoluntatem praedicabant, secum ueniens adtulit' (388. 33–390. 3), so it is conceivable that the bishops at Hatfield reproduced, in whole or in part, the decisions of that Roman

Council in their reply to Pope Agatho. The note on Caedmon's dream (iv. 24) notes that Bede 'chose ... to see the miracle in divine inspiration conveyed in the traditional vehicle of a dream' (p. 166). A reference could profitably have been made to Nora Chadwick, 'Dreams in early European literature' in *Celtic Studies. Essays in memory of Angus Matheson 1912–1962*, edd. J. Carney and David Greene (1968), pp. 33–50, though Mrs Chadwick, rather surprisingly, made no reference to Caedmon. Again, to the note on paganism in p. 171: 'Cuthbert's rustics were formally Christians; what they reverted to in time of stress was not the formalized practices of such as Redwald but hedge-paganism which never could be wholly eradicated', there could usefully have been added the words of the rustics to St Cuthbert in the incident of the rafts: 'Let no man pray for them, and may God have no mercy on any one of them, for they have robbed men of their old ways of worship, and how the new worship is to be conducted, nobody knows' (*Bede's Prose Life*, 3. 165 Colgrave). Finally, Wallace-Hadrill, in discussing Wilfrid's acquisition of Ripon through King Alhfrith (v. 19) is content to say: 'Bede's account of the reason for the Irish abandonment of Ripon is not in Eddius' (p. 193), without any reference to the fact that among those expelled were Abbot Eata and St Cuthbert (*Prose Life*, 8. 181 Colgrave). We have here a classic example of Bede's discretion, as a *uerax historicus*, in avoiding unedifying details. Furthermore, the observation that 'Bede does seem to admire Wilfrid though not to like him' (pp. 191–2) could have been supported by a reference to the incident at Hexham which provoked the *Epistola ad Pleguinam*, when Bede was accused of heresy in the presence of Wilfrid who,it would appear, made no comment on the matter (*Ep. ad Pleguinam* 17. *CCSL* cxxiiiC. 626). Such silence would try the patience even of a Bede.

No commentary on a great historical work can ever aspire to be final. Fresh discoveries and new interpretations will constantly provide modifications for received judgements. Equally, however, no really great commentary is every wholly superseded. It was said earlier in this review that Plummer's commentary will continue to be consulted by students of the *Ecclesiastical History* even with Wallace-Hadrill's complementary volume. In similar fashion it is likely that we shall continue to turn to Wallace-Hadrill in coming years to test our new theories by his judgements and to draw upon a scholarship which, like Plummer's, was of the heart as well as of the head.

Let me end on a detail of text-transmission. At the beginning of the commentary, in default of the introduction that Wallace-

Hadrill did not live to write, is reproduced (pp. xv–xxxv) his paper on 'Bede and Plummer', read at the Bedan Conference in Durham in 1973 and published in both his *Early Medieval History* (1975) and *Famulus Christi* (the proceedings of the Bedan Conference) (1976). On p. xxxiv there is a reference to 'Dean Liddon'. When the paper was sent for inclusion in *Famulus Christi* the present reviewer pointed out that H. P. Liddon was never a dean and, although a canon of St Paul's, did not like the 'newfangled fashion' of using Canon as a title ('Please do not Canonize me', he said to a friend). Accordingly, with Michael Wallace-Hadrill's agreement, the 'Dean' became 'Dr'. Now the error, trivial in itself but an error nevertheless, has been perpetuated. No better example could be found of the difficulty of eradicating minor slips from the historian's text.

XIV

Bede and his Legacy*

Less than ten years after the battle of Hastings had brought to an end the old English state and ensured that henceforth the destiny of England would, for better or worse, be linked with the mainland of Europe rather than with Scandinavia, a party of monks left Evesham Abbey in Worcestershire on a journey to Northumbria, there hoping to revive the monastic life which had been destroyed by the Viking raids of the ninth century. For such a venture the party, composed of only three members, must have seemed hopelessly inadequate as it travelled on foot, with its scanty baggage – books and mass- vestments – borne on the back of a single donkey. Yet there was one feature of the composition of the group which was a significant and hopeful pointer to the future: it was multinational, being composed of two Englishmen and a Norman. Already, less than a decade after the Conquest, the two peoples were working together in a common religious cause. Furthermore, the leader of the group was an Englishman. This is a circumstance which invites us to look at the three individuals a little more closely.[1]

First, the Norman. His name was Reinfrid and he was, according to Symeon, the monastic historian of Durham, *ignarus litterarum* – 'ignorant of letters' – a description which could suggest that he was no more than a simple lay-brother. In fact he was a socially well-connected knight[2], whose illiteracy was the result of an upbringing in which writing, like the art of shoeing horses, was a useful accomplishment, but no part of a gentleman's education.[3] One kept clerks to do one's writing, just as one had a smith to shoe one's horse. Reinfrid had already visited Northumbria, perhaps as a participant in King William's harrying of the North in 1069-70.

---

* A public lecture delivered in the University of Durham on 6 March 1985 in commemoration of the twelve hundred and fiftieth anniversary of the death of Bede.

1 The account of the settlement comes from Symeon of Durham, *Historia Dunelmensis Ecclesiae* III, 21 (ed. Arnold, Rolls series, I 108-10).

2 See D. Knowles, *The Monastic Order in England*[2] (Cambridge 1963), 166 note[4]. Knowles describes the Northern monastic revival with characteristic felicity, pp.165-71.

3 See V.H. Galbraith, 'The Literacy of the Medieval English Kings', British Academy Lecture for 1935, reprinted in *Studies in History*: British Academy Lectures Selected and Introduced by Lucy S. Sutherland (London 1966), 78-111.

There he had seen the deserted site of St. Hilda's abbey at Whitby, being much distressed by its neglected state. He determined to become a monk and entered the monastery of Evesham, then under the rule of Aethelwig, the great English abbot whose reputation stood too high to permit the Normans to remove him. Here he would have encountered Aelfwig, monk and deacon, the second member of the party.

p.220

The third, and its leader, was Aldwin, a monk of the Gloucestershire house of Winchcombe. He was a man of good social standing who had rejected honours and riches for the sake of voluntary poverty and contempt of the world. From Bede's writings he had learned that Northumbria had once been the home of many monks and holy men and this had aroused in him a desire to visit their deserted dwellings and live there in imitation of their example. Aldwin came to Evesham seeking companions for his venture and was joined by Aelfwig and Reinfrid. Abbot Aethelwig gave his blessing to the venture, subject to the condition that Aldwin should be the leader and spiritual father of the party. Accordingly, some time between 1072 and 1074 the three monks set out on their ambitious undertaking.

The sequel may be briefly told. The trio travelled to the North and initially settled on the north bank of the Tyne at Monkchester (the modern Newcastle).[4] This spot, although within the diocese of Durham, came under the secular jurisdiction of Waltheof, Earl of Northumberland, to the dissatisfaction of Bishop Walcher of Durham, who wished to have the monks entirely under his control. He therefore presented them with Benedict Biscop's monastery of St. Paul, Jarrow. They found the church roofless, and covered it with unhewn timbers and thatch, constructing a little hut for themselves, to serve as dormitory and refectory. Here they lived in poverty, in marked contrast to the comforts which they had enjoyed in the South. But the appeal of this elected poverty proved infectious. Others joined them; a few from Northumbria, many from southern England. Among these was Turgot, an English cleric from a distinguished Lincolnshire family, destined to become bishop of St. Andrew's. With Turgot as a companion, Aldwin, once his community at Jarrow was well-established, removed himself to Melrose, perhaps attracted by the memory that this had been the house where the novice St. Cuthbert was trained by the Irish prior Boisil. Difficulties were, however, encountered with King Malcolm III (Canmore), when Aldwin and Turgot declined, as religious, to swear allegiance to him, and in about 1076-1078 they were persuaded by Bishop Walcher to return to Northumbria, where the bishop presented them with Benedict Biscop's first foundation at Monkwearmouth which they restored as they had previously restored Jarrow.[5] Finally, in

4 Symeon, *HDE* III, 21 (Arnold 109).

1083, Walcher's successor, Bishop William of St. Carilef, brought Aldwin and his monks to Durham, there to renew the monastic tradition of the family of St. Cuthbert. On Whit Sunday, 28 May 1083, Aldwin and his community renewed their monastic vows and took a vow of stability at the shrine of St. Cuthbert.[6] Thus began the career of Durham Cathedral Priory, destined to become one of the most famous religious houses in England, until its suppression by King Henry VIII in 1539.

I have dwelt at some length on the northern monastic revival initiated by Aldwin because it is the most dramatic illustration of the influence of Bede in the early Middle Ages. It was not, of course, the earliest manifestation of his legacy. From the time of his death in 735, Bede's influence was felt, not only in England, but on the Continent of Europe, as is shown by the famous letters of St. Boniface and Lul, his successor in the see of Mainz, asking for copies of the writings of Bede, that 'most skilful investigator of the Scriptures' and 'candle of the Church'.[7] In the Jarrow Lecture for 1982 Mr Malcolm Parkes argued most persuasively that the more easily written Insular Minuscule hand superseded the traditional Capitular Uncial in the scriptorium of Wearmouth-Jarrow in order to enable the monks to cope with a new and heavy demand from outside the community for copies of their almost too successful house-author, Bede.

> 'They suddenly found that they had a best- seller on their hands and a prolific best seller at that, and because the demand came from outside the house it could not be so easily controlled as the demand from within.'[8]

In the Carolingian Empire Bede's writings were in great demand, and many of our oldest surviving manuscripts are of ninth-century Continental origin, the oldest English examples having perished in the Viking invasions.[9] With such a European reputation, there was no danger that Bede's influence would pass away in England with the Norman Conquest. We have already seen how Aldwin was moved to attempt the revival of Northumbrian monasticism by his reading of the *Ecclesiastical History* – a work which, it may be added, was no less popular on the European mainland than in the country of its origin[10] where, in the twelfth

---

Ibid, III, 22 (Arnold 111-13).

Ibid, IV, 3 (Arnold 122).

Boniface, *Ep.* 76 *(Briefe des Bonifatius, Willibalds Leben des Bonifatius*, ed. and tr. by R. Rau (Darmstadt 1968), 237); cf. *Ep.* 91 (Rau 310). Both letters tr. in *The Letters of St. Boniface*, tr. with an introduction by Ephraim Emerton (Records of Civilization No. XXXI) (New York 1940), 133-4, 168-9.

M.B. Parkes, *The Scriptorium at Wearmouth Jarrow* (Jarrow Lecture 1982), 22.

See Dorothy Whitelock, *After Bede* (Jarrow Lecture 1960), 13.

0 M.L.W. Laistner and H.H. King, *A Hand-List of Bede MSS.* (Ithaca, N.Y. 1943), 94.

p.221 century, it inspired William | of Malmesbury, perhaps the greatest English medieval historian, to continue the work of Bede.[11] Throughout the Middle Ages, Bede remained a leading theological author. In the sixteenth century the Catholic apologist Thomas Stapleton, whose translation of the *Ecclesiastical History* – the first ever made into English – was published at Antwerp in 1565, attempted, rather optimistically one would have thought, to use the evidence supplied by Bede to influence Queen Elizabeth against the Reformation. Yet it was as a scriptural commentator and computist that Bede became one of the classic authors in medieval libraries. His commentaries on Scripture remained popular from the eighth to the early sixteenth century, while as late as 1537 his works on the computus (the science of calculating the correct date of Easter) were published at Cologne by Noviomagus, not as a piece of antiquarian scholarship, but as a practical guide to paschal calculations which continue to be employed to the present day.[12]

Modern scholarship has confirmed and enhanced Bede's reputation as the teacher of the Middle Ages by exploring fields of study like his writings on Latin grammar and poetic metre and their influence on the schools of the Carolingian renaissance;[13] the character of his hagiographical writings;[14] and his qualities as a historian.[15] It may be fairly said that Bede's reputation has never stood higher than at present, not

---

11 *De Gestis Regum Angliae, Prologus* (ed. Stubbs, Rolls Series, 1-2). See Antonia Gransden, 'Bede's Reputation as an Historian in Medieval England', *The Journal of Ecclesiastical History* xxxii (1981), 397-427.

12 See C.W. Jones, *Bedae Pseudepigrapha: Scientific Writings Falsely Attributed to Bede* (Ithaca, New York 1939), 1 and 7.

13 C.W. Jones, 'Bede's Place in Mediaeval Schools' in *Famulus Christi: Essays in Commemoration of the Thirteenth Centenary of the Birth of the Venerable Bede*, ed. by G. Bonner (London 1976), 261-85.

14 B. Colgrave, 'Bede's Miracle Stories' in *Bede. His Life, Times and Writings*, ed. A. Hamilton Thompson (Oxford 1935), 201-29; B. Ward, 'Miracles and History: A Reconsideration of the Miracle Stories used by Bede' in *Famulus Christi*, 70-76; R. Gardner, 'Miracles of healing in Anglo-Celtic Northumbria as recorded by the Venerable Bede and his contemporaries: A reappraisal in the light of twentieth century experience' in *British Medical Journal* 287 (24-31 December 1983), 1927-33.

15 W. Levison, 'Bede as Historian,' in *Bede. HLT*, 111-51; J. Campbell, 'Bede' in *Latin Historians*, ed. T.A. Dorey (London 1966), 159-90; L.W. Barnard, 'Bede and Eusebius as Church Historians' in *Famulus Christi*, 106-24; Roger D. Ray, 'Bede, the Exegete, as Historian,' ibid. pp. 125-40; 'Bede's *Vera lex historiae*' in *Speculum* lv (1980), 1-21; R.A. Markus, *Bede and the Tradition of Ecclesiastical Historiography* (Jarrow Lecture 1975); G. Tugène, 'L'histoire "ecclesiastique" du peuple anglais' in *Recherches Augustiniennes* xvii (1982), 129-72; J. McClure, 'Bede's Old Testament Kings' in *Ideal and Reality in Frankish and Anglo-Saxon England. Studies presented to J.M. Wallace Hadrill*, ed. P. Wormald (Oxford, 1983), 76-98.

simply as a scholar, or even as a canonised saint, but as a human being, at once modest and of heroic stature, who took advantage of the uniquely favourable circumstances in which he found himself – it should not be forgotten that, without the excellent education which he had received at Jarrow and the remarkable library with which Benedict Biscop had equipped his twin-foundation, Bede would have laboured in vain – to transmit to future generations of Christians the treasures of the past. I use a phrase which amounts to a cliché deliberately, to indicate both the extent and the limitations of Bede's endeavours. He was, from first to last, a Christian writing for Christians. If by chance he passed on some part of the legacy of the pagan world, this was by accident – Bede was no humanist like Erasmus.[16]

Bede saw his task as the transmission of the teachings of the great theologians of an earlier age – he was not, by intention, an original thinker. It is, of course, true that he put the stamp of his own personality on his works, but this was by accident, not design. Bede's desire was to follow in the steps of the Fathers of the Church, whose teaching he sought to transmit to those unable – or too lazy[17] – to read the works on which he drew at first hand. He was, if the term may be permitted, a kind of theological middle-man, even a populariser, and there is no reason to think that he would have shrunk from such a description, for he was singularly without personal vanity. Like other scholars he was aware of his own scholarship, could reply sharply when it was impugned, and speak severely of a teacher whose doctrine he deemed to be untrue;[18] but his general style is one of studied modesty. He knew his | own worth; he believed that it was the gift of God and not of his own creation; and was therefore able, at one and the same time, to value the gift and to evaluate the user, in the light of God's grace bestowed upon humanity in Jesus Christ.

p.222

The theme of this lecture is Bede and his legacy, more succinctly, the man and his work. To understand the work, we have to know the man, which we can do only through the work. Our information about Bede

16 See G. Bonner, 'Bede and Medieval Civilisation,' *Anglo-Saxon England* ii (1973), 82f.

17 Bede, *Explanatio Apocalypsis, Praef.*: 'Nostrae siquidem, id est, Anglorum, gentis inertiae consulendum ratus, quae et non dudum, id est temporibus beati Gregorii papae, semen accepti fidei, et idem quantum ad lectionem tepide satis excoluit, non solum dilucidare sensus, verum quoque stringere, disposui. Nam ei aperta magis brevitas quam disputatio prolixa memoriae solet infigi.' *PL* xciii, 134 AB.

18 See his *Ep. ad Plenguinam* (*CCSL* cxxiii C, 617-26) as the example of his sharp reaction to ignorant criticism and his remarks about Isidore of Seville: 'Nolo ut pueri mei mendacium legant, et in hoc post meum obitum sine fructu laborent,' quoted in Cuthbert's *Epistola de obitu Baedae* (in *Bede's Ecclesiastical History*, edd. B. Colgrave & R.A.B. Mynors, Oxford 1969, 582) as illustrating his ability to criticise severely, on which see P. Meyvaert, 'Bede the Scholar' in *Famulus Christi*, 58-60.

personally is scanty, though one need not be too pessimistic about the limited amount of biographical material available. It is true that our major source is the all too brief autobiographical sketch appended in 731 to Book V of the *Ecclesiastical History*, with its priceless bibliography of Bede's compositions to that date,[19] and this brief autobiography can be supplemented by the famous letter of Bede's disciple, Cuthbert, afterwards Abbot of Wearmouth and Jarrow, describing the master's last days and death in language not inferior to Bede's own in eloquence and pathos; and to these two primary documents, both of which were reproduced in their entirety by Symeon in his history of the Church of Durham,[20] may be added various autobiographical touches, such as his description at the beginning of the fourth book of his commentary on Samuel of how the brief relaxation which he had allowed himself from writing after completing the third had been prolonged by the distress of mind caused by the departure of Abbot Ceolfrith from Northumbria, intending to end his days at the shrine of St. Peter at Rome in 716.[21] However, these general biographical details, limited as they are, can be illuminated by the general tone of the whole corpus of Bede's writings, to provide a picture of the saint which we may reasonably feel to be convincing, even though it must inevitably be subjective.

Bede does not say much about himself in his writings, but his personality comes through his works to a far greater degree than in the case of many more egotistical writers. Probably Charles Plummer's judgement: '... throughout the works of Bede, the characteristic which strikes us most is the simple and unfeigned piety of the writer'[22] is as good as any. It is difficult to see how anyone can dissent from this verdict who has read Bede with any attention. One of the most delightful anecdotes about him is that related by Alcuin: that Bede would never absent himself from the Divine Office, explaining as his reason: 'I know that the angels visit the canonical hours and the assemblies of the brethren. Will they not say: "Where is Bede? Why does he not come to the devotions laid down for the brethren?"'[23] I personally find this story wholly convincing, especially in view of the fact that the Benedictine Rule which, although it was not actually in use at Wearmouth-Jarrow, undoubtedly affected Bede's thought and style, speaks of the presence of God and His angels at the Divine Office.[24]

---

19 *HE* V, 24 (Colgrave & Mynors 566-7).

20 Symeon, *HDE* I, 14 and 15 (Arnold 42, 43-6).

21 *In Primam Partem Samuhelis* IV, Praef. *CCSL* cxix, 212. E.T. by Charles Plummer in his ed. of the *Historia Ecclesiastica* (Oxford 1896), i. pp. xv, xvi.

22 Plummer, op.cit. i, p. lxv.

23 Alcuin, *Ep*. 16. *MGH Epp.* IV, 443.

And this *aperçu* of Bede provided by another may be complemented by Bede's own remark to Bishop Acca of Hexham in the dedication of his commentary on Luke, that owing to a shortage of assistants he was compelled to be his own author, notary and copyist – author, shorthand-typist and compositor would be the modern equivalent.[25] Busy as he was, the worship of God came first in Bede; his writing, important though it might be, took second place.

Charles Plummer, Bede's great Victorian editor, writing in 1896, called Bede 'the very model of the saintly scholar- priest',[26] an estimate which was echoed, whether consciously or not I do not know, by Sister Mary Carroll fifty years later: 'Lofty as was Bede's appreciation of [the monastic] state of life, he valued still more his life as a priest, and his writings turn frequently to the duties of the clergy.'[27] With these judgements in mind, let us consider Bede as an author. | p.223

The first thing which must strike a reader is the range of Bede's writings: apart from his biblical commentaries, which constitute by far the greater part of his works, he is a hagiographer, writing lives of St. Anastatius (now lost), St. Felix of Nola and, of course, St. Cuthbert –two lives, one in verse and the other in prose; an historian, the author of *The History of the Abbots of Wearmouth and Jarrow* as well as the more famous *Ecclesiastical History*; a writer of school text-books – *De Orthographia, De Arte Metrica* and *De Schematibus et Tropis*; a geographer, describing the sacred sites of Palestine (*De Locis Sanctis*); and a scientist and computist (*De Natura Rerum*, *De Temporibus*, *De Temporum Ratione*). To these larger compositions may be added his hymns and poems, his letters and sermons. The result is a remarkable total, alike for its quantity and its variety.[28] The only field which is neglected is that of dogmatic theology, which Bede may well have considered to have required a theologically more

---

24 *RB* 16. 6, 7: 'Ergo consideremus qualiter oporteat in conspectu divinitatis et angelorum eius esse, (7) et sic stemus ad psallendum ut mens nostra concordet voci nostrae.' *SC* 182, 536. On the Rule in Anglo Saxon England see H.M.R.E. Mayr-Harting, *The Venerable Bede, the Rule of St. Benedict, and Social Class* (Jarrow Lecture 1976), 6ff.

25 *In Luc. Prologius*: '... 'ipse mihi dictator simul notarius et librarius existerem ...' *CCSL* cxx, 7.

26 Plummer, op.cit. i. pp. lxxvii-xix; but see the comment of J.M. Wallace Hadrill, 'Bede and Plummer' in *Famulus Christi*, 369: 'Of Plummer's personal identification with Bede I have said almost enough. He believed that Bede was the same type of "saintly scholar-priest" as R.W. Church and H.P. Liddon. These were very considerable men. Nonetheless, Bede was something more than a saintly scholar- priest. His learning was a route to objectives that scarcely put us in mind of a Victorian scholar, however enlightened.'

27 *The Venerable Bede. His Spiritual Teachings*. (Catholic University of America. Studies in Medieval History, N.S. Vol. 9) (Washington D.C. 1946), 257-8.

28 See Peter Hunter Blair, *The World of Bede* (London 1970), esp. pp. 197-297.

highly-instructed readership than he was generally likely to find in eighth-century England, though it is also possible that, with a copy of St. Augustine's *Enchiridion* in the library at Wearmouth- Jarrow,[29] he may have felt that anyone requiring a handbook of Christian doctrine might as well come directly to one of the masters of Christian thought rather than consult an exposition by himself, which would only paraphrase his great authority.

Recognising then Bede's piety and pastoral concern and the remarkable range of his productions, let us now look a little more closely at the background to his achievement. He entered the cloister as a child oblate at seven, in about 680, was made deacon in his nineteenth year and priest in his thirtieth. Throughout his whole life (to borrow his own well-known words) it was his constant pleasure to learn or teach or write.[30] His career, then, was what in modern terms would be called an academic one, with all that implies, being at one and the same time widely-ranging and restricted.

It was widely-ranging because of Bede's training and library resources. We know virtually nothing about his education, but it is clear that he must have had excellent teachers to produce his easy command of Latin; and once he had mastered the universal language of the Western Church and scholarship, he had at his disposal the library founded by Benedict Biscop and enriched by his successor, Ceolfrid. No catalogue of that library survives; but its general character was reconstructed by M.L.W. Laistner in a famous article in 1935, which later scholarship can modify, but is not likely substantially to alter.[31] It is impossible to exaggerate the importance of that library for Bede's literary achievement. Without it he would either have had to abandon the thought of scholarship altogether, or to have become a *vagans*, a wandering scholar, seeking books in Ireland, or in other parts of England, or on the Continent (we know from the *Letter to Egbert* that he visited York in 773 to consult books there).[32] As it was, Bede had at his disposal at Jarrow a library which a modern patristic scholar would not despise, and of which he made good use,

---

29 *Ench.* xxx, 115, 116 is quoted by Bede, *In Luc.* III (*CCSL* cxx, 227-8, lines 2393-2428); xxi, 80 in *In Luc.* V (*CCSL* cxx, 381 lines 890-895); xxii, 93 in *In Cant. Cant.* I (*CCSL* cxix B, 179 lines 482-4).

30 *HE* V, 24 (Colgrave & Mynors 566).

31 M.L.W. Laistner, 'The Library of the Venerable Bede,' in *Bede. HLTW*, 237- 66; G. Bonner, art.cit. note[16], p.79 note[5].

32 *Ep. ad Ecgbertum Episcopum* 1: 'Memini te hesterno dixisse anno, cum tecum aliquot diebus legendi gratia in monasterio tuo demorarer, quod hoc etiam anno velles, cum in eundem devenires locum, me quoque, ob commune legendi studium, ad tuum accipere colloquium ...' (Plummer i. 405).

providing an example of how a man of books, in a recently-converted barbarian kingdom on the fringe of the Roman civilisation could be an heir to the ages and – to use a phrase he would certainly have rejected – a citizen of the world. The fact that he wrote a book on the Holy Places of Palestine[33] from the information of others without having been there himself at least indicates a horizon wider than Northumbria.

On the other hand, in another sense, Bede's world was a narrow one. Physically speaking it was bounded by Lindisfarne to the north and York to the south – there is no evidence that he ever travelled beyond these bounds. His knowledge of the events of his own age was curiously circumscribed. He was aware of the condition of the Church in Northumbria, as appears in his letter to Bishop Egbert of York, written at the end of his life to urge the need for reform. He was also aware to a certain degree of the Anglo-Saxon mission to the Continent, and speaks of the two English missionary-martyrs, Hewald the White and Hewald the Black, and of St. Willibrord, Archbishop of Utrecht;[34] but amazingly, in the light of history, he does not mention his contemporary St. Boniface, the Apostle of Germany, who had worked with Willibrord in Frisia and had been consecrated bishop, on a visit to Rome, in 722. The reason | why Bede ignores Boniface can perhaps be explained by the fact that while the two Hewalds and Willibrord were Northumbrians, Boniface was a man of Wessex, and would therefore be unlikely to be mentioned in the reports which reached Bede from the Continent through Northumbrian sources.[35] Bede's apparent ignorance of Boniface presents an ironic contrast with the admiration for Bede's work which Boniface was later to express in requests for copies of Bede's scriptural commentaries. The man of letters was mightier than the man of action.

p.224

33 *Liber de Locis Sanctis. C.S.E.L.* xxxix, 301-24.

34 *HE* V, 10, 11 (Colgrave & Mynors, 480-87.

35 See Franz Flaskamp, 'Die frühe Friesen- und Sachsenmission aus northumbrischen Sicht. Das Zeugnis des Baeda,' *Archiv fur Kulturgeschichte* 51 (1969), 183-209 and note his observation (p.187): 'Von diesem frühen frankischen Christenum in Friesland erfuhr der Westsasche Wynfreth bei seinem frieischen Versuch 716 an Ort und Stelle, Baeda dagegen im sehr abgelegenen Wearmouth- Jarrow, soweit ersichtlich, rein nichts. Nach seiner Information ging die Christianisierung Frieslands, ausschliesslich auf seine northumbrischen Landsleute zurück ...' T. Reuter, 'St. Boniface and Europe' in *The Greatest Englishman*, ed. T.R. (Exeter 1980), 91 note[63]: 'The fact that Bede, who had good contacts with the Frisian mission ... does not mention Boniface is suggestive.'

This parochialism on Bede's part with regard to the events of his own time is reflected on a larger scale in the character of his writings, for Bede's outlook is a narrow one, not merely in the sense that any specialist, theological or otherwise, is professionally narrow, but in the sense of deliberately seeking to exclude a whole department of human experience – the non-Christian – from his considerations. Bede's view of Christian culture is essentially that proposed in the patristic age by St. Augustine in his work *De Doctrina Christiana*: secular learning in general, and pagan learning in particular, are to be cultivated by the Christian exegete only insofar as they serve to elucidate the biblical text or the doctrines of the Church. Augustine, however, differed from Bede in one important respect: unlike Bede he had received the traditional Roman classical education and had indeed taught it himself before becoming a Catholic Christian and a Christian bishop. Bede, so far as we can tell, proceeded directly from the study of the Latin grammarians to that of the Bible and the Fathers of the Church without any intervening period of studying the classical authors, of whom his knowledge was essentially superficial.[36] One of the most remarkable, but also one of the most disconcerting, contributions of Peter Hunter Blair to Bedan studies was to call into question that there must have been a copy of Virgil in the library of Wearmouth-Jarrow. Hunter Blair showed that almost all the citations of Virgil in Bede can be found quoted by the Latin grammarians whom he would have studied as a schoolboy.[37] Nor would it be surprising, in itself, if there was no copy of Virgil in Bede's library – it was a library intended for monks, not humanists, for a monastery, not a college of liberal arts. What is significant is Bede's personal attitude to classical studies, of which he fundamentally disapproved, while admitting that they might have some value for cultivating eloquence in orthodox Christian teachers. Christianity comprehended all that was good in pagan classical culture, and so that culture could be ignored. There are no good grounds for questioning Bede's sincerity in this evaluation, though it is not necessary to be a diehard classicist to feel that his declaration that the Old Testament writings surpass the works of Virgil, Lucretius and Homer, not only by their divine authority, *sed et antiquitate et ipsa positione dicendi*[38] – by age and style – is open to debate.

---

36 See Bonner, art.cit. note[16], 83.

37 Hunter Blair, 'From Bede to Alcuin,' *Famulus Christi*, 243-50.

38 *De Schematibus et Tropis*, ed. Halm, *Rhetores Latini Minores* (Leipzig 1863), 60.

Bede's critical attitude towards the pagan classics extends into the whole field of the secular order. He does not reject it outright; indeed, he seems in the *Letter to Egbert* to be concerned for the well-being of the Northumbrian kingdom, which was imperilled by the existence of fraudulent monasteries, in which dishonest men evaded their military service, as well as for the Northumbrian Church.[39] On the other hand, there can be no question that Bede approves of conduct in highly-placed persons which, if widely practised, would have been prejudicial both to social relationships and to political order. Thus he commends – indeed he admires – Queen Ethelthryth's decision to retire into the cloister against the wishes of her husband, Egfrith of Northumbria;[40] and he has no criticism of King Sigeberht of East Anglia, who entered a monastery from which he had forcibly to be dragged in order to command his army – unsuccessfully and disastrously – against King Penda of Mercia.[41] It would be an exaggeration to say that Bede is hostile to the secular on principle; he admires Christian kings like St Oswald and King Oswine of Deira; but there is an ambiguity in his outlook, not different, perhaps, | fundamentally from the ambiguity which any devout Christian may feel about the secular order, but which inevitably coloured Bede's theology in general and the philosophy underlying the *Ecclesiastical History* in particular.[42]

p.225

The *Ecclesiastical History* has a particular interest for a number of reasons. In the first place, it is by far the best known of all Bede's writings – for many people, the only one. Again, it has been commended by modern scholars as a piece of historical scholarship altogether in advance of its time, to be judged by the criteria which would be applied to a contemporary work. Thirdly, it is an important primary source for early English history – without it, indeed, we could not hope to describe the century of the conversion. Finally, the *Ecclesiastical History* is one of those works like *The Canterbury Tales* and the *Morte d'Arthur* which make up what may be called the Legend of England: that idea of England and its heritage, founded upon history and imagination, which has for centuries conditioned the view which the English take of themselves.[43] Such a view is a myth; but it is the

---

39 *Ep. ad Ecgbert. Ep.* 11-13 (Plummer i. 414-7).

40 *HE* IV, 19[17] – 20[18] (Colgrave & Mynors 390-401).

41 Ibid. III, 18 (Colgrave & Mynors 266-9).

42 See G. Bonner, 'The Christian Life in the Thought of the Venerable Bede,' *Durham University Journal* lxii (1970), 39-55; J. Davidse, *Beda Venerabilis interpretatie van de historische werkelijkheid* (Amsterdam 1977) (English summery 190-4); Clare Stancliffe, 'Kings who Opted Out' in *Ideal and Reality in Frankish and Anglo-Saxon Society. Studies presented to J.M. Wallace Hadrill*, ed. P. Wormald (Oxford, 1983), 154-76.

43 A classic exposition of this view is provided by Rudyard Kipling in *Puck of Pook's Hill*. Cf. also David Jones, *In Parenthesis*, where the poet draws upon a double heritage of English

sort of myth by which a cultural tradition lives. Like *The Canterbury Tales* and the *Morte d'Arthur* the *Ecclesiastical History* is a major work of art. A distinguished scholar has said of Bede's Latin verses: '... his was not a poetical nature.'[44] The same cannot be said of Bede's prose-style in the *Ecclesiastical History*, with its felicitous descriptions of scenes and speeches which never fail to move – the speech of the nameless thegn who, in the debate before King Edwin as to whether Northumbria should accept the Christian Gospel likens the life of man to the flight of a sparrow through a lighted banqueting-hall on a winter's night is a classic example, but there are many others – and there can be few readers with a feeling for literature who do not, at the end of the *Ecclesiastical History*, feel that they have been in contact with an author who, in another age, might have been a major novelist.

We are, however, immediately concerned with the *Ecclesiastical History* considered as history. As such, it has been highly praised by no less a judge than Sir Frank Stenton;[45] but in recent years questions have been raised about Bede's fundamental approach to the writing of history. If we compare the *Ecclesiastical History* with the *History of the Franks* by the sixth-century writer, Gregory of Tours, we notice a difference of atmosphere: the world which Gregory describes seems distinctly more savage and brutal than that of Bede. Are we to understand from this that seventh-century England was more gentle and humane than sixth-century Gaul? There is no good reason to think that it was.[46] The English and the Franks were of a common stock, and there are no grounds for supposing that the English way of life was milder than the Frankish. Indeed, there are hints in Bede of a native savagery to rival anything that the Franks could offer, as in his account of the conquest of the Isle of Wight by King Caedwalla of Wessex, who then exterminated the local population and replaced it by his own followers.[47] Why then does Bede differ from Gregory, who spares us nothing of the depravity of the Frankish rulers, whose careers he describes? The answer seems to be that Bede deliberately omits many details which he deems to be unedifying, with an apparent disregard for what he calls 'the true law of History': 'to hand down simply

---

and Celtic tradition to provide the background to his description of a London Welsh regiment in France in 1915-16.

44 F.J.E. Raby, *A History of Christian-Latin Poetry*^{2} (Oxford 1953), 146.

45 *Anglo-Saxon England*^{3} (Oxford 1971), 187).

46 See M. Wallace Hadrill, 'Gregory of Tours and Bede' in *Fruhmittelalterliche Studien* ii (1968), 31-44, reprinted in *Early Medieval History* (Oxford 1975), 96-114, esp. p. 110; D.P. Kirby, 'Northumbria in the time of Bede' in *St. Wilfrid at Hexham*, ed. D.P.K. (Newcastle upon Tyne 1974), 1-34.

47 *HE* VI, 16[14] (Colgrave & Mynors 382-5).

in writing, for the instruction of posterity, those things which we have gathered together from common report.'[48] Bede elsewhere styles himself a *verax historicus* – a truthful historian.[49] Today it would be generally agreed that the historian is under no less an obligation to record things unfavourable to his own party or nation than to celebrate their virtues and achievements. Bede's behaviour in this respect can be explained and, in the light of the thought of his day, defended, as we shall see hereafter. For the moment, let us consider the reasons which have caused him to be acclaimed as a great historian by modern scholars.

p.226

The first thing which must strike us, in considering the *Ecclesiastical History*, is the methodology: Bede begins his work with acknowledgements to many people, like Abbot Albinus, the priest Nothelm, Bishops Daniel and Cynibert, and the monks of Lastingham and Lindisfarne, who have provided him with material, either written or oral. These acknowledgements create an impression of contemporaneity – Bede might be a modern scholar expressing his thanks to those who have helped him. But there is more to this list of sources than the mere appearance of modernity: they testify to Bede's extraordinary skill in assembling and then combining disparate pieces of information in a coherent narrative.[50] This is, perhaps, his outstanding gift as an historian, and one which any historian may envy.

Again, one may note the geographical introduction to the *Ecclesiastical History*, with its description of the island of Britain, based upon a variety of authors like Pliny the Elder, Gildas, Solinus and Orosius. Bede starts, in a very modern fashion, from the geography of the whole region in which the events he is describing occurred, and not simply of the parts of Britain inhabited by the English, together with its neighbour Ireland, about which he is much less informed as regards details. He recognises that environment determines history. To this geographical information he adds references to the languages in use in the British Isles – English, British, Irish and Pictish, with Latin as the common ecclesiastical tongue – and the races which speak them. Although his subject is the English people, Bede is prepared to devote space to other peoples, and his work is free from racial prejudice – his complaint against the British, to whom he shows a hostility not displayed to other races, is that they made no attempt to convert the English to the Christian faith; they failed in their Christian duty.[51] Bede's hostility – whether justified or not is a debatable question – arises from moral, not nationalistic, considerations.

---

48 *HE* I, *Praef.* (Colgrave & Mynors 6-7).

49 *HE* III, 17 (Colgrave & Mynors 264-5).

50 Stenton, *Anglo-Saxon England*³, 187.

51 *HE I, 22 (Colgrave & Mynors 66-9); II, 2 (134-42); V, 22 (554-5).*

Yet again, the modern historian will notice, and approve, Bede's readiness to quote his sources, even – it may be thought – excessively, as when he gives the reader, at wearisome length, the whole text of the letter of Abbot Ceolfrith to the Pictish king, Naiton, in 710, on the Paschal question;[52] though it must be remembered, if Bede seems to quote to excess, that he did not have at his disposal that priceless tool of scholarship available to the modern author through the invention of printing, the footnote. However, when all criticisms are made, Bede's readiness, not only to state, but actually to supply his authorities, must commend him to any modern scholar making use of his works.

From the foregoing it will be apparent why Bede has been hailed as an historian in advance of his time, so that the implication that he does not live up to his own claim to be a *verax historicus* becomes particularly distressing. Yet Bede's deficiencies from the viewpoint of the modern historian become explicable if we avoid anachronistic expectations and try to understand Bede in his contemporary setting.

Bede, I have maintained, did not seek to be original, but to stand in the tradition of the Fathers of the Church. This was what he sought to do in his biblical commentaries, which constitute the greater part of his literary output, and were of all his productions those which his contemporaries especially valued. When he came to write the *Ecclesiastical History* he likewise looked to the past for inspiration and example, and found it in the fourth-century *Ecclesiastical History* of Eusebius of Caesarea, the Father of Church History, which he knew in the Latin translation made in the early fifth century by Rufinus of Aquileia. Eusebius, when he began work on his history, was aware that he was attempting something new, and his work shows it – it was he who invented those long citations from original documents, a device unknown to classical historians, which provided Bede with an example. He was also, I suspect, the authority – or at least an authority – for Bede's decision to omit unedifying details from his own history.

At the beginning of his eighth book Eusebius comes to describe the persecution of the Christian Church under the Emperor Diocletian: the churches demolished, the Holy Scriptures publicly burned. Of the faint-hearted and apostate he writes (in the version of Rufinus):

> ... it is not my business to describe the many sorts of injuries which were inflicted upon the priests of God, just as I have not thought it my business to reveal in detail how greatly the madness of dissension burned among us before the persecution. This alone is history permitted to hand on: that we experienced the divine hand by the just judgement and necessary correction of God. Neither is there any profit to bring to public notice the things for

52 *HE* V, 21 (Colgrave & Mynors 534051).

> which the hurricane of persecution was let loose, or those individuals whom the tempest of infidelity overwhelmed and broke in pieces. I will only record those things which will edify me as the narrator, or others as the hearers. For this reason I will now briefly describe, so far as I can, the divinely-inspired combats of the most blessed martyrs.[53]

The principle here laid down is charitably to avoid dwelling on the bad, and to concentrate on those things which make for edification – a not inappropriate principle for a Church history. If Bede followed it, it was precisely because he was writing a *Church* history – the *Ecclesiastical History* of the English people. This fact helps to explain certain features of his work which have puzzled scholars who have vainly sought in the pages of Bede the sort of information about the secular aspect of society which he had no intention of supplying. Bede's work, it has been said, was an 'adjunct to scriptural study.'[54] Fundamentally, I would agree; but I would prefer to say that, following the pattern of Eusebius, it grew out of scriptural study, showing how the dominical command to preach the gospel to the nations had been fulfilled, in the case of the English, and how after their conversion, they themselves wished to convert their kinsmen still living on the European mainland.[55] Nor do I think it necessarily an accident that the narrative portion of the *Ecclesiastical History* ends with the adoption of the Roman Easter by the Picts[56] and the conversion to its use and the adoption of the Roman tonsure by the monks of Iona.[57] The desire to share the faith with their pagan kinsmen in Europe is a measure of the effect of Christianity, in Bede's opinion, on the English; but so too is the conversion of Iona, the monastery from which St. Aidan, the great missionary of the Northumbrians, had come; for in Bede's view the observance of the correct date of Easter was a matter on which a man's salvation might depend, and by bringing the community from which the people of Northumbria had derived so much spiritual benefit to the right observance, the Northern English had shown that mutual charity which St. Paul commends to Christians (Gal.6:2).

p.227

It is therefore clear that the *Ecclesiastical History* is, as it says, an ecclesiastical history, and must be judged by the standards which apply to works of this genre, and not by those pertaining to avowedly secular compositions. It may readily be conceded that Bede, through his personal genius, produced a work which transcended the boundaries conventionally set to compositions of this type and by the quality of his achievement has

53 Eusebius/Rufinus, *HE* III. *GCS* Eusebius, 2 er Bd., 2 er Teil (Leipzig 1908).

54 W.F. Bolton, *A History of Anglo-Latin Literature* (Princeton, N.J. 1967), 172.

55 *HE* V, 9-11 (Colgrave & Mynors 474-87).

56 *HE* V, 21 (Colgrave & Mynors 632-53).

57 *HE* V, 22 (Colgrave & Mynors 552-5).

caused himself to be judged by the standards of another age intending to produce another class of work; but he should not be blamed for not doing what he never set out to do. His intentions were different from those of Gregory of Tours. It may be regretted, from out standpoint, that he did not share the opinion of the fifth-century Church historian, Socrates Scholasticus, who saw a peculiar and intimate relationship between Church and state, so that when one was disturbed, the other was also affected by a kind of sympathy;[58] but the *Historia Tripartita* of Cassiodorus ad Epiphanius, which contains extracts from Socrates, was not available to Bede at Wearmouth-Jarrow, and omits this particular passage.[59] Furthermore, Socrates was an East Roman, affected by that notion of the relationship between Church and state which was later to be expressed in the Byzantine Empire, while Bede stood in the tradition of St. Augustine's *City of God*, with its tendency to see Christian affairs in terms of salvation history, and to regard the temporal and secular as irrelevant to man's eternal destiny.

It follows from this that if we are to understand Bede – as opposed to using Bede as a source for modern reconstructions of early English history – we need to approach him, not through the *Ecclesiastical History* but rather through his more directly theological writings, his commentaries on the Bible. Much of the material in these comes, not from Bede but from earlier commentators; but the fact that Bede uses them is an indication of the cast of his mind, and to these may be added the direct self-revelation of his own words.

In discussing Bede as a biblical commentator it is necessary to keep in mind the principles which governed his exegesis: that while he accepted the sacred text as the word of God, and believed it to be literally true, he was more concerned to understand it spiritually, as the inspiration of faith and as a guide to Christian living, than to dissect it historically, as modern biblical scholars do. The Christian life, for Bede, is one of faith and works,[60] lived within the fellowship of the Church, which is the City of | God[61] and which is symbolised in Solomon's temple at Jerusalem.[62] In the

p.228

58 Socrates, *HE* V, *Praef.*: 'This we do for several reasons ...; but more especially that it might be known that whenever the affairs of the state were disturbed, those of the Church, as if by some sympathy, were likewise troubled.' *PG* lxvii, 564 A, 565 A.

59 *Historia Tripartita*: the text goes from Socrates IV, 38 (*CSEL* lxxii, 490) to V, 1 (493), with a table of chapter-headings between (491-2). Laistner thought that this work was in the library at Wearmouth-Jarrow; but see Wilhelm Levison, *England and the Continent in the Eighth Century* (Oxford, 1946), 141 Note 1.

60 Bede, *De Templo* I: '... neque fides sine operibus neque sine fide Deo possunt opera bona placere ...' (*CCSL* cxix A, 190. 1715-6); *De Templo* II: '... non nisi per fidem et opera iustitiae nos ad superna gaudia vitae posse pervenire' (*CCSL* cxix A, 199, 307-8).

love of God it is necessary that we have both faith of truth and purity of good actions, *for without faith it is impossible to please God; and faith without works is dead.* Moreover, in the love of the brotherhood patience and kindness must be preserved, as says the Apostle: *Charity suffereth long and is kind.*[63] – this is Bede's teaching, expressed in *De Templo*, his commentary on the construction of Solomon's temple described in I Kings and II Chronicles. The obligation of faith and works is, naturally, laid upon all the faithful, but especially on teachers (*doctores*) and the ordained ministry; their duty involved both action and teaching (*operatio et doctrina*)[64] for, says Bede, 'the whole perfection of the priest is grounded in works and in the teaching of truth, according to what the blessed Luke, after he had written his Gospel, says: that he had "*made* a *treatise* of those things *that Jesus began to do and teach*"'.[65] It is, however, to be noted that Bede recognises that the First Epistle of Peter does not confine the notion of priesthood to the ordained ministry, but extends it to all the faithful as *an elect race, a royal priesthood, a holy nation, a people for God's own possession.*[66] 'By shepherds', he says, speaking of Luke 2:18, 'we must

61 Bede, *De Tabernaculo* II: '... ecclesia quae angelis sanctis et hominibus constans partim adhuc peregrinatur in infirmis partim in aeternas patria regnat' (*CCSL* cxxix A, 72. 1213-4); *In Esram et Neemiam* I: '... et si omnes electi de potestate tenebrarum eruti ad libertatem pertinent gloriae filiorum Dei, omnes ad societatem sanctae civitatis, id est ecclesiae, se adnumerari laetantur, non tamen omnium sed perfectorum solummodo est in aedificationem eiusdem ecclesiae etiam aliis praedicando laborare' (*CCSL* cxix A, 248. 273- 8).

62 Bede, *De Templo* I: 'Domus Dei quam aedificat rex Salomon in Hierusalem in figuram facta est sanctae univeralis ecclesiae quae a primo electo usque ad ultimum qui in fine mundi nasciturus est cotidie per gratiam regis pacifici sui videlicet redemptoris aedificatur quae partim adhuc peregrinatur ab illo in terris partim evasis peregrinandi aerumnis cum illo iam regnat in caelis ubi peracto ultimo iudicio tota est regnatura cum illo.' (*CCSL* cxix A, 147. 1-7).

63 Ibid.: 'In dilectione Dei etenim fidem veritatis et puritatem necesse est ut habeamus bonae operationis. *Sine fidem enim impossibile est placere Deo: et fides sine operibus mortua est* (Iac.2:26). In amore autem fraternitatis patientia est et benignitas servanda dicente apostolo, *caritas patiens est benigna est* (I. Cor. 13:4).' *CCSL* cxix A, 189, 1698-1703.

64 Bede, *Ep. ad Ecgbert. Ep.* 2 (Plummer i. 405-06): 'Exhortor itaque tuam, dilectissime in Christo antistes, sancitatem, ut gradum sacrosanctum quem tibi Auctor graduum et spiritualium largitor charismatum committere dignatus est, sacrosancta et operatione et doctrina confirmare memineris'; *In Ezram et Meemiam* II: '... mens electorum gratia spiritus sancti illustratur ut ad perfectionem bonae operationis perveniat cum fide sanctae et individuae trinitatis sicque laetabunda dedicationem beatae retributionis expectat.' *CCSL* xcix A, 299, 453-7.

65 Bede, *De Tabernaculo* III: '... tota perfectio sacerdotis in operibus et doctrina veritatis consistit iuxta hoc quod beatus Lucas descripto evangelio dicit fecisse se sermonem de his *quae coepit Iesus facere et docere.*' *CCSL* cvix A, 110. 697-111. 700.

66 Bede, *De Templo* II: 'Neque enim episcopis solis et presbiteris verum omni Dei ecclesiae loquebatur apostolus Petrus cum ait: *Vos autem genus electum regale sacerdotum gens sancta populus adquisitionis* (I Pet. 2:9). *CCSL* cxix A, 194. 88-91; cf. *Exp. Apocalypsis* 20: 'Alio

here understand not only bishops, priests and deacons, or even monastic superiors, but all the faithful, however small their house may be, are rightly called shepherds, insofar as they rule over that house with watchful care.'[67]

The key for understanding the Scriptures, for Bede as for the Fathers of the Church whose teaching he sought to follow, is Christ: 'by the Lord's passion the vast abyss of the Scriptures has been laid bare to us.'[68] An example of how the thought of Christ will determine Bede's understanding of an apparently pedestrian detail, transforming it into an account of the progress of the Christian life from baptismal regeneration to heaven, is afforded, in his commentary on Ezra and Nehemiah, by his exegesis of I Kings 6:8: *The door of the middle side was on the right side of the house; and they went up by a winding stair into the middle chamber, and out of the middle into the third.*

> Our Lord and Saviour has willed to open to us the door of salvation in the right side of His Body, so that, being cleansed and sanctified by His sacraments, we might be able to enter the loftier hall of the heavenly kingdom. For we ascend through the door of the middle side into the higher chamber when, being consecrated by the water of | baptism and the cup of the Lord's chalice, we arrive at the heavenly life of souls from this terrestrial way of life. We also enter into the third chamber when, by the reception of immortal bodies, we complete the blessedness of our souls.[69]

p.229

This is, of course, a thoroughly fanciful piece of exegesis; yet in it Bede has contrived to remind his reader of how the Christian life is lived in the sacramental fellowship of the Church; and even if we feel that in this particular instance, Bede goes too far in the employment of an allegorical understanding, the same can hardly be said of his exposition of Israel's deliverance from Egypt as a figure of the Christian's liberation from the

---

Editio habet, *Sacerdotes Dei et Christi*. Non autem de solis episcopis et presbyteris dictum est, qui proprie vocantur in Ecclesia sacerdotes, sed sicut omnes Christi dicimur propter mysticum chrisma, sic omnes sacerdotes, quoniam membra sumus unius sacerdotis. De quibus apostolus Petrus: *Plebs,*, inquit, *sancta, regale sacerdotium*.' *PL* xci, 192 C. Bede is here quoting verbatim Augustine, *De Civitate Dei* XX, 10 (*CSEL* xl (2), 455.2-7).

67 Bede, *Hom.* I, 7: 'Non solum pastores episcopi presbyteri diaconi vel etiam rectores monasteriorum sunt intellegendi sed et omnes fideles qui vel parvulae sua domus custodiam gerunt pastores recte vocantur in quantum suae domui sollicitas vigilantia praesunt.' *CCSL* cxxii, 49. 104-8.

68 Bede, *In Ezram et Neem.* III: '... per passionem domini scripturarum nobis est abyssus patefacta ...' *CCSL cxix A, 352. 514-5.*

69 Ibid. II: 'dominus et salvator noster ianuam nobis salutis in dextro sui corporis voluit aperire per cuius sacramenta abluti ac sanctificati altiorem regni caelestis aulam possemus intrare. Ascendimus namque per ostium lateris medii in superius cenaculum quando per aquam baptismatis et poculum dominici calicis consecrati ab hac terrestri conversatione ad caelestem animarum vitam pervenimus a superiore quoque in tertium penetramus cenaculum (III Reg. 6:8) cum beatitudinem animarum etiam corporum immortalium perceptione cumulamus.' *CCSL* cxix A, 301. 517-25.

power of Satan through the sacrifice of Christ, which stands in the great tradition of Christian typology:

> For we too went forth from servitude in Egypt by the blood of a Lamb that we might come to the land of promise when, having been baptised into the sacrament of the Lord's passion, we shook off the heavy yoke of sin, that being adopted *into the glorious liberty of the sons of God*, we might be able to be heirs of the heavenly kingdom. We remained a long time living in tabernacles and in tents, journeying through the desert until we should come to our fatherland when renouncing in baptism, not only Satan, as though he were the king of Egypt – that is, of darkness – but also all his works and the works of this age, we promised that we should be as pilgrims in this world, and wayfarers of another life, of which, by the Lord, we hoped to be citizens.[70]

Let us consider a third example of Bede's exegesis: his understanding of the allegorical interpretation of the *daily burnt offerings* of Ezra 3:4[3] for the Christian.

> ... we offer a *burnt offering* to the Lord upon His altar when, with whole devotion to His faith established firmly in our hearts, we toil with good actions. And we do this *morning and evening* when we remember that we ourselves most certainly received from Him the beginnings of our saving efforts, and that we cannot complete those things which we have begun except by the help of His grace, and therefore offer to Him due prayers of thanks in all things, with a burning longing of devout conduct. Likewise we offer a morning burnt offering when, by virtuous living, we make a thank-offering to our Creator for the light of spiritual knowledge which we have received, and an evening offering when we burn with unquenching zeal for the eternal rest which we hope to receive in Him after performing good works.[71]

These passages – and they could easily be multiplied – illustrate the character, not only of Bede's exegesis, but of Bede himself. Bede uses allegory, but to a practical end: to move others to the same love and

70 Bede, *In Ezram et Neem*. I: 'Egressi enim sumus et nos per sanguinem agni de Aegyptia servitude ut veniremus ad terram repromissionis cum in sacramentum dominicae passionis baptizati iugum grave praevaricationis abiecimus quatenus *in libertatem gloriae filiorum Dei* (Rom. 8:21) adoptati heredes regni caelestis esse possemus. Manebamus in tabernaculis et tentoriis per desertum longo tempore iter agentes donec veniremus ad patriam cum in baptismo renuntiantes non solum satanae quasi regi Aegupti, id est tenebrarum, sed et omnibus pompis eius atque operibus huius saeculi velut peregrinos nos in hoc mundo ac viatores alterius autem vitae quam a domino speraremus cives esse promisimus.' *CSSL cxix A 267. 1056-268. 1067.*

71 Ibid.: 'Offerimus namque holocaustum domino super altare ipsius cum stabilita in corde nostro fidei eius integra devotione bonis actibus operam damus. Et hoc mane ac vespere facimus cum nos pro certo meminerimus et initia salutiferae intentionis ab illo accepisse et non nisi per auxilium gratiae eiuis ea quae inchoavimus bona posse perficere ideoque illo vota gratiarum in omnibus cum ardente desiderio piae conversationis referimus. Item mane holocaustum facimus cum pro lumine accepto spiritalis scientiae conditori nostro vicem bene vivendi rependimus, vespere holocaustum facimus cum pro requie sempiterna quam nos in illo post bona opera accepturos speramus incessabili studio flagramus.' *CCSL* cxix A, 266. 1010-22.

devotion which he himself felt for God and his neighbour. It is this lov and devotion which underlies all his writings and explains features like th omission of unedifying details in the *Ecclesiastical History* – to record then would not make for edification, or help others to progress in faith, hop and charity. Given Bede's views, if they have been rightly interpreted, i would seem fitting to close this lecture with one of his prayers. The famous prayer which concludes *Ecclesiastical History* (V,24) is too familiar. Let me therefore quote Bede's conclusion to his commentary on Ezra and Nehemiah, less familiar, but hardly less moving:

> And do Thou, great *Father of lights*, from whom *every good gift and every perfect gift cometh down*, Who hast given to me, the humblest of Thy servants, both love for *the wonderful things of Thy law* and aid in meditating upon them, and Who, in the treasury of the prophetic volume, hast furnished me with the grace, not only to embrace *things old*, | but also in very truth to find *new things* under the veil of the old and to bring them forth for the use of my fellow- servants, *remember me, O my God, for good.*[72]

p.230

This may fitly end the academic part of my lecture; but speaking on the subject of Bede and his legacy to a Durham audience in 1985, I would not wish to omit the name of a great Durham scholar and lover of Bede: Bertram Colgrave, Doctor of Letters and Emeritus Reader in the University, who died in 1968. Throughout his long career in Durham, Colgrave laboured, by word and pen alike, to advance the study of early Christian Northumbria and, in particular, of the works of Bede. It was altogether appropriate that, when the Jarrow Lecture series was instituted in 1958 by the late Canon George Beckwith, Rector of Jarrow from 1955 to 1964, he should have been invited to deliver the first lecture on *The Venerable Bede and his Times*. But Colgrave's devotion to Bede did not confine itself to *doctrina*, study; it expressed itself in *operatio*, action. It was through his urging that Wilhelm Levison (1897-1947), one of the greatest medieval historians of the twentieth century, was invited to come to Durham from Germany in 1939, to become an Honorary Fellow of the University and thus escape the fate that overwhelmed millions of his fellow Jews on the Continent of Europe between 1939 and 1945. With a generosity as generally rare as it was, in him, characteristic, Levison left his library to be divided between his old university at Bonn and his later university of Durham. He lies buried, with his wife, Elsa, in the little cemetery on the corner between Potter's Bank and Elvet Hill Road. May I suggest that in

72 Ibid. III: 'Et tu summe *pater luminum* a quo *omne datum optimum et omne donum perfectum* (Iac. 1:17) descendit qui mihi humillimo servorum tuorum et amorem dedisti et auxilium considerandi *mirabilia de lege tua* (Ps. 118:18) quique in thesauro prophetici voluminis non solum *vetera* amplectendi verum et *nova* (cf. Matt. 13:52) sub velamine veterum donaria inveniendi atque in usus conservorum meorum proferendi indigno mihi gratiam praestitisti *memento mei Deus in bonum* (Neh. 14:31).' *CCSL* cxix A, 392. 2108-15.

the lives and writings of Bertram Colgrave and Wilhelm Levison we can see that the legacy of Bede continues to exercise an influence in our own day, no less than in the eleventh century, when it brought Aldwin and his companions to the North, to revive the monastic devotion of which they had read in the works of Bede?

XV

ANGLO-SAXON CULTURE AND SPIRITUALITY

A Paper read at the Fellowship Conference in Winchester, 1973

It is generally agreed that every Englishman knows one medieval date—1066. The student of national psychology will note that what seems to have impressed itself most firmly on the English mind is a national disaster; but the historian can only record his satisfaction with English historical judgement, since there can be no question of the importance of the events of this year for the subsequent history of England. By defeating and killing his rival, Harold Hardrada of Norway, at Stamfordbridge on 25 September, Harold Godwinson of England ended the very real possibility that England would be drawn into the Scandinavian cultural and political orbit. His own defeat and death at the hands of Duke William at Hastings on 14 October ensured equally decisively that England would participate in a French-speaking culture, of which the Duchy of Normandy was an integral part,[1] and become subject to influences which would determine her future in every part of national life, not least in religion. In a very real sense the events of that October day have determined the course of English history for nearly a thousand years.

In historical retrospect we may say that the outcome of the Battle of Hastings was to the advantage of England, and that the English in the long run gained more than they lost by their defeat. No doubt they felt differently at the time; indeed, forty years later the victory of Tinchebrai gained by

King Henry I over his brother, Duke Robert of Normandy, seemed a providential reversal of the English defeat at Hastings;[2] and it is possible for the modern historian, not only to sympathise with the Old English in their subjection to a foreign invader, but also to feel that something was lost as well as gained in the Norman victory. The Old English state which came to an end at Hastings was far from being the uncultured polity of Norman imagination. In many fields—for instance, in book-painting and embroidery, and in the development of a vernacular literature—the English were superior to their conquerors, while the English Church was by no means the decadent and simoniacal institution depicted by the propaganda employed by William of Normandy to justify his aggression.[3] Here in Winchester, the capital of the Kingdom of Wessex, famous for its association with King Alfred and with St. Swithun and St. Aethelwold, for its religious houses and for its famous school of illumination, it is possible to feel a sense of fellowship with the vanished society of pre-Conquest England, especially in connection with a conference which has for its theme that of Transfiguration, of making all things new in Christ. Perhaps I may borrow some lines from G. K. Chesterton's dedication of *The Ballad of the White Horse?*

> Lady, by one light only
> We look from Alfred's eyes.
> We know he saw athwart that wreck
> The sign that hangs about your neck,
> Where One more than Melchizedek
> Is dead and never dies.

(The image of the crucifixion in this stanza is particularly appropriate for our purposes in view of the importance of the Cross in Anglo-Saxon art and poetry.)

A monastic faith and culture

My theme is Anglo-Saxon culture and spirituality, and I must begin with a warning. We talk very easily about Anglo-Saxon England, forgetting that this term denotes a period of some six centuries, a period, that is to say, rather longer than that which has elapsed from the death of Edward III to the present day. There is always a temptation in dealing with far-away epochs like that of Anglo-Saxon England to attribute to them a uniformity and a homogeneity which we would not ascribe to more recent periods. Yet clearly, the England of King Oswald and St. Cuthbert was different from that of Alfred, and that in turn was different from the England of St. Dunstan or Edward the Confessor. In this paper I propose to generalise, to do no more than point out certain characteristics of the Old English Church. I do not claim that they were peculiar to that Church, still less that the early English were especially holy and better than other men. In fact there was as much brutality and wickedness in Anglo-Saxon England as in any other part of Europe at that time, as can be seen from the pages of Bede who was, in all probability, more anxious in his *History* to lay stress on the deeds of good and holy men from a desire to encourage others to live virtuously than to dwell upon the crimes and follies of the vicious.[4] In all societies and at all times, the saints are in a minority. Nevertheless, the saints are apt to set the spiritual tone of any age; and ordinary Christians, who cannot rise to their heights, may nevertheless participate in their achievements through a common membership of the Body of Christ. Bede expresses this notion with singular felicity in a sentence which might provide the theme of my paper. "By the wonderful grace of the divine dispensation it comes about that we, *on whom the ends of the age have come,* may with sincere affection also love those who were faithful at the very beginning of the age, and receive them in the bosom of our affection no less than those who live with us at present, and we may believe that we too can be received by them through the embrace of charity." [5] Again, more briefly, he remarks: "We too ought to make the exalted life of the elect our own, which we can follow by imitation, by rejoicing with it and by reverencing it." [6]

Let me begin by making certain generalisations about the character of Christianity in early England, refering you for details to the fine study recently published by Henry Mayr-Harting, *The coming of Christianity to Anglo-Saxon England* (London 1972). Whether or not there was any survival of Romano-British Christianity in the areas occupied by the English—and my own belief is that there probably was some survival—it seems clear that the English experience of Christianity came from missionary activity from without, notably from Rome and Ireland, though with some influence from Gaul. Some very important consequences stemmed from this; for it meant that the English, from the beginning of their conversion, experienced Christianity as part of an encounter with another, higher culture, the culture of the Christian Roman Empire. That culture was the same whether it was transmitted by the Roman mission of Augustine or the Irish mission of Aidan; and all our evidence shows that the English responded enthusiastically to what the missionaries had to offer. As a result, English Christianity had, from the first, an international flavour; and it was not only to their immediate neighbours in Gaul that the English looked, as to the source of their conversion, Rome. English princesses with a monastic
* vocation like St. Hilda might go to Gaul to learn about the religious life at Faremoutiers-en-Brie or Chelles, and Benedict Biscop sojourn at Lérins to the same ends, but Rome remained the goal of pilgrimage for English kings and nobility. Thus we find Caedwalla of Wessex, the blood-stained conqueror of the Isle of Wight, abdicating his throne and making a pilgrimage to Rome where he was baptised just before his death in 689,[7] while in 853 the future King Alfred, then aged four, was sent by his father Aethelwulf to visit Rome, where Pope Leo IV invested him with the insignia of a Roman consul.[8] In the previous century the English missionaries to the Continent, St. Willibrord and St. Boni-

face, had deliberately placed themselves under the authority of the Apostolic See,[9] and there can be no question that, from the first, the English regarded themselves as being particularly beholden to the bishop of Rome, since it was a Roman bishop, Gregory the Great, who had first sought the conversion of the English nation.

I have said that the English conversion to faith was also accompanied by a conversion of culture, a conversion to the culture of the Christian Roman Empire. Unlike Constantine and Methodius, the Apostles of the Slavs, the Roman and Irish missionaries did not attempt to give their converts a vernacular bible or liturgy, and the very considerable vernacular literature which later developed was the creation of the English themselves. This development was wholly for the good. It meant that the English were culturally as well as ecclesiastically part of the Western Church, and ensured that scholars like Aldhelm and Bede could more than hold their own with their neighbours on the Continent. But the Latin culture which the English received was of a peculiar character, which was destined to a very great degree to colour the whole of Anglo-Saxon spirituality: it was monastic; that is to say, it regarded all learning and study as being directed to one end: the worship and praise of God, expressed and symbolized in the public worship of the Church and the study and exposition of the Bible. The programme of study required for the acquisition of such a culture did not provide for any acquaintance with the Latin classics. It envisaged a transition from the study of the Latin grammarians to that of the Bible and the Fathers of the Church without any intervening period of the study of secular authors.[10] This did not lead (as some humanists might suppose) to a barbaric style—for, after all, a system which could produce the prose of Bede or of the famous letter in which Bede's disciple Cuthbert describes the master's death is clearly not to be despised—but it did mean a deliberate limitation of cultural interests, and precisely the sort of limitation we should expect in monastic circles. A French scholar has very shrewdly remarked that one cannot accept the charge of an historian of classical studies that the Anglo-Saxons handed on "a mutilated antiquity" for they had no desire to be the heirs of the ancient world.[11] Much of their artistic achievement tells the same story. If we look at some of their finest manuscripts, we find that they are all motivated by religious devotion. Bishop Eadfrith of Lindisfarne copied and illuminated the Lindisfarne Gospels "for God and St. Cuthbert"—and one must envisage him sitting in the scriptorium of Lindisfarne, a mud-and-wattle building in the Irish fashion with unglazed windows, at work on his superb artistic achievement. Abbot Ceolfrid of Wearmouth-Jarrow caused the great Bible, commonly called the Codex Amiatinus, and regarded by some as the finest Latin uncial manuscript in existence, to be written for presentation to the Pope at Rome. It has been calculated that 1550 calves would have been needed to provide the vellum for this and for the two similar volumes which Ceolfrid made for use at Wearmouth and Jarrow respectively, and this amazing total not only provides some indication of the wealth of this great twin-house at the beginning of the eighth century, but also of the willingness of its possessors to devote it to the glory of God.[12] Again, we may consider a manuscript of that other great period of English book-painting, the tenth–eleventh centuries, the famous Benedictional of St. Aethelwold, of which the scribe, the monk Godeman, wrote in a prefatory poem :

> A bishop, the great Aethelwold, whom the Lord had made patron of Winchester, ordered a certain monk subject to him to write the present book. Knowing well how to preserve Christ's fleecy lambs from the malignant art of the devil; illustrious, venerable and benign, he desires also to tender as a good steward full fruit to God, when the Judge who sifts the acts of the whole world, what each has done, shall come and give such reward as they deserve : to the just eternal life and punishment to the unrighteous. He commanded also to be made this book with many frames well adorned and filled with various figures decorated with numerous beautiful colours and with gold. This book the Boanerges aforesaid caused to be indited for himself and in order that he might be able to sanctify the people of the Saviour by means of it and pour forth holy prayers to God for the flock committed to him, and that he may lose no lambkin of the fold, but may be able to say with joy : "Lo, I present to Thee myself and the children whom Thou didst give to keep; by Thy aid not one of them has the fierce ravening wolf snatched away . . ." [13]

The point of works like the Lindisfarne Gospels, the Codex Amiatinus and the Benedictional of St. Aethelwold, is that they are monastic productions in every sense of the word, made for religious reasons and for a religious end. Professor Knowles has remarked that book-copying is the manual labour of the cloister *par excellence* and the products of the Old English scriptoria amply justify his observation.

To speak, however, of Anglo-Saxon manuscripts inevitably brings one to the circumstances which produced the earliest and what many would regard as the greatest of them : the Christianization of Northumbria, and the fruitful encounter between Roman and Irish Christianity which occurred there and which provoked that extraordinary flowering of Christian culture associated with such productions as the Lindisfarne Gospels, the Ruthwell and Bewcastle Crosses and the writings of Bede. The bitter dissensions over the date of Easter, incomprehensible as they must seem to the majority of us today—though they were far from being so to the disputants at the time—must not conceal the debt of the Northumbrian Church to the Irish mission or obscure the very real influence which the Irish tradition exercised. A shrewd observer has pointed out that in the *Ecclesiastical History* Bede gives special prominence to three saints who may serve as models to the monks and bishops of his own day: John of Hexham; St. Cuthbert; and, above all, the Irish St. Aidan.[14] Bede wanted Christian poverty in the clergy of his day and it was in the Irish mission and in the English inspired by the Irish that he found it. He records that St. Aidan travelled about his diocese on foot and when King Oswine gave him a horse—a valuable gift, equivalent to a car at the present day—he gave it away to a poor man who asked for alms.[15] In a like manner St. Chad of Lichfield, himself trained by Aidan, was accustomed to travel on foot until Archbishop Theodore—with that passion for efficiency which marks the true Greek—forcibly placed him on horseback with his own hands.[16] We can see the influence of the Irish tradition in the life of St. Cuthbert, the greatest of the Northern saints, who was trained at Old Melrose, a dependency of Lindisfarne, by the Irish Prior Boisil and who was at one time expelled from the monastery of Ripon for observing the Celtic Easter. Cuthbert is Irish in his asceticism, in his perambulation as a bishop of his diocese, and his eventual retirement to a hermit's life on Farne. There is something very Irish, too, in Cuthbert's relations with the animal world, as in the charming story of how, on a visit to the monastery of Coldingham, Cuthbert rose stealthily in the night and went out to keep vigil in the sea, standing up to his neck in the dark hours; and a certain brother who had followed him secretly observed that when at daybreak Cuthbert came out of the sea and knelt on the sand to pray, two otters came up, warmed his feet with their breath and attempted to dry them with their fur;[17] or the episode on Farne, when Cuthbert rebuked some ravens which were tearing the thatch off the guest-house, and the penitent birds brought him a lump of lard with which he could grease his boots.[18] But behind this Irish ascetic tradition there is an older tradition, going back to St. Martin of Tours and beyond him to the monks of Egypt, and above all to St. Antony, the great father of hermits, whose life had such a profound effect upon eastern and western asceticism alike. One can find literary proof of this in Felix's life of St. Guthlac (674–715), in which the account of the demonic assaults on Felix in his Fenland hermitage of Crowland is clearly modelled upon those described in Athanasius' life of Antony.[19] Here then we find the English keeping alive that ancient ideal of the hermit: the holy man, living in solitude to contemplate God, and yet exercised by the attacks of the demonic forces, with whom he engages in a victorious struggle through the grace of Christ.

The Life-giving Cross

To talk of demons—known to the English as the Seed of Cain,[20] monsters like Grendel who haunt the misty moorlands and prey upon mankind—leads us, by an easy transition, to their sovereign antidote: the life-giving cross. It is in their crosses that the Anglo-Saxons have provided one of their most enduring art-forms and one of the noblest. "On the estates of nobles and good men of the Saxon race," wrote the English nun Huneberc of Heidenheim, "it is the custom to have a cross, which is dedicated to our Lord and held in great reverence, erected on some prominent spot for the convenience of those who wish to pray daily before it." [21] Professor Rosalind Hill has shown that many of the Northumbrian crosses were placed near harbours, or on Roman roads, or at natural meeting places for sheep-farmers.[22] To these might come a priest or a bishop to preach or to administer the sacraments; and it seems very probable that the portable altar found in the coffin of St. Cuthbert and now exhibited in the Monks' Dormitory at Durham and perhaps the little chalice which may be seen at Hexham Priory in Northumberland were intended for use when travelling, and would be used for celebrations at one of the crosses. The earlier crosses were wooden, like the majority of Anglo-Saxon buildings; but by the eighth century, stone crosses were being erected and decorated with magnificent carving. Of these, two have obtained an unchallenged artistic pre-eminence: the Bewcastle Cross in Cumberland and, supremely, the Ruthwell Cross in Dumfriesshire. This last can, in a certain sense, symbolize the Christian culture and the spirituality of early Anglo-Saxon England, in that it is at once expressive of the native genius of Christian Northumbria and also of the common Christian culture of Europe. One sees this in the decoration, the so-called inhabited vine-scroll ornamentation, which is of Mediterranean origin. Again, the iconography includes, besides various biblical scenes—John the Baptist; Christ in Judgment; the Flight into Egypt; the Visitation; Mary Magdalene washing Christ's feet; the Annunciation and the Crucifixion—a scene from monastic history: SS. Paul and Antony breaking bread in the desert—a reference to an incident in the *Life of St. Paul of Thebes* written by St. Jerome between 374 and 379.[23] One could hardly have a more vivid epitome of the monastic culture of Northumbria, based on the Bible and borrowing from classical antiquity only what it required to do glory to God. And the inspiration came from the Eastern Church: for the iconography derives from Byzantium as does the whole cultus of the True Cross. Traditionally, you will recall, the Cross on which Christ was crucified is said to have been discovered by St. Helena, the mother of Constantine, the "most exalted and most successful of the world's great archaeologists," as Sir Steven Runciman has pleasantly described her. Whether the Helena tradition is historically true is uncertain. What is clear is that by the middle of the fourth century a cross had been discovered at Jerusalem and pieces of the wood were being dispersed to other Christian centres. Eastern veneration of the cross spread to the West in the seventh century, after the Emperor Heraclius recaptured the True Cross from the Persians, who had seized it when they took Jerusalem in 614. In 701 the Syrian Pope Sergius I was led by a vision to discover a jewelled reliquary containing a fragment of the True Cross large enough to put Rome on an equal footing with Constantinople in the matter of relic worship; and it is to be noted that

Abbot Ceolfrith of Wearmouth-Jarrow was at Rome that same year and may well have witnessed the celebrations.[24]

There is, however, another aspect of the Ruthwell Cross. On the shaft, in runic letters, are to be found four citations apparently taken from the poem considered by many scholars to be the greatest of Old English religious compositions: *The Dream of the Rood.* In it the poet has a vision in the night of Christ's cross which tells the story of the Passion; how it was once a tree and was then cut down and made into a gallows—"Strong foes took me, fashioned me to be a spectacle for them, bade me raise up their felons"; how Christ, "the young Hero," stripped Himself and mounted the high cross in order to redeem mankind.

> I have endured many stern trials on the hill; I saw the God of hosts violently stretched out; darkness with its clouds had covered the Lord's corpse, the fair radiance; a shadow went forth, dark beneath the clouds. All creation wept, lamented the King's death. Christ was on the Cross.

Then the cross was taken down with those of the two thieves and buried in a deep pit; but afterwards the followers of the Lord found it and decked it with gold and silver.

> Now, my loved man, thou mayest hear that I have endured bitter anguish, grievous sorrows. Now the time has come when far and wide over the earth and all this splendid creation, men do me honour; they worship this sign. On me the Son of God suffered for a space; wherefore now I rise glorious beneath the heavens, and I can heal all who fear me. Long ago I became the severest of torments, most hateful to men, before I opened to mankind the true path of life. Lo! the Prince of glory, the Lord of heaven, honoured me then beyond the trees of the forest, even as Almighty God also honoured his mother Mary herself above the whole race of women. Now I bid thee, my loved man, to declare this vision unto men; reveal in words that it is the glorious tree on which Almighty God suffered for the many sins of mankind and the old deeds of Adam.[25]

The relation of the *Dream of the Rood* to the Ruthwell Cross is a notorious problem of scholarship. The poem as a whole exists in a West-Saxon dialect form in a manuscript of the late tenth century now in the Cathedral Library at Vercelli in Italy (an interesting example, it may be remarked in passing, of the way in which manuscripts travelled in the past); the extracts on the Ruthwell Cross are in the Northumbrian dialect of the late seventh or early eighth century. Clearly, this presents a problem of relationship. It does not follow that because certain passages existed in the late seventh century that the poem as a whole necessarily had been composed at that time—it is conceivable that the longer version was inspired by the Ruthwell passages. However, the conclusion of a recent editor is that the Ruthwell inscription "has all the appearance of reference to or quotation from some familiar text," [26] and if this is the case, we can see the Anglo-Saxon crosses as being something more than a symbol to denote a meeting-place for Christian worship. Rather, we may see them as theological statements in stone, intended to serve the same purpose as the pictures which Benedict Biscop brought back from his fifth visit to Rome in 678, pictures of the Virgin Mary and the twelve apostles, and of scenes from the Gospels and the Apocalypse, which were exhibited in Monkwearmouth Church so that, in the words of Bede, "all those who entered the church even though ignorant of letters, wherever they turned their gaze might contemplate, even though only in an image, the beloved aspect of Christ and of His saints; or might with more vigilant mind recall the grace of the Incarnation; or else, having before their eyes the great danger of the final testing, might remember to examine themselves more strictly." [27]

Now these words of Bede, if they are applied—as I think it is right to apply them—to the Northumbrian crosses, raise a very interesting train of thought with regard to the *Dream of the Rood.* Here again we are confronted with a textual difficulty: many scholars, including Bruce Dickens and Alan Ross, have considered the later part of the poem, from lines 78 onward, including the passage which I recently quoted beginning: "Now, my loved may, thou mayest hear that I have endured bitter anguish, grievous sorrows," to be a later addition, inferior in quality to the rest. This view has, however, been strongly criticized by J. V. Fleming in an article published in 1966, who argues that the last part records the reaction of the poet to the vision:

> Then glad at heart I worshipped the cross with great zeal, where I was alone with none to bear me company. My soul was eager to depart; I felt many yearns within me. It is now the hope of my life that I, alone more often than other men, may go to the cross, worship it fittingly. Great is the desire for that in my heart, and to the cross I turn for help.[28]

In this reaction Fleming sees the significance of the theology of the poem. As a result of an article published by Miss Rosemary Woolf in 1958,[29] the suggestion has been made that *The Dream of the Rood* is a carefully-argued orthodox formulation of Christ's dual nature and the contrasting aspects of the Crucifixion, divinity and triumph on one hand and humanity and suffering on the other, which takes account of the Monophysite and Monothelite controversies which were still raging in the Greek East in the seventh century. Fleming is sceptical about this; and in my opinion—speaking simply from the position of a student of Bede—rightly so. I can see no literary evidence for holding that the early English were deep students of Christology. I do not mean by this that they were not orthodox Chalcedonians; but I do not think that they had the subtle theological understanding which Miss Woolf suggests.

What then is the theological point of the poem? It seems to me that Fleming makes an important point when he reminds us that "going to the cross" was a common penitential practice in early monasteries; and that this practice reflects the same mental outlook which was expressed in the custom of praying either standing or prostrate, with the arms outstretched in the form of a cross. The dreamer goes to the True Cross in a vision of the night; from the Cross he hears of the salvation of mankind by Christ's death upon the Cross and by His Resurrection; and by this vision he is given comfort and hope in the present age, looking for the time

> when the Lord's cross, which erstwhile I saw here on earth, will fetch me from this fleeting life, and bring me then where there is great gladness, joy in heaven, where God's people are placed at the feast, where there is bliss unending.

However, the point which Fleming makes above all is that "the poem is characterized by a cast of thought and to some extent by a vocabulary that is not merely vaguely 'Christian,' but which is specifically monastic in its spirituality."[30] This verdict upon a vernacular poem exactly agrees with the impression which we should form from the Latin culture of early England which I have described as monastic. A monastic culture and therefore a monastic spirituality; and within that spirituality there will inevitably be considerable emphasis laid upon contemplation.

Pastoral and Missionary Concern

If, however, we examine the teaching of so distinguished an exponent of early English monasticism as Bede, we notice a rather curious fact. Bede is aware, following the tradition of the Fathers, that there are two lives: the active and the contemplative, and that the contemplative is the higher, in that unlike the active it does not end with this life, but continues throughout eternity. Nevertheless, so far as the coenobitical life is concerned, Bede seems to regard the natural life of the monk as being an active one, a life of good works. This, I take it, is the point of his remark in a sermon that while the active life is common to all the people of God, very few come to the contemplative and those who do are the more exalted if they come after a full accomplishment of pious action.[31] I believe myself that Bede considered his own monastic life to be an active one—he was, after all, still teaching and translating on his death-bed; and this pattern holds good throughout the Anglo-Saxon period. In the tenth century, for example, we have such notable reforming bishops as Dunstan (*c.* 909–988), Aethelwold (*c.* 909–984) and Oswald (d. 992), all monks by origin, and Aelfric, Abbot of Eynsham (*c.* 950–1020), famous as the author of the *Catholic Homilies,* composed between 990 and 995 and designed to provide sermons for all the Sundays and festivals of the Church's year. Indeed, of 116 bishops known in the period 960–1066, no fewer than sixty-seven are known to have been monks and only fourteen to have been secular clergy.[32]

I do not want to try to make too much of this, since this monastic concern with the active life in the early Middle Ages is not peculiar to England. I do, however, want to emphasise the extent to which the monastic profession carried with it an element of pastoral concern in Anglo-Saxon England. The pages of Bede's *History* are full of examples: St. Aidan, St. Boisil of Melrose, St. Cuthbert, to name only a few. And this pastoral concern was of a missionary character; for one of the most admirable features of the Anglo-Saxon Church is the fact that the English, once converted, were not content to keep the good news of the Gospel to themselves, but were anxious that their heathen kinsmen on the Continent of Europe should also share in the Christian hope. So we have the heroic story of the Anglo-Saxon mission to the Continent, in which the names of St. Willibrord (658–739) and St. Boniface (*c.* 675–754) are the most famous, the latter setting the seal on his devoted labours by martyrdom, since he was murdered by a heathen band at Dockum near the Frisian coast on 5th June 754. According to his biographer Willibald, Boniface encouraged his companions to meet death with the words: "Brethren, be of stout heart, fear not them who kill the body, for they cannot slay the soul, which continues to live for ever. Rejoice in the Lord; anchor your hope in God, for without delay He will render to you the reward of eternal bliss and grant you an abode with the angels in His heaven above. Be not slaves to the transitory pleasures of this world. Be not seduced by the vain flattery of the heathen, but endure with steadfast mind the sudden onslaught of death, that you may be able to reign evermore with Christ." [33]

The story of the Anglo-Saxon mission to the Continent is too long to recount here, but I would point to certain features which conform to the picture I am trying to create of early English Christianity. First, there is the notion of a *peregrinatio pro Christo,* voluntary exile from one's native land for the sake of Christ, a notion firmly fixed in Irish monasticism which was responsible for the creation of such Irish houses on the Continent as St. Gall, Luxeuil and Bobbio. This was the motive which had brought St. Columba to Iona (*pro Christo perigrinari volens enavigavit*) [34] and an Irish poet at a later date put an imagined farewell into the saint's mouth with great poignancy:

> There is a grey eye
> That will look back upon Erin:
> It shall never see again
> The men of Erin nor her women.
>
> I stretch my glance across the brine
> From the firm oaken planks:
> Many are the tears of my bright soft grey eye
> As I look back upon Erin.[35]

Rather curiously, it was a Northumbrian named Egbert, who had made a pilgrimage for Christ's sake into Ireland, who first conceived the idea of the German mission. He wished himself to go, but was forbidden by a vision and had to be content with sending others, just as Gregory the Great had been forced to send Augustine and his companions to England when he would rather have gone himself. Thus it was that the Irish were responsible in large measure for bringing Christianity to northern England, and that it was a Northumbrian resident in Ireland who first concerned himself with bringing Christianity to the heathen homeland of the English race. There is here a remarkable spiritual continuity.

Again, one must observe the Roman loyalty of the English Continental missionaries. Willibrord and Boniface alike sought consecration at Rome and the latter, at his consecration in 722, took an oath of loyalty to the Roman see such as was commonly taken by newly-consecrated suburbicarian Italian bishops, but without any promise of loyalty to the East Roman emperor such as they commonly gave.[36] I have sometimes thought that the English must take a good deal of responsibility for the creation of the medieval papacy through their work in Germany. The important point, however, for our purposes, is the sense of the English missionaries of being part of a universal Church which has its centre of authority at Rome. There is, of course, nothing extraordinary about the papalism of Willibrord and Boniface. The English Church had received her first missionaries from Rome; by the decision of the Synod of Whitby of 664 she had elected to follow the Roman practice and tradition; and Rome, as we have seen, rather than the neighbouring churches of Gaul, was the obvious inspiration of English Christianity, both ecclesiastically and culturally. To these considerations may be added the thought of the Bishop of Rome as being the "lord" and the missionary as his "man", a notion so congenial to Anglo-Saxon society. But whatever the reason, there can be no question that one of the characteristics of the English mission to the Continent was a doctrine of obedience to and respect for the Roman see, which went hand in hand with the first principles of the Christian faith.

Finally, one sees in the English mission that same concern for monastic culture which marks the home-church. Manuscripts illuminated in the Hiberno-Northumbrian tradition, like the famous Echternach Gospels, appear on the Continent, and we find examples of the English uncial and insular minuscule hands coming from German scriptoria, written by scribes who were either English or trained by an Englishman.[37] Furthermore, as an aftermath of the English mission to the Germans, we have the invitation of the Englishman Alcuin by Charlemagne to his dominions, there to help the king in his attempt to revive learning and to hand on the traditions of the school of York, which in turn derived its learning from Bede. It has been said of Alcuin that he rapidly became and long remained the spiritual ruler of Europe; but he drew upon a great tradition of learned spirituality going back to the earliest days of

Christian Northumbria. Indeed, the English mission to the Continent might well have taken for its motto the words of Bede: "We cannot either rightly love one another without the faith of Christ, nor can we truly believe in the name of Christ without brotherly love".[38]

I have spoken of certain characteristics of Anglo-Saxon spirituality: its monastic quality; its culture—a real, if limited, one, which could express itself in artistic and literary productions of the first order; and of its pastoral concern, manifested in the lives of notable bishops and teachers both in England and on the Continent. I have also noted as an historical fact its papalism, using the word quite simply to denote loyalty to the Roman see without any particular theological overtones. One can also detect various pointers to the future. For example, it is an English monk of Whitby, writing the earliest life of St. Gregory the Great, who first tells the story of the Mass of St. Gregory—destined to furnish a very popular theme for later medieval artists—in which a Roman matron who doubted the reality of the change in the eucharistic elements at the moment of consecration was convinced by seeing on the altar what appeared to be the fragment of a little finger, covered with blood.[39] Aelfric of Eynsham, who tells this story in his Paschal homily, together with the even more extraordinary one from the Fathers of the Desert, of how two doubting monks who, after the consecration, saw a child lying on the paten and an angel with a knife dismembering him, is at pains to emphasise that the sacrament is Christ's body by the power of God's word and not by any substantial change; but Aelfric's view—not original, but borrowed from Ratramnus of Corbie[40]—was not destined to prevail; and as in the case of obedience to Rome, the Anglo-Saxon Church was in the vanguard of thought in its day. Again, and perhaps even more curiously, it was the English Council of Hatfield * of 680, meeting under a Greek Archbishop of Canterbury, Theodore of Tarsus, which in its denunciation of Monotheletism, solemnly declared its belief in the double procession of the Holy Spirit from the Father and the Son—a belief which could be found in Latin theologians from St. Augustine of Hippo onwards, but which was not at the time professed by the Roman see.[41] On the other hand, so far as the Virgin Mary was concerned, the pre-Conquest English were more cautious. Thus Aelfric, speaking of the Conception, merely says: "What shall we say of the birth-tide of Mary, save that she was begotten by father and by mother as other persons, and was born on the day that we call the eighth of September? Her father was named Joachim and her mother Anna, pious persons according to the old law; but we will not write further concerning them, lest we fall into any error."[42] It was left to another Englishman writing after the Norman Conquest, Eadmer, the biographer of St. Anselm, to draw portentous theological conclusions from the Feast of the Conception of the Mother of God and to propose the doctrine of the Immaculate Conception.[43]

This World and the World to Come

Limitations to time require me to begin to draw to a close. I am conscious that I have left unsaid many things I would like to say about the religious characteristics of the early English Church which could, indeed, be made the subject of a book. I shall therefore in the last part of this paper speak of what appear to me to be two of the principal characteristics of Anglo-Saxon religion in pre-Conquest times.

The first is a positive, affirmatory contribution to the national life. This expresses itself in many ways: for example, in Bede's *History,* which is an *ecclesiastical* history of the English people; and in the concern which he expressed towards the end of his life at the neglect of their secular obligations by high-born persons under a specious pretext of religion, which could only result, in Bede's opinion, in harm to the Kingdom of Northumbria. Again, we can see the close link between the English Church and the English state in the practice which so shocked the Norman reformers of the bishop sitting with the earl in the shire court and administering temporal justice. The other side of this episcopal intervention in secular affairs is one with which the reformers would not have quarrelled: a concern by the king for the affairs of the Church. One thinks of St. Oswald in the seventh century, who became one of the royal saints of early England with a cultus which extended beyond the boundaries of England to the Continent; but the inevitable, if rather obvious, example is Alfred; and it is difficult to withhold admiration for a man who, after defeating the Danes, heroically attempted to revive the English Church, which had suffered so greatly in the Danish invasions, and who commissioned and participated in the programme of translation from the Latin for the benefit of those who, though ignorant of Latin, were nevertheless literate.

The fruits of Alfred's attempts at reform were seen in the century which followed his death; and here, as in former times, it is the monasteries which provided the power-houses of revival. Alfred's own attempts at restoring the religious life in his own dominions had not been very successful. He had made his daughter, Aethelgifu, abbess of the nunnery which he founded at Shaftesbury; but for his foundation for men at Athelney, he was forced to rely on monks from the Continent, since the English were apparently unwilling to live in so deserted a spot. However, in the tenth century a revival took place, with which the names of Dunstan at Glastonbury, and Aethelwold at Abingdon are particularly associated and, as we have seen, both these men subsequently became bishops.[44] Aethelwold was consecrated bishop of Winchester in 963 where he soon displayed a masterful temperament, expelling the secular clerks from the Old Minster on account of their undisciplined way of life and replacing them with monks, carrying out a similar reform at the New Minster (founded in 903 as a monastery but affected by a loss of enthusiasm) and insisting on a stricter discipline at Nunnaminster, the Winchester house for women. It is likely that he probably was the principal author of the *Regularis*

Concordia, the book of liturgical customs borrowed from the continental practice of houses like Fleury, Ghent and Lorraine, which was intended to provide a uniform practice for English religious houses.[45] In the *Regularis Concordia* we can see how the wheel has come full circle in the relations of England with the Continent. In the eighth century English missionaries took the Christian faith and Christian culture to the Continent; in the tenth, after the Carolingian reforms, England goes to the Continent to find a model for her own practice.

This is true of English art. In later Saxon times, the centre of gravity for manuscript illumination had shifted from Northumbria to southern England, and the Winchester school of painting, its supreme representative, was a direct product of the monastic revival. The southern artists did not look back for inspiration to the Hiberno-Northumbrian tradition of the Lindisfarne Gospels; rather they looked to the Continent, and to the inspiration of Carolingian and Ottonian art. The new style is already to be seen in an illuminated copy of Bede's *Life of St. Cuthbert,* copied about 937 and probably of Winchester provenance. Its first clear manifestation is in King Edgar's Foundation Charter of the New Minster at Winchester, written and illuminated in 966, and it reaches a high point in the Benedictional of St. Aethelwold, written at a date between 971 and 984.[46] Like King Edgar's Charter, the Benedictional is written in a Carolingian minuscule hand, and not in the famous Insular script which had grown up in England.[47] Again, the leafy ornament which frames the miniatures and the decorated pages of the Benedictional is quite unlike the Celtic motifs which may be found in earlier manuscripts, even if written in the south of England.[48] But despite borrowing from the Continent of script and decoration, the Benedictional is an original English creation, expressed in a wonderful drawing technique which will be developed in later products of the
* Winchester School, like the Grimbald and Weingarten Gospels. In all these we can see the artistic genius of Anglo-Saxon England offered to God, and that sensitivity to beauty which can be found in the earliest expression of English vernacular literature, the famous hymn of Caedmon the cowherd, recorded by Bede in the *Ecclesiastical History.*[49]

But besides this appreciation of the created world there is another, equally or perhaps more characteristic: a world-denying strain which regards this world as no more than a "thoroughfare of woe" and which ardently desires, with the Apostle, to be dissolved and to be with Christ. One finds this is Bede who, despite his active life of scholarship which, by his own admission, gave him great joy, always looked forward eagerly to death, which would bring him to his true fatherland. For Bede, writing in a tradition which looks back to the great ascetics of the Egyptian Desert, the experience of God is often manifested by a supernatural light, brighter than any earthly illumination, and frequently manifested at the deaths of the saints. This experience is not, of course, only to be found in the pages of Bede; we find it at the death of

St. Columba, as described by his biographer Adomnan.[50] Again, it was the vision of the soul of St. Aidan, being borne to heaven by angels in a globe of light, which caused St. Cuthbert to forsake his shepherd's life for that of a monk.[51] We find the divine light yet again in Bede's account of the nun of Barking dying of the plague of 664 who called on her companions to put out the lamp which burned in her room since she beheld the house filled with such a light that their lamp seemed in comparison to be but darkness[52] This experience of supernatural light is not uncommon in the literature of religious experience and I will not dwell upon it; but it provides a background to Bede's exposition of the words of the *Song of Songs: Until the day break and the shadows flee away.*

> *Until the day break,* etc. That is, until the eternal light of the age to come arises, and the *shadows* of this present life, by which even the faithful who use the lamp of the Word of God are often blinded, *diminish* that they may pass away. . . . Nor is this comparison of the present life to the shades of night and the future to the day contrary to the word by which the Apostle testifies to the life which we now live and says: *The night is far spent, the day has drawn near* for, to put it briefly, this present life of the faithful who, casting away *the works of darkness* are clothed with *the armour of light* is indeed day in comparison with the faithless, who neither know nor love anything of the true life; but in comparison with the future blessedness, when the true light is beheld without end, it remains deepest night.[53]

The theme of this Conference is Transfiguration, of a change to a better state, from the natural to the supernatural, from the mortal to the immortal. It is a process which, although begun in this life, is completed only in the life to come; for we reach the haven of the New Jerusalem only by crossing the stormy sea of death. It seems fitting to let Bede speak the last word:

> *God,* therefore, *gave unto us eternal life;* but to those who are still pilgrims on the earth he gave in hope what he will give to those coming to him in heaven in reality.[54]

NOTES

[1] R. W. Southern, *The Making of the Middle Ages* (London 1953), p. 17: "As a result of the Norman Conquest England had been effectively added to the French-speaking world".

[2] Note the comment of William of Malmesbury, *Gesta Regum Anglorum* V, 398: "Idem dies ante quadraginta circiter annos fuerat, cum Willelmus Hastingas primus appulit; provido forsitan Dei iudicio, ut eo die subderetur Angliae Normannia, quo ad eam subiugandum olim venerat Normannorum copia" (Rolls Series 90 (2)).

[3] See R. R. Darlington, "Ecclesiastical Reform in the late Old English period", *English Historical Review* li (1936), 385-428; Frank Barlow, *The English Church 1000–1066. A Constitutional History* (London 1963).

[4] See James Campbell, "Bede", in *Latin Historians,* ed. T. A. Dorey (London 1966), pp. 159-90.

[5] Bede, *De Tabernaculo* II (*Corpus Christianorum Series Latina* cxix A, 62. 801-806).

[6] Bede, *In Ezram et Neemiam* III (*CC* cxix A, 375. 1427-29).

[7] Bede, *Historia Ecclesiastica* V, 7 (ed. Colgrave & Mynors, pp. 468-73).

[8] See W. H. Stevenson, *Asser's Life of King Alfred* (Oxford 1904), pp. 179-85.

[9] John Godfrey, *The Church in Anglo-Saxon England* (Cambridge 1962), p. 235: "There was never a clearer case of an Englishman dedicating himself to the service of the Holy See" (of the consecration of Boniface by Gregory II in 722).

[10] See Pierre Riché, *Education et culture dans l'Occident barbare VIe–VIIIe siècles,* 2nd ed. (Paris 1962), pp. 433-43.

[11] ibid., p. 443 (referring to M. Roger, *L'enseignement des lettres classiques d'Ausone à Alcuin* (Paris 1905), p. 309).

[12] See E. A. Lowe, *English Uncial* (Oxford 1960), pp. 8-13; Henry Mayr-Harting, *The coming of Christianity to Anglo-Saxon England* (London 1972), p. 155.

[13] Translation by Francis Wormald, *The Benedictional of St. Athelwold* (London 1959), p. 7.

[14] Campbell [op. cit. n. 4], p. 175.

[15] Bede, *HE* III, 14 (Colgrave & Mynors, p. 258).

[16] ibid., IV, 3 (Colgrave & Mynors, p. 337).

[17] *Vita Cuthberti Auct. Anon.,* II, 2; *Vita Cuthberti Bedae,* 10 (ed. B. Colgrave, *Two Lives of St. Cuthbert* (Cambridge 1940), pp. 78-82, 188-90).

[18] *Vita Cuthbert. Anon.,* III, 5; *Vita Cuthbert. Bedae,* 20 (Colgrave, pp. 100-102, 222-24).

[19] Felix, *Vita Sancti Guthlaci,* 19-34 (ed. Colgrave, *Felix's Life of Saint Guthlac* (Cambridge 1956), pp. 82-111; see note on cap. 29, p. 184).

[20] ibid., 31: "semen Cain" (Colgrave, p. 106). Professor Dorothy Whitelock, *The Audience in Beowulf* (Oxford 1951), p. 80, draws attention that the same expression occurs in *Beowulf,* lines 103-10, 1261-66 (note by Colgrave, p. 185).

[21] Huneberc of Heidenheim, *The Hodoepericon of St. Willibald,* tr. by C. H. Talbot, *The Anglo-Saxon Missionaries in Germany* (London 1954), p. 155.

[22] Rosalind Hill, "Christianity and Geography in early Northumbria", *Studies in Church History* Vol. III, ed. G. J. Cuming (Leiden 1966), pp. 136-39.

[23] Jerome, *Vita Sancti Pauli,* 11 (*PL* xxiii, 26A).

[24] See editorial note in *The Dream of the Rood,* ed. by Michael Swanton (Manchester/New York 1970), pp. 42-52, for a convenient summary of the history of the cult of the True Cross.

[25] I cite from the translation by R. K. Gordon, *Anglo-Saxon Poetry* (London 1926), pp. 261-64, with a slight modification in the rendering of lines 122-31 in accordance with the suggestion of J. V. Fleming, art. cit. infra, n. 28.

[26] Swanton, ed. cit. n. 24, p. 41.

[27] Bede, *Historia Abbatum,* 6 (ed. Plummer, pp. 369-70).

[28] J. V. Fleming, "*The Dream of the Rood* and Anglo-Saxon monasticism", *Traditio* xxii (1966), 43-72.

[29] Rosemary Woolf, "Doctrinal influences on the *Dream of the Rood*", *Medium Aevum* xxvii (1958), 137-53.

[30] Fleming, art. cit., p. 71.

[31] Bede, *Hom.* I, 9 (*CC* cxxii, 64. 145-51).

[32] David Knowles, *The Monastic Order in England,* 2nd ed. (Cambridge 1963), Appendix IV, pp. 697-701.

[33] Tr. by Talbot, *The Anglo-Saxon Missionaries in Germany,* pp. 56, 57.

[34] Adomnan, *Vita Columbani. Secunda praefatio* (ed. by A. O. and M. O. Anderson (London 1961), p. 187).

[35] Kuno Meyer, *Selections from Ancient Irish Poetry,* 2nd ed. (London 1959), p. 85.

[36] Boniface, *Ep.* 16 (ed. Tangl), tr. by Talbot, *Anglo-Saxon Missionaries in Germany,* pp. 70, 71.

[37] On the Echternach Gospels, see Lowe, *Codices Latini Antiquiores* ii (2nd ed. 1972), pp. xviii-ix; on English scribal influence on the Continent see Lowe, *English Uncial,* pp. 13, 14.

[38] Bede, *Exp. in Primam Ep. Iohannis* (*PL* xciii, 105A).
[39] *The Earliest Life of Gregory the Great by an Anonymous Monk of Whitby*, c. 20 (ed. B. Colgrave (Lawrence: The University of Kansas Press 1968), p. 106).
[40] *The Homilies of the Anglo-Saxon Church* by Benjamin Thorpe: *Homilies of Aelfric* (London 1846-48) ii, 273. See A. J. Macdonald, *Berengar and the reform of sacramental doctrine* (London 1930), pp. 247-49. The legend of the dismembered child is *Vitae Patrum* V: *Verba Seniorum* Lib. xviii, 3 (*PL* lxxiii, 978 D-980 A).
[41] Bede, *HE* IV, 17 [15] (Colgrave & Mynors, p. 386). See J. N. D. Kelly, *Early Christian Creeds*, 2nd ed. (London 1960), pp. 362, 363.
[42] Aelfric, *Catholic Homilies*, ed. B. Thorpe, ii. 467.
[43] See Hilda Graef, *Mary. A History of Devotion and Doctrine* i (London 1963), pp. 215-21; on the English contribution to the liturgical side of Marian devotion, see Edmund Bishop, "On the origins of the Feast of the Conception of the Blessed Virgin Mary", *Liturgica Historica* (Oxford 1918), 238-59.
[44] On Dunstan see Eleanor Shipley Duckett, *St. Dunstan of Canterbury* (London 1955) and J. Armitage Robinson, *The Times of St Dunstan* (Oxford 1923).
[45] *Regularis Concordia* ed. Thomas Symons (London 1953). See David Knowles, *The Monastic Order in England*, 2nd ed., pp. 31-56.
[46] On the Winchester school, see O. E. Saunders, *A History of English Art in the Middle Ages* (Oxford 1932), pp. 30-35 and Margaret Rickert, *Painting in Britain: The Middle Ages* (London 1954), pp. 34-45 and *La miniature anglaise* (Milan 1959), pp. 22-23, Pl. X.
[47] On English Caroline minuscule in general, see T. A. M. Bishop, *English Caroline Minuscule* (Oxford 1971) and for the Benedictional of St. Aethelwold, ibid., pp. xxi-xxii, Pl. X.
[48] See Rickert, *La miniature anglaise*, p. 23; Wormald, *The Benedictional of St. Ethelwold*, p. 13.
[49] Bede, *HE* IV, [22] (Colgrave & Mynors, p. 529).
[50] Adomnan, *Vita Columbani*, III, 23 (ed. Anderson & Anderson, p. 529). The whole of the work abounds in accounts of manifestations of supernatural light.
[51] *Vita Cuthberti Auct. Anon.*, I, 5; cf. *Vita Cuthberti Bedae*, 4 (Colgrave, pp. 68, 164-66).
[52] Bede, *HE* IV, 8 (Colgrave & Mynors, p. 358). Cf. IV, 7 (pp. 356-58) and III, 8 (p. 238) (the death of Eorcengota).
[53] Bede, *In Cantica Lib.* III (*PL* xci, 1116B).
[54] Bede, *Exp. in Primam Ep. Iohannis* (*PL* xciii, 116A).

Corrigenda

p. 545, l. 27, the date 679 seems to be more favoured.

XVI

Schism and Church Unity

Schism may be defined as division within a Christian community, which may lead to external separation but does not involve disagreement over fundamental doctrines. It is this doctrinal element which essentially distinguishes schism from heresy; for heresy (at least in the opinion of the disputants, which may not be endorsed by later historians) involves radical disagreement over articles of faith essential for salvation. In the early Church, however, the boundaries between schism and heresy were not absolutely defined or clearly established. There was a tendency, particularly on the side which emerged as 'orthodox' and so set the pattern for later orthodox evaluation, to feel that schism contained within itself the seeds of heresy. Thus St Jerome (347[?]–420) declares that heresy involves perverse dogma, schism episcopal dissension, 'but, for the rest, there is no schism that does not devise a heresy for itself'.[1] In similar fashion St Augustine (354–430) could argue that while schism initially arises from disagreement over opinions, 'schism grown old becomes heresy'.[2] While both Jerome and Augustine had theological axes to grind, their declarations are a reminder that schism in the early Church did not result only from personal antagonisms, but frequently involved theological considerations whose full implications were only gradually appreciated. Thus, for example, a good many schisms in the early Church, such as Novatianism, arose initially from disciplinary considerations: should a penitent guilty of mortal sin be readmitted to communion, or ought he to spend his life in perpetual penance? But this disagreement over discipline had ecclesiological implications: Ought not the Church Militant to be a pure Church? Had she authority to pronounce absolution in God's name? In early Christian thought, heresy was concerned largely with belief about the doctrines of God and the creation of the world, with the Trinity, and with the incarnation. Ecclesiology was defined by pastoral practice rather than by theological reflection; but in order to justify pastoral practice it was necessary to theorize, and so open lines of theological investigation which were to be increasingly developed in later centuries, until they came in practice to be deemed as much a test of right belief as the relation of the Son to the Father in the Trinity, or of the human to the divine in the person of Jesus Christ.

An example of such development is provided by the thought of St Cyprian, bishop of Carthage from 248/9 to 258. In the course of the disputes which arose in the wake of the Decian persecution of 250, Cyprian composed his treatise *On the Unity of the Catholic Church*, probably in support of his Roman colleague Cornelius, who was harassed at Rome by the antipope Novatian. Cyprian's argument, designed to have a profound influence on both African and later western theology, is rooted in the conviction that there can be no spiritual life outside the Catholic Church. Had there been safety from the waters of the Flood outside the Ark of Noah there might be salvation for the heretic or the schismatic; but there was none. Some years later, in 256, Cyprian found himself in dispute with Cornelius' successor, Stephen, on the question of the manner of receiving converts from heretical and schismatic churches. Cyprian followed a practice of rebaptizing them (in his view, baptizing them for the first time), which had been introduced into Africa by his predecessor Agrippinus in the early third century. Stephen maintained the Roman custom, in which the convert was not rebaptized, but received by the imposition of the bishop's hands. In the dispute between them, Stephen appealed to tradition to justify his practice: 'Let no innovation be made!'[3] Cyprian, despite his belief that a bishop enjoyed full autonomy in his diocese provided that he was orthodox in doctrine, nevertheless continued to press Stephen to adopt the African practice, apparently because he had been convinced by his own arguments, and wished to change Roman tradition on theological grounds. In the event, he failed; but his theorizing provides an illustration of the way in which pastoral practice could be questioned on theological grounds, and the distinction between schism and heresy effectively removed by an ecclesiology which regarded the one Catholic Church as the sole channel of divine grace.

Nevertheless, this narrowness of Cyprian's doctrine of the Church was the result of a passionate devotion to the ideal of

Christian unity, the natural development of St Paul's exhortation 'that there should be no schism in the body' (1 Cor. 12.25). The early Church normally recognized and respected local divergencies of practice, and St Ambrose of Milan (339–397) could say roundly to a questioner: 'When I am here, I do not fast on Saturday; and when I am at Rome, I do. If you do not wish to cause scandal, observe the local practice of any church which you may visit,'[4] and tell his congregation, when expounding the Milanese practice, not observed at Rome, of washing the feet of the newly baptized: 'We are well aware that the Roman church does not have this custom . . . I say this, not to criticize others, but to commend my own practice. In general I desire to follow the Roman church; yet we too are not without common sense, and what other places have rightly retained, we also rightly maintain.'[5] Yet Ambrose did not hesitate to follow the example of the Roman church on all major issues so that, during the fourth-century schism in the church of Antioch, in common with the western Church as a whole and Alexandria in the East, he supported the minority Catholic congregation in that city led by bishop Paulinus, and refused to recognize Meletius, the bishop of the great majority of the Antiochene Catholics, who enjoyed the support of the bishops of Asia and Syria. The idea that the two congregations might be equally members of the one Catholic Church never occurred to him.

S L Greenslade, in his *Schism in the Early Church*, discussed the causes of schism under five headings: Personal; Nationalism, Social and Economic Influences; The Rivalry of Sees; Liturgical Disputes; and Problems of Discipline and the Puritan Idea of the Church. These divisions, which suited the pattern of Greenslade's book, are perhaps too refined, and are certainly controversial. Many scholars, following A H M Jones,[6] would regard the notion of a possible nationalistic element in early Christian schism as open to question, and Greenslade himself was constrained to admit that 'there was some tension between the opposing ideals of liturgical uniformity and liberty in the early Church . . . but not much schism'.[7] Essentially, the causes of schism are personal and ideological, though it is to be doubted whether either of these factors ever wholly excluded the other. Any schismatic leader, however ambitious, is likely to urge some issue of principle as a justification of his actions, while on the other hand personalities may well render insoluble an issue which, left to other men, could be resolved with a little goodwill on both sides. Goodwill was not lacking in the early Church. During the late fourth century, a very small schismatic sect, known as the *Tertullianistae*, was quietly received back into the Catholic church of Carthage, apparently without account being taken of the belief of their alleged founder, the third-century African theologian Tertullian, that the human soul, and God himself, were bodies.[8] Here was a case when a minor theological error was not deemed to turn a schism into a heresy.

It will be helpful to consider certain well-known early schisms, in order to understand their origins and characteristics; and it is convenient to begin with that in the church of Corinth, which provoked the celebrated letter of the church of Rome, to be dated around AD 95, and written anonymously by Clement in the name of the Roman church. As the oldest non-biblical Christian writing that we possess (unless the *Didache* is older), Clement's letter is of particular interest.

Our knowledge of the Corinthian schism derives solely from Clement's letter. It appears that there had been 'an abominable and unholy sedition (*stasis*)'[9] in the church of Corinth, through which certain presbyters had been removed from their office. Since no motive other than *zēlos kai phthonos* (jealousy and envy) is given, it may be guessed that the issues were personal rather than ideological, and that the Corinthian church, after a period of peace and stability ('You were sincere and innocent, and bore no malice to one another. All sedition and all schism were abominable to you,' declares Clement),[10] was again manifesting the contentiousness which had formerly distressed St Paul (1 Cor. 1.11–13).

Clement's remedy is to commend mutual charity and submission to duly constituted authority. He likens the Church to an army, in which all serve within the military hierarchy. 'Not all are prefects, nor tribunes, nor centurions, nor in charge of fifty men, or the like; but each carries out in his own rank the commands of the emperor and the generals.'[11] We have no direct information about the effect of Clement's letter; but since it was apparently held in high esteem in the Corinthian church some seventy years later, being read in church as though it were a work of Scripture,[12] it may be concluded that it was successful in bringing about a reconciliation in the church to which it was addressed.

A feature of the Corinthian schism is that it involved factions within the Church, and not secession from it. With the Montanist movement of the second century, we have to do with a group which was eventually expelled and became a separate communion. Schism here led to separation, though only after attempts to obtain recognition by the Great Church had failed. Montanus, a Phrygian convert of the mid-second century, began after his baptism to speak in ecstasy, declaring that his utterances were the voice of God. He was shortly followed by two women, Prisca and Maximilla. Their prophecies, though not characterized by any particular profundity ('The Holy Spirit seemed to say nothing of any religious or intellectual value to his prophets'),[13] attracted many followers in Asia, and the movement subsequently spread to North Africa, where it made a notable convert in Tertullian.

However, although in itself the claim to speak with divine inspiration was not heretical, both the unbridled enthusiasm of Montanism, which was calculated deliberately to provoke the pagan authorities, and its ferocious asceticism, aroused opposition in the Asiatic church, with the result that two parties struggled for mastery, and at one time, in the reign of Pope Zephyrinus (199–217), Montanism came near to obtaining recognition by Rome. Eventually it failed; and at some later date, two Asiatic councils at Iconium (perhaps about 230) and Synnada (date unknown) decided not to recognize Montanist baptism. Thus a movement which began within the Church became an external schism and was eventually branded a heresy.

A curious feature of this progression is that it was the mood of Montanism – ecstatic, eschatological, and ascetic – rather than its doctrines, which gave offence. It appears to have been one of those revivalist movements which, from time to time, disturbed the life of the Church, and as such was rather a menace to order and established authority, than a deliberately secessionist sect.

With the Novatianist schism of the mid third century, we come to a movement which was determined both by personalities and principles. Novatian was a distinguished Roman presbyter, the author of a work on the Trinity. The Decian persecution of 250 left Church leaders everywhere with the pastoral problem of how to deal with penitent apostates who now sought reconciliation with the Church. Opinion on this matter was divided. Many Christians believed that with a mortal sin of such gravity as apostasy, no reconciliation was possible, and the repentant sinner ought to spend his remaining years in lifelong penance, in the hope that, at the last, God would give him the pardon which the Church Militant dared not pronounce. However, the great majority of the bishops decided that it was better to absolve such penitents, in order that they might be encouraged and sustained by the sacramental fellowship of the Catholic Church. From this policy Novatian vehemently dissented. He contrived to have himself consecrated bishop of Rome, in opposition to the reigning Pope, Cornelius, and so founded a schismatic Church which was to endure to the fifth century and enjoy a certain measure of respect, even from members of the Great Church.[14]

Novatian's character has naturally been unflatteringly depicted by his Catholic opponents; yet even allowing for bias, it is difficult not to feel that personal ambition, as well as zeal for a pure Church, played its part in leading him into schism.

With Donatism we come to what is probably the most famous schism of the early Church. Here again, the issue was one of ecclesiastical discipline, but one that was debated in a particular area – Roman North Africa – where rigorism enjoyed a great degree of popular support, to such an extent that some historians have interpreted Donatism as an expression of African national feeling in religious terms. The theological debate turned upon the status of those clerics who, in the Diocletianic persecution (300–11), had surrendered copies of the Scriptures for destruction to the secular authorities. Such surrender (*traditio*) was regarded by the Donatists as equivalent to apostasy and, in a tradition which looked back to the teaching of St Cyprian, these 'handers-over' (*traditores*) were deemed to have forfeited the power to administer valid sacraments. Accordingly, sacraments administered by *traditores* were not merely inefficacious but positively defiling, and anyone baptized in the Catholic Church needed Donatist baptism to cleanse him of his unremitted sins. Caecilian, the bishop of Carthage who initially provoked the controversy, was alleged to have had among his consecrators one Felix of Apthungi, an obscure bishop whose sole historical distinction is that he was alleged (untruly) to have been a *traditor*. The fact that Felix was acquitted by both ecclesiastical and secular enquiries made no difference to the enemies of Caecilian: in their eyes he had been consecrated by a *traditor*, and anyone who communicated with him, or with his successors, shared the taint of *traditio*.

Initially, the Donatist movement claimed to be a party within the

African Church, holding a common theology, but divided on a point of discipline. It also claimed – correctly – that it stood in the doctrinal tradition of St Cyprian, the great hero of African Christians. It was thus, technically, a schism; though its own claim, naturally, was to be the true African Church, and that its Catholic opponents were the schismatics. The fact that it attracted no support outside Africa, apart from a tenuous foothold at Rome, made no difference to its supporters, who were prepared to believe that true faith had perished in the Roman world and was preserved only in Africa. For that reason its fundamental principles made Donatism nearer to heresy than other early schismatic movements. But now secular considerations entered an ecclesiastical dispute. Since the conversion of the emperor Constantine, at the beginning of the fourth century, Christian emperors had shown a steadily increasing determination to enforce what they deemed to be right belief upon their subjects. This process had culminated in 392 by the law of Theodosius I against all heresies, which decreed that heretical clergy were to be fined ten pounds of gold (a huge sum) and the places where heretical rites were celebrated with the owner's consent were to be confiscated – a severe deterrent to lay patrons of heresy.[15] The question was: Were Donatists liable under this law? In the preceding decades, emperors had legislated spasmodically against rebaptism, but had not regarded Donatism as being in itself heretical. An action brought in 404 by Augustine of Hippo and his friend Possidius, bishop of Calama, against Crispinus, the Donatist bishop of that city, eventually procured a decision that the law was applicable, and so Donatism became legally liable as heretical.

The legal decision, although from the Catholic point of view a useful threat, did not involve an equivalent theological change of outlook. The Catholics passionately desired to see the Donatists restored to the universal Church. The Donatists were equally determined to remain apart. In consequence, both sides tended to minimize the theological differences between them, the one in order to forward the work of reconciliation, the other to avoid the operation of the imperial laws. Eventually the Catholics decided to have recourse to the secular arm, ostensibly – and perhaps sincerely – as a protection against Donatist terrorists; and after a conference between both churches at Carthage in 411, at which the imperial commissioner, Count Marcellinus, decided that the Catholics were the true Church of Africa, the work of forcible reintegration went ahead with considerable, though by no means complete, success, until the invasion of Africa by the Arian Vandals in 429 gave both disputants other matters to think about.

The history of Donatism is of an internal schism in a local Church which passed outside and soon became an independent Church, not only claiming to be theologically in the right, as did other schismatic Churches, but also seeking to be officially recognized as the lawful Church of Africa by the Roman government. The Donatist attitude to the secular world was a curious mixture of fundamental hostility and occasional opportunism. In essence, Donatist theology was based upon the ideal of a pure Church which, by its very character, would be persecuted by an inevitably pagan state, and Donatism was unable to adapt its thinking to the new conditions presented by a Christian Empire. It was therefore, by its very temperament, separated from the Catholic Church, which both could and did. It is here that there is a possibility, which by its very nature does not admit of proof, that the Donatist outlook made an especial appeal to the indigenous Berber population of North Africa.

This being said, it is also clear that personal factors played a part in initiating and consolidating the schism. Caecilian, whose consecration provided the pretext for Donatist opposition, seems to have been unpopular with a section of the Christian population of Carthage. Donatus the Great, the consolidator though not the founder of the schism, was accused by Augustine of having 'desired to obtain control of all Africa',[16] when he sought recognition as the legitimate bishop of Carthage from the emperor Constantine. Furthermore, throughout the controversy, individual Donatist leaders generally displayed a fundamentalistic hostility to any attempt at reconciliation.

Compared with Donatism the fourth-century schism in the Church of Antioch was a storm in a teacup; but it is important, in that it brought about a long-continued division among the great sees of Christendom. In 330 Eustathius, the bishop of Antioch, a strong supporter of Nicene trinitarian theology, was banished from his see, allegedly for political reasons. At his departure he urged his people to accept whoever should be set over them as their bishop. A small group, led by the presbyter Paulinus, showed its loyalty to Eustathius by disobeying his injunction and worshipping apart from the rest of the Christian congregation. A generation later, in 360, Meletius, bishop of Sebaste, was translated to Antioch, supposedly as an opponent of Nicaea. Once enthroned, he revealed that his theology was effectively Nicene, with the result that he was exiled and an uncompromising Arian named Euzoius put in his place. The majority of the Antiochene Christians, however, remained loyal to Meletius. In 364, on the accession of the Catholic emperor Jovian, Meletius and a group of Syrian bishops presented him with a statement of faith, declaring their adherence to the Creed of Nicaea of 325. Meletius then attempted to enter into communion with St Athanasius (*c.* 296–373), the great champion of Nicene trinitarian doctrine. The attempt failed, for reasons which are not clear, and Athanasius then communicated with Paulinus, who had recently been made a bishop by Bishop Lucifer of Cagliari (d. 370/1). Lucifer was himself later to found a schism, called the Luciferians, composed of those rigorist supporters of Nicaea who refused to be reconciled with penitent Arians. Thus from 364 onwards there were two Nicene bishops of Antioch: Paulinus, recognized by Alexandria and, subsequently, by Rome; and Meletius, recognized by the bishops of Asia and Syria. St Basil of Caesarea (*c.* 330–79), a friend of Meletius, laboured to have him accepted by Rome and Alexandria, and died embittered by the obstinate refusal of Pope Damasus (*c.* 304–84). Paradoxically, it was the defeat and death of the emperor Valens at Adrianople in 378 which helped to resolve the impasse, for it brought to the East the emperor Theodosius I who, when he discovered the strength of support for Meletius, accepted him as the legitimate bishop of Antioch. Meletius died unexpectedly at the Council of Constantinople of 381 and St Gregory of Nazianzus (329–89), who succeeded him as chairman, endeavoured to persuade the bishops to accept Paulinus as his successor. They refused, and nominated Flavian, thereby ensuring that the schism would continue. Paulinus continued to enjoy the support of Rome and the West, and before his death in 388 irregularly consecrated Evagrius as his successor. It was only in 393 that a council held at Caesarea in Palestine recognized Flavian, and Theophilus, the reigning bishop of Alexandria, then accepted him. Rome finally gave way some time before 398. It is sad to record that Flavian was ungenerous in his victory, and declined to recognize the orders of those whom Evagrius had ordained.

The Schism of Antioch is an excellent example of how personalities can affect the course of history. But for Paulinus' obstinacy in remaining loyal to Eustathius against the specific injunctions of the latter, it need never have arisen. If Lucifer of Cagliari had not consecrated Paulinus, or if Athanasius and Meletius had been able to agree in 364 (and the fault seems to have lain with Meletius), the division could have ended then. Again, had the bishops at Constantinople been willing in 381 to accept the urging of Gregory of Nazianzus to recognize Paulinus as Meletius' successor, the dispute would have ended. Finally, if Paulinus had not consecrated Evagrius uncanonically, the schism would have died with him. The whole story is a sad one, especially when we remember that, after 364, both Paulinus and Meletius subscribed to the Creed of Nicaea, with the result that there were two orthodox bishops in opposition in the same city, while the great sees of the Christian world, divided in their support, made little effort to bring the unhappy division to an end.

This survey of certain notable schisms in the early Church indicates the diversity of their origins. Some seem to have been essentially personal and internal, like that at Corinth, and to have been fairly easily resolved by a personal appeal. Others, like Montanism, were an expression of religious enthusiasm, innocent in itself, but distasteful to some Christians and a threat to any hope of toleration of Christianity by the Roman state,[17] so that an eventual break with the Great Church was almost inevitable. In Novatianism, and Donatism, disagreement on ecclesiastical discipline is the expression of deep underlying theological divergences about the nature and the powers of the Church which, in the case of Donatism, may have been exacerbated, though not actually caused, by social and psychological factors. Finally, the Schism of Antioch shows that, in an age of theological controversy, individual commitments and personal loyalties in a common cause could lead to deep and long-continued divisions among the great sees of Christendom, which lasted for many years and long resisted efforts to resolve them.

NOTES

1 Jerome, *On the Epistle to Titus*, 3, 11. PL 26.598.
2 Augustine, *Against Cresconius*, 2, 7, 9. PL 43.471.
3 In Cyprian, *Letters*, 74, 1. CSEL 3 (2), 799.
4 Augustine, *Letter* 36, 14, 32. PL 33.151.
5 Ambrose, *On the Sacraments*, 3, 5. PL 16.432–3.
6 'Were Ancient Heresies National or Social Movements in Disguise?',

The Journal of Theological Studies, New Series x (1959), 280–98.

7 Greenslade, *Schism in the Early Church*, (London, SCM, 1964^{2}) p. 98.

8 Augustine, *On Heresies*, 86. PL 42.46.

9 1 Clement, 1, 1. Text and trans. by Kirsopp Lake, *The Apostolic Fathers* (Loeb Classical Library edn), vol. 1, pp. 8–11.

10 ibid., 2, 5. Kirsopp Lake, pp. 12–13.

11 ibid., 37, 3. Kirsopp Lake, pp. 72–3.

12 Eusebius, *Ecclesiastical History*, IV, 23, 10–11. PG 20.388C–389A.

13 Greenslade, op. cit., p. 109.

14 One such was the fifth-century Church historian, Socrates Scholasticus.

15 *Theodosian Code*, XVI, 5, 21.

16 Augustine, *Psalmus contra Partem Donati* ('Psalm against the Party of Donatus'), lines 101–03 (ed. R. Anastasi, Padua 1957, p. 52).

17 'At the best the movement upheld important features of biblical Christianity; at its worst it was incredibly silly and its enthusiasm took pagan forms' (Greenslade, p. 223.).

BIBLIOGRAPHY

Cavallera, F, *Le Schisme d'Antioche*. Paris, 1905.

Evans, R F, *One and Holy. The Church in Latin Patristic Thought*. London, SPCK, 1972.

Frend, W H C, *The Donatist Church*. Oxford, Clarendon Press, 1971^{2}.

Greenslade, S L, *Schism in the Early Church*. London, SCM, 1964^{2}.

Labriolle, P. de, *La crise montaniste*. Paris 1913.

Walker, G S M, *The Churchmanship of St Cyprian*. London, Lutterworth, 1968.

XVII

The Extinction of Paganism and the Church Historian

Any period of history which later ages deem to have been significant is apt to gather to itself a mythology. To the medieval Church the first three Christian centuries appeared as a period of continuous slaughter, in which legions of martyrs preferred to perish rather than deny their faith in Christ. With such an assumption it was inevitable that the extinction of paganism during the years which followed the conversion of Constantine should be seen as a pious work undertaken in conformity with God's will – *gesta Dei per Christianos* – and when Julian the Apostate attempted to turn back the tide, he was duly slain by two warrior saints sent for the purpose from heaven[1] – a legend which had sufficient vitality eventually to find its way into the Ethiopic *Miracles of the Virgin Mary*, with Julian transformed into a gigantic artisan named Gôlyâd, who threatens to destroy a monastery and is slain by a martyred knight raised by Our Lady to that end.[2] On the pagan side we have the well-known story of how Serena, wife of Stilicho and favourite niece of Theodosius the Great, took a necklace from the image of the Great Mother for her own adornment and mocked and humiliated an aged vestal virgin who denounced her. At a later date, when Alaric the Goth threatened Rome, Serena was suspected of treachery and strangled. To the pagan historian Zosimus her fate was the reward of her impiety, and it seemed fitting that the neck which had usurped the goddess's ornament would at the last be encircled by the executioner's rope.[3] The factual truth of these stories is not, for our purposes, important. What matters is the witness that they provide to the mythological – or, if you prefer it, the theological – interpretations which were early given to the victory of Christianity.

[1] N. H. Baynes, 'The death of Julian the Apostate in Christian legend', *Byzantine Studies and Other Essays*, London 1955, 271–81.

[2] *One Hundred and Ten Miracles of Our Lady Mary*, trans. by E. A. Wallis Budge, London 1933, 220–1.

[3] Zosimus, *Historia Nova*, v. 38.

Journal of Ecclesiastical History, Vol. 35, No. 3, July 1984

It is interpretations of this character, together with the fact that, as a consequence of the victory of Christianity, the greater part of our information about the extinction of paganism has a Christian bias, which constitute the great problem facing the church historian when he attempts to describe and, still more, when he attempts to explain the end of paganism. The ancient historian can study the ending of the old religion as an episode in the history of Greco-Roman culture, interesting both in itself and as an influence on classical studies in the Middle Ages and at the Renaissance. The ecclesiastical historian, on the other hand, unless he is prepared to treat the death of paganism as a mere episode in the general course of church history, cannot do that. He needs to study paganism as an aspect of the world of the early Church, and, in determining why it ceased to be, he may hope to come to a deeper understanding of the nature of early Christianity. Nevertheless, the church historian who addresses himself to the problem of the end of later paganism in the Christian empire is faced with two great obstacles.

First, the character of paganism itself. I take it for granted that the modern ecclesiastical historian, whatever his personal opinions may be, will seek to avoid any discrimination in favour of Christianity. Indeed, I suspect that his temptation will be all the other way and that he will lean over backwards to do paganism justice, and rather more than justice. Unfortunately – and this is the difficulty – the later paganism does not readily commend itself to the modern observer, who generally lacks that nostalgia for dying paganism experienced by an earlier generation nourished on romanticism and a classical education, and who finds it hard to discover in paganism anything that he would regard as constituting genuine religion. Perhaps it should be added that the leading figures of the later paganism are apt to appear more than a little absurd in historical retrospect. Sir Maurice Bowra in conversation once likened the Emperor Julian to a 'dotty Colonel of Engineers' of the sort who finds religious enlightenment through studying the dimensions of the Great Pyramid;[4] while Ferdinand Lot even more unkindly dismissed the grave Symmachus as an imbecile.[5] Harsh words; but, when all is said and done, there is a certain unreality and artificiality about these last defenders of a dying cause, and it is uncommonly difficult, all theological odium laid aside, to see how anyone gained anything specifically religious by transferring, as Julian did, from Christianity to paganism.

A second difficulty arises, partly from the first, but still more from an inherited tradition of historiography. Instinctively, we are apt to regard the relations between paganism and Christianity as being in the nature of a duel to the death, an encounter between two great systems which could only end in the destruction of one or the other. Now in an obvious sense

[4] Julian's religious tendencies seem to have been essentially of an occultist character. See E. R. Dodds, *The Greeks and the Irrational* (Sather Classical Lectures, vol. 25), Berkeley, California 1951, appendix II, p. 288.

[5] F. Lot, *La Fin du monde antique et le début du moyen âge*, Paris 1927, 209.

this impression is correct. No one who reads the denunciations of paganism by the Fathers of the Church will be left in any doubt about their attitude, any more than one can, on the other side, misunderstand the attitude of the pagan rhetorician, Helladius, who used to boast that he had killed nine Christians with his own hand at the destruction of the Serapeum at Alexandria in 391.[6] But in another sense the impression is a misleading simplification of a long-continued process, which began before the Constantinian revolution and which was characterised by what contemporary theological jargon calls dialogue as well as by polemics. There were areas of contact in which the two enemies influenced and learned from one another, and when Christianity was finally left in possession of the field it had been profoundly influenced by its vanquished rival. The two systems were, in a certain sense, 'united in the strife which divided them'. For this reason the church historian, if he is to do justice to paganism and Christianity, must of necessity become an historian of religion and see the eventual triumph of the Christian Church – with all theological considerations duly guarded – as part of the religious history of the Mediterranean world, an episode in a religious development which looks back to prehistoric times and on to the rise of Islam, itself an heir to Christianity even as Christianity was an heir of paganism. Such an approach is inevitably non-theological in the conventional sense and must be controlled by the evidence provided by the historian of doctrine, which alone can bring out the particular quality of Christianity, the new element which the Gospel message brought into the religious world. At the same time, too much emphasis on theology, the factor which more than any other differentiates Christianity from paganism, will leave unexplained how anyone – apart from a few intellectuals – ever became a Christian except under the pressure of the coercive legislation of the Christian Empire. But converts not infrequently hope that their new religious profession will fulfil at least some of their former hopes and ideals as well as rejecting and extirpating others, and it is clear that some Christian converts did indeed see Christianity as the fulfilment and completion of what they had desired and experienced as pagans.

At the outset the ecclesiastical historian is faced with the difficulty of defining exactly what is to be understood by the words 'pagan' and 'paganism'. I am not here thinking of the long debate on the history and philology of the word *paganus*:[7] whether it meant a rustic who has not heard the Christian message or whether – as seems unlikely – it was a piece of * military slang for a civilian, adopted by the Christians who considered themselves to be *milites Christi* – but quite simply asking: what are the characteristics of a pagan? The only comprehensive answer to such a

[6] Socrates, *H.E.*, v. 16. On the other hand, Helladius was apparently prepared to teach Christian pupils, including Socrates himself.

[7] On this word, see H. Grégoire, P. Orgels, J. Moreau and A. Maricq, *Les Persécutions dans l'Empire roman*, 2nd edn, Brussels 1964, 188–220, and W. E. Kaegi, *Byzantium and the Decline of Rome*, Princeton, N.J. 1968, 62 n. 1.

question seems to be that a pagan was anyone within the Roman Empire – or for that matter without – who was not a Christian or a Jew. That such a definition is, by any standards, imprecise is in some degree helpful, inasmuch as it emphasises that paganism was not simply, or even primarily, a matter of religious commitment but of conformity with a particular tradition. We might call it a way of life or better still adopt Gilbert Murray's expression which has been given currency by Professor Dodds, the 'Inherited Conglomerate'[8] – a set of beliefs and conventions, rather broadly based upon certain religious assumptions, generally accepted, and rejected only at the price of becoming a social outsider. It was the refusal of the Christians to conform, quite apart from any question of atheism or criminality, which had constituted their offence in the eyes of many pagans in the pre-Constantinian period. Equally, it was the very wide range of beliefs and practices which was influenced by the Inherited Conglomerate which caused thorough-going Christians to seek to reject the society in which they lived *in toto*. Hence the doubts and hesitations long felt by conscientious churchmen about adopting the traditional system of education ('Not only by burning incense do we worship the demons but by too ardent reading of the poets')[9] and also the apparent irrelevance of so much Christian polemic to the actual conditions of paganism in the later Empire.[10] Antiquarian and academic it may well have been; irrelevant to the immediate issues it most certainly was; but given the character of the Inherited Conglomerate, its all-inclusiveness and lack of definition, it is understandable that Christian controversialists should have devoted their energies to demolition-work which now seems to us to have been irrelevant. It did not seem irrelevant to them; nor, perhaps, to their pagan opponents.

This is not to maintain that the later Roman paganism was devoid of genuine religious feeling: the difficulty is to locate and to define it. Two obvious focal points would seem to be in popular devotion – often in a form which could be treated with some disdain by more educated pagans – and in a species of occultism, clothed in the philosophical language of Neoplatonism. In contrast with Christianity it might be said that the former type of paganism was comprehensive, the latter selective. In the eyes of popular paganism, Christianity was atheistical and exclusive; in the eyes of intellectual paganism, it was superstitious and indiscriminating.[11]

[8] Gilbert Murray, *Greek Studies*, Oxford 1946, 67, cited by Dodds, *The Greeks*, 179.

[9] Isidore of Seville, *Sententiarum Liber*, iii. 13. 1: 'Ideo prohibetur Christianis figmenta legere poetarum, quia per oblectamenta inanium fabularum mentem excitant ad incentiva libidinum. Non enim solum thura offerendo daemonibus immolatur, sed etiam eorum dicta libentius capiendo.' P.L., lxxxiii. 685A–686B.

[10] See R. A. Markus, 'Paganism, Christianity and the Latin classics in the fourth century', in *Latin Literature and the Fourth Century*, ed. J. W. Binns, London 1974, 7–8: 'To read the various formal set pieces, the *contra paganos* type of literature from the pens of Christian apologists, is to enter a world of almost total unreality. We are the spectators of shadow-boxing.'

[11] This is the burden of the complaint of the pagan grammarian, Maximus of Madaura *apud* Augustine, *Ep.* 16.

Julian,[12] and after him Zosimus,[13] could denounce Christianity for having accepted Constantine, guilty of the blood of his kin, while Julian's friend Salutius, at the beginning of his manual of pagan theology, requires that the catechumen should have been well instructed from childhood.[14] In making such a requirement Salutius was, of course, merely following a tradition which looked back to Celsus, when he rebuked the Christians for receiving the ignorant, the stupid and the uneducated;[15] but in so doing he reveals the self-imposed disability under which the intellectual pagans laboured in their struggle with Christianity. They were snobs.

Julian and Salutius are, however, representatives of a particular phase in the struggle between paganism and Christianity: the short period between 361 and 363 when, for the last time, a professed pagan ruled over the entire Roman Empire and attempted to procure a religious revival. He failed, as – more spectacularly – did Nicomachus Flavianus and the pagan party of Rome at the River Frigidus in 394. But the essential problem is whether the events of the fourth century, dramatic as they were, were truly decisive. Even if Julian had survived the Persian campaign; even if Nicomachus Flavianus and not Theodosius had been victorious at the Battle of the Frigidus, it is difficult to see that they could have reversed, or even long delayed, the slow tide of Christian progress. The issue had already been decided.

To understand this it is necessary to look back before the conversion of Constantine to the third century. This was a period of Christian advance, accompanied by spasmodic, if occasionally violent, persecution, which seems to a considerable degree to have been related to, and perhaps inspired by, the political situation of the Empire. Decius may himself have been anti-Christian; but his order to sacrifice applied to all Roman citizens and may be regarded as an attempt to secure national solidarity in the face of external menaces by a common homage to the Roman state religion. The persecution of Valerian, more directly aimed at the Christian Church, was to a large degree motivated by financial considerations and affected only the clergy and the richer laymen. It was, in any case, speedily terminated by the capture of Valerian by the Persians and the succession of the tolerant Gallienus. Then follows a period of more than forty years of peace for the Christians until the outbreak of the Diocletianic persecution in 303. The precise motive for this outbreak – the worst and longest of all – is not clear; but one feature of the Great Persecution which distinguished it from its predecessors is the attempt by Maximin Daïa to revive paganism. Maximin, surely one of the more perceptive and intelligent of the persecuting emperors, recognised that it was no longer a matter of merely suppressing Christianity. If paganism were to survive, a religious revival was necessary, and to that end Maximin anticipated Julian by attempting to institute a pagan ecclesiastical organisation,

[12] Julian, *Caesares*, 336 A B. [13] Zosimus, *H.N.*, ii. 29.
[14] Salutius, *De Diis et Mundo*, I. I (Rochefort, p. 4).
[15] Celsus *apud* Origen, *C. Celsum*, iii. 44 (trans. Chadwick, p. 158).

closely resembling – if not directly copied from – that of the Christian Church. To this he added a propaganda campaign, circulating forged reports allegedly emanating from Pontius Pilate and discreditable to the founder of Christianity, and forced confessions of Christian enormities by women of ill-fame.[16] Maximin's methods have a curiously modern flavour.

To the evidence afforded by these measures, in themselves an admission of the decline of paganism, may be added that provided by the toleration edict issued by Galerius on his death-bed in 311.[17] This revealing document, which shows little of the remorse which has sometimes been read into it, puts the official case in a nutshell. The Christians have been possessed by such wilfulness (*voluntas*) and folly (*stultitia*) that they have refused to follow ancestral practice, and very many have persevered in their determination even in the face of ruin and death. As a result they have both refused to worship the gods of Rome and have been prevented from worshipping their own God to the general detriment of society. In such circumstances it seems best to permit the Christians to exist again (*ut denuo sint Christiani*), if only to ensure that they pray to their God for the good of the state. Here, in the formal language of the Imperial Chancery, we have a dignified confession of the failure of paganism to extirpate Christianity, a failure which would be consummated by the victory of Constantine over his rivals and his emergence in 324 as the Christian ruler of a united empire.

The conversion of Constantine and his victory over Licinius were seen by Christian contemporaries as decisive events, as indeed they were. Through Constantine the Catholic Church became, not indeed the official religion of the Roman Empire, but a favoured sect, enjoying the privileges of the official state cultus and the patronage of the Emperor. For the first time an opportunity was offered to Christian bishops to influence, in some degree, the policy of the government; and it is remarkable how easily divines like Ossius of Cordoba and Eusebius of Nicomedia seem to have been able to move in court circles, as if to the manner born. There was, of course, no question at this time of Christians outnumbering the pagans – this would not come until the fifth century; but they now had a sense of confidence, an *élan*, which is reflected in the last chapter of Eusebius's *Church History*, with its note of *magnus ab integro saeclorum nascitur ordo*. Furthermore, they enjoyed the incomparable advantage of being a well-organised body with an established organisation and a creed which, if not finally formulated, was at least clear on the issues which separated Christianity from paganism. They were, in fact, the equivalent of a modern political party, with a well-defined programme; and however much they might quarrel among themselves, they could always be relied upon to come together against the heathen, as Julian was to discover to his cost.

In such a situation it was inevitable that the idea of the forcible

[16] Eusebius, *H.E.*, viii. 14. 9; ix. 4. 2–5. 2; Lactantius, *De Mort. Persecut.*, 36.

[17] On this edict, see J. Moreau, *Lactance, De la Mort des Persécuteurs* (Sources Chrétiennes, no. 39), ii. 388–95.

suppression of paganism should arise in Christian minds, for Christianity was, by its very nature, intolerant in a way that paganism could never be. The dialogue into which the Christian apologists had entered in the second century had been necessitated by the fact that the pagans had the upper hand, rather than by modern notions of toleration. Tertullian might tell Scapula that it was no part of religion to constrain religion,[18] but the general tenor of his works makes it difficult to believe that he would have boggled at religious coercion if he had lived under a Christian emperor in the fourth century. There was, indeed, a fundamental difference in outlook between paganism and Christianity. Whatever popular hostility there might be against the Christians, and whatever the character of legislation against them, there was no sustained prejudice against them or their God. Their offence lay, not in the fact that they followed a particular cult, but that they refused to recognise the worship of others. For the Christians, on the other hand, the gods of the pagans were demons,[19] and their worship was an outrage in itself. This view is expressed, with brutal clarity, by the converted astrologer Firmicius Maternus in the manifesto for intolerance which he addressed to Constans and Constantius about 346, with the logical corollary that, since the pagans will benefit from the suppression of their superstitions, any objection that they might make should be disregarded.[20] This outlook seems to have been widely held among the Christians, and at a later date St Augustine could seek to justify the coercion of the Donatists by reminding them that they had no objection to the imperial laws against paganism.

Curiously, however, the pagans seem to have long been unaware of the danger in which they were placed by the advance of Christianity – a further proof of the failure of the vitality which Maximin Daïa had sought to remedy. Perhaps the only positive development in favour of paganism during Constantine's reign was his revival of the influence of senators after the Diocletianic absolutism.[21] From this revival were to come the aristocratic

[18] Tert., *Ad Scapulam*, 2: 'Nos unum deum colimus, quem omnes naturaliter nostis, ad cuius fulgura et tonitrua contremiscitis, ad cuius beneficia gaudetis. Caeteros et ipsi putatis deos esse, quos nos daemonas scimus. Tamen humani iuris et naturalis potestatis est unicuique, quod putaverit, colere; nec alii obest aut prodest, alterius religio. Sed nec religionis est cogere religionem, quae sponte suscipi debeat, non vi: cum et hostiae ab animo libenti expostulentur.' P.L., i. 777AB.

[19] See Tertullian's comment, quoted above. Cf. Ambrose's reply to Symmachus: 'Uno, inquit, itinere non potest perveniri ad tam grande secretum. Quod vos ignoratis, id nos Dei voce cognovimus.' *Ep.* 18. 8. Text in J. Wytzes, *Der Streit um den Altar der Viktoria*, Amsterdam 1936, 78. 25–80. 2.

[20] Firmicius Maternus, *De Errore Profanarum Religionum* 16. 4: 'nolunt quidam et repugnant et exitium suum prona cupiditate desiderant, sed subvenite miseris, liberate pereuntes: ad hoc vobis Deus summus commisit imperium, ut per vos vulneris istius plaga curetur. facinoris eorum periculum scimus, erroris notae sunt poenae, sed melius est ut liberetis invitos quam ut volentibus concedatis exitium.' *C.S.E.L.*, ii. 100.

[21] See M. T. W. Arnheim, *The Senatorial Aristocracy in the Later Roman Empire*, Oxford 1972, 72–3: 'Perhaps it would not be altogether unreasonable to suggest that the appointment of nobles to high office was an attempt to mollify their hostility to the advent

leaders of the pagan revival under Julian and the last revolt in the days of Theodosius. Yet there seems to have been no attempt to prepare any resistance to the mounting pressure of Christianity. At a time when both the Emperor and the Church were in alliance the pagans stood and waited to be attacked.

They did not have long to wait. Constantine, although he closed some temples which gave rise to scandal and confiscated their revenues to his own use, seems in general to have observed the promise of religious toleration made in 315 and 324. His sons had no such scruples. In 341 Constans and Constantius issued the famous law requiring that *superstitio* should cease and that the madness of sacrifice be abolished.[22] The precise scope of this law has been variously estimated. For Johannes Geffcken it was 'a turning-point; for the first time imperial legislation was directed in the sharpest strain against sacrifices'.[23] Other scholars are more reserved in their evaluation, pointing to the fact that when the law was promulgated, Constans was away from Rome campaigning against the Franks and may have aimed at pagan intrigues involving sacrifice for the purpose of divination[24] – always unpopular with Roman authority, whether pagan or Christian – a supposition which is supported by the imprecision of the word *superstitio* which, like *deisidaimonia* in Greek, is susceptible of a very wide range of employment. It may indeed be that this imprecision was deliberate. In such a matter the government had to feel its way and religious zeal to be quantified by political caution. Similarly, Constantius' law of 354,[25] which ordered the closure of temples and threatened to punish sacrifice with the death penalty, seems to have been less a legislative decree than a pious declaration of intent, which was allowed to lapse after the emperor's visit to Rome in 357.[26] The succession of Julian four years later brought an end to this first attempt at the legal proscription of paganism.

But the assault upon paganism came from below as well as from above. Imperial legislation afforded the Christians a pretext for physical action. That this occurred as a result of the law of 341 is suggested by another of 342, addressed by Constans and Constantius to Catullinus, the Urban Prefect of Rome, and decreeing that, although all 'superstition' must be eradicated, temple buildings outside the walls of the City must remain untouched and uninjured.[27] The edict of 341 had presumably proved a

of an emperor with pro-Christian leanings. Would it be surprising if Constantine preferred to have these possessors of landed wealth and local influence on his side rather than against him?'; 73, n. 1: '...Far from giving him a firm basis of support, Constantine's Christianity placed him in a weak position; hence the need to placate the rich, influential and very pagan senatorial aristocracy.'

[22] *Codex Theodosianus*, xvi. 10. 2 (hereafter cited as *CT*).

[23] J. Geffcken, *Der Ausgang des griechisch-römischen Heidentums*, 2nd edn, Heidelberg 1929, 97.

[24] K.-L. Noethlichs, *Die gesetzgeberischen Massnahmen der christlichen Kaiser des vierten Jahrhunderts gegen Häretiker, Heiden und Juden*, Cologne 1971, 54.

[25] *CT*, xvi., 10. 4. For the date, see Noethlichs, op. cit., 273 n. 389.

[26] Noethlichs, op. cit., 65.

[27] *CT*, xvi. 10. 3.

too potent source of inspiration for some Christians, who were unwilling to leave the destruction of pagan temples to the state. This strain of anti-pagan violence continues throughout the fourth century and into the fifth. The activities of Circumcellions in Africa and the monks of Syria and Egypt are notorious.[28] George of Cappadocia's celebrated question uttered in 360 before the temple of the Genius of Alexandria, which ultimately helped to provoke his lynching by the exasperated pagans: 'How long shall this sepulchre stand?' was far from being merely rhetorical, given both the law of 354 ordering the closure of temples and the activities of the *Dux Ægypti* Artemius who, encouraged by George, had despoiled the Serapeum of its treasures and employed troops against the resentful worshippers.[29] In Gaul the missionary journeys of Martin of Tours during the reign of Gratian were marked by the destruction of pagan temples, often in the face of considerable hostility.[30] Sometimes the pagans turned on their persecutors. In 391 the philosopher Olympius and a group of supporters occupied the Serapeum at Alexandria, which was faced with destruction by the Patriarch Theophilus, in an heroic attempt to postpone the inevitable.[31] Again, when the Christians of Colonia Sufetana in Numidia attacked a statue of Hercules, probably encouraged by the law of 399 commanding that pagan temples should be destroyed, the pagans retaliated and killed no less than sixty of them.[32] In 408, again in Numidia, the pagans of Calama rioted and attempted to lynch the bishop Possidius.

The sequel to this outbreak was rather curious. A patriotic citizen of Calama, Nectarius, himself a pagan, appealed to Possidius' friend, Augustine of Hippo, asking him to use his influence to preserve the innocent from the punishment which threatened those guilty of the riot. In itself such an appeal by a pagan to a bishop was not new – Symmachus himself had made use of the services of the Novatianist bishop Leontius to avert the wrath of Theodosius in 388;[33] but Nectarius' argument is interesting. It is a bishop's duty, he points out, to promote the welfare of men, to concern himself in a legal case only for the benefit of the parties and not to their detriment, and to obtain for other men pardon of their sins from God. One may suspect a degree of irony in the argument; but the important fact is that it was used at all in those circumstances. A pagan was prepared to expect the good offices of a bishop.[34] The Christian minister had become taken for granted to an extent which Augustine himself had not appreciated, as was shown by his disappointment on discovering that a letter couched in Christian phraseology by the

[28] One may note that even before the Peace of the Church, Africans like Purpurius of Limata and Silvanus of Cirta were prepared to rob a temple of Serapis (*Gesta apud Zenophilum* in Optatus, ed. Ziwsa, app. I. *C.S.E.L.*, xxvi. 195–6).

[29] Sozomen, *H.E.*, iv. 30. 2; Theodoret, *H.E.*, iii. 18; Amm. Marc., xxii. 11. 3–11; Julian, *Ep.* 60 (Bidez-Cumont).

[30] Sulpicius Severus, *Vita Martini*, 13–15. *C.S.E.L.*, i. 122–5. See É. Mâle, *La Fin du paganisme en Gaule*, Paris 1950, 33–48.

[31] Sozomen, *H.E.*, v. 14.

[32] Augustine, *Ep.*, 50 (for date, see Goldbacher, *C.S.E.L.*, lviii. 18).

[33] Socrates, *H.E.*, v. 14.

[34] Nectarius, *apud* Aug., *Ep.* 90.

citizens of Madaura was nothing more than epistolary politeness and did not mean that they had become Christians.[35]

Yet it is in exchanges like those between Augustine and Nectarius and the citizens of Madaura that we may, perhaps, find a clue to the answer to the critical question in the extinction of paganism: how were the masses won over? Was conversion essentially a matter of state coercion and Christian pressure, which eventually dragooned the bulk of the population into formal conformity, or was the process less clearly defined, a matter of transition as much as of compulsion?

We should not underestimate the importance of state coercion. The old Roman assumption that membership of the state involved formal adherence to the state religion died hard, and once Christianity became the state cult in the late fourth century many people would doubtless have conformed as a matter of routine. The Church certainly learned a lesson, as the later missions to the Germanic peoples showed, when the initial appeal was made to kings and nobles. Equally the contribution of influential individuals must be recognised. In a society where patronage was so strongly developed as in the later Roman Empire, some communities would have their religion determined by the faith of the landlord. *Cuius regio, eius religio.*[36] But while recognising such factors, is it possible to find something more, a deeper psychological factor which helps to explain a great religious transformation?

The answer may perhaps be found in the class of persons called semi-Christians (*demi-chrétiens*) by Charles Guignebert in an article published over sixty years ago.[37] These were persons well disposed towards the Christian faith and to the Church, who could even adhere to them quite firmly, but who nevertheless still clung to the old faiths to a greater or lesser degree. Guignebert – while admitting that this was not easy – wished to distinguish such semi-Christians from those sincere converts who, while accepting Christianity for better or worse, continued to retain some of their old customs and habits of thought. I think that the distinction is both a valid and an important one, and that the paganised Christians – as I shall call them for lack of any more suitable title – played an important part in the conversion of the Roman Empire by creating a milieu within the Church in which the semi-Christians could eventually feel at home. Probably the most obvious dividing-line between the paganised Christians and the semi-Christians (which is, however, not an infallible test) is the willingness to accept baptism or martyrdom, and particularly the former, since a failure in courage in the face of the threat of death can happen to otherwise sincere and dedicated people. On the other hand, to refuse

[35] *Apud* Aug., *Ep.* 232 (*post* 407): 'Optamus te, domine, in deo et Christo eius per multos annos semper in clero tuo gaudere.' *C.S.E.L.*, lvii. 512.

[36] See F. Van der Meer, *Augustine the Bishop*, Eng. trans. by B. Battershaw and G. R. Lamb, London 1961, 29.

[37] C. Guignebert, 'Les Demi-Chrétiens et leur place dans l'Église antique', *Revue de l'Histoire des Religions*, lxxxviii (1923), 65–102.

to accept baptism, and with it the day-to-day restraints and liabilities imposed by a fully Christian life, while at the same time adhering, in some degree, to the Church, is an indication of the sort of reserve which characterises the semi-Christian and which stands in sharp contrast to the spirit of the paganised Christian, who was prepared to commit himself to Christ, even if he did not fully comprehend the Christian faith and its implications.

The influence of the paganised Christians can be seen in many aspects of the life of the early Church. Two admirable examples come from Africa. One is the vision of Deinocrates, brother of St Perpetua who had died at the age of seven and who was delivered from a place of subterranean torment by the intercession of Perpetua while she was awaiting martyrdom. In an article published in 1930, F. J. Dölger argued convincingly that the sufferings of Deinocrates were due, not to any grave post-baptismal sin, as later theologians including Augustine believed, but to the fact that he had died before his time.[38] 'The dream of Deinocrates' sufferings is based less on Christian pictures of Purgatory than on ancient pagan notions about the thirsty dead and the fate of those who die untimely',[39] and it is significant in this context that Perpetua and her companions were catechumens at the time of their arrest and were baptised only a little before their execution. Yet the vision of Deinocrates was destined to become a document of palmary importance in subsequent discussion of the doctrine of Purgatory, and a pagan view of the after-life thus came to influence Christian theology.

The other example of paganised Christianity to be cited here is provided by the famous tomb of Timgad, probably that of the Donatist bishop Optatus, with a hole pierced in the grave-slab to enable offerings of wine to be poured into the mouth of the corpse below.[40] Here we have a pagan practice which goes back beyond the classical period to Mycenaean and even Minoan origins,[41] a practice whose crudity has caused Professor Dodds to write: 'When the archaic Greek poured liquids down a feeding-tube into the livid jaws of a mouldering corpse, all we can say is that he abstained, for good reasons, from knowing what he was doing; or, to put it more abstractly, that he ignored the distinction between corpse and ghost – he treated them as "consubstantial"'.[42] Yet we find this wholly pagan practice in use among the African Donatists who were by first principles fanatically hostile to paganism; while their Catholic neighbours, if they refrained from this particular custom, were no less enthusiastically devoted to the cult of the martyrs. To a hostile observer like Faustus the Manichee, the Catholics had taken over the whole

[38] F. J. Dölger, 'Antike Parallelen zum leidenden Deinocrates', *Antike und Christentum*, ii (1930).

[39] E. R. Dodds, *Pagan and Christian in an Age of Anxiety*, Cambridge 1965, 52.

[40] See H.-I. Marrou, 'Survivance païennes dans les rites funéraires des donatistes', in *Hommages à Joseph Bidex et à Franz Cumont* (Collection Latomus, vol. II), Brussels 1949, 193–203.

[41] Ibid., 195.

[42] Dodds, *The Greeks*, 136.

apparatus of pagan worship and were a schism from paganism;[43] and the anxiety shown by Ambrose and Augustine to abolish the feasts at the tombs of the martyrs is a proof that they recognised the force of such an accusation.

Now these pagan ideas and practices, however distasteful to trained theologians and conscientious bishops, can be seen in historical retrospect as having served a useful purpose in the life of the Church: they cushioned the psychological shock experienced by converts from paganism by providing some element of continuity in the religious life of the new Christian, and as time went by – and especially after the Peace of the Church – more and more material was borrowed from the secular world which, in its original associations, was pagan. The crowning of the bride and bridegroom in the marriage service of the Eastern Orthodox Church is an attractive ceremony; but it would have scandalised the author of the *De Corona Militis*. Tertullian was always a puritan.

The paganised Christians were within the circle of the Church; the semi-Christians were on the fringe. In general one may guess that they were better off and better educated, with more to lose by professed adherence and less inclined, in any event, to set so much store by formal membership. An excellent example, in his pagan days, is the Platonist Marius Victorinus who, before his conversion, was accustomed to declare that he was already a Christian and to respond to the challenge to demonstrate this by the query: 'Do walls then make Christians?' Victorinus was, at the time, 'a venerator of idols and a participant in the sacrilegious rites by which almost all the Roman nobility was inspired', and his refusal to make a public confession of Christianity was due to a reluctance to offend his pagan friends.[44] Indeed, Victorinus might almost be regarded as the archetype of the semi-Christian, torn between two irreconcilable factions and reluctant to sever his links with one by declaring for the other – though in his case, at the last, he made his decision and was baptised.

Semi-Christians existed in the pre-Nicene age and after the Peace of the Church their numbers considerably increased, partly because there was no longer the threat of persecution to deter the faint-hearted, and partly because of the tendency to extend the catechumenate over a very long period of time, and even to the hour of death. As a result, it is often difficult to decide where a man's religious commitment lay, and it may plausibly be argued that many of the religiously ambiguous figures of the fourth

[43] Faustus *apud* Aug., *C. Faustum* xx. 4: '...sacrificia vero eorum vertistis in agapes, idola in martyres, quos votis similibus colitis; defunctorum umbras vino placatis et dapibus, sollemnes gentium dies cum ipsis celebratis, ut Kalendas et solstitia. de vita certe mutastis nihil: estis sane schisma a matrice suo diversum nihil habens nisi conventum', *C.S.E.L.*, xxv (1). 538. Cf. Julian's gibe, representing a pagan view of the matter: 'You have filled the whole world with tombs and sepulchres, and yet in your scriptures it is nowhere said that you must grovel among the tombs and pay them honour' (*C. Galil.*, 335C).

[44] Aug., *Conf.*, viii. ii. 3–5.

century were, in fact, semi-Christians. One may mention, for example, Augustine's father Patricius, who was still only a recent catechumen when Augustine was sixteen,[45] but who had allowed his wife to bring up their children as Christians. A similar case is that of the poet Claudian, of whose Easter hymn Professor Cameron has written: 'It certainly looks as if Claudian either considered himself or wished to be considered as Christian.'[46] The explanation, to my mind, is provided by the idea of the semi-Christians, and explains why both Augustine and Orosius regarded Claudian as a pagan.[47] By their standards, he was. But an even more interesting example of a semi-Christian is provided by Ausonius, whose religious convictions have long been a matter of controversy. Much which can be urged as evidence for Ausonius being a pagan – his use of classical mythology, his occasional gross obscenity, the lack of any hope of a future life in his elegies – accords very well with the concept of semi-Christianity. Helen Waddell expressed the matter with characteristic felicity: 'For his religion, Christian and pagan are words too absolute: he will write of Easter or a Vigil of Venus with the same temperate pleasure',[48] and it is precisely for that reason that the break with Paulinus of Nola caused him such distress, for Paulinus had determined to follow Christ whatever the cost.[49]

But perhaps the greatest of the semi-Christians, and certainly the most influential, is Constantine the Great himself. His life bears all the marks of the breed: a catechumenate lasting from his conversion to his death-bed; a concern for the Church which went hand-in-hand with many unchristian actions; and a lack of understanding of the significance of theology in Christianity reflected in his handling of the dispute between Alexander and Arius. Indeed, Constantine's view of the Church was essentially a pagan one: when its ministers offer worship to God they confer an incalculable benefit upon the state.[50] What other purpose did the Roman state religion serve? Here Constantine illustrates Guignebert's observation about the semi-Christians: they are not given to syncretism and make no effort to harmonise their differing beliefs (as did the Gnostics), but simply juxtaposed them.[51]

The existence of the semi-Christians in the Roman world makes

[45] Ibid., ii. iii. 6.

[46] A. Cameron, 'Claudian', in *Latin Literature of the Fourth Century*, 155.

[47] Aug., *De Civ. Dei*, v. 26; Orosius, *Hist. adv. Paganos*, vii. 35. 21.

[48] Helen Waddell, *The Wandering Scholars*, London 1927, 7.

[49] See W. H. C. Frend, 'The two worlds of Paulinus of Nola', in *Latin Literature of the Fourth Century*, 100–33; but note the genuine affection shown by Paulinus for Ausonius in *Carm.*, XI: 'Ego te per omne quod datum mortalibus.'

[50] Eusebius, *H.E.*, x. 17. Professor Markus reminds me that this view was shared by the whole Theodosian dynasty, Socrates, Sozomen, and almost everyone in the fifth century and probably later. This observation seems to me to be further confirmation of the pervasive effect of pagan thought upon men who had been brought up as Christians in a society where Christianity was apparently dominant.

[51] Guignebert, 'Les Demi-Chrétiens', 69.

attempts to calculate the proportion of pagans to Christians at the time of the conversion of Constantine – a thankless task at best – rather unhelpful in estimating the causes of the eventual victory of Christianity. It seems reasonable to suppose that during the fourth century the pagans outnumbered the Christians while in the fifth the ratio was reversed. What one would like to know would be the proportion of semi-Christians to avowed Christians and pagans at the beginning of the fourth century. The canons of the early fourth-century councils regarding *flamines* who have been baptised and who subsequently sacrifice or subsidise gladiatorial or stage shows; women who beat their slaves to death; persons who practise magic or divination; and the ineligibility for ordination of those who wait for a grave sickness before they are baptised and afterwards recover,[52] all suggest that there was a considerable number of semi-Christians even before the Peace of the Church, so that besides the nucleus of convinced Christians, essential for any eventual assumptions of power, there was also an element of men of good will who, without being prepared to commit themselves wholly, were generally prepared to further the interests of the Church and to provide moral, and sometimes more than moral, support. It is conceivable, though utterly unprovable, that there was more sympathy for Christianity than is generally supposed. After the conversion of Constantine the number of semi-Christians must have increased substantially, and the undesirable predilection of their flocks for the heathen entertainments of the arena and the theatre becomes a theme for Christian preachers. The trouble about these fair-weather patriots was that, having dual loyalties, they were inevitably prone to follow the lead of the reigning emperor. It was they, and not the dedicated elements of the population, whether pagan or Christian, who were most likely to be swayed by the pressure of imperial legislation. It is in this context significant that during the greater part of the fourth century the reigning emperors were Christians.

These considerations may throw light upon two famous cases of Christian apostasy under Julian. First, that of Pegasius, bishop of Troy, who has the melancholy distinction of being the only recorded bishop to have lapsed and become a pagan priest. Pegasius might be dismissed as a mere time-server if we did not know, from Julian's own account, that when Julian visited Troy in 354 he was already worshipping the sun-god in secret while publicly discharging his episcopal functions and prepared to defend pagan veneration of Hector by an analogy with the Christian cult of the martyrs.[53] In the circumstances it seems fair to regard Pegasius as having always been a Philhellene who, with a pagan emperor on the throne, could no longer suppress his deepest enthusiasms. More doubtful is the case of Hecebolius, the rhetorician who was an ardent Christian

[52] Council of Elvira, canons 2, 3, 5, 6; Council of Ancyra, canon 24; Council of Neo-Caesarea, canon 12 (J. Stevenson, *A New Eusebius*, London 1963, nos. 265, 267, 268, pp. 305–6; 312–3).

[53] Julian, *Ep.* 79 (Bidez-Cumont).

under Constantius, an equally ardent pagan under Julian, and who then reverted to Christianity under Jovian. On the face of the evidence Hecebolius would seem to have been an unprincipled adventurer; but it is just possible that he was carried away by the pagan renaissance under Julian – which affected him personally when Julian forbade Christians to teach in the schools – and found that his Christianity was only superficial.[54] At all events, between 381 and 383 Theodosius I found it necessary to issue three laws against apostates from Christianity[55] and this suggests that reversion to the old faiths did not end with Julian but continued in the reign of Valens, who was tolerant towards paganism if not to orthodox Christianity. 'It was now possible to enter the Church without any profound changes of mental furniture and spiritual orientation and, if Julian or Eugenius was in power, to leave the Church with equal ease.'[56] Certainly, if we are to accept the assertion of the anonymous author of the so-called *Carmen adversus Flavianum*, the final rally of paganism at Rome at the end of the fourth century produced a crowd of apostasies by those who hoped to benefit from a restoration of the old order of things;[57] but the pagan forces were defeated by Theodosius and the last hope of a restored paganism was gone. Already, even before Eugenius' rebellion had broken out, Theodosius had begun the series of edicts designed to outlaw paganism, both in public worship and private devotion.[58] Slowly and fitfully, but inexorably, the pagan cults were suppressed, even though very considerable pockets of resistance lingered alike in East and West until the sixth century.[59]

The Christian Church, for obvious reasons, profited from this state of affairs. The waverers and the half-committed, being deprived of any effective religious alternative and subjected to legal and social pressures,

[54] For Hecebolius, see Socrates, *H.E.*, iii. 1, 13, 23; Guignebert, art. cit., 73.

[55] *CT*, xvi. 7. 1–3. Valentinian III was forced to renew previous legislation against apostasy, *CT*, xvi. 7. 6.

[56] A. D. Nock, *Conversion*, Oxford 1933, 158–9.

[57] *Carmen*, lines 78–83:

> christicolas multos voluit sic perdere demens
> qui vellent sine lege mori, donaret honores
> oblitosque sui caperet quos daemonis arte
> muneribus cupiens quorundam frangere mentes
> aut alios facere prava mercede profanos
> mittereque inferias miseros sub Tartara secum.

On the *Carmen*, see J. F. Matthews, 'The historical setting of the *Carmen contra Paganos*', *Historia*, xix (1970), 464–79.

[58] *CT*, xvi. 10. 10 (24 February 391). See Noethlichs, *Die gesetzgeberischen Massnahmen*, 173–82.

[59] In Gaul Caesarius of Arles found it necessary to continue the work of Martin of Tours. See Césaire d'Arles, *Sermons au Peuple*, tom. I, ed. M.-J. Delage (Sources Chrétiennes, no. 175), 138–42. In the year of Caesarius' death (542) John of Ephesus was appointed as an official missionary to the pagans of Asia, Caria, Lydia and Phrygia. See D. J. Constantelos, 'Paganism and the state in the age of Justinian', *Catholic Historical Review*, lx (1964), 372–80; A. H. M. Jones, *The Later Roman Empire*, Oxford 1964, ii. 939.

finally made their home in the Church; but inevitably they did so, to a considerable degree, on their own terms, without abandoning the habits and pleasures to which they were accustomed. And so the Church, although left in possession of the field, was forced to accept whole departments of life which had previously been denied to Christians. There was, of course, a limit to what could be accommodated. In the field of popular entertainment, for example, the gladiatorial contests had to go. They were too obviously incompatible with the profession of Christianity and were suppressed in the East (which had never much cared for them) in 326 and in the West in 404.[60] However, the theatre – particularly offensive to serious Christians because of its paganism and indecency – continued, despite the danger to the souls of the spectators and, still more, of the performers.[61] All that could be done was to ensure that entertainment was denied on Sundays in the pious hope that people would be driven to church in the absence of anything else to do.[62]

Even more significant for the future was the fact that the victory of Christianity left the general structure of education intact. Whatever hopes some Christians may have entertained of replacing the pagan classics by the Scriptures were never realised, and the work of the two Apollinares, father and son, fell into oblivion as soon as Julian was dead. Only in the West, after Roman rule had ended, was it possible in a monastic environment to provide a system of training which led the student directly from the grammarians to the study of the Bible and the Fathers without any intervening stage of classical reading. In certain circumstances the system worked. It produced one author of the calibre of Bede of Jarrow; but its inadequacies for any education outside the cloister – and indeed within it, so far as the ordinary student was concerned – were too apparent, and the Carolingian renaissance saw a return to the classical authors with all their pagan allusions as part of the general programme for educational revival. So the various patristic ideas about the education of the young had to be practised in the home rather than in the school and the old, harsh system, so vividly described by Ausonius and so feelingly by Augustine, easily survived the transition from a pagan to a Christian society.[63]

The survival of the classics as the foundation of education was perhaps the most enduring legacy of paganism; it provided a tradition which was not finally ended in Western Europe until the twentieth century. But the

[60] Prohibited in the East by Constantine in 326 (*CT*, xv. 12. 1) and in the West by Honorius in 404 (Theodoret, *H.E.*, v. 26).

[61] See Jones, op. cit., ii. 977, 1020–1.

[62] *CT*, ii. 8. 20 (393); ii. 8. 23 (399); ii. 8. 24 (405).

[63] On this, see M. L. W. Laistner, *Christianity and Pagan Culture*, Ithaca N.Y. 1951, *passim*, and the Homily by John Chrysostom, *On Vainglory and the Right Way for Parents to Bring up Their Children*, translated therein 85–122. Pierre Riché, *Education et culture dans l'Occident barbare 6e–8e siècle* (Patristica Sorbonensia 4), Paris 1962, 48–9, draws attention to the fact that Christianity, by following the teaching of Christ, might have changed the spirit of ancient education. Its failure to do so indicates the tenacity of the ancient system.

dying paganism affected the Christian Church of the patristic period more immediately in two ways, one positive and the other negative. The positive contribution was its effect upon Christian theology through the influence of Neoplatonism. It is generally agreed that the longest-lasting and most embittered opposition to Christianity came from the pagan intellectuals, and especially from the teachers of philosophy whose uncompromising adherence to the old faith finally led Justinian to order the closure of the schools of Athens in 529.[64] Indeed, the Neoplatonism which they professed represented the last attempt to provide an intellectual framework within which the old cults could continue; but it was more than that. As formulated by Plotinus in the third century it had been 'an attempt to reconcile a mystical intuition of God with a rationalistic explanation of the physical universe'[65] and, as such, it offered material to Christian divines as well as to pagan philosophers. Certainly there were features of Neoplatonism which could never be reconciled with Christian revelation and these had to be discarded; but there remained a considerable body of Neoplatonist thought which was not merely acceptable to Christians but was positively welcome to the theologians of the fourth and fifth centuries in their discussions about the nature of the Godhead. It may well be, as Jean Daniélou maintained in a famous work,[66] that verbal agreement between the Fathers and the Neoplatonists does not necessarily prove an underlying agreement of thought; and it is certain that for most Christian theologians Neoplatonism was, at best, an ancillary discipline, an instrument which could, in certain circumstances, illuminate problems raised by theological speculation. Yet the influence exercised by Neoplatonism over Christian thinkers like Gregory of Nyssa, Ambrose and Augustine, and the fact that it finally brought into the Church – admittedly with some intellectual reservations – Synesius of Cyrene,[67] is impressive evidence of its power. Yet even more remarkable is the influence which this pagan philosophical system exercised through the writings of the Pseudo-Dionysius, not only upon medieval theology, but upon a modern Orthodox theologian like Vladimir Lossky. A whole tradition of Christian theology has been determined by a product of the thought-world of later paganism.

The negative effect on the Church of the passing away of paganism was a dilution of the quality of Christian living brought about by an influx of converts with a semi-Christian outlook, which in turn led to a sharp reaction against the decline in standards from a smaller group of

[64] Alan Cameron, 'The last days of the Academy at Athens', *Proceedings of the Cambridge Philological Society*, no. 195 (New Series, no. 15) (1969), 7–29, questions the effectiveness of Justinian's decree, arguing that the Academy continued to function. This, if true, does not affect my argument.

[65] Laistner, op. cit., 23–4.

[66] J. Daniélou, *Platonisme et théologie mystique*, Paris 1944.

[67] On Synesius see H.-I. Marrou, 'Synesius of Cyrene and Alexandrian Neoplatonism', in *The Conflict between Paganism and Christianity in the Fourth Century*, ed. A. Momigliano, Oxford 1963, 126–50; Geffcken, *Der Ausgang des griechisch-römischen Heidentums*, 218, 242.

uncompromising Christians who wished to maintain the discipline of the heroic days of the persecutions, which were already being regarded as the true Golden Age of the Church. In the West this reaction was expressed in Pelagianism – a movement which failed; and in East and West alike by monasticism, which increasingly came to be regarded as the only valid form of the Christian life, the only one lived in accordance with the spirit of the Gospel. In a world which had become nominally Christian the cloister replaced the local Christian community as the place where salvation was to be found, and the Church tacitly admitted its failure to win the world for Christ. The true Christians still remained a minority and the salvation of the ordinary layman was a doubtful and a difficult business.

These considerations suggest, to me at least, that the extinction of paganism and its supersession by Christianity, despite the factors of legal coercion and physical violence which accompanied them, are best understood not as a catastrophic event but as an evolutionary process. The Christian Roman Empire which finally emerged was indeed a new species; but it bore many of the characteristic features of its pagan predecessor. The decline of paganism had set in even before the conversion of Constantine, and the virtual absence of any pagan martyrs confirms the impression that paganism was already dying even before the Christian emperors of the fourth century launched their attack upon it. Had there been any real vitality in paganism, any determination by its numerous adherents to maintain the cults which they practised, then it is inconceivable that the limited resources of the Christian emperors would have availed to sweep them away. As it was, many pagans grumbled and some actively resisted; but the total effort was too little and too late.[68] Nevertheless, although paganism had failed to incorporate Christianity within its comprehensive framework, as it had incorporated so many other Oriental religions, it did contrive, involuntarily, to cause Christianity to introduce a good deal of pagan culture and not a little pagan religious practice into the state Church of the later Roman Empire. From the strictly religious standpoint Professor Dodds was, of course, correct when he wrote: 'In a material sense the Inherited Conglomerate did not in the end perish by disintegration; large portions of it were left standing through the centuries, a familiar, shabby, rather lovable facade, until one day the Christians pushed the facade over and discovered that there was virtually nothing behind it – only a faded local patriotism and an antiquarian sentiment';[69] but if one understands paganism in a wider, cultural sense, as I would wish

[68] 'Paganism was not a heroic faith, and could boast few martyrs... Nevertheless passive resistance was widespread, and pagans were prepared to pay, if not to suffer, for their faith' (Jones, *The Later Roman Empire*, ii. 943). Ramsay MacMullen, *Paganism in the Roman Empire*, New Haven and London 1981, 134, draws attention to the fact that 'the enormous thing called paganism...did not one day just topple over dead' and to the mysterious character of its demise. This supports my own view that the conversion to Christianity was essentially an evolutionary process.

[69] Dodds, *The Greeks*, 244.

to do, the victory of Christianity is better regarded as the imposition of a wholly new way of thinking upon a civilisation. To quote Professor Dodds again: 'A new belief-pattern very seldom effaces completely the pattern that was there before: either the old lives on as an element in the new – sometimes as an unconfessed or half-conscious element – or else the two persist side-by-side, logically incompatible, but contemporaneously accepted by different individuals or even by the same individual.'[70]

[70] Ibid., 179.

XVIII

The End of Ancient Christianity
By Robert Markus. pp. xvii + 258.
Cambridge University Press, 1990

THE title of this work is ambiguous. When did Ancient Christianity—whatever that is—come to an end? With the composition of the Second Epistle of Peter? With the conversion of Constantine? With the publication of Luther's ninety-five theses? Or even, as some might hold, with the Second Vatican Council? In fact, the theme here is rather more restricted. Ancient Christianity, in this context, is that of the later patristic era, and essentially that of the Western, Latin-speaking provinces of the Roman Empire, and it came to an end, in Markus's view, in the time of Pope Gregory the Great. 'What was it', he asks, 'about Gregory's world that so changed the framework of thought, the assumptions about the world?' (p. xi). For him, the essence of the change is what he calls 'a drainage of secularity ... produced by minds which see as "sacred" (or its contrary, "profane") what had earlier been counted as "secular". ... The secular became marginalised, merged in or absorbed by the sacred, both in discourse and in the social structure and institutions' (p. 226). 'The massive secularity of John Chrysostom's and of Augustine's world had drained out in Gregory's. There was little room for the secular in it' (p. 228). In his earlier, and admirable, work *Saeculum* (1970; 2nd edn. 1989), which will greatly help the reader of the present study to understand the argument, Markus addressed himself to the question of how Augustine viewed the relationship between Church and State in the 'Christian times' brought about by the legislation of Theodosius I, and saw him providing a '"secularisation" of the realm of politics [which] implies a pluralistic, religiously neutral civil community' (*Saeculum*, 173). The Christian Middle Ages sought to suppress the 'open, pluralist, secular society'. Markus,

[Journal of Theological Studies, NS, Vol. 43, Pt. 2, October 1992]

in his new study, seeks to trace the process of what he calls de-secularization, 'the absorption of the "secular" in the "sacred" as ascetic norms came to penetrate wide sections of Christian society and to colour aspirations far beyond the walls of the cloister. The ascetic take-over signals the end of ancient Christianity' (p. 17).

The development of Markus's argument is subtle and complicated, and any attempt to epitomize it runs the risk of misrepresentation; but an attempt must be made if the book is to be reviewed at all. Fundamentally, Markus sees the Constantinian revolution as presenting the Church with a crisis of identity, that curious experience which enables individuals who are ill at ease with the world to express their discomfort in intellectual terms. (More ordinary souls are content to accept the fact that they do not always feel at home in this vale of tears and get on with the job in hand.) Christians, in the post-Constantinian world, 'needed to reassure themselves that their Church was the heir of the persecuted Church of the martyrs' (p. 24) and did so, partly through the cult of the martyrs, and partly through an extension of asceticism, in which the ascetic succeeded the martyr and became, like him, a hero and intercessor. (Markus says that 'Christian communities in late Antiquity did not feel conscious of a need for individuals who could mediate privileged access to the divine to them' (p. 26), but the episode of Dinocrates in the *Passion of SS. Perpetua and Felicity*, 7–8 suggests that the idea was at least in the air at the beginning of the third century.) This extension of the appeal of asceticism raised the question of the nature of the Christian life and the definition of paganism—how much renunciation did being a Christian involve? Markus contrasts the rigorism which produced the teaching of Pelagius and his circle with what he calls Augustine's 'defence of Christian mediocrity'—one might equally well say 'Augustine's pastoral experience', remembering that the saint's predestinarian theology fundamentally excluded asceticism except as an expression of the working of God's grace. The famous *Da quod iubes* of *Confessions* x. xxix. 40, which so distressed Pelagius, epitomizes Augustine's attitude to asceticism. Nevertheless, despite Augustine, asceticism prevailed. 'Western Christianity, ...acquired a pronounced streak of distrust of the body and of sexuality' (p. 58) (was it, in fact, any greater than that of the Christian East?). Furthermore monasticism, which had in its origins been a flight from 'the City' to 'the Desert', now re-entered the City, and monastic experience became increasingly seen as the proper training of a bishop. (In theory this remains true to this day in the Eastern Orthodox Church.) This in turn meant that ascetic principles were applied to the lives of the laity. Markus contrasts Pope Leo I's attack on Christian participation in the Roman civic festival of the Lupercalia which, by his day, no longer had any religious import in the eyes of its Christian participants, with its celebration at Constantinople in the tenth century 'as a mobile spring festival in which civic, political and religious elements were combined without the least tension' and speaks of 'the papal attempt to impose on the lay world clerical norms which left no room for the neutral world of the "secular"' (p. 134).

Christianization extended to the realm of space and time. The cult of relics meant that the dead were brought into the city, whence pagan fears of pollution had excluded them (by the nineteenth century it became necessary to exclude them again for fear of another, secular form of pollution, and the churchyards of the city churches had to be closed). The need to see the post-Constantinian Church as the heir to the Church of the martyrs led to the compilation of Christian calendars to replace the religious festivals of the pagan year, and to attacks on popular festivals like the Kalends of January which, if not overtly pagan, distracted people's minds from Christian devotion. Again, 'Christian culture in the early medieval centuries became essentially and radically biblical in a way that it had not been before. ... As Christian discourse shrank to scriptural, so the world of which it spoke shrank to the sacred. The secular became marginalised, merged in or absorbed by the sacred, both in discourse and in the social structure and institutions' (pp. 225, 226).

Markus's book, as might be expected of the author, is vastly learned and raises a host of ideas and questions. He has isolated a great many features which differentiate the early medieval West from Late Antiquity, and would regard such changes, if I have understood him correctly, as being essentially due to the progress of the ascetic ideal and the attempt to impose that ideal, so far as possible, upon Christians, whether or not they were professed religious. Few historians would, I imagine, deny that this was an important element in the formation of early medieval society; but I find it difficult not to feel that it is only a partial explanation of a phenomenon which is at once more complicated and more simple than Markus describes.

There is first the meaning of the term self-definition, which Markus sees as a key to the development of the post-Constantinian Church. To what extent is it an active or a passive quality in an individual or an institution? One might say—and Peter Brown has said—that Quintus Aurelius Symmachus 'defined himself ... by a passionate identification with the Senate and its pagan traditions'.[1] One could also say that the Emperor Honorius defined himself by a rather un-royal interest in chicken farming. But did either of these individuals choose his particular interest to differentiate himself from other men, or was his choice not rather due to an enthusiasm which brought about the differentiation? When we ask this question about an institution, the answer is even more difficult to formulate. Self-definition may be a matter of deliberate choice; but it may also be due to a compelling principle, which constrains a group, perhaps against its inclinations, to stand apart from its fellows. Tertullian, at least in theory, preached separation. The author of *The Epistle to Diognetus* commended integration, so far as Christian conviction permitted. Throughout the early Christian centuries the Church had to reckon with both these possible alternatives; but it is not easy to see why it had to have an identity crisis in the fourth century, when it had both successfully weathered the Diocletianic Persecution and then could rejoice in the conversion of Constantine. Far from doubting its identity, the Church could truly say with the Psalmist: *The lot is fallen unto me in a fair ground: yea, I have a goodly heritage*. This is the mood of Eusebius' *Ecclesiastical History* and it is hardly a mood to encourage doubts about one's identity. (The crowds who gathered at the Cenotaph in Whitehall every 11 November between the two World Wars were concerned to honour the fallen, not to reassure themselves about their own relationship to them.) No doubt the influx of opportunist Christians disturbed some devout persons, and especially ascetics; but asceticism was not a post-Constantinian development. On the contrary, it had existed before the Peace of the Church, just as there had been lukewarm Christians before the Peace of the Church, as the Decian Persecution embarrassingly revealed. One could denounce such Laodicean Christians without necessarily supposing that they imperilled the very existence of the Church. Of course, some Christians did so suppose—the Novatianists in the third century, the Donatists in the fourth; but the Great Church was able to comprehend such weaker brethren, the fulminations of moralists like Jerome and the Pelagians notwithstanding. If asceticism prevailed in the late patristic period it was because it represented a tendency which had existed in the Church from its origins. 'There are to be found at the heart of Christianity', wrote Norman Baynes, who was no mean judge, 'a stark asceticism and a staggering confidence.'[2] This

[1] Brown, 'Pelagius and his supporters: aims and environment', *JTS*, NS, 19 (1968), repr. *Religion and Society in the Age of St Augustine* (London 1972), 186–7.

[2] Baynes, 'Idolatry and the early Church' in *Byzantine Studies and Other Essays* (London 1955), 124.

confidence was never more assured than in the fourth century, when it appeared that everything favoured the Church in its struggle with the world.

There is, however, another consideration. The self-definition of the Church was not simply a matter of moral conduct but of theological belief. The Christian community was a credal community and theologians were concerned to establish what was, and what was not, doctrinally acceptable. The Church had hardly become politically acceptable when it embarked upon the long-drawn-out Arian Controversy, whose conclusions were to shape the character of orthodox Christianity throughout the Middle Ages and for long afterwards. In that controversy, the name of Athanasius is justifiably famous and his influence decisive. Yet although Athanasius undoubtedly played a major role in defining the Church, he would have been surprised indeed to be told that that was what he was doing. He saw himself as fighting for Christian truth.

Accordingly, it would seem highly questionable to regard ecclesiastical self-definition as being a conscious exercise. Rather, Christian leaders saw themselves as upholding true faith and Christian morals. Even asceticism sought, and eventually found, a theological foundation—men went into the Desert to express a faith which they already possessed.

Again, the understanding of the words sacred and secular would seem to require deeper analysis than Markus devotes to them. Modern thinkers take the secular and the sacred for granted. Earlier ages recognized them pragmatically but did not necessarily regard the distinction as desirable. Neither orthodox Judaism nor Islam makes the sort of distinction between the sacred and the secular which Western Christians have learned to accept by bitter experience. Such experience in the early Church arose from the fact that it was living in a society whose religious norms it could not accept, but with which it was constrained, lacking the privileges of Judaism, to have dealings. Hence St Paul's principle regarding meat offered to idols: since an idol is, in itself, nothing, its offerings are harmless and may safely be eaten by believers, providing that this eating does not encourage idolatry among simple believers (1 Cor. 8). One could say that St Paul, in emancipating Gentile Christianity from the constraints of Jewish formalism, created a conception of secularisation which approached, and perhaps even went beyond, that of most practising Christians at the present day. But, clearly, the situation was in practice more complicated, given the extent to which religion permeated the ancient world, which was inclusive rather than tolerant, as the

Christians found to their cost, when charged with atheism, and in which a simple action, like blowing a kiss to a sacred stone, could have profound implications (Minucius Felix, *Octavius* 2, 4). Furthermore, from the first there existed a spirit of intolerance among many Christians, which meant that any recognition of a secular sphere, indifferent to religion, was no more than a temporary concession, made because they were unable, like the Jews, to retreat into a kind of intellectual ghetto, situated within, but not partaking of, the pagan order. Of course there were sincere Christians who were also tolerant, so far as their religion permitted; and no doubt there were Christians who were tolerant because, in the last resort, their Christianity did not go very deep; but given the mood of those influential in Western Christianity—the Tertullians and the Cyprians—there is no reason for surprise that, once Christianity gained the upper hand, it set about eradicating paganism and replacing it with its own sacred objects and practices.

In this matter the East Roman Empire, deliberately excluded by Markus from consideration, makes a striking contrast with the West; for while Christian East Rome was as thoroughly desecularized as the Occident, it did maintain a sense of what we would now call the secular because of its continuity with the imperial past. It was the emperor, not the patriarch, who dominated Byzantium. Furthermore, the Empire had not so much been desecularized as re-sacralized on Christian lines. Christianity had been substituted for paganism, though the firm remained under the old management. Accordingly, in East Rome, there was a civic side, outside the control of the Church, even though within the political framework as a whole there was no freedom of religion. Indeed, it might be argued that there cannot be any real secular area, in the modern sense, as long as one religion, and one religion alone, holds sway.

Finally, it seems to the reviewer that Markus's account does not adequately take into consideration political factors in determining religious developments. Certain features of the Late Antique period which had militated against a complete Christian take-over were simply swept away by the barbarian invasions. If Christian bishops took over the leadership of their political communities, it was because there was no one else to do so. Markus notes that in the cities of Gaul and Spain which fell to the barbarians the spectacle of the games, always a source of distaste to the Church Fathers, was destroyed (p. 172). In Italy the Gothic War led to the decline of senatorial patronage and to an exodus of many aristocrats to the East, which 'seems finally to have sapped the strength of the foundations on which the old secular traditions of urban living no less than literary culture rested' (p. 217). This helps to explain the emergence of the predominantly biblical culture of the early Middle Ages—there was little alternative talent to the ascetic leaders who moved from the monastery to the episcopate. Indeed, Justinian's *reconquista*, designed to bring the West back into political and cultural relations with the East, was a total failure. 'The second half of the sixth century was not only a time of lost hopes. The world of the 530s had vanished for ever' (p. 219). James O'Donnell has painted a sad picture of Cassiodorus' last years at Vivarium, at work on the *De Orthographia*—a spelling-book for the use of his monastic community.[3] The social situation was wide open to a take-over by the Christians, who by now had their own culture, albeit of biblical inspiration; there was effectively no opposition, unlike the East, where the tradition of secular studies continued, and where political leaders, unlike the kings and nobles of the Western Middle Ages, were literate and educated men. In the West, literacy represented no necessary part of a ruler's education. Perhaps the most remarkable fact, in these circumstances, is the survival of the Latin classics, despite all the disapproval of zealous churchmen. Here was one field where the secular, in the sense of pagan, survived, to emerge after some centuries as an essential propaedeutic to Christian education.

In 1884 Thomas Hardy observed:

> Is not the present quasi-scientific system of writing history mere charlatanism? Events and tendencies are traced as if they were rivers of voluntary activity, and courses reasoned out from the circumstances in which natures, religions, or what-not, have found themselves. But are they not in the main the outcome of *passivity*—acted upon by unconscious propensity?

No one will accuse Robert Markus of writing, or seeking to write, quasi-scientific history; but it seems to me that in *The End of Ancient Christianity* he does not sufficiently allow for the element of contingency in determining historical processes. I do not myself find any difficulty in accepting the rapid and remarkable diffusion and acceptance of the cult of the martyrs and saints (and of the demonic supernatural, about which Markus has little or nothing to say) or the popularity of asceticism as the arbiter of Christian living—we have, after all, seen analagous developments in religious tastes in our own day; a recent biographical notice of David Knowles records how, 'with a rueful smile he observed that of all things in his world he had supposed the Latin Mass and the

[3] O'Donnell, *Cassiodorus* (Berkeley and Los Angeles/London 1979), 229 ff.

steam engine the most stable and lasting—and both were gone'[4] but I am persuaded that, in this sublunary world, the element of chance in the development of human affairs is greater than historians, and perhaps Church historians more than others, care to admit. In short, there may be a greater continuity between the outlook of the age of Gregory the Great and that of the earlier Latin Fathers than Markus suggests, and the marked changes of the late sixth century may well have come about because essentially political and social factors provided the Christian Church with the opportunity to take over the religious control of the barbarian kingdoms of the Latin West and to exploit it with an intolerance which most Christians today would find unattractive.

XIX

Christianity and the Modern World-View

Habet enim et scientia modum suum bonum, si quod in ea inflat vel inflare assolet aeternorum charitate vincatur.

(St Augustine, *De Trinitate* XII, xiv, 21)

IN A PAPER read at the Inter-Orthodox Conference at Brookline, Massachusetts, in September 1970, of which an English translation appeared in the Spring number of the *Eastern Churches Review* of 1971,[1] Dr Christos Yannaras discussed the relation between Eastern Orthodoxy and the West, understanding by that term the basic human stance or attitude towards the world which has developed in Western Europe (and, by extension, the American culture which has developed from and with Western Europe) as a result of the 'liberal spirit of the Renaissance and the rise of the positive sciences and technology', and which has produced 'a deep wedge between religion and life, a kind of "spiritual schizophrenia" which basically characterizes the Western stance toward the world and history'.[2] This development is commonly associated with the scientific revolution in thought and technology of the 17th century; but for Dr Yannaras it derives from Descartes and ultimately from Scholasticism – 'man's claim by intellectual effort to secure mastery over the whole realm of accessible truth, and his tendency to define and distinguish the boundaries between man's capacities and the transcendent reality of God'.[3] Against this stance Dr Yannaras sets the 'eschatological reality of the Church', the 'continuous building-up of the Church, the fulfilment of the perspectives of history by the reality of the "little leaven" '[4] (notably lacking, one may add, in the Church Militant today). 'The role of Orthodox theology', he says, 'within the historical and cultural milieu of the West is to draw attention to the eschatological witness of the Church as embodied in the parish.'[5] Dr Yannaras, it must be observed, was addressing a conference of his own Church and was not, on that occasion, seeking to engage in discussion with other Christians. I am here concerned, not with his views on the role of Orthodoxy in the world today, upon which it would be improper for me to comment, but with his analysis of the causes of what he calls the Western stance. In the same issue of the *Eastern Churches Review* Fr Robert Murray gently objected to Dr Yannaras's historical picture:

1C. Yannaras, 'Orthodoxy and the West', *ECR* iii (1971), pp. 286–300.
2*Ibid.*, pp. 286, 288.
3*Ibid.*, p. 287.
4*Ibid.*, p. 298.
5*Ibid.*, p. 300.

The determinative antecedents of Descartes, as of the Reformers, are in decadent scholasticism rather than in the great syntheses of the 13th century. It must be said with regret that Dr Yannaras's account of 'scholasticism' is a caricature as rhetorical and unjust as that repeatedly offered by Berdiaev, whose undisciplined and arbitrary pronouncements Dr Yannaras rightly criticizes. It is both incorrect and unjust to ascribe to St Thomas Aquinas, for example, either the views or tendencies alleged, or responsibility for developments of from three to seven centuries after his death. On all the major issues raised by Dr Yannaras, St Thomas is essentially one with his sources, the Fathers of the undivided Church.[6]

In the following number of the *Eastern Churches Review* there was printed a letter from Sir John Lawrence, welcoming the discussion between Yannaras and Murray and expressing the opinion that Dr Yannaras 'had touched on something that is fundamental, not only for the Churches of the East and West, but also for the future of humanity. . . . It . . . seems to me', wrote Sir John,

that Western medieval philosophers were sometimes following a false track and that we are still suffering for that. I am not a medievalist . . . but it looks to me as if from the time of Anselm Western Christian philosophy expected human reason to be able to do more than it can. The Eastern Church never made that mistake. . . . In my own life it was H. A. Pritchard's lectures on the Theory of Knowledge, reinforced by devastating tutorials with Horace Joseph, that brought me up against the limits of the human mind forty years ago. It now seems to me that this was part of my preparation for the reception of Orthodox apophatic theology twenty years later.[7]

In the present paper, some attempt will be made to consider the contention that the present Western world-view is derived from tendencies in Latin theology from the time of St Anselm onwards, and to evaluate the role of apophaticism in theology. From these consideration we shall attempt, however briefly and inadequately, to consider the significance of secular studies and technology for theology and the attitude which the Christian thinker – and especially the theologian – should adopt towards them.

It may be said at the outset that the suggestion of Sir John Lawrence that from the time of St Anselm Western Christian philosophy has expected human reason to do more than it can would appear to receive confirmation from a number of distinguished medievalists. Thus, the President of St John's College, Oxford, has observed that Anselm 'spoke . . . the language of rational argument, leaving no question unattempted however trivial or however fundamental, and never failing in the end to give some kind of answer'.[8] Professor Christopher Brooke asserts that Anselm was 'able to blow away the cobwebs which surrounded the doctrine of the Atonement'[9] (a revealing phrase, if we remember that Gustav Aulén, in a famous study, considered that Anselm's theory

[6]R. Murray, 'A Brief Comment on Dr Yannaras's Article', *ECR* iii (1971), p. 306.
[7]*ECR* iii (1971), pp. 491–2.
[8]R. W. Southern, *Medieval Humanism and Other Essays* (Oxford 1970), p. 13.
[9]C. Brooke, *The Twelfth Century Renaissance* (London 1969), p. 34.

represented a departure from the classical doctrine of the Fathers),[10] and has emphasized the importance of the impact of dialectic, especially as employed by Abelard, in determining the theology of the 12th century.[11] Again, Dom Jean Leclercq, in a beautiful and learned book on early medieval monasticism in the West, has contrasted the claustral theology of the early Middle Ages – humane and experimental, with that of the Schools which succeeded it – metaphysical, impersonal and universal;[12] and has remarked that 'more and more [monastic theology] appears to be a prolongation of patristic theology'.[13] St Bernard is, indeed, the last of the Fathers,[14] so far as the West is concerned.

On a broader cultural front the Austrian historian, Friedrich Heer, has drawn attention to the fact that in the 12th, and to a large extent still in the early 13th century, Europe had the characteristics of an open society, despite the breach between the Greek and Latin Churches in 1054;[15] and one may in this context recall the comment of the Russian historian T. I. Uspenskii that 'the circle of ideas in which the European mind was working from the eleventh to the thirteenth century was the same that we find in Byzantium'.[16] But the most startling apparent confirmation of Sir John Lawrence's suggestion comes from an essay by Dr Southern, which regards the period from about 1100 to about 1320 as one of the great ages of humanism in the history of Europe, an age which saw a recovery of the sense of the dignity of human nature; of the dignity of nature itself; and of the order and rationality of creation:

> . . . The whole universe appears intelligible and accessible to human reason: nature is seen as an orderly system, and man – in understanding the laws of nature – understands himself as the main part, the key-stone, of nature. Without this understanding it is hard to see how man can experience that confidence in human powers that humanism implies.[17]

Dr Southern points to the development of secular studies in the 12th century, and contrasts Peter Lombard's *Sentences*, the principal theological

[10] G. Aulén, *Christus Victor*, ET by G. Hebert (London 1965), pp. 1–2: 'The real beginnings of a thought-out doctrine of the Atonement are found in Anselm of Canterbury, who thus comes to hold a position of first-rate importance in the history of dogma. By the theory of satisfaction developed in the *Cur Deus Homo?* he repressed, even if he could not entirely overcome, the old mythological account of Christ's work as a victory over the devil; in place of the older and more "physical" idea of salvation he put forward his teaching of a deliverance from the guilt of sin; and, above all, he taught an "objective" Atonement, according to which God is the object of Christ's atoning work, and is reconciled through the satisfaction made to His justice.' Cf. pp. 81–92 and note Aulén's conclusion (p. 87): 'It is . . . essential to the theory of Anselm that the Incarnation and the Atonement are not organically connected together, as they were in the classic view.'

[11] Brooke, *op. cit.*, pp. 30–50.

[12] J. Leclercq, *The Love of Learning and the Desire for God*, ET by C. Misrahi (New York: Mentor Omega Books 1962), pp. 224–5.

[13] *Ibid.*, p. 189.

[14] *Ibid.*, p. 114.

[15] F. Heer, *The Medieval World: Europe 1100–1350*, ET by J. Sondheimer (New York: Mentor Books 1963), pp. 17, 18.

[16] T. I. Uspenskii, *Essays in Byzantine Civilization* [in Russian] (St Petersburg 1892), cited by A. A. Vasiliev, *History of the Byzantine Empire*, 2nd ed. (Madison, Wisconsin 1958), vol. ii, p. 475.

[17] Southern, *Medieval Humanism and Other Essays*, p. 32.

work of the middle of that century, which quotes almost entirely from the Fathers, with the *Summa Theologica* of Thomas Aquinas, which contains about 3500 quotations from Aristotle.[18] In a sense, he says, the two Summae of St Thomas represent the highest point of medieval humanism:

> The work of Thomas Aquinas is full of illustrations of the supremacy of reason and nature. His judgements nearly always give the natural man rather more than his due. He reversed the ancient opinion that the body is the ruined habitation of the soul, and held with Aristotle that it is the basis of the soul's being. Everywhere he points to the natural perfection of man, his natural rights, and the power of his natural reason. The dignity of human nature is not simply a poetic vision; it has become a central truth of philosophy.[19]

From the foregoing, one could construct an intellectual history of Western Europe which would appear to justify the suggestions of Dr Yannaras and Sir John Lawrence. It might go somewhat as follows. Greek and Latin Christianity share a common heritage, derived from the Apostolic Church and the Christian Fathers. However, in the West, towards the end of the 11th century, there develops a particular approach to theology, conditioned by a confidence in the power of human reason and dominated by the science of dialectic. This finds expression in Scholasticism, and its development is powerfully aided by the recovery of the Aristotelian *corpus* through translations from the Arabic. The approach reaches its extreme form in the Nominalism of the Ockhamists of the 14th century, which placed an absolute division between faith and reason. This division was retained at the Protestant Reformation by Luther, himself a product of the Nominalist school, with his emphasis on faith alone, and by the Calvinist doctrine of the total corruption of human nature, which left no place for any contact between truth as understood in the world of fallen man and truth as revealed by divine grace. But in the secular world the confidence in the powers of human nature which had marked the early days of Scholasticism survived, and was enhanced by the technological achievements which have distinguished Western European culture from the 17th century onwards. With the decline of religious belief in modern industrial society, an abyss has opened between Christianity and unbelief which Western Christians, whether Protestant or Catholic, are unable to bridge, and which has caused some of them to capitulate, and to adopt a theology of secularization. This failure to be able to speak to the secular world comes from the abandonment of that synthesis of faith and reason effected in the Patristic Age and maintained today in the Eastern Church, when she is being true to herself and not led

[18] *Ibid.*, p. 46.

[19] *Ibid.*, p. 50. Cf. the comment of William Temple, 'Thomism and Modern Needs', *Blackfriars* xxv (1944), p. 91: 'Whatever may be true of St Thomas himself, the Thomist tradition as commonly presented does not adequately convey the awful pervasiveness and penetrating potency of sin in all departments of human life, including in its sphere of poisonous influence even our worship and our generosity.' But note the reply of Victor White, OP, in the same issue (p. 105): 'The present-day disciple of St Thomas has not only to develop and supplement the original "map" of St Thomas, he has also to restore it.' White points (p. 109) to St Thomas's own emphasis on the 'disintegration of human nature wrought by the Fall'.

astray by the fashionable philosophies of the West. Eastern Orthodoxy, like Latin Christianity, was threatened by Scholasticism in the 14th century in the person of the Nominalist philosopher Barlaam of Calabria, but was saved by the religious genius of Gregory Palamas. 'If Barlaamism had triumphed, it might have led the Eastern Church along the paths down which William of Ockham's Nominalism did lead the West, and it might have entailed, perhaps even more quickly, the same consequences.' Such is the judgement of the distinguished Russian theologian Fr Meyendorff.[20]

Such an account of the intellectual origins of the present outlook of the West appears plausible and persuasive and has been maintained, with certain refinements, in at least one book published in recent years.[21] Dr Yannaras, apparently, would carry the implications of this view a stage farther, for he would regard technology as the embodiment of the stance implied by the terms 'West' and 'Western man' and hold it to be ultimately derived from the philosophical implications of Scholasticism and, as such, exactly opposed to the view of the world and history which is presupposed by the experience of the Orthodox Church.

> If we accept that, as the Orthodox Church teaches, man's relation to God is not simply an intellectual and ethical relation, but a relation entirely and realistically based on the acceptance and use of created things, that is to say, on a eucharistic-liturgical utilization of the world, then it is technology, with its particular stance and character, which constitutes the basic theological problem in the encounter between Orthodoxy and the West.[22]

Accordingly, it is particularly important that we should consider whether the sketch of the development of Western European thought which has just been given is convincing; and the answer, so far as the present writer is concerned, must be that it is not.

In the first place, the picture as a whole suffers from simplification and selectivity. It takes no account of the complexity of historical processes, particularly in the realm of ideas. St Anselm's rationalism – as Dr Southern recognizes in the essay from which I previously quoted – was far removed from the rationalism of the present day,[23] and so far as Anselm himself was concerned, belief preceded understanding. What he was concerned to

[20] J. Meyendorff, *A Study of Gregory Palamas*, ET by G. Lawrence (London 1964), p. 237.

[21] Philip Sherrard, *The Greek East and the Latin West* (Oxford 1959).

[22] Yannaras, 'Orthodoxy and the West', p. 291.

[23] See the comments of Frederick Copleston, *A History of Philosophy*, vol. ii: *Medieval Philosophy: Augustine to Scotus* (London 1964), p. 158: 'If by rationalism one means an attitude of mind which denies revelation and faith, St Anselm was certainly no rationalist, since he accepted the primacy of faith and the fact of authority and only then went on to attempt to understand the data of faith. If, however, one is going to extend the term "rationalism" to cover the attitude of mind which leads to the attempt to prove mysteries, not because the mysteries are not accepted by faith or would be rejected if one could not prove them, but because one desires to understand all that one believes, without having first clearly defined the ways in which different truths are accessible to us, then one might, of course, call the thought of St Anselm "rationalism" or an approximation to rationalism.' The difficulty about any facile judgement about the thought of St Anselm is demonstrated by the fact that a critic no less demanding than Karl Barth does not consider that Anselm's teaching leaves any place for unaided reasoning independent of faith. Barth may be mistaken; but his argument is still of significance for our purposes.

do was to try to meet and answer possible objections to Christianity by unbelievers who could not be met by a simple exhortation to believe.[24] Again, the sketch takes no account of the continuance of the Augustinian tradition during the later Middle Ages in thinkers like St Bonaventure or Giles of Rome, or of the rich flowering of mysticism in the same period, which represents a devotional spirit very different from that of the Schools, having much in common with Eastern spirituality. Again, and in very different context, the break-down of the European 'open society' of the 12th century to which Friedrich Heer alludes, cannot be understood simply, or even primarily, in terms of intellectual alienation. Brutal material factors like the capture of Constantinople by the Latin Crusaders in 1204 or the Mongol invasion of Russia in the 13th century would have broken European unity independent of any idealistic considerations.[25] Dr Southern would, indeed, regard the period of Western medieval humanism as coming to an end in the early 14th century with a loss of confidence in the system and its aims,[26] a loss which was only exacerbated, and not brought about, by the Black Death and its aftermath. Finally, the sketch is unsatisfactory in that it does not take account of the complexity of the situation within the Eastern Church itself during the Middle Ages. G. P. Fedotov, in his famous study *The Russian Religious Mind,* gives a remarkably unflattering portrait of Byzantine religion in general and of the shape which it took among the Slavonic peoples who embraced Orthodoxy. In particular he lays emphasis on the formalism of Byzantine Christianity (' . . . a tremendous gap in the Byzantine religion: the weakness of ethical life'),[27] a formalism which, when transported to Russia and embodied in canonical codes, themselves dependent upon Greek originals, produced a set of rules remarkable for their superstition and narrow legalism.[28] Reading Fedotov, the western ecclesiastical historian experiences a depressing sense of familiarity: the Russian Church of the 12th century only too closely resembled the West in much of its legislation.[29]

It may be suggested, from the examples which have been given – and it

[24]Southern, *Medieval Humanism and Other Essays,* pp. 13, 16–17. Cf. the remarks by M. J. Charlesworth, *St Anselm's Proslogion* (Oxford 1965), pp. 30–40.

[25]Heer, *The Medieval World,* pp. 23–24.

[26]Southern, *op. cit.,* pp. 58–60.

[27]G. P. Fedotov, *The Russian Religious Mind* (New York: Harper Torchbooks 1960), p. 35.

[28]*Ibid.,* pp. 179–201. I am, of course, fully aware of those other aspects of Russian Christianity so movingly described by Nicolas Arseniev, *Russian Piety,* ET by A. Moorhouse (London 1964) – its 'contemplation of the glory of the Incarnate Word' (p. 28), its 'active, true compassion' (p. 91), and its 'Christocentric orientation' (p. 118). But Arseniev is conscious of the danger of extreme ritualism, to which the Russians are prone and which finds expression in the great Russian schism of the Old Believers in the 17th century (pp. 61–64). It is, indeed, precisely these contrasts in Russian religion which afford a warning against any simplistic evaluation of Eastern Christianity.

[29]For example, the 12th-century Novgorodian canonical compilation which goes under the name of Kirik forbids a woman who has given birth to a child to enter the church for forty days – a prohibition based upon the notion of ritual impurity (Fedotov, p. 192). Precisely the same issue was raised by Augustine of Canterbury in his letter to Pope Gregory I five centuries earlier; though in this instance Gregory replied, with characteristic magnanimity, that if the mother were to come to church to give thanks in the very hour of her delivery she would not commit sin (Bede, *HE* i, 27; ed. Colgrave & Mynors, p. 90). It may be noted that Archbishop Theodore of Canterbury (668–90) – a Greek – forbade a woman to enter church for forty days after giving birth (Haddan & Stubbs, *Councils* iii, p. 189).

is impractical to go into more detail here – that any simplified view of the progress and development of Western Christendon and the scientific and technological civilization of the West is untenable. Let us now consider the cardinal issue of this thesis: was the rise of Scholasticism in fact decisive in bringing about the conditions from which modern technology has developed? Here, at the outset, it is important to be clear what is implied by the term Scholasticism. In so far as it represents the dominant characteristic of later medieval education and learning, the word may be used very loosely, and a poet like Dante could be termed a Scholastic; but such usage is hopelessly imprecise for our purposes. It is important not to call Scholastic what was, in fact, the common intellectual heritage of the Middle Ages. For example, the Scholastics believed in the Ptolemaic system of the universe; but so did pre-Scholastic medieval thinkers like Isidore of Seville and the Venerable Bede. Equally, to equate Scholasticism with Aristotelianism, as is not infrequently done, would mean that there was no real Scholasticism before the 13th century and so deprive Peter Lombard of any claim to be called a Scholastic. To avoid such difficulties, it seems best to regard Scholasticism as being fundamentally a method: that is to say, a set of teaching procedures used in medieval universities involving the technique of the *quaestio* – the formal question of the meaning of a text and, pre-eminently, of the text of the Bible, to be answered according to the rules of logic.[30] Such a definition will cover all the great Scholastics, including those who were religiously orthodox, like St Thomas Aquinas, and those whose orthodoxy is more controversial, like Siger of Brabant and Boethius of Dacia.

Now it is clear that Scholasticism as so understood has in common with modern science an assumption of a certain order and causality in the world and in the universe, but modern science differs from Scholasticism in one vital particular: in its combination of theoretical speculation and experimental verification. It is upon this combination that the great advances of modern science depended and depend, and it was a combination which, if not unknown to, was certainly undeveloped in the Middle Ages. Certain Scholastics – Robert Grosseteste and Roger Bacon are among the most famous[31] – had interests which we should today call

[30]See Leclercq, *The Love of Learning and the Desire for God*, pp. 11–13; David Knowles, *The Evolution of Medieval Thought* (London 1962), pp. 87–90.

[31]See A. C. Crombie, *Robert Grosseteste and the Origins of Experimental Science* (Oxford 1953), and note his conclusion (p. 318) that 'despite the enormous increase in power that the new mathematics brought in the seventeenth century, the logical structure and problems of experimental science had remained basically the same since the beginning of its modern history some four centuries earlier'. But cf. the judgement of the same author, *Augustine to Galileo*, 2nd ed. (London 1961), vol. ii, p. 119: 'By taking the empirical phenomena of motion seriously as a problem and seeing the solution through to the end, [the 17th-century physicists] had no alternative but to reform the whole of cosmology, to invent new mathematical techniques in the process, and to provide the eminent example for the methods of science as a whole. This, it may be suggested, was the advance made by the *virtuosi* of the seventeenth century over the clerics of the medieval universities to whom in other ways they owed so much.' Note also the judgement of A. R. Hall, *The Scientific Revolution 1500–1800* (London 1954), p. 163: '. . . traditional ideas continued to satisfy the majority until the seventeenth century and the philosophic conception of empiricism was a very different thing from its application to scientific problems. No important re-statement of scientific method was made during the sixteenth century. The medieval tradition continued to run strong.'

scientific; but the great step in bringing about the scientific revolution – an event which, in the words of Professor Butterfield, 'outshines everything since the rise of Christianity and reduces the Renaissance and Reformation to the rank of mere episodes, mere internal displacements, within the system of medieval Christendom'[32] – occurred in the 17th century. The decisive break with the medieval outlook took place in the realm of astronomy, and this depended upon the development of the telescope and of mathematics.[33] Some of the later Scholastics may have contributed to this break by denying any distinction between the Aristotelian sublunary world of nature and the heavenly world and by maintaining that, in consequence, general laws governed the whole of the universe, both above and below the sphere of the moon; but this was of far less importance than the discoveries of Copernicus and Galileo, and the theories of Newton.[34] Newton's First Law of Motion states that every body continues in its state of rest or of uniform motion in a straight line except insofar as it is compelled by impressed force to change that state. The significance of this law, for our purposes, is that it represents a decisive rejection of the traditional Aristotelian formula: Every body continues in its state of rest except so far as it is compelled by impressed force to change that state.[35] This notion had been very much the essence both of medieval cosmology and, in a broader sense, of the whole medieval world-view: 'everything has its right place, its home, the region that suits it, and, if not forcibly restrained, moves thither by a sort of homing instinct'.[36] Such a view had been held by the Scholastics and by their predecessors. In rejecting it Newton struck a blow at one of the traditional proofs of the existence of God by eliminating the need for any Prime Mover; but it is difficult to discover any reason for thinking that he formulated his Law under the influence of Scholastic philosophy. Far more important for Newton was the evidence of practical experiment, like Galileo's famous refutation of the Aristotelian theory that heavy bodies fall more quickly than light ones by the dropping of weights from the leaning tower of Pisa. Equally, more exact astronomical observation, made possible by the invention of the telescope, helped to break down the medieval outlook – the observation of the Nova in Cassiopeia in 1572 was of great importance in this connexion;[37] but this observation had begun millennia before the

[32]Herbert Butterfield, *The Origins of Modern Science* (London 1949), p. viii.

[33]Crombie, *Augustine to Galileo*, vol. ii, pp. 124–5: ' The internal revolution in scientific thought that took place during the sixteenth and seventeenth centuries had, then, two essential aspects, the experimental and the mathematical, and it was precisely those branches of science which were most amenable to measurement that showed the most spectacular developments.'

[34]See *Entretiens sur la renaissance du 12e siècle sous la direction de Maurice de Gandillac et Edouard Jeauneau* (Decades du Centre culturel international de Cerisy-la-Salle, NS 9, Paris 1968), pp. 112–13; Butterfield, *op. cit.*, pp. 7–14.

[35]A. N. Whitehead, *An Introduction to Mathematics* (London 1911), p. 44.

[36]C. S. Lewis, *The Discarded Image* (Cambridge 1964), p. 92.

[37]See F. R. Johnson, *Astronomical Thought in Renaissance England* (Baltimore 1937), p. 154, cited by Lewis, *The Discarded Image*, p. 4, n. 1; Butterfield *The Origins of Modern Science*, p. 53: '. . . a greater shock to European thought than the publication of the Copernican hypothesis itself'.

Scholastics were born, and the great discoveries of the 16th and 17th centuries would have been made even if the Scholastics had never been.

Limitations of space preclude a more extended discussion of this topic; but I hope that I have said enough to cast doubt upon the view that the modern, rationalistic outlook of the West is a product of medieval theology, and to refute the suggestion that the scientific revolution of the 17th century is ultimately a product of Scholasticism.[38] It is true that certain assumptions were common both to early modern science and to Scholasticism – for example, the assumption of a universe governed by natural laws; but this does not mean that science inherited such an assumption from Scholasticism to any greater degree than from the common philosophical tradition of Antiquity. Furthermore, the suggestion that Scholasticism was, in a sense, rationalistic might not unreasonably be reversed; for it could be argued, in the light of the evidence, that the real triumph of the great Scholastic theologians was that they met and contained the threat of an Aristotelian-dominated philosophy by using Aristotle while at the same time leaving the final word to revealed truth. It would, after all, be difficult to accuse the author of the *Adoro devote* and the *Pange lingua* of leaving no place for a faith based upon revelation in his theological system.

Let us turn now to our second topic, namely apophatic theology. Sir John Lawrence has recorded its effect upon him twenty years after his undergraduate studies in philosophy, and one can well believe that it would come as a refreshment to many Western Christians, and especially to those Protestants whose religious tradition has left little room for any sense of mystery and awe.[39] Nevertheless, there seems reason to question the assumption that it is the theological method *par excellence.*

Let it first be noted (as indeed Dr Yannaras recognizes)[40] that the emphasis on apophatic theology in modern Orthodoxy is very much a mark of the theologians of the Russian diaspora. Here Vladimir Losskii's great book, *The Mystical Theology of the Eastern Church,* has been especially influential, for Losskii based his exposition upon the teaching of Pseudo-Dionysius, whom he elsewhere described as a 'Christian thinker disguised as a Neo-Platonist [standing] . . . in the tradition of the great Cappadocians, of St Basil and especially St Gregory of Nyssa'.[41] For

[38] I am not here concerned with the question why the intellectual developments of the 17th century took place as they did – this is a real problem, as Crombie notes, *Augustine to Galileo,* vol. ii, p. 124: 'The existence of motives and opportunities, even when they brought fundamental scientific problems into prominence, does not explain the intellectual revolution which made it possible for scientists to solve these problems, and the history of the interaction between motives, opportunities, skills, and intellectual changes that brought about the Scientific Revolution has, in fact, yet to be written.' When it is written, it is to be hoped that the theological implications will not be ignored.

[39] 'In an early novel by Benjamin Swift the Roman Catholic remarked that Protestantism was too coldly logical: it seemed to walk round its God in complete comprehension' (N. H. Baynes, *Byzantine Studies and other Essays* [London 1955], p. 4).

[40] Yannaras, 'Orthodoxy and the West', p. 296.

[41] Losskii, *The Vision of God,* ET by A. Moorhouse (London 1963), pp. 99, 100.

Losskii, 'negative theology is not merely a theory of ecstasy. It is an expression of that fundamental attitude which transforms the whole of theology into a contemplation of the mysteries of revelation'[42] and, as such, must take precedence over affirmative theology.

In considering this view it may be remarked in passing that negative theology is not peculiar to the Greek Fathers but can be found, for example, in the thought of St Augustine, as Losskii himself recognized.[43] But it is difficult to see, in considering the writings of the Fathers as a whole, that it occupies the place in their theology which it does in that of Losskii. Rather, they employ it partly as an indication of the utter transcendence of God, and partly as a warning against the sort of facile speculation to which certain heretics, notably the extreme Arians, were prone.[44] 'I do not hinder continual recollection of God,' said Gregory of Nazianzus, 'but only theological discussion; and not as if such discussion were wrong in itself, but only what is unreasonable. Nor do I object to teaching, but only to want of judgement in so doing';[45] and, in a famous image, he likens the act of theological investigation to the vision of God's back, which was seen by Moses, but only from the cleft in the rock which is, for Gregory, the Incarnation.[46] It is against the background of Arian disputatiousness and loquacity that we should understand the warnings of the Fathers; for it was, after all, the orthodox and not the heretics who introduced the word *homoousios,* with all its controversial associations, into the creed of Nicaea, to the scandal of conservative theologians who objected to the use of a non-biblical word; and it was Catholic theologians like the Cappadocians who were prepared to expound the mystery of the Trinity in terms of *ousia* and *hypostasis.* Thus St Basil can write:

> The distinction between *ousia* and *hypostasis* is the same as that between the general and the particular; as, for example, between the animal, man, and a particular man. Accordingly, in the case of the Godhead, we confess one *ousia* so as not to give a variant definition of existence; but we confess a particular *hypostasis,* so that our conception of Father, Son and Holy Spirit may be without confusion and clear.[47]

Basil is, of course, well aware that such language is only figurative; but he uses it because, if we must try to talk about God, we should use the best theological terms that are available. So in his treatise on the Holy Spirit he writes:

> Either let the ineffable be honoured by silence or let holy things be numbered with befitting reverence. There is one God and Father, one only-begotten Son,

[42]Losskii, *Mystical Theology,* ET (London 1957), p. 42.

[43]Losskii, 'Les éléments de "Théologie négative" dans la pensée de saint Augustin', *Augustinus Magister: Congrès international Augustinien, Paris 21–24 septembre 1954* (Paris 1954), vol. i, pp. 575–81.

[44]The notorious example is that of the Eunomian Aetius who, having sat at the feet of an Aristotelian philosopher at Alexandria, subsequently applied dialectical reasoning to the understanding of divine matters and made theology a geometrical exercise. A specimen of his theological method is preserved by Epiphanius, *Haer.* lxxvi, 11 (MPG, xlii, cols 533C–545B).

[45]Greg. Naz., *Or.* 27, 4 (ed. Mason, 7. 1–4).

[46]*Ibid., Or.* 28, 3 (Mason, 24. 8–25. 5).

[47]Basil, *Ep.* 236, 6 (MPG, xxxii, col. 884A).

one Holy Spirit. We proclaim each of the *hypostases* singly; but when it is necessary to reckon them together, we are not carried away by unintelligent arithmetic to a polytheistic conception of God.[48]

Considerable confusion can be created by the fact that the term 'apophatic theology' can be used in two senses. First, it can be used as a description of contemplation, in which the mind is emptied of all carnal images and waits for God in a darkness. This is Dionysian contemplation, going back ultimately to Gregory of Nyssa,[49] and has had considerable influence on Western mystics like St John of the Cross and the author of the *Cloud of Unknowing.* To speak of the value of this method is not the intention of the present writer – it must be left to followers of the Way; though it is to be noticed that Christian mystics usually lay stress upon the fact that they see God (as Gregory of Nazianzus would put it) through the cleft in the rock, the Incarnation.[50]

The second use of apophaticism is in the field of dogmatic theology. Here, it has a vital role in reminding the theologian that he is, at best, talking of the ineffable; but it can never be the only theological method, since pure apophaticism would simply reduce us to silence and the palm of theology might well be awarded to the Gnostic Basilides who, with a ruthless logic, spoke of a non-existent God who, without intelligence, without sense, without will, without choice, without passion, without desire, wished (without actually wishing) to make a universe. 'Thus the non-existent God made a non-existent universe out of the non-existent.'[51] The Catholic Fathers understandably rejected this sort of language on account of its absurdity;[52] but a difficulty about its employment in a more orthodox context was well expressed by a writer quoted in Abbot Cuthbert Butler's famous work *Western Mysticism*:

> The mystics heap up terms of negation – darkness, void, nothingness – in endeavouring to describe the Absolute which they have apprehended. It may be, of course, that their apprehension had such a fullness and richness of content that in human language it could only be described negatively. But one may, at least, point out that their method is the very opposite of the characteristically Christian one of affirmation; that where they say 'darkness' St John says 'light', and that St John says 'fulness' where they say 'void': and St Paul stresses, not ignorance, but enhanced knowledge, as the result of religious experience.[53]

48 *De Spiritu Sancto,* xviii, 44 (ed. Pruche, *Sources chrétiennes* xvii, p. 192).

49 See Jean Daniélou, *Platonisme et théologie mystique* (Paris 1944), esp. pp. 189–99.

50 So Gregory Palamas was 'forced to introduce a Christocentric corrective into Dionysius. . . . [H]e understands Dionysius in a Christological sense' (Meyendorff, *A Study of Gregory Palamas,* pp. 133, 152. See further pp. 149–84). Equally, in the case of St Maximus the Confessor, his Christology is the basis of all his theology (see Lars Thunberg, *Microcosm and Mediator. The Theological Anthropology of Maximus the Confessor* [Lund 1965], esp. pp. 350–463). The case of Maximus the Confessor is particularly interesting, since his teaching played an important part in the development of St Bernard's mysticism. See E. Gilson, *The Mystical Theology of St Bernard,* ET by A. H. C. Downes (London 1940), pp. 17, 25, 26, 132.

51 Basilides, *apud* Hippolytus, *Ref.,* vii, 21. 1–5 (*CGS: Hippolytus Werke,* 3er Bd., 196. 15–197. 16).

52 There is an amusing parody of a Gnostic system – in this case Valentinianism – by Irenaeus, *C. Haer.,* I, xi, 4 (MPG, vii, cols 567A–568A).

53 C. Butler, *Western Mysticism,* 3rd ed. (London 1967), p. 123.

St Gregory Palamas, although he considered that negative language comes nearer to describing the ineffable Divine Nature than positive theology,[54] nevertheless recognized that negation by itself is not enough.[55] Many Western Christians, following the writer quoted by Abbot Butler, will feel that the frequent employment of affirmative language in the Bible gives cataphatic theology a higher standing than some Eastern theologians seem willing to allow it, while at the same time acknowledging the inadequacy of human language to express the ineffable. But it must be emphasized that no use of affirmative theological language is at any time to be understood as implying a rational comprehension of the divine mysteries. We speak because we have to; we use, wherever we can, the language of biblical revelation; and we submit our formulas to the judgement of the Holy Spirit in the universal Church of Christ.

This brings us to the third topic for consideration: the significance of secular studies and technology for theology, and the attitude which the Christian thinker should adopt towards them. Dr Yannaras, it will be recalled, regards technology as constituting the basic theological problem in the encounter with the West, and contrasts it with the 'eucharistic-liturgical utilization of the world' taught by the Orthodox Church.[56] We must discuss the implications of this contrast.

In the first place, it would be well to be clear about what we are to understand by technology. Fundamentally, I take it, the word describes the design and employment of mechanical aids to make human life more comfortable, more safe, and more efficient, and to provide man with freedom from laborious and uninspiring drudgery in order to pursue a more humane and creative existence.[57] In that sense technology has been with us as long as the species *homo sapiens,* and the ox-drawn plough and the spinning-wheel are as much part of technology as the computer and the air-liner. If, of course, by technology one understands the greedy exploitation of this planet by mechanical and chemical devices without regard for anything other than immediate enrichment and enjoyment, then it is easy enough to agree with Dr Yannaras; but the fault here lies not in the machines, but in their misuse. In any case, the exploitation which Dr Yannaras would deplore is by no means confined to Western technologists. Primitive peoples are as capable of harming the planet as are men equipped with machines, as the deforestation and consequent desiccation of North Africa by the medieval Arab invaders bears witness, and the only difference in the case of a technologically-developed society

[54]Greg. Pal., *Cap. Phys.,* 106 (MPG, cl, col. 1192D). He points out, however, that apophatic theology does not destroy but defines affirmative language, *op. cit.,* 123 (col. 1205D).

[55]For examples, see Meyendorff, *A Study of Gregory Palamas,* pp. 206–7.

[56]See above, n. 22.

[57]I do not forget the boredom and degradation imposed upon the worker in certain types of mass-production industry. Here there is clearly an ethical issue as to whether such methods of production are justifiable. But this moral consideration does not in itself condemn industrial development as a whole; and it is hardly necessary to point out that boredom and degradation through slavery, serfdom and sheer poverty, were only too familiar in pre-industrial society.

(and it is, admittedly, a formidable difference) is that it can do more long-lasting harm in a shorter time. Dr Yannaras might reply that this is precisely what he has in mind: it is the task of Christians to teach their fellow men the doctrine of a eucharistic-liturgical utilization of the world and this, he would claim, Western Christianity is incapable of doing.

But, one might reply with all humility, is there any reason to think that Orthodoxy is any better equipped to speak to modern secular man than Roman Catholicism or Protestantism? The present writer sees no reason to suppose that his English fellow-countrymen are more likely to be impressed by Orthodoxy than by the forms of Christianity with which they are familiar. The fundamental difficulty is that large numbers of Western Europeans have become secularized, not primarily for intellectual reasons but because of developments in society, and particularly because of the great increase in population-density, which have accompanied the change from an agrarian to an industrialized society which does not provide for religion any place such as it enjoyed in the agrarian economy of an earlier date.[58] If the citizens of a society conditioned by applied technology are to be reached, it cannot be by simply commending to them the practice of a religion which, so far as the majority are concerned, looks very much like a survival, picturesque but outdated, from another age, with little relevance to their daily existence, though capable of adding dignity to the decisive moments of a man's life: birth, marriage and death.

Dr Yannaras speaks of the witness of the parish, and such witness is unquestionably of the greatest importance in recommending Christianity to non-Christian neighbours; but the Church cannot rest there. One of the features of the present *malaise* in Christianity in the West is a lack of intellectual confidence, which expresses itself in the rather pathetic attempt by some light-weight theologians to persuade themselves and others that the assumptions and values of a de-Christianized society must be taken up and approved if Christianity is to make any sort of impression on contemporary men. It can only be said of such tactics that they have not, to date, produced any very remarkable results; and one cannot but suspect that they are calculated to arouse contempt in some of the people to whom they are addressed. 'Any compromise to bring them in' is not a very inspiring slogan for the Church of the Risen Christ.

If the Christian Church is to make any impact on modern society, it must be able to demonstrate that it has an intellectual grasp capable of understanding the categories of thought of that society. Besides the day-to-day witness of professing Christians, it is essential for Christian theologians to seek to bridge the gap between a technological society and the Church by endeavouring to understand the intellectual presuppositions upon which that society is based and by trying to understand them in the light of Christian revelation. An example of what I have in mind is

[58] I have tried to discuss this to some extent in my paper 'Divided Christendom: the contemporary Background', *Sobornost'*, series 5, no. 7 (1968), pp. 511–25.

provided by a recently-published work by Dr A. R. Peacocke. Dr Peacocke is both a biochemist and a theologian; and he is not prepared to compromise the standards of either discipline. In his book he provides an account of the scientific origins of the universe, the world and man, conducting his reader through quantum mechanics and relativity, cosmology, the origins and evolution of life with an admirable lucidity which does not – so far as a non-scientist can judge – involve any loss of academic rigour. He then discusses the Christian view of Creation and of the Incarnation, and in the light of these theological and scientific perspectives finally considers the question of matter:

> . . . on the one hand, that which God has brought into existence, the stuff of the cosmos, is seen through the sciences to be the matrix and necessary condition for the appearance of purpose, mind, self-consciousness and values – all that characterizes the human person; and, on the other, the Christian revelation affirms that this character of the stuff of the cosmos is so fundamental that God expressed His being in, and acted through, the perfect culmination of this process in the person of Jesus of Nazareth. Indeed, in Jesus we really see what personalness amounts to. The two enterprises converge in a view of the cosmos which can therefore be properly called 'sacramental'. . . . The eucharist focusses and summarizes the sacramental character of the whole existence and thereby enhances our appreciation of that character: it does not subtract from it. Thus in the eucharist is expressed the Christian understanding of *all* human activity, which is in accordance with God's creative purposes, as the end of man and as man's proper fulfilment.[59]

It will be observed that Dr Peacocke here affirms a eucharistic-liturgical utilization of the world no less than Dr Yannaras; and that though he is led to that view by the light of revelation, he finds it in no way opposed to his studies as a scientist. As I see it, Dr Peacocke's views add weight to the general concern felt at this time among thoughtful people for a responsible attitude towards the material world in which they live. But he also recognizes that it is both the privilege and the duty of man to develop that world, and quotes with approval William Temple's remark that it was the products of nature *transformed* by the work of man (bread, not wheat, wine, not grapes) which are the sacramental symbols in the Eucharist.[60] But the significant fact about Dr Peacocke's book, for our purposes, is that he does not hesitate to use both the evidence of science and the evidence of theology to present a Christian world-view in the terminology of the modern age. The name of Thomas Aquinas does not appear in the index of his book, and Dr Peacocke might be embarrassed to be compared with the great Scholastic theologian; but it seems to me that he is attempting to do in the 20th century what St Thomas tried to do in the 13th: to take a secular discipline (in the one case Aristotelian philosophy, in the other modern science) and to consider it in the light of Christian revelation, in order to present a coherent, Christian system. I would not presume to judge how far Dr Peacocke has

[59]Peacocke, *Science and the Christian Experiment* (London 1971), pp. 186, 187.
[60]*Ibid.*, p. 195.

succeeded; but I am quite sure that he is right in making the attempt.

This brings me to a final point. In the light of such considerations I hold that it is wrong to disparage unduly the intentions and the achievements of the Scholastic theologians of the Middle Ages. It may be conceded that their labours led into a blind alley, so far as posterity is concerned; but it does not follow, for that reason, that they were in error in trying to apply the dialectic to Christian theological reasoning, or in seeking to integrate the newly-discovered Aristotelian writings into the Christian philosophy of their day. The Scholastics assumed – in my opinion rightly – that the Christian faith was capable of taking and using all that was best in pagan philosophy, in rather the same way that the great Anglican scholars of the 19th century, Westcott, Lightfoot and Hort, assumed that the Christian faith could take and use the most rigorous methods of historical investigation without prejudice to the truth of Christian revelation. It is possible that the labours of the Scholastics may seem less helpful to our present age than do those of Westcott, Lightfoot and Hort; but I think we owe them a debt of gratitude for their undertaking, even if we feel that our own efforts to reconcile Athens and Jerusalem must take a different form.

ADDITIONAL NOTES

I p.382 lines 11–12: 'The present writer inclines to denial rather than to affirmation'. Today (1996) he inclines to affirmation rather than to denial. See his article, 'Augustine and Mysticism', *Collectanea Augustiniana: Augustine, Mystic and Mystagogue*, ed. F. van Fleteren, J. C. Schnaubelt & J. Reino (New York: Peter Lang, 1994), 113–57.

XI p.80 line 17: 'and no one could have kept him out'. See the reservations of Peter Hunter Blair, 'From Bede to Alcuin', Famulus Christi. *Essays in Commemoration of the Thirteenth Centenary of the Birth of the Venerable Bede*, ed. G. Bonner (London: SPCK, 1976), 243–52.

p.89 lines 10–11: 'nor did he have the *De Trinitate*'. I was wrong: he quotes it in the *De Natura Rerum* and in the *De Temporum Ratione* (references in *CCSL* 123 C, 723) and in the *Expositio Actuum Apostolorum* (refs. in Laistner's ed., Cambridge: The Medieval Academy of America 1939), 165.

XII p.1 Since this lecture was delivered, thirty years ago, a considerable number of critical editions of Bede's writings have been made available in the *Corpus Christianorum, Series Latina* by the labours of Charles W. Jones and Dom D. Hurst. See the list in Benedicta Ward, SLG, *The Venerable Bede* (Outstanding Christian Thinkers Series) (London 1990), ix–xii.

p.2 Sparks did not produce an edition, but one is currently being undertaken by Dr Thomas W. Mackay of Brigham Young University, Provo, Utah.

p.7 Primasius. Dr Adams's edition was published in 1985 in *Corpus Christianorum Series Latina* 92.

p.10 line 30. The passage is from Cyprian, *Ep*.56. *CSEL* 3(2), 649.

XV p.535 lines 34–5: 'with a monastic vocation like St Hilda'. J. M. Wallace-Hadrill, *Bede's Ecclesiastical History of the English People. A Historical Commentary* (Oxford: The Clarendon Press, 1988), 232, doubts whether St Hilda could have intended to enter Chelles in 647.

p.547 lines 27–8: '... later products of the Winchester school'. This book may be a Canterbury rather than a Winchester product; see *The Golden*

Age of Anglo-Saxon Art, ed. J. Backhouse, D. H. Turner & Leslie Webster (London: British Museum Publications, Ltd., 1984), p.72, no 55.

XVII p.341 line 38: ' – as seems unlikely – ', but see *contra,* Robin Lane Fox, *Pagans and Christians in the Mediterranean World from the second century AD to the conversion of Constantine* (Penguin Books: Harmondsworth, Middlesex, 1986), 30–31.

My views about the semi-Paganism of Ausonius (p.351 lines 10–21) are rejected by Robert Markus, *The End of Ancient Christianity* (Cambridge University Press, 1990), 33–6. I am not persuaded. Carolinne White, in her excellent *Christian Friendship in the Fourth Century* (Cambridge University Press, 1992), 151, suggests that 'although Ausonius was apparently never persuaded to follow his friend in his new commitment, it is likely that their friendship came to an end, not because of their disagreement but because of Ausonius' death'. Timothy Barnes, *Eusebius and Constantine* (Cambridge, Mass., 1981), regards Constantine as a genuine Christian. It seems to me that Alistair Kee, *Constantine versus Christ. The Triumph of Ideology* (London, 1982), makes a convincing case for seeing Constantine as a religious man, but not a Christian in any deep sense of the word.

XIX Christos Yannaras replied to this article in the *Eastern Churches Review* 6 (1974), 162–9, drawing attention to the writings of the French Dominican M.-D. Chenu and Erwin Panovsky, on the connexion between Western technology and medieval Scholastic theology, and the relation of Scholastic thought to Gothic architecture: p.168: 'Historically Gothic architecture is the first significant example of the cultural and – more specifically – the technological implications of the man-centred world-view of the medieval Latin theologians. On the foundation of this world-view rests the whole structure of Western or technological civilization'. Dr Yannaras then goes on to describe environmental pollution as 'the most significant stage in the historical evolution of [the] new relationship between man and the world ... inaugurated by medieval scholastic theology'. Clearly, this matter is too large to be discussed here. I can only say that, to be convinced, I would require a far more widely documented demonstration of Yannaras's thesis than reference to two scholars, however learned and distinguished they may be.

In any case, theological opinions founded on architectural styles are inevitably subjective. P.N. Ure, *Justinian and his Age* (Penguin Books: Harmondsworth, Middlesex, 1951), remarks (pp.220–21): 'George Herbert could find heaven in Salisbury cathedral. Even he could hardly have done so in some of [Justinian's] churches just mentioned, at least not in any sense in which the experience is the direct result of the architecture. The cathedral of the Holy Wisdom (Sancta Sophia) at Constantinople is another proposition. It is in every sense of the word a great church.' Ure, however, also saw Sancta Sophia at Constantinople as a technological triumph: 'What makes Sancta Sophia so exciting a building is that its architects were not only great artists but also great and adventurous engineers' (p.223); so it would seem that, *pace* Yannaras, technology can be employed to the greater glory of God in the East no less than in the West.

INDEX